Manfred S. Frings

THE MIND OF MAX SCHELER

The First
Comprehensive
Guide
Based on the
Complete
Works

ETHICS
SOCIETY
KNOWLEDGE
RELIGION
SCIENCE
EVOLUTION
REALITY
LOVE
RESENTMENT
CAPITALISM
FUTURE
TIME
DEATH

MARQUETTE
UNIVERSITY

PRESS

MARQUETTE STUDIES IN PHILOSOPHY
No. 13

ANDREW TALLON, SERIES EDITOR

Library of Congress Cataloging-in-Publication Data

Frings, Manfred S.
 The mind of Max Scheler : the first comprehensive guide /
based on the complete works by Manfred S. Frings.
  p. cm. — (Marquette studies in philosophy ; 13)
 Includes bibliographical references and indexes.
 ISBN 0-87462-613-7 (pbk.)
 1. Scheler, Max, 1874-1928. Title. II. Series.
B3329.S484F72 1997   97-4682
193—dc21

MARQUETTE UNIVERSITY PRESS
MILWAUKEE

The Association of Jesuit University Presses

To my wife Karin, with love

TABLE OF CONTENTS

Preface 5
Introduction 9
  a) A Short Biography of Max Scheler 9
  b) Max Scheler in the United States 12

CHAPTER I
ETHICS OF VALUES AND THE PERSON

Prefatory Remark 19
1) The Functional Existence of Values 22
  a) The Non-Existence of Values Per Se 22
  b) The Ranks among Values 26
  c) The Emotive *A Priori* 35

2) The Peculiarity of Moral Values. Good and Evil in the Realm of Values 39
  a) Good and Evil and the Five Ranks of Non-Moral Values 39
  b) The Temporality of Good and Evil. The Being of the Person. The Basic Moral Tenor and Conscience. 41
  c) The Call of Repentance 54

3) The Quintessence of Imperative-Free Ethics of Values and the Person. The Order of Love (*Ordo Amoris*) The Call of the Hour (*Kairos*) 58
  a) The Functionalization of Moral Experience 58
  b) The Order of Love. Space. Time and Fate 63
  c) The Refraction of the Order of Values in the Order of Love of the Individual Person 66

4) The Vehicles of Moral Growth. Exemplars of Person. Model Persons and Role Models 71
  a) Discussion of the General Problematic 71
  b) Discussion of the Specific Problematic of Exemplars of Person...76

CHAPTER II
PHENOMENOLOGICAL INTERSUBJECTIVITY

Prefatory Remark 81

The Primordiality of the Other in Emotive Experience 81
1) The Genesis of the Problem of the Other in Philosophical Litera-
ture .... ⌐ ⌐
2) The Argument for the Phenomenon of Communality and the ...
Other Self 83
3) The Other, the Self, and the Role of the Lived Body 86
4) The Four Levels of Sympathetic Feelings 91

CHAPTER III
THE FOUR SOCIAL FORMS OF
TOGETHERNESS WITH OTHER PERSONS

Prefatory Remark 99
1) The Mass 101
2) The Life-Community 101
3) Society 108
4) The Encompassing Person 114

CHAPTER IV
PHENOMENOLOGY OF RELIGIOUS EXPERIENCE

Prefatory Remark 121
1) Controversial Aspects of Phenomenology 122
2) The Immanent Regions of Consciousness and the Region of the
Absolute 125
3) The Special Place of the Religious Act in Consciousness 129
   a) The General Character of Religious Acts 129
   b) Faith and Belief 136
   c) The Dwindling of Faith and the Therapist of the Age 139

CHAPTER V
RESSENTIMENT

Prefatory Remark 143
1) The Emotive Structure of Ressentiment 145
2) Delusions of Value Judgments in the Ethos of Society 151
   a) Ressentiment and Humanitarianism 151

b) The Inversion of Life-Values and Values of Sensible Pleasures, Usefulness and Technology 154

c) The Value of What is Self-Earned and the Absence of Moral Solidarity 159

d) Egalitarianism. Subjectivation of Values 163

CHAPTER VI
CAPITALISM AND ETHICS.
THE WARPED MORAL TENOR OF SOCIETY

Prefatory Remark 167

1) The Origin of Capitalism: The Modern Mind Set 168

2) Arguments For and Against Capitalism as a Mind Set 172

3) *Homo Capitalisticus* 175

CHAPTER VII
SUBLIMINAL PHENOMENOLOGY

Prefatory Remark 181

1) Specifics of Scheler's Phenomenology 182

2) A Glimpse at the Dionysian Reduction 192

CHAPTER VIII
THE FORMS OF KNOWLEDGE AND SOCIETY

Prefatory Remark 193

A) Problems of a Sociology of Knowledge 195

1) The Structure of the Investigation 195

2) Sociology of Culture 196

3) Some Formal Problems 197

4) Some Material Problems 206

B) Cognition and Work 212

1) Outline of the Relationship between Cognition and Work. The Concept of Pragmatism 212

2) The Nature of Knowledge and Cognition 216

3) The Three Types of Knowledge 220

4) Pragmatism 221

a) Critique of Pragmatism 221

b) The Justification of Pragmatism 226
5) The Theory of Perception. Transconscious Phantasmic Images
(*Bilder*). Perception Sensation 236
6) The Condition of Perception: Drives 244

CHAPTER IX
THE LAST VISION:
THE BECOMING OF GOD, OF WORLD, AND THE COS-MIC PLACE OF HUMAN EXISTENCE

Prefatory Remark 249
1) Clarification of Terms: Metaphysics, Philosophical Anthropology,
Met-Anthropology 253
2) Philosophical Anthropology: General Discussion 257
3) Philosophical Anthropology: Specific Discussion 260
a) The Role of Human Self-Understanding in History 260
b) Absolute Time 263
c) The Sketch: Emergence of Ideas 268
d) Evolution: Vital Becoming 273
e) The "Isomorphic Analogy" of the Structure of Spirit 280
f) Meta-Physics, Meta-Biology and the Inanimate Level of
Impulsion 282
g) Metaphysics and Science 285
h) Metaphysics and the Ground of Being 289
i) Death 295

BIBLIOGRAPHIES

Collected Works (*Gesammelte Werke*) of Max Scheler 299
Current English Translations 300
Selected Secondary Literature (from 1955 to Present) 302

INDEXES

Index of Proper Names 315
Index of Subject Matter 319

PREFACE

This book has been written with two purposes in mind:

1) It fills a long-standing gap in contemporary philosophical literature in that it provides a first comprehensive look in the philosophy of Max Scheler (1874-1928) as it appears in the original text of the recently completed German Collected Edition (*Gesammelte Werke*), consisting of fifteen volumes. The book is based, therefore, exclusively on the German originals and respective manuscripts.

(2) The book is meant to address a) specialists who are provided with a web of cross-references pertinent to the above Edition and to English translations whenever they are available. The book is meant to address b) beginners to Scheler studies, the number of which has grown considerably of late, both home and abroad.

Our work here is the result of almost three decades of investigation into the mind of Max Scheler as manifest in his Collected Works and thousands of posthumous manuscript-pages that I have been studying: not only to bring to light the unity of his thought but also to show his familiarity with a vast literature, including that which lies outside the strictly philosophical. During the process of creating the present text, it inadvertently became clear to me that it is for the benefit of the reader that references to secondary literature, and the arguments, comments and contentions that accompany it, should not becloud an already challenging text.

By proceeding in this fashion, I hope to have succeeded in opening a clear view of an entire, rather complex, system of thought of early twentieth century philosophy that has remained in the background of investigations made by such thinkers as Heidegger, Husserl, Levinas, Merleau-Ponty, Nietzsche, Russell, Sartre, Wittgenstein and others no less important than the ones just mentioned.

The author wishes, therefore, to apologize that the names of many of his colleagues and the titles of secondary literature do not appear in the text. Instead, he has chosen to add a selected list of recent secondary literature for the reader's convenience. Collegial thanks are extended here to all of these authors and many more for what I have learned from their own studies.

As we approach the dawn of a third millennium—leaving behind us centuries marked among others by evils of war, starvation, social upheavals, waning of faith and a holocaust, but also marked by the realization of the highest values of art, culture and inventions that have benefitted humanity's well being and health owing in part to the advances of technology—the question of what and who we humans are is foremost in philosophical investigations. This character of modern philosophy was inaugurated by Descartes and Pascal, and is rooted in the fact that humans increasingly realize that they live their lives between so many opposing forces, such as good and evil, justice and injustice, poverty and wealth, faith and atheism, abortion and the right to life, among many others. This human situation is paradoxical if not tragic and calls for philosophical answers. Furthermore, modern humanity lives in the aura of technology that is itself beset with paradoxes and on which humanity heavily relies, yet sometimes repudiates, but which perhaps more than we may realize outlines the direction of our future.

Today we are familiar with pictures of our tiny planet taken from the darkness of outer space. The Greek word *planetai* literally refers us to the fact that our planet is "wandering." The word "planet" aptly conveys the paramount modern experience of living in the vastness of space and time. This cosmic experience along with the credence modern humanity has in technology, particularly Western culture, has gradually replaced an experience of living under God or, for that matter, with gods as was the case during ancient eras of mythology.

If we were to look from outer space at the beauty of our wandering blue, white and sometimes reddish colored planet earth, we might get a different impression, however, if, in a simple mental experiment, we blocked the planet off and replace it with humanity seen floating alone on the background of the silence and uncanny darkness of the universe. In this scenario, one is instantly startled by the incredible amount of human perversion, immoralities, and foolish self-destruction that drifts along with humanity's positive accomplishments on earth.

Such a celestial view of human history immediately prompts one to think of the question that concerns us all as we approach the gateway leading into a new millennium: could it be that—in the vastness of the universe—we earthlings are totally alone?

As we shall see, Max Scheler, as so many contemporary philosophers, was keenly aware that more than ever humans are increasingly asking about the meaning of their existence. At the end of his life, he acknowledged that the questions of "*Was ist der Mensch?*" (What is the human being?) and "What is his place in nature?" had occupied him more deeply than any other philosophical question.

Scheler confronted this question of the nature of our own being not only in terms of philosophy but also in terms of sociology, metaphysics, philosophy of religion, psychology, ethics and anthropology. Within the context of his book, *On the Eternal in Man*, he articulated what may be an essential trait of modern humankind, namely, the very existential feeling of cosmic isolation: "For the first time humanity feels *alone* in the wide universe."

Scheler's thought has remained somewhat overshadowed by that of his contemporaries who subscribed to existential loneliness and negativism that punctuated twentieth century philosophy to this day. Scheler's philosophy is a positive alternative to that of his contemporaries and later phenomenological and hermeneutical developments, including present day deconstruction. Contrary to the latter's assertions, for Scheler there were indeed privileged texts and cultures that were not the result of just social construction. His philosophy is largely an unswerving attempt to preserve the individual value of the person as irreplaceable. Thus, egalitarian movements are under continuous scrutiny and suspicion in his thought.

My deeply felt thanks for the completion of this text extend not only to the many scholars listed in the bibliography but equally to the many students who attended my seminars on Max Scheler. From their philosophical questioning I have learned a great deal.

I alone remain responsible for whatever errors that may have occurred.

Albuquerque, New Mexico, March 1996.
M.S.F.

INTRODUCTION

A Short Biography of Max Scheler

Max Scheler was born in Munich, Germany on August 22, 1874. His mother was of Jewish extraction. His father was Protestant. As an adolescent he was drawn to Catholicism, probably because of Catholicism's teachings on love. By 1922, however, he had fallen away from Catholicism in favor of a metaphysical attempt to explicate the Divine as "becoming" in history. He renounced the notion of a Christian Creator God.

The year 1922, therefore, roughly divides his productivity into a first and second period of philosophical inquiry. The year also roughly divides his personal life, which was not without drama, misunderstanding and tragedy. He received his doctorate in 1887 at Jena University. His advisor was Rudolf Eucken who lectured in Europe and America on the task of achieving a unity of mankind in order to prevent the destructive forces that worked in modern society. For this Eucken was awarded the Nobel Prize for Peace in 1908. Scheler was stimulated by a number of Euckenian thoughts, including his support of the League of Nations.

Scheler wrote his habilitation-thesis in 1899, also at Jena University, and began his teaching career there. In December 1906 he taught at the then predominately Catholic University of Munich. He met here a number of early phenomenologists, but he had already at that time distanced himself from a number of facets of the understanding of phenomenology generated by "the father of phenomenology," Edmund Husserl.

Due to the dissolution of his first marriage with Amalie von Dewitz-Krebs, who was a divorcee seven years his senior and subsequent to controversies between the University and political parties not favorable to Catholicism, he lost his position in Munich in 1910. There were two sons of this first marriage; one died early, the other had, according to Scheler, inherited only negative traits of his parents; from his mother hysteria and parsimony; from himself a weak will lending itself easily to lustful inclinations. The son died between 1938 and 1940 in a Nazi concentration camp near Oldenburg, partly because he had a Jewish grandmother, partly because he had been classified as a criminal psychopath.

Having lost permission in Munich to teach at a university, Scheler became a private scholar, lecturer and free-lance writer between 1910 and 1919. This was a most productive period for him. Having no income, he went to Göttingen in 1911 to give private lectures, often in hotel rooms rented by his friend D.v. Hildebrand. He met a number of the early members of the fledgling phenomenological Göttingen circle, among them H.Conrad-Martius, Th.Conrad, J.Hering, R.Ingarden, A.Koyré, H.Lipps and A. Reinach.

A captivating orator, he kept his audience spellbound. His private lectures in Göttingen laid the foundation of Edith Stein's conversion to Catholicism. Her characterization of Scheler in Göttingen sums up the excitement for Scheler among students and the general audience there. She reports that Scheler's influence on her went far beyond philosophy. Although Scheler was baptized but a non-practicing Catholic, it was he who motivated her to turn to the Catholic faith and to shed all rational prejudices. Her first impressions of Scheler made her think that he represented in person the phenomenon of a genius. As a Jew converted to Catholicism, the nun Edith Stein—Theresia Beneticta a Cruce—was killed in 1942 in the Nazi concentration camp Auschwitz.

Scheler's lectures in Göttingen provoked feelings of envy in the more retiring and recognizable Professor Husserl, who at the time lectured on principles of phenomenology at Göttingen University. During his first period of production, Scheler's fame was growing fast. He had published numerous treatises, among them "Ressentiment in the Structure of Moralities," "The Idols of Self-Knowledge," "Phenomenology and Theory of Knowledge," "Death and After-Life," "Repentance and Re-Birth," "The Causes of Hatred of Germans by Others," "The Meaning of the Feminist Movement," "The Idea of Man," and "The Future of Capitalism." In addition, he published various books, *The Genius of War, Phenomenology and Theory of Feelings of Sympathy and of Love and Hatred, Formalism in Ethics and Non-Formal Ethics of Values* and his major work on the philosophy of religion entitled *On the Eternal in Man* in 1921. These publications roughly comprise the first period of his productivity and will be referred to below.

After the breakdown of his first marriage and after his Göttingen experiences he went back to Munich in 1911. He married Maerit Furtwängler in 1912, who was seventeen years his junior. He idealized Maerit as his great love, which is testified by early sonnets he wrote for her and by a large amount of correspondence. Scheler had a strong liking to Edgar Allan Poe. He was admittedly always deeply touched whenever he read Poe's *Annabel Lee*, especially its last two strophes, which Poe—destroyed by endless drinking—devoted to his deceased wife. Scheler felt he had psychological affinities to Poe. He felt he had not given his most precious friends and loves their due; he felt he was "wrapped in weaknesses and guilt" and that a drive to die got stronger during all the human conflicts he suffered.

Despite his hopes, Scheler and Maerit had no children. On the occasion of a party in 1919 when he was invited by the University of Cologne to join its faculty, he met a young student, Maria Scheu. She became his assistant and he fell in love with her. Already at the time Scheler felt his life was falling apart. He suffered his first heart attack. Although he tried to do justice to both Maerit and Maria, Maerit divorced her husband in 1923 on the ground that she could no longer stand the triangular relationship. Scheler maintained correspondence with Maerit until his death. In 1924 Scheler married Maria Scheu who was eighteen years his junior and they had a son.

After having accepted in 1928 a professorship at the University of Frankfurt-on-the-Main, Scheler died of a heart attack on May 19. Maria Scheler, until her death in Munich in 1969 at seventy-seven years of age, devoted her entire life to editing, transcribing and classifying the many manuscripts that her husband had left behind. In 1954 the first volume of Max Scheler's *Gesammelte Werke* (Collected Works) appeared. Without Maria's indefatigable endeavors of deciphering and editing, our understanding of Scheler's philosophical project would have remained fragmentary.

Max Scheler's thought covered the following areas of investigation: ethics, philosophy of religion, phenomenology, sociology, political thought, metaphysics and philosophical anthropology. Especially toward the end of his life Scheler engaged in the political issues of his time. In this regard he proved to have a rare gift of prediction. He wrote negatively about the rising National Socialists as early as 1924. In 1927, six years before Hitler assumed power over Germany, he had already publicly warned of Fascism and National Socialism. He seems to have been the only academic of rank in Germany to have been outspoken on the subject. From 1933 to 1945, Scheler's work was suppressed by Nazi authorities.

Max Scheler's demise was seen as an irreplaceable loss by almost all European philosophers at the time. Ortega y Gasset referred to him as the greatest mind that lived in Europe; Martin Heidegger regarded him as a most seminal thinker to whom all others, including himself, were indebted. Despite the praise of his thinking at the end of the European twenties, his fame, like the brief sight of a comet, faded rapidly. His life and times saw growing social turmoil during the German roaring twenties to be followed by formidable events that lead to Hitler's dictatorship in 1933 and World War II (1939-1945).

Post World War II trends toward existentialism, philosophy of science, Marxism, analytic philosophy, Husserlian phenomenology, structuralism and deconstruction kept a revival of Scheler's thought in Germany at a slow pace up to the early nineties. However, in many other countries such as China, France, Japan, Poland and the United States his thinking became more known and recognized. Translations of Scheler into the languages of these and other countries continue to appear.

Max Scheler in the United States

One might not immediately expect there to be a detailed record on what might be regarded to be a substantial influence that Max Scheler exercised not only on European but also on the American philosophical community of his and subsequent time.

On the North American continent, his name appeared first in a review in 1913 by H. Wodehouse of Scheler's *Phänomenologie und Theorie der Sympathiegefühle und von Liebe und Hass* 1913, in *Mind* XXII, 1914. In it, the author expresses the hope that Scheler would carry on and amplify on the conceptions he had developed in this work, which dealt with the phenomenology of feelings. Possibly owing to the outbreak of World War I (1914-1918), further attention in America to new Continental European philosophers came temporarily to an end. This may have been a blessing in disguise because Scheler, like many German intellectuals, expressed enthusiasm for the decision of the Imperial German government to declare war. Scheler did so openly in a book, *The Genius of War* (1914). But he soon tempered his unreasonable judgements of Germany's enemies, especially England, in a second edition of the book in 1916. His evaluation of war as a "moral thunderstorm" that would bring people to its senses were motivated by the general martial spirit in Germany. However, Scheler's excitement for the war soon ran out. As early as 1917, the third year of World War I, he published an in-depth study entitled *Die Ursachen des Deutschenhasses* (The reasons of hatred of Germans by Others), a theme not especially welcome in Germany when thousands of her soldiers were being killed and the war began to be a hopeless game played by the Imperial government.

The first noteworthy effect Scheler made on the American philosophical community was in 1927 when the late distinguished Editor of *The Library of Living Philosophers*, Paul A. Schilpp, sent Scheler a letter asking whether he could participate in Scheler's seminars and lectures at Cologne University in preparation for writing his dissertation on Scheler at Stanford University. Scheler welcomed the young American. But as Schilpp noted in a letter to me of September 8, 1978, the very day he left New York harbor for Cologne on May 19, 1928, Scheler died. He learned about Scheler's death only on his arrival in Europe. He then decided to write a dissertation on Kant.

Schilpp had already published three articles on Scheler—among the first ones in the United States. In the *Philosophical Review*, 2, Vol. XXXVI, 1927, Schilpp gave an elaborate account of Scheler's *Problems of a Sociology of Knowledge* (1926). As we will later see in detail, this standard work of Scheler's contends that "mind" exists only in individual groups; there is no universal mind as had been held throughout German Idealism. It is only when the mind's ideas enter into function with factors providing a fertile ground from which and with which ideas can touch base, so to speak, (such as the realizing factors of economy, population, race, political realities, geographic patterns, etc.) that ideas become realities themselves. Without such factors, the mind does not exist. Albeit by coincidence, Scheler's sociological investigation shared some essentials features of American Pragmatism, for instance, with William James' essays "Does Consciousness Exist"? and "The Notion of Consciousness." Scheler considered William James to be a "genius."

We wish to emphasize that Scheler was the only thinker of rank in Europe who already early this century regarded American Pragmatism to be a viable philosophy. He was familiar with a number of German translations of James's works and also with some of Peirce's and other pragmatists' works. Indeed, his own manuscripts on pragmatism date back as far as 1909. He elaborated on them during his whole lifetime. This research culminated in a book-length article "Cognition and Work: An Investigation into the Value and Limits of the Pragmatist Motive of the Cognition of the World" (1926). This work along with *Problems of a Sociology of Knowledge* he referred to as "gateways" to his metaphysics. There is no doubt that both are indispensable for evaluating his thought as a whole.

Schilpp published on Scheler also in the *Journal of Philosophy*, 10, 1927, and an obituary article in the *Philosophical Review*, XXXVIII, 1929. Schilpp unwittingly joined a large number of European luminaries, including the then leading expert of Romance philology and Scheler's friend Ernst Robert Curtius, who held that the modern world could ill afford to have lost him.

Chronologically, however, the very first exchanges of thought with Max Scheler in America appear to have been those of Albion W. Small and Floyd N. House in the *American Journal of Sociology* 1925/ 26 and 1926/27 respectively. Both Small and House singled out the significance of Scheler's contribution to the *Problems of a Sociology of Knowledge*. Albion Small of The University of Chicago reviewed Scheler's 1924 text that had appeared in a collection of essays on the Sociology of Knowledge that Scheler had personally edited under the auspices of the *Forschungsinstitut für Sozialwissenschaften* at Cologne University, of which Scheler was director.

Albion Small remarked on Scheler's sociological research that "At all events, this book opens up vistas of social relations compared with which our own sociological teachings have thus far been parochial" (*The American Journal of Sociology*, 31, 1925-26. See also the same Journal, 27, 1921, where A. Small reviews Scheler's *Kölner Vierteljahreshefte für Sozialwissenschaften*). In this connection we must mention also Wilhelm Jerusalem who was one of the contributors to said collection and who, like H. Münsterberg at Harvard as well as R. Eucken, who had been Scheler's thesis advisor and kept correspondence with W. James, was a major source for Scheler on information about the United States. Scheler was also familiar with William James's book *A Pluralist Universe* by way of a 1914 German translation by J. Goldstein.

It was W. Jerusalem who first used the German term "*Soziologie der Erkenntnis*" (Sociology of Cognition) in a paper written in 1909, which later Scheler published in the first issue of his *Kölner Vierteljahreshefte für Sozialwissenschaften*, 1, 1921. Jerusalem also used the term "*Soziologie des Wissens*" (Sociology of Knowledge) in a letter to William James, dated May 2, 1909, at the time when he published a translation into German of James's *Pragmatism*. Scheler's manuscripts of *Problems of a Sociology of Knowledge* first published in 1924, date back to 1921. His life-long interest in pragmatism is also evidenced in a brochure issued in 1909 at the University of Munich. In it, Scheler is listed with a lecture entitled *Arbeit und Erkenntnis* (Work and Cognition) just the reverse word order of the title of his main 1926 publication, *Erkenntnis und Arbeit* (Cognition and Work). In the 1909 lecture at the University of Munich, Scheler covered— among other subjects—"Origins of the Modern Mind-Set of Work," and "The Anglo-American Movement of Pragmatism." At the time this was almost a risk for a young assistant professor to lecture at a German university.

Scheler's untimely death in 1928 halted further discussion in America of his sociology of knowledge and of his prognostications of future humanity. Inasmuch as his *Erkenntnis und Arbeit* is not yet available in English, special attention will be paid to this work later.

The final years of Scheler were marked by what at the time was diagnosed as a deteriorating heart muscle condition, which overtook him at the age of only fifty-four. With his oncoming death an end was put to what was no doubt developing into an active personal contact with the American philosophical community. In a warm invitation extended to him by the Committee of the Sixth International Congress for Philosophy at Harvard University, September 13 to 17, 1926, he was slated to give the keynote address at one of its four sessions. Scheler's physician had to press him not to journey overseas as it was inadvisable under the medical circumstances to pursue such a trip. Scheler canceled the reservations he had already made with White Star Line.

Scheler did not only intend to participate in this international Congress during his final years. It is possible that he was also going to Chicago for further contacts. In one of his sixty-seven notebooks (Archive No. B II, 63, p. 34) we find the address in Flint, Michigan, of Howard Becker who might have personally suggested to Scheler to visit Chicago. The entry also shows the title of a number of his works likely to be suggested for English translations. While living in Cologne, Howard Becker made but one English rendition of Scheler's 1927 essay *"Das Weltalter des Ausgleichs"* (The World Era of Adjustment), that projected the inevitable global confluence of nations, cultures, civilizations and races. It was the first rendition into English of one of Scheler's works, and Becker called it, "The Future of Man" (*The Monthly Criterion* 7, 1928). Becker also published synopses of Scheler's work in the *American Journal of Sociology* and *The Journal of Abnormal and Social Psychology*.

Scheler's itinerary abroad was also to incorporate an invitation from the Imperial Government of Japan to lecture on the Sociology of Knowledge for two years at Tohoku University, Sendai. In a letter addressed to the administration of Cologne University, he wrote that he wanted to accept this invitation and utilize his stay in Japan to finish in a more "tranquil environment" his projected *Metaphysics* and *Philosophical Anthropology*. There was an almost concurrent invitation from Moscow, extended to him by Leo Trotzki and Georgij Tschitscherin to lecture at the University there. His agenda for Moscow shows the following subjects of lectures: six lectures on "God and the State;" lectures on "The Nature of Man," containing basic ideas of his projected *Philosophical Anthropology*; and again six lectures were planned on "Questions of Ontology and Theory of Knowledge."

Apparently, Max Scheler's thought was in high demand during the twenties. To be added to his foreign schedule were also talks in his own country—personal meetings he had with people like N. Berdyaev, the young Heidegger and, especially, with his students.

I wish to highlight the latter point in particular because Scheler did not have the lofty and serious style German Herr Professors were noted for at that time. Students had a difficult time gaining access to them for answering questions, unless the student's name had been listed early enough in the professor's appointment schedule. By contrast, Scheler's lifestyle was one of direct involvement with not only students but with anybody, as long as there was something that could be learned from a discussion. He was easy-going, and not infrequently gave the impression of a child's innocence. Ideas literally befell him all the time to the effect that it was difficult for him to record them in order. While reading books, he would tear out pages to make notes on, or use train tickets or whatever for that purpose. Carefree as his lifestyle sometimes was, Scheler did not pay much attention to his attire either; wearing mismatched socks was not unusual. His widow tells us that his preoccupation with students' concerns was sometimes so intense that he would on occasion inadvertently neglect his colleagues in his discussions with students. On one such occasion she repeatedly had to poke his knees under the table to make him turn his attention to his colleagues. Scheler did not get the point. He innocently asked his wife, "Why do you keep on kicking my knees under the table?"

As we said earlier, Scheler's fame was short lived. His life and times saw growing social turmoil of the German roaring twenties. With prophetic perspicuity—characteristic of all of Max Scheler's thought—he spoke up against spreading Fascism and Marxism in a lecture given in the German Ministry of Defense in Berlin in 1927, entitled: "On the Idea of Eternal Peace and Pacifism." He felt that a portentous omen of a World War II had already begun to overshadow Europe's political horizon. He urged Europeans to think European, to form a "European University," where international scholars and international students were to bridge political and other national differences. He was far-sighted enough already to envision a "United States of Europe" at the end of his life in order to thwart the threat of dictatorship.

Five years after Scheler's death, the Nazi regime then in power in Germany suppressed his philosophy till 1945; but his widow Maria defied the regime by doing the aforementioned invaluable editorial work in seclusion. Her work lead to the first volumes of the critical German Collected Edition, the *Gesammelte Werke*, in 1954. A number of manuscripts and items of correspondence of Scheler were lost during air raids on the city of Cologne.

Despite the Nazi suppression that lasted until the end of World War II, Scheler's thought was revisited in the United States in 1941 with the publication of a symposium on his thought, consisting of a number of papers published in *Philosophy and Phenomenological Research* in 1941/42. Alfred Schütz, who studied Scheler's works intensively especially toward the end of his life, contributed with a paper on Scheler's theory of the alter-ego, a cornerstone of the Sociology of Knowledge, and Scheler's aforementioned book on the phenomenology of sympathy. The issue of the Journal contains essays on Scheler by Becker, Dahlke, Dunker, Guthrie, Hafkesbrink, Koele and Williams.

But this did not impress its editor, Marvin Farber, a student of Husserl who initiated the Husserlian direction of phenomenology in the United States, diverting it away from Scheler. Farber maintained a hostile attitude against Scheler, which he likely got from his master Husserl. Apparently joining Farber's misgivings, V.J. McGill and G.N. Shuster questioned Scheler's philosophical and political intentions. Indeed, Farber went so far as to charge Scheler with having been a Proto-Nazi in an entry on Scheler in *Encyclopedia Americana*. It was first Herbert Spiegelberg who raised strong doubts over the monstrosity of these charges in a chapter on Max Scheler in his well known study, *The Phenomenological Movement*. His doubts were later verified in Volumes IV and IX of the *Gesammelte Werke*. Despite this passing criticism against Scheler, professional occupation with him in the United States ever since has remained on the increase. A first introduction in English on Scheler's thought appeared in 1965, followed by numerous other works on him since then. This was also accompanied by numerous studies made on Scheler's philosophy in China, France, Italy, Japan, Poland, Russia, Spain and others. The works of his that have been translated into English are listed at the end of this book.

At the time of Maria Scheler's demise (1892-1969), the German Collected Edition comprised six volumes. Since 1970 the edition expanded in Chicago by nine volumes and was completed in Albuquerque with Volume XV. It is the only edition of a major European figure in philosophy of this century that has in its larger parts been edited in the United States.

CHAPTER I

ETHICS OF VALUES AND THE PERSON

Prefatory Remark

It amounts to a startling fact that the scope of the philosophical literature of our century—far exceeding that of any previous century—shows only a modest occupation with the *foundation* of the discipline of ethics itself. Most philosophers of rank whom one associates with this century's philosophy either refer to ethics parenthetically, implicitly, or look at it as a discipline subordinated to their own thought.

The lack of research into the foundations of ethics amounts to a striking, perhaps frightening, phenomenon. No doubt, in an age of technology, steadily intensifying internationalization and communication among peoples, there is dire need for philosophers to look into the origins of the present disarray of values and their perceptions. The recent growth of specialized professional ethics of business, medicine, law and others, did not, despite their usefulness for society, contribute to uncovering these origins, because to touch upon the foundations of ethics was not their goal.

Yet this charge that the majority of the great thinkers of our time did not concern themselves with ethics as they should have can also be countered in light of the history of ethics itself since ancient Greece. This history does indeed show unrelenting endeavors of ethicists to find ways of improving the moral status of the human race of their time. Aristotle, Bentham, Brentano, W.James, Kant, Meinong, Mill, G.E. Moore, Rashdall, Socrates and Spinoza, to mention only some, provide us with rich resources for assessing the moral problems of their times. And the same intention, it can further be argued, has also been pursued by a number of more recent thinkers such as R.Brandt, W.Frankena, N.Hartmann, Ortega, H.Reiner, P.Ricoeur and, of course, the thinker whose ethics we are going to present here in some detail. All of them did advance their own views on the discipline of ethics itself, but they also revisited some perennial questions and attempted to solve them in light of the day. All of them focused, more or less, on the ultimate moral question of ethics, namely, what the human being, at any of its moments and situations, *ought* to do. As we shall see, Max Scheler came forth with an entirely novel, hitherto only little-known but most challenging conceptualization of the moral category of oughtness and values and their function in the *kairos* of the moral moment. J.P. Sartre, it should be added, was especially indebted to Scheler as he stated in his 1983 *Les carnets de la drôle de guerre*, although Sartre never completed a work on ethics proper. Scheler's ethics lead him to the comprehension of the importance of the nature of oughtness and values that guide all our actions and judgement. On the basis of this, he stated, in ethics there is nothing else left to be done but "to start all over anew" (Il ne restait plus qu'à tout recommencer.)

But ethicists disagree on the conceptualization of the foundation of ethics and, therefore, on the role and essence of oughtness. One need only look at the discrepancies between Aristotle and Kant, between utilitarian or theological ethics, or between eudaimonist and logical ethics. Indeed, the recent infusion of professional ethics into the field of ethics per se only adds to the confusion over the role and essence of the category of oughtness, which is found only in humans.

It was perhaps this ubiquitous diversity in conceiving the foundations of ethics in the past that made many thinkers of our time hesitant to take up the question of ethics. Martin Heidegger (1889-1976), for instance, throughout his work never tackles the question of the foundation of ethics, except by pointing to the Greek tripartition of early philosophy into logic, ethics and physics proposed by Xenocrates. Of course, if one takes ethics to be a discipline subordinated to others, say to ontology as did the early Heidegger, and the later Edmund Husserl (1857-1937), the solution to the question of the foundation of ethics is simply set aside. But is this commendable today in light of the unstoppable, fast progress of technology which affects *moral* decision-making which, in essence, cannot be in step with technology's fast pace. Medical technology has brought into relief such paradoxes in human behavior as that of abortion, surrogate motherhood or manipulation of the human gene, to such an extent that even the professional ethics of medicine or of law do not suffice to come to grips with these paradoxes.

Notwithstanding the valuable insights made by so many contemporary philosophers into the nature of human existence and its world, there remain moral issues pressing with a vengeance for solutions to be found *in* that existence. The aforementioned moral issues of abortion, genetic engineering, and surrogate motherhood as well as of profit-making, of war, of legal or medical malpractice, of smoking, of capital punishment, of drugs, of euthanasia, are but a few of many. They are closely associated with equally pressing social problems, one of them being the unequal distribution of the values of earthly goods like nutrition whose recognition belongs, in large part, to the center of the foundation of an ethics of values before us. It is just an aberration in the moral perception of values itself that a global, multi-billion dollar entertainment industry—as compared to elemental needs of hungry children and of their health care—appears as an incredible mammon that considerably obscures such needs in our planetary life. The ethics before us will recognize such imbalances in human behavior as a surreptitious growth of social shortcomings and sometimes evils stemming from a deep-seated disorder in the feeling of values.

Throughout all of his philosophy, our thinker has directly and indirectly confronted these issues in light of their moral, sociological, political, cultural and religious facets—that is, in light of the order and the dislocation of *values* in modern society. The German title Scheler gave to his ethics reads: *Der Formalismus in der Ethik und die materiale Wertethik: Neuer Versuch der Grundlegung eines ethischen Personalismus* (*Formalism in Ethics and Non-Formal Ethics of Values. A New Attempt toward the Foundation of an Ethical Personalism*).

The title has two parts. The first, "Formalism in Ethics and Non-Formal Ethics of Values," refers in part to Scheler's critique of formalism in ethics in general and, in particular, to the formalism of Kant. The first part of the book deals with (1) the role values have in moral experience and (2) with their initial givenness in feelings, not reason. In his 1916 foreword to the book, Scheler tells us that his critique of Kant is only of marginal interest to him. What is of importance is the determination of the nature and function of values themselves, i.e., as peculiar contents inseparably tied in with feelings or emotive experiences. In the first part of the title, the German word "*materiale*" refers to the "contents" of values that are able to be experienced. The German word has nothing to do with matter or material, nor with a connotation of importance it might have in English. The English translation as "non-formal" therefore indicates the opposition to "formal," which was Scheler's intention in the title and the critique of Kant.

The subtitle is of equal importance. It refers to the nature of the person as the "bearer" of all values. The analysis of the human person is covered in Part II of the book. Inasmuch as the person's existence consists solely in the execution or "acting out" of acts, actions. The analysis of the person is also an implicit critique of the fledgling phenomenological movement that began to form around Edmund Husserl at the beginning of the century, and for whom the human sphere of personhood was only secondary to the human ego. In addition, Scheler was also opposed to the contentions Husserl had made in his first major work, *Ideas I* (1913) in which he conceived of human consciousness as "pure." The year that his value-ethics was first published, Scheler held that a pure consciousness by itself is a fiction: we have no other experiences of it in our consciousness other than that it is of a *person*. In sharp contrast to Husserl, therefore, person is "form" of consciousness. Scheler thus foreshadowed Heidegger's analyses of "Dasein" as described in his *Being and Time* (1927), which is also a hidden but strong critique of Husserl's emphasis on the ego. "Dasein," too, like the person, is more primordial than the ego.

Let us now turn to the pivots of Scheler's ethics of values and of the person. We stated that the foundation of ethics must address the question of how the moral category of oughtness must be conceived. As we may already expect from what has been said, Scheler's elucidations of the nature of values will show that whatever we "ought to" do, or ought not to do, presupposes the *value* of that which ought to be done, or not. Hence, an analysis of the foundations of ethics based in the experience of values and in the self-execution of the person through its acts and actions must first clarify the very being of values, their origins, and their ranks. As is customary in the literature on Scheler, we will refer to his ethics, as he himself did, simply as "Formalism."

1. The Functional Existence of Values
a) The Non-Existence of Values Per Se

With establishing the functional existence of values, an entirely new domain for exploring the foundation of ethics can be delineated at the outset by listing the following points:

1. Scheler's *Formalism* is a first attempt to put the discipline of ethics on a phenomenological footing.
2. While formal laws of logic hold for values considered to be formal objects, the laws of logic fail to have universal application when they are shown to be the immediate contents of feelings, i.e., in emotive experiences.
3. An ethics based in part on the experience of specific contents of values, that is, on "value-phenomena" indissolubly knotted in acts of feeling, must question moral imperatives and definitions of the good as they have appeared in the history of ethics. No matter how clear or obvious the latter may appear to human reason, they have not improved the moral status of humanity.

4. For this and other reasons yet to be seen, a phenomenological ethics of values does not set up a moral imperative. A moral imperative presupposes the *value* on which it rests.

5. The task of scrutinizing foundations of ethics must a) not only address moral but also the existential, historical, religious, and social dimensions of the person as the "bearer" of values and, b) it must equally address the being of values and of the person.

Let us begin with the question: What is a value?

The genesis of Scheler's ethics of values and the person has its roots in his doctoral Dissertation of 1887 entitled *Contributions toward Establishing the Relations between Logical and Ethical Principles* in translation. In the dissertation Scheler states:

> As to the question: "What is a value?" I submit the following answer: Insofar as in the question the word "is" refers to existence (and not only to being as mere copula), a value "is" not at all. The concept of value does not allow more of a definition than does the concept of being (I 98 translation mine).

A value, therefore, is originally neither a property of a thing, nor is a value itself a thing; nor is a value a logical abstraction. For this reason, the somewhat confusing term "objective values" which Scheler uses throughout *Formalism* does not pertain to objective things. Just as it would be a prejudice to argue that anything "objective" in pure mathematics must also exist "as" a thing-object, so also it is prejudicial to consider anything "objective" in the realm of values as necessarily existing like an object. We wish to keep this in mind in order to draw a line between what we will henceforth call the "functional existence" of values as described below, on the one hand, and the existence of everyday objects, on the other. What is functional existence?

A second quotation taken from *Formalism* assists us in getting a first view of this particular type of "existence" of values:

> No more than the names of colors refer to mere properties of corporeal things—notwithstanding the fact that appearances of colors made in our [everyday] natural ways of looking at the world come to our attention only insofar as they function as a means for distinguishing various corporeal, thing-like entities—do the names of values refer to mere properties of the thing-like given in unites that we call goods. (II 35/F 12)

The two quotations given tell us two things. Values as such do not exist and values are not properties inherent in things. These are two negative statements. We must therefore ask: What, then, are values?

The answer to this question lies in what we referred to as the functional existence of values. Functional existence of something is at hand whenever this something must enter into a function with something else for it to become extant. A color, for instance, does not exist unless it is spread out on a surface. It exists in function with a surface that we see. As such, the color "green," for example, is given to us only in "seeing" it on the surface. "Green" is accessible only in visual perception. One cannot hear the color green. The color "green" that is seen, however, does not compel us to think that the surface itself has the inherent property of being green. The surface will also turn red or any other color on certain conditions.

The analogy between values and colors verifies Scheler's dissertation statement and amounts to a principle of his value ethics: values must enter into a function with something in order for them to be. By themselves, they are not objective entities.

Hence, values are *independent* of objective things. The same holds, of course, for colors. Things like a cloth and a lawn are independent of "green." Both can be brown. The independence of things from colors as well as the independence of things from values is reciprocal. "Green" does not care whether it is of the lawn or the cloth. A value like "holy" likewise does not care whether it pertains to God, to a saint or a fetish. The independence that values have of things also has a negative aspect: it begets the possibility of deceptions in value experiences. We will address these later.

At first sight, the independence holding between values and things and things and values suggests that there cannot be an order among values in such independent functional existence. This is not so and can be explained for the time being with the help of the above analogy between values and colors. All nuances of colorations rest on an order of spectral colors which are only rarely visible as in rainbows or crystal. Nevertheless, spectral colors, too, require substrates as the air in a rainbow or the crystal in order to be iridescent. They must enter this function with something. If there are no substrates for spectral colors, there are no spectral colors either. Even visible light cannot exist without a surface. Sent through a vacuum, light waves remain dark. Light exists when it enters into an operational function with something that "resists," to use a Schelerian expression, its rays. In everyday human experiences, the order of spectral colors remains mostly hidden behind the visible, functional colorations. The visible colorations *conceal* the mostly invisible order of the spectrum. But, on the other hand, the order of the color spectrum is necessary for visible colorations. It also *un*-conceals by setting visible colorations free. The same state of affairs can be translated to the functional existence of values. Values, including value-deceptions, have an order to them, which is mostly concealed to human beings. We went perhaps a little too far in ontologizing the being of values as we did. But the being of values can be approached in terms of the mutual independence of values and things, which Scheler stresses. Yet, what Scheler has in mind concerning the status of values is something different. He claims there is a *primacy* of the givenness of contents of values over any other acts of consciousness. Feeling values is basic to the mind's acts; emotive experiences are not internal chaos (Kant) but are suffused with an order of contents of values very different from the laws of logic pertaining to reasoning and thinking. Scheler's argument is like this: just as colors can only be given to us "in" seeing them, so also values are given to us only "in" the feeling of them. Without "seeing" there are no colors. Without "feeling" there are no values. The priority of feelings over thinking and willing, for that matter, is one of order, not one of sequence.

If this is so, there is a far reaching philosophical consequence in *Formalism*. If the human being is essentially egological, as in Descartes, German Idealism or Husserl, and if the ego is conceived to be a purely rational ego without feelings, then the human being would be without values except those given in rationality. Scheler launched the charge of slovenliness in matters of feelings on values in philosophy. This would also pertain to the last of the great philosophers Scheler knew in person, to Heidegger, whose "Dasein" qua human being is bare of feeling, and therefore of values. (A brief remark concerning a spurious argument often made in texts dealing with the history of phenomenology should be added at this point, but will be resumed in detail later.)

There is no question that in *Formalism* Scheler was out to determine the essence of values as they are given in feeling. Given the above analogy, one could have expected him to apply the well known Husserlian phenomenological method of "bracketing" things from values in order to bring into focus "values themselves," as Husserlians often assert. Had it been at all possible chronologically for Scheler to have read Husserl's *Ideas I* while he was writing his *Formalism* (both works published in 1913) and had he approved of Husserl's *Ideas I*, which he did not, he might, under such conditions, have considered applying Husserl's method then and in subsequent writings. But, as we shall see, Scheler denounced methods of phenomenology and came up with very different intentions and goals of what phenomenology should and could pursue.

b) The Ranks among Values

Keeping in mind that values do not exist by themselves, we are now in a position to establish a first peculiarity of the nature of values.

There are five different *kinds* of value-contents that are spectral in all valuations. Scheler refers to the value-ranks also as "modalities" (*Modalitäten*).

Each of the five value-ranks is correlated with five different kinds of feeling. Furthermore, to feelings of values there attach self-generating "feeling-states" (*Gefühlszustände*). All feelings and their correlative referents, values, and accompanying feeling-states fall into two basic groups:

1) There are values that only a person can feel, and there are feeling-states that only a person can have.

2) There are feelings of life-values and those which can be felt only in the lived body or animal organisms. Their respective feeling-states are always relative to life, not to personhood. Many of them we share with animals.

Let us look into the five ranks and their respective feelings in descending order. Each rank entails a positive and its opposite negative value.

1) The highest value-rank encompasses the values of the "holiness" and the unholy. It is given in religious feelings such as feelings of repentance, of humility, worship, or in the act of praying for something. Given the independence that values have, the value of holiness is not only felt with regard to a God of a particular religion. Holiness may be felt with regard to particular animals like cows or birds and even in regard to inanimate objects. But no matter what is felt to be holy, the feeling of the *value* of holiness itself is restricted only to feelings a person can have.

The feeling-state of the experience of holiness is blissfulness or, in the event of a lack of such experience despair, no matter how slightly this feeling-state may permeate a person's being.

2) The second highest value-rank contains all values of the mind. They are what Scheler calls spiritual values (*geistige Werte*) and spiritual feelings. They fall into three groups:

a) aesthetic values spanning beauty and ugliness,

b) juridical values spanning right and wrong,

c) philosophic values of the cognition of truth.

These values can be experienced only in personal feelings. This may best be shown with regard to the negative value of injustice. Injustice, is given "in" a feeling of personal injury, and not in sensations as bodily pain would be able to be felt. A felt personal injustice can show that feelings can be independent of logical arguments, say in a court. This feeling is not congruent with a legal adjudication. It can remain unaffected by any and all rational counsel and remain for a long time with an individual or a group having dealt an injustice. Indeed, this feeling may go far beyond what any law or religion can do to crush it. Antigone's conscience is a prototype of how the conflict felt between personal injustice and the law of the state as it has been rationally conceived.

Although one tends to think that these values of the mind are the product of rational conceptualization, Scheler stuck to the principle that conceptualizations and perceptions are preceded in the order of their givenness to the person by "value-ception" (*Wertnehmung*).

The feeling-states of this rank (of whatever degree) are "spiritual joy" when the positive values of this rank are realized and "melancholy" when they are not.

3) The next rank of values in descending order is that of vital or life-values. They play not only an important role in modern society, but also with a number of especially German *fin du siècle* philosophers. In particular, it was Nietzsche who declared the value of life to be the highest value, for which reason "God is dead." Mental values of the second rank are perspectival interpretational fictions for Nietzsche, including truth which is proclaimed to be error.

Life-values show two aspects:

a) They can be felt within one's organism,

b) they can be felt as appearances of external objects. Many of the former we share with animals. The latter are felt only by humans. These values range from what is "noble" down to what is "ignoble."

Feelings of life-values suffuse the whole organism rather than occurring in only one area of the organism. Therefore, they are not localizable in organs. They spread through the whole of the lived organism as strength, health, fatigue, exhaustion, anticipation of the continuous decline of one's energy and, of course, of oncoming death. Because vital-values are expressive of objects, the value of nobleness may shine through an old oak tree, a wonderful horse, through the imperial looks of a lion used as symbol for a nation, or through the tranquility of a beautiful sunset. One factor that makes life-values important today is their presence in the environment. Violations of these values are felt as intrusions of technology into clean air, water, earth, etc. Such intrusions are anchored in a value-deception consisting in an emotive preferring of what is useful and profitable over what is not useful or profitable, but noble. Life-values are strictly

speaking found only among humans when they take on the character of heroism: Homer's *Iliad* and *Odyssey*, a medieval knight as Roland
or Jeanne d'Arc, or in any war. War is a defense of life-values of war-
ring parties. Indeed, a whole culture may be characterized by a special sensitivity for this value-rank. Nietzsche justifiably espoused the
Italian Renaissance and elevated life-values to "will to power" in nature itself. So did Oswald Spengler and many thinkers and poets of
Romanticism. Needless to emphasize, modern society is the sociological arena in which a war for or against life-values is being waged.
The feeling-states of this rank are persistent vitality and ineptitude.

4) Like the former ranks, the two lowest value-ranks are also relative to life (*daseinsrelativ*). The values of the fourth rank span usefulness and what is not useful. They are pragmatic values. While Scheler
did not yet articulate in *Formalism* what the feeling of usefulness and
non-usefulness is because he did not assign to them a separate rank,
it can be argued that these values are given in feelings of self-preservation
and of subliminal anticipations for success in practical activities.

These values also pervade the animal kingdom. A bird collecting
useful material for building a nest, or a chimpanzee using a rock to
crack nuts indicates utilitarian values in pursuit of preservation.

But with human beings, this value rank manifests itself much more
distinctly in that they make tools and technical equipment for better
manipulation of these values. This value-rank obviously encompasses
the values of primitive tools used by animals and stone-age man to
contemporaneous space-technology. The exceptionally high level of
sensitivity for these values that humans living in society motivated
their common self-understanding as *homo faber*, as a toolman, along
with a fledgling variation of it as "machine man" (*La Mettrie*), or later as
the "organization mind." The *homo faber* idea will occupy us later in the
exposition of Scheler's *Philosophical Anthropology*.

The feeling-states of this rank, never mentioned by Scheler, must,
on the basis of the feeling we believe these values are given in, pertain
to feeling-states of success or of failure.

The modern self-understanding by humans as *homo faber* is reflected in the abundant use of means and methods designed to realize values of usefulness. The idea of tool-man is also implicit in
Heidegger's "Dasein" in his *Being and Time* (1927). Dasein is with
pragmatic values before anything else. Heidegger avoids the term
value, because he falsely thought that all values are objective thing-
values. For Heidegger, tools, utensils, the stuff around us (*das Zeug*),
even "disclose" Being. Values of holiness, mental and vital values play
no role in the pragmatic everyday-world of Dasein, because, in its

essence it is exposed to how utensils and the stuff are "at-hand" (*zuhanden*) or, secondarily, "present-to-hand" (*vorhanden*). Scheler once stated that if he were only Dasein, he would rather not live. Dasein's supposedly only pragmatic existence had, however, already been conceived by Scheler as early as in *Formalism*. Whenever he refers to "milieu-things" they are "*Brauchbarkeiten*," which is just another word for what Heidegger is talking about. Heidegger's assumption that Being is disclosed through things at-hand amounted for Scheler to a gross distortion of the order of value-ranks we are discussing here.

5) The lowest value-rank is that of sensible values. They are given in sensible feelings. They range from what is comfortable, pleasant, and agreeable for the body to the opposites of discomfort, the unpleasant or the disagreeable. What is peculiar to this rank is that its values are not communicable to other individuals. One cannot feel another's pain; perhaps, at best, one can imagine how one would feel it oneself, that is, in vicarious feelings.

Things that are comfortable or uncomfortable vary according to the independence that values have among each other, from individual to individual, and from species to species. What is comfortable, tasty and nutritious in one species may be poison for another. An easy chair may be comfortable to one individual whereas it is not so for another. The range of sensible values allows for infinite nuances and shades of intensity.

Modern society is very sensitive to these two lowest value-ranks. These ranks are its pivot or "polar-star" (X 266/PV 138). Karol Wojtyla, Pope John Paul II, who extensively lectured and published on Max Scheler's *Formalism* at Krakow University, Poland. He had written his habilitation thesis on *Formalism* in Rome in which he criticized the modern, pervasive meaning of "good." He pointedly stated in Denver, August 14, 1993, that "good" has come to mean what is "pleasing or useful at a particular moment" and that "each person can build a private system of values" while the higher value-ranks are receding in the backgrounds of human experience.

The respective feeling-states of the lowest value-rank are pleasure-feelings experienced in the body and their opposite, physical pain.

In descending order, the five value-ranks can now be listed as follows:

1. The value-rank of the holy and unholy,
2. The value-rank of values of the mind:
   a) juridical values,

b) aesthetic values,
c) values of knowledge,
3. The value-rank of life values: noble—ignoble
4. The value-rank of utility values: useful—not useful
5. The value-rank of sensible values: comfort—discomfort

Besides the mutual independence that things and values have, there is yet another peculiarity running through all ranks. This point lies beyond the description of values just presented. It pertains to the essence of values. The peculiarity concerned is significant insofar as it prepares us to focus on the moral values of good and evil which we have not yet mentioned.

The peculiarity concerned consists in the undeniable fact that already lower sensible feelings through which sensible values are given, possess an *inner pre-rational preference of their own* toward higher values and feelings *within their own rank*. It is impossible, for example, that a sensible feeling could by itself prefer the uncomfortable to the comfortable. Our lived bodies do not simply "prefer" pain over pleasure. This subliminal, quasi- automatic emotive preferring is already "in" the feeling; that is, the preference is essential to value feeling in that it is stretched, as it were, always between at least two values. Feeling of values has its foundation, says Scheler, in the preferring and not in choosing (II 107/F 89). Although there are rare cases of bodily preferring of what is painful, as in cases of sadism and masochism, the temporary preference of discomfort over comfort in such cases is still felt as a positive phantom value in terms of seeking gratification from the phantom enjoyment. Such psychoanalytical cases are akin, strangely enough, to persons seeking forgiveness of sins by self-flagellation. The flagellation is a phantom value in the lived-body schema of preferring positive value feeling and states.

Already, therefore, the lowest feelings of sensation possess an *inherent* drift of their own toward "preferring" of what is comfortable. Indeed, the entire realm of animality is "fated," says Scheler, by the organismic feeling of preference of comfort over discomfort.

What we referred to as the inherent drift toward positive values "in" sensible feelings that have their foundation in pre-rational preferring is also at work in all the other ranks. That is, within each rank there prevails a pre-rational activity of "preferring" positive values over negative values. Let this preferring that happens on only one rank be called "horizontal," for instance, sitting on a comfortable chair happens within the lowest value-rank. But this does not mean that the "chair" is comfortable. Rather, our lived body "comfortables" the chair "in" preferring comfort over discomfort.

On the other hand, there is also a pre-rational "vertical" drift running through all ranks. Although we are not aware of this in practice, preferring higher ranks to lower ranks is an *a priori* relationship "among" ranks as it is "among" values of one rank.

Yet, this vertical preference ranging from the rank of sensible values to the ranks of the sacred is not easily convincing. This is because the vertical preference among ranks is mostly covered up by peculiar value preferences characteristic of one or another individual, of an age or a civilizations with their conventions and customs. An age like ours, having a strong emotive penchant toward values of comfort, pleasure and entertainment, is not prone to indulge in concerns of transcendence or *a priori* contents sitting in discussions of higher and lower values in economics. Conversely, a culture having much less concern for entertainment and pleasure values, such as India, is not prone to indulge in endless productions of implements and gadgets serving comfort or pleasure.

The essence of the order of values as being inherent in both vertical and horizontal subliminal preferences can at this point be brought into relief by making use again of the value-color analogy. The vertical preference among ranks of values can be compared to the role light plays in visual perception. Just as the sense of sight by itself prefers what is lit up over what is not, so also value ranks by themselves tend to invoke us to prefer higher ranks to those given in a practical situation.

This allows us to catch a glimpse into the structure of the *a priori* of value-feelings: the emotive *a priori* pertains to preferring among the values belonging to only one rank but conjoined with preferring higher value-ranks. Hence, the *a priori* of emotive, pre-rational preferring among values is, in contrast to a rational *a priori*, twofold: it is both horizontal and vertical. That is, the *a priori* in feelings is transverse.

Let us now look into another contention of Scheler's. He tells us that the heights among the five value-ranks also possess objective, rational criteria that reflect the order in feeling them.

A first measure for the heights of value ranks is their *divisibility*. Values of the lowest rank, for example, are very divisible because one technically produces them, say, pleasure by intoxication, libations, foods and drugs. Because of this these values are producible, measurable and of potentially high effectiveness in individual situations. This even obtains in part among life values. The same holds for the high degree of quantification and division among the pragmatic values of the second rank. Without this criterion no technology to speak of could be made possible. Divisibility runs even through the life values although not to the degree as in the two lowest value ranks. Artificial fertilization and insemination would, for example, be a case in point. But life values as heroism or courage are not mechanically producible to such an extent. In the two highest value-ranks a production of their feelings and values play little or no role. The emotive experience of the value of beauty of a work of art cannot be technically produced. It hits people spontaneously. One cannot say to a person who is not affected by the beauty of a work of art that he can and must like it. Nor can one make a person enamored with its beauty nor command not to be enamored. One cannot technically extinguish, as we saw, a feeling of injustice either. While we can allay painful sensations, resist excessive pleasures, the feelings of the person tied to the two highest ranks do not allow of technical controls. One may at best sleep over a feeling of injustice but it will well up later all the same.

The lack of value-quantification is most evident in religious feelings. Scheler considers technical management of group worship in churches of secondary if not of no religious significance. Planning and organizing group-worship is, sociologically, a phenomenon of society. Spontaneous feelings of worship occur in the individual, not in a group. The values of the highest rank, such as humility, repentance, devotion, thankfulness for one's existence, etc., cannot be quantified and timed as to when they should occur. Both the experience of holiness and of mental values are not controllable by clock-time.

As was suggested, there exists a sociological implication in the objective criteria of quantifiable and non-quantifiable values. Whenever a group of people is suffused with a strong sensitivity for lower value ranks, such a group tends to be divided. As we shall see, Scheler's sociology of knowledge will tell us that in this respect society is *not* the highest value of human togetherness. What unifies groups most is their feeling of the value of holiness and their religions even though this is not so obvious in the international legal relations among societies and diplomacy. On this point, Scheler is quite supportive of Nietzsche who also argued that history is ultimately carried in the name of religions. Sociologically, religions easily survive the changing times of quantified values and groups.

This leads us to another measure for the heights among value-ranks: the higher they are, the longer they last in time; or: the higher values are, the more they are characterized by duration. The lower they are, the more transient values are. Whatever may be comfortable and useful to generations is surpassed by the indivisible values of justice, beauty, knowledge and the holy. Or, as Scheler puts it, the values of the person have the "ability to exist through time." The lower the ranks are, the more they can be manipulated to come into and pass out of measurable time.

A third measure of heights among value-ranks is their degrees of giving humans fulfillment and satisfaction. By comparison to the values of the person, the lower value-ranks are less fulfilling because their fulfillment is only short. Because of their vital relativity they do not reach the core of the person. All forms of unrelenting pleasure-seeking are unmistakable tokens of deepseated deficiencies and weaknesses of persons and groups concerned. The degree and intensity of feelings for pleasure, comfort and entertainment is reciprocal to the depth of personal dissatisfaction and unfulfillment that engender such hedonist motivation. This point can be heard everywhere today, especially by educators. Scheler seems to get to the core of it when he states in *Formalism:*

> Indeed, one can say that the number of means designed to produce sensible pleasure and to remove sensible pain (e.g., narcotics) increases as unhappiness and negativity in vital feeling become the inner *fundamental attitude of a society* (II 347/F 345-346).

And Scheler continues by referring to the opposite state of affairs also. A group which is not indulging in pleasure-values is one of personal joy and fulfillment. Such people freely settle around the holy man, and ignore quantifiable values of profit, etc. In addition, it must stated, Scheler continues, the more joy that is central to a person, the less joy requires external, i.e. divisible and manageable, stimuli.

Lastly, the relationship that exists between relative and absolute values would give evidence to the emotive order of values and their ranks. Absolute values are felt only in "pure" feelings, preferring and loving; that is, in feelings which are, as the literal meaning of the word "absolute" indicates, "detached" from sensibility.

Absolute values, therefore, have no place in the value ranks relative to life. The value of justice, for instance, is a value accessible only to and to be experienced by a person and, as such, is not relative to life in its biological meaning. Any experience of values detached from life as a whole is able to be felt only by persons. "Personal feelings" and the absolute values given in them, are therefore a distinct class of values given in personal feelings.

Since all values are either positive values or negative values, and since positive values are preferable to negative ones, we must ask how "oughtness" is to be understood, or why one "ought" to realize higher values. Clearly, positive values and goods ought to be and negative values and ills ought not to be. Scheler's explanation of the nature of oughtness rests on the axiom that every positive ought is directed toward the exclusion of a negative value that ought not to be realized. While one ought to realize a positive value, one excludes a negative value that ought not to be realized. For example, the proposition, "I ought to do justice" does *not* posit the value of justice. The reason for this is that whenever we say that something ought to be or ought to be done, this something is felt and grasped as *not* yet existing. On the other hand, when we say that something ought not to be, it is felt and grasped as *existing*. In other words, if the positive ought pertains to values and goods given as not existing, every positive proposition about the ought must pertain to non-existing values.

But formal axioms existing among values mentioned in *Formalism* also hold that "the being of a positive value is itself a positive value," and that "the non-being of a positive value is a negative value." Therefore, all positive propositions of the ought must pertain to *negative* values. When we say that something ought to be, the non-existence of the positive value and the good concerned must, on the basis of the above formal law, be a negative value. When we say that something ought not to be, the "existence" of the negative value that ought not to be must also, then, be a negative value.

Oughtness can never itself determine what positive values are, simply because the ought by itself cannot provide means for the realization of a positive value-content that ought to be. If it were possible for the ought to bring about a realization of a positive value by itself, the ought would refer to an already existing positive value or a good in reality and, hence, defeat its very moral role of prompting or bringing about a value not yet existing. Whenever the person experiences the moral power to realize a positive value, such person is virtuous; or, virtue is the experienced *power* to be or to do something that ought to be or to be done. Conversely, vice is the experienced *impotency* of doing something that ought to be or ought to be done.

These above axioms pertain equally to the distinction to be made between the two types of oughtness there are.

There is (1) an ideal ought and there is (2) an individual ought. An example for the ideal ought is: "Injustice ought not to be." An example for the individual ought is: "Thou shalt not do injustice." The second type of ought is dependent on the first. In both types of oughtness, the ideal universal and the individual, the ought has its foundation, however, in the *value* of what ought to be or what ought not to be. And in both cases the ought excludes a negative value.

c) The Emotive A Priori

Since a work on ethics is for Scheler a "judgemental" formulation of what is given in moral insight, this includes also his own ethics. Therefore, his ethics must provide a clarification of the "emotive" *a priori*. Accordingly, we will now address the emotive *a priori* in addition to what has already been said about its transverse character. Since we restrict ourselves in what follows to only the emotive *a priori*, we must defer a presentation of his phenomenology as a whole in which the enormous difference it has from Husserlian phenomenology will be shown.

In the ethics before us, the *a priori* resides in the emotive contents of values present in value-ception (*Wertnehmung*). We are fortunate that Scheler provided in *Formalism* and later works an elaborate presentation of the *a priori* rarely found in phenomenological literature. He first supplies the difference between a non-formal *a priori* and a formal one. He then gives some details of his own elucidation on the subject. Since we cannot cover the entire section on the *a priori* of *Formalism*, we must highlight some of the essential features of it for our purposes. To this end, we look first at the phenomenological *a priori* of meaning-contents and its givenness in pre-rational, i.e., emotive experience.

1. Phenomenological "experience" goes beyond empirical experience. Phenomenological experience pertains to processes of consciousness, and only secondarily to empirical experience. While the *a priori* in its classical formulation refers to data "prior to" empirical experience, the phenomenological *a priori* is more radical in that it pertains to *any* experience occurring in consciousness. This means that the traditional formal *a priori* is restricted to empirical experience and, therefore, fails to incorporate experiences in "consciousness-of-something." This "something" is, phenomenologically, anything consciousness has awareness "of," including values of emotive consciousness. For Scheler the phenomenological phrase "consciousness–of," in contrast to the formal *a priori*, means that the non-formal *a priori* is neither a constitutive activity of formation, nor a synthesis generated by a self. What consciousness is "of" can be *any* content, be it something rational, senseless, meaningless, logical, illusionary, fictions, fantasies in dreams, blurry contents in day-dreaming, or whatever. It is also true that the formal *a priori* is "of" something; but its content is absorbed by a "form" that imposes itself *onto* its contents. While the non-formal *a priori*, like the formal *a priori*, admits of having formal laws also, they are shown to be of only secondary importance.

This is because non-formal contents of the *a priori* go beyond formal laws. The non-formal *a priori* is therefore said to have a wider range than *a priori* formal laws.

The non-formal *a priori* is, according to Scheler, self-given by way of an *instantaneously intuited* content, not arrived at by a method of reduction. This aspect refers to the core of Scheler's phenomenological *a priori*: it does not prompt the Kantian question of what "can" be given, nor the Husserlian question of how something is given; rather, the phenomenological focus is fixed on what "is" given in consciousness. Scheler's stress lies on what is factually "*there*" in consciousness (X 381/PE 138), a usage of "there" that foreshadows, to be sure, Heidegger's ontological facticity of There-being or *Da-sein*, articulated some fourteen years later in his *Being and Time*.

By focusing on what consciousness is "of," phenomenology can also set aside or "bracket" every conceivable condition for the occurrences of meanings in consciousness; Scheler also proceeds in this fashion, but when he does, the ego has no constitutive basis as it has for Husserl. What is given in consciousness is tied to intentional acts, not to an ego. Therefore, in contrast to the rational *a priori*, the contents of what is given *a priori* in consciousness are devoid of any "positing" (*Setzung*) of subjects, of objects, or of what is real or unreal. There is *nothing but* an unmediated content in phenomenological view. The *a priori* is a "pure," self-given content in consciousness only—what Scheler often phenomenologically calls a "fact." It is grasped only "in" consciousness itself as a self-given meaning-content (*Bedeutungsinhalt*). These facts in consciousness can be of both universal validity and individual validity. Indeed, a non-formal *a priori* content of value may be given to only one individual at only one time and never by anyone else. Since the *a priori* meaning-contents can neither be defined nor described, it is an unmediated *a priori* always already "there" before descriptions or definitions can address it. Hence it is a favorite way of Scheler to use examples to show what the story of the *a priori* is all about. At this juncture in particular, we avail ourselves of a case of deception. Let us suppose that while taking a walk we see suddenly a person who draws our immediate attention and we do not know why this person stands out so much from all others. Let us also suppose that at a split second we may realize that this person to be just a dummy. There are two components in such an experience of deception. First there was a live person and then there was an inanimate dummy. Yet, the dummy was first experienced as "alive" and *without* mediation. The "aliveness" (*das Lebendigsein*) of the person was an unmediated or intuited "content" in the deception of the dummy. The apriority in this deceptive experience is the self-given *phenomenon* of aliveness despite there having been a dummy. The example shows two things: first the *a priori* intuited aliveness of the dummy in the deception and, second, the undeceiving (*Ent-täuschung*) of the deception. In both phases of the experience involved, the phenomenon of aliveness is unaffected, or *a priori* to what has happened. This is also the reason why a phenomenon, which for Scheler is always non-formal *a priori*, is "there." This example may suffice at this point also to show why the contents of *values* are phenomena. But values do not only constitute part of outer perception as the phenomenon of aliveness did in the given example. Values likewise constitute the moral status of the inner being of the person and of communities of persons, that is, their moral tenor and ethos. While the phenomenon of "aliveness" stays translucent in the deception, it is also translucent in such trifle things as cartoons on a screen, or in the plastic doll to which a young girl talks and the doll that talks to the girl.

The nature of an *a priori* phenomenon implies that no mediated experience could ever be made accessible as an intuited "immanent" fact. For only what is "intuitively" given in acts is a phenomenon for Scheler. In this immanent experience both what is "given" and what is "meant" wholly coincide. That is, what is given is meant, and what is meant is given. It is in this coincidence that the phenomenological *a priori* consists. And it is in this coincidence that there is self-evidential "truth," without its antithesis of falsehood. Scheler repeatedly refers to Spinoza in saying that truth is the criterion of itself *and* of falsehood.

We can now investigate the emotive *a priori* of the being of values. We already referred briefly to the transverse character of the emotive *a priori*. The *a priori* was said to pertain to the heights of value-ranks and to the positive and negative values of each rank. But it was not yet clear how the *a priori* of self-givenness of value-meanings is to be understood.

The self-given value *a priori* lies in the unmediated act of preferring, which is the foundation of the feeling of values. Only values given in acts of preferring can be felt (II 107/F 89).

The word "preferring" as used in *Formalism* is, like its German counterpart "*vorziehen*," somewhat misleading because of the everyday usage of the word as meaning "choosing." Phenomenological preferring used in *Formalism*, however, is said to occur in the absence of deliberate choosing, willing and conations. Its meaning comes close to when we say that we are "leaning toward" something that intimates a positive value. Indeed, preferring always relates to values. In this sense, one cannot "lean toward" a negative value. We can choose or will something only after the preferring of a value has taken place. In this, we are simultaneously "attracted" by a positive value, pulling us toward it while it flashes out *in and during* preferring.

While the act of preferring is the foundation for feeling, preferring has its own foundation in the act of *love*. Loving is distinct from preferring in that love does *not* require a second term for it to occur. We do not love something over something else, but *something*. This may best be illustrated by the indivisible moment of love at *first sight*. There is no need for another term of comparison; rather, love's arrow shoots straight forward to one, and only one, value-object in the absence of any other object. Preferring, however, requires at least the possibility of another value-term, even if this possibility is very remote. Choosing requires even two objects for it to occur.

The above instance of a value-deception occurring in the phenomenon of "aliveness" provides us with another clue as to the apriority of values. Preferring is *a priori* if it occurs *between* two different values and between nothing else. This is why we had stressed the transversality of the emotive *a priori*. The being-higher of a value lies *in* its being preferred and vice versa. The height of a value lies in its own essence. In the value-deception mentioned above, "aliveness" is preferred. The dummy's "usefulness" for the store in the mall is not at all self-given in the experience concerned. The value-height is itself a phenomenon in the preferring. Yet, a deception takes place. The dummy is mistaken for a live person. Whenever such value-deception takes place it can have serious consequences for the entire life of a person and a whole civilization. Scheler was the only phenomenologist who focused on deception and error from a phenomenological viewpoint (III 213-292; PE 3-97). We will cover these topics in Chapter five dealing with human resentment.

On the surface, there appears to be a contradiction in Scheler's emotive *a priori*. It consists, on the one hand, in maintaining that historical systems of preferring are variable, and on the other hand, that the ranks among values are invariable. He calls a variable system of preferring an "*ethos*" and maintains that there are various preference systems throughout history. How can the *a priori* residual in preferring allow of such variations of an ethos? In the respective section of the "Dimensions of Variations of Ethos," Scheler does not refer to such residual in preferring. One would have to think that the *a priori* in preferring is not variable. Or is it? Its variability consists in preferring itself. Preferring allows of both vertical and horizontal positive values. Thus the *a priori* does not mean that it can shift at any time. Rather, the *a priori* lies in the being-higher of a given value; this allows the historical relativity among value-preferences, or the so-called "relativity of value-estimations," an area that Scheler leaves for further research. He indicates, however, that the relativity of value-estimations may at first look like a "palette daubed with paint," but that seen from an appropriate distance it would gradually assume the profile of a grandiose painting, or fragments thereof, making translucent the invariable order of value-ranks to mankind, mixed and daubed as it is itself by races, nations, cultures and religions. In other words, while the order of value-ranks is invariable, and while the most important *a priori* relations consist in the order of their rules of "preferring," the *a priori* relations are, by contrast, variable. Preferring can focus on any particular value-rank or value.

Given the inseparability of preferring and the heights of the value *a priori*, we can now see that the variable structure of preferring values, or of not preferring values, "circumscribes" the feelings of values that humans can have. Feeling has its own, albeit secondary, apriority. We "feel" that mental values are higher and more enduring than non-mental value ranks, no matter how much we can be deceived to prefer the latter.

Scheler's critique of the formalism in ethics culminates in a moot historical observation he makes of modern Western civilization. The formal apriority is deeply conjoined with a Kantian attitude expressive of a "hostility," "distrust," and "angst" of the world that is believed to be in dire need of rational formation and organization. It is a distrust of the so-called chaos in the realm of feelings articulated since Descartes. This Western distrust gives rise to a hatred of the world which, in turn, engenders an unceasing drive for "lawmaking" and "forming" so that man and world can be brought under relative control. The modern era lacks, therefore, what Scheler considers to be the heart of the well-being of the human race: "*love* of the world, of trust in and loving *devotion* to the world" (II 85/F 67).

2. The Peculiarity of Moral Values.
Good and Evil and the Realm of Values
a) Good and Evil and the Five Ranks of Non-Moral Values

The values of the two highest ranks, mental and religious values, are not the only values given and felt only by the human person. To be added to them are the central values of ethics: good and evil. They, too, are *a priori* phenomena, but of a peculiar nature.

On the basis of the explication of the act of preferring one could expect that good and evil are correlative objects of this act. Indeed, one can prefer good over evil and can will and choose good at any time. However, good and evil do not belong to any of the five value-ranks as listed. Accordingly they must have a special status distinguishing them from all other values. This is indeed the case. They do not belong to the five value-ranks because their occurrence possesses a special status. They are purely temporal or, in present day phenomenological terminology, they "constitute themselves." They arise by themselves. They are no objects to be realized in any act correlated to the values of the five value-ranks. This novel explanation of good and evil deserves much attention because in our own times there is still a lingering belief that good and evil are to be realized by acts and actions or that they are secondary to the values of right and wrong. We retain Scheler's terminology of good and evil as "moral values" while the values of the value ranks are termed non-moral values. This terminology indeed simplifies matters, although one cannot, strictly speaking, readily accept the expression "non-moral values" in the discipline of ethics when such an expression refers to positive values.

Good and evil occur as values in spontaneous and genuine value-realization. But they also appear in a realization of a value which is not genuinely spontaneous. The latter is the case when a person has a deliberate intention of purposefully realizing goodness. Through non-spontaneous value-realizations there are many possibilities of self-deception. Someone who utilizes an opportunity to show that he is good by extending help ostentatiously for displaying goodness, perhaps even marketing his goodness, Scheler calls a pharisee. Within the fabric of personality, the person may subconsciously just want to "appear" good to others. This does not exclude the possibility that such a person has a good will; but it does indicate the slippery paths which can lead to self-deceptions about one's own self-value. These slippery paths have a prominent role in society. As we shall see, the very nature of contrived humanitarian attitudes are not infrequently riveted in a deep-seated individual "impotency" of extending spontaneous, Samaritan aid without having any publicity in mind.

What are those moral values of good and evil, and why are they not contained in the value-ranks? Why do they occur exclusively in human existence?

In contrast to the values of the five ranks, good and evil do not require a necessary relation to things. The relationship that the values of the five ranks have to material things increases in the descending order of the ranks. The value of holiness may, but does not necessarily require a modest role of material things, such as a cup, bread, a statue, a symbol. The second highest rank of values of the mind requires more things, such as paper, books, paint, marble, records. The third rank from the top, that of life values, has numerous ties to things in nature—although life itself is not a thing. Utilitarian and pleasure values, however, are inseparable from things.

No comparable relation to things pertains to good and evil. For this reason they are purely personal. Indeed, no "thing" can be morally good or evil, unless used as a means in a moral situation. Even in this there is doubt. In its essence it can at best be practically good or bad as being useful, efficient, practical, or the opposite. Nevertheless, good and evil do occur in conjunction with acts of preferring non-moral values, whereas non-moral values themselves are restricted to their proper ranks, save for cases of value-deceptions.

This point deserves more attention than it has hitherto been paid because, as was stated earlier, things have a pervasive function throughout all value-ranks, although this function contains much room for the independence that exists between values and things. We are faced here with an antithetic situation concerning the moral values of good and evil, on the one hand, and things, on the other. Whereas good and evil are detached from things, good and evil are, nevertheless, in a relation with things.

While good and evil are not given in sensible feelings at all, they nevertheless occur in conjunction with the lower ranks. An example may serve to illustrate this. When a person living in an underdeveloped country prefers the utility value of building a shelter out of concern for his impoverished family over values of pleasure, he evidently realizes a moral good in preferring the utility value of the shelter to sensible pleasure. In this case, good and evil appear to be connected with the material things of which the shelter is made, despite the independence of good and evil from things because they can occur only with a person. But in this case they occur unmistakably with the person's *use* of things which are necessary to realize the higher value of the well-being of the family. Let us keep in mind that the relation between the moral values of the person and their relation to things is problematic.

b) The Temporality of Good and Evil. The Being of the Person. The Basic Moral Tenor and Conscience.

Besides the peculiarity of good and evil with regard to things, another argument for their unique character can be advanced that has been overlooked by almost all twentieth century philosophers. It will clarify Max Scheler's contention that ethics must do justice to the irreplaceable self-value and dignity of the individual person as the bearer of all values in an ever changing moral world. Scheler says:

> We must emphatically reject Kant's assertion that good and evil are *originally* attached only to acts of willing. That which can be called *originally* "good" and "evil," i.e., that which bears the non-formal values of "good" and "evil" prior to and independent of all individual acts is the "*person*," the *being* of the person itself. (II 49/F 28)

Only the *being* of the person, not an individual act itself, such as one of the will, can be good or evil. What, then, does "person" mean if the person alone can be good and evil?

To answer this question let us first see where Scheler locates good and evil in the structure of the universe. In so doing, he belongs to a tradition that started with the German Mystics and which was followed by Schelling and Berdyaev. These attempts are interesting because good and evil are seen in a metaphysical or an ontological light.

Scheler gives a concise description of the ontological dimension of good and evil at the beginning of his essay, "Shame and Feelings of Modesty," published in 1913 (X 65-164/PV 385). Compared to what Jean-Paul Sartre and Nietzsche say about human shame, one must give credit to Scheler's essay. It is without doubt the finest piece ever written in philosophical literature about the phenomenon of shame. Scheler may well have been reflecting how shame is becoming a rare manifestation of being human in modern society.

At the beginning of this essay we read that the place of being human in the structure (*Stufenbau*) of the universe is between divinity and animality. There is no human feeling except that of shame which can betoken this location so clearly. This location spans man's "spirit" and the dark feelings of life, many of which we share with animals. Only when the light of consciousness is "existentially" bound up with a living organism, as is the case in the embodied person, and only when this light shines down on the wellings of our inner life, there is the basic condition for shame, and the obscure origins of its occurrence. Disregarding what one may be ashamed of, and disregarding the various kinds of shame Scheler elaborates, shame occurs when we are lost in personal values and acts and when we, all of a sudden, become attached to our animal-like and bodily existence which is limited in time and space. This reattaching occurs in a sudden *turn* (*Zurückwendung*) from personal existence *back* onto vital existence, no matter if this turn starts in us or is caused by something else.

Shame also occurs in the opposite case when we are lost in our bodily existence but suddenly disturbed by someone else. Whenever shame occurs, this turning back from a purely mental to a plain of vital existence and vice versa reveals the very condition for the occurrence of shame. This condition is a *disharmony* and imbalance between the sphere of the person and that of our lives. Moreover, maximum good is only present in God and maximum evil is personified only in the devil: neither God nor the devil can feel shame. God is only good and lacks evil. The devil is only evil and lacks goodness. Man, however, is between God and the devil and is, therefore, a "bridge" between good and evil and *must* shame. The location of good *and* evil in man is, therefore, to be seen when man is conceived to be a "bridge" between good and evil. While this bridge may look like it has an infinite span, it does not touch either end because man is never perfectly good nor completely evil. He partakes in both, and this makes possible the feeling of shame. We have presented this picture of shame as located between good and evil because it sets the stage for what Scheler will tell us about them in more detail in *Formalism*, where good and evil are seen in light of the nature of human personhood.

What is called "person" exists only in and through the *execution* of acts. "Act" has the common phenomenological meaning of an activity of the mind in which there is "consciousness-of-something." But in the Schelerian sense, the term extends it to include pre-conscious acts of feeling and preferring. Such acts of consciousness are, for instance, "thinking," "willing," "loving," "hating," "remembering," "expecting," "dreaming," "hallucinating," "lying," "paying attention," "understanding," "believing," "wishing," "thanking," "praying," etc. Different acts can also overlap as, for example, an act of hating something while being in an act of remembering it. It is of utmost phenomenological importance to keep in mind that while the person exists "in" executing any act or acts, the person "varies" in and through the differences acts have among them. The person suffuses every act with its uniquely individual traits and, reciprocally, every act is suffused by the individual person. This Schelerian position is in sharp contrast to Husserl for whom the "ego" does not allow of personal variations. For Husserl, the ego precedes what he understands to be "person."

We can see already at this point that Scheler's *Formalism* must be fundamentally different from Husserl's point of departure in *Ideas I* of 1913. (These hitherto often misunderstood differences will be discussed later.)

An example may pinpoint the practical meaning of the person's "variation" while executing acts. Suppose a number of persons are writing down the same sentence at the same time. Each written sentence reveals a different handwriting. The action of writing down the same sentence varies with each person. No two persons write the sentence in the same way. This would support Scheler's argument that every individual person is mirrored in the execution of any one act, just as metaphorically the person is mirrored in the style of handwriting. The person varies in the act being acted out. A person in an act of loving varies when he hates. A person known to me only as a strict teacher varies when I see him enjoy dancing. All this seems simple, but throughout all possible variations of an individual person in all acts which a person is possible to execute *there remains one and the same person*. One may call this personal "identity in variation." Each person varies uniquely in every act. The individually unique execution of any act as different from any other act that is executed provides us with a clue for Scheler's contention that every person has its own "irreplaceable" self-value.

It would follow from the existential dynamics of the person as an "act-being" who as a whole is the sole bearer of good and evil that one specific act, such as the act the will, is not the seat for the occurrence of good and evil, as Kant had held. Good and evil are not necessary for there to be an act of willing. Moreover, one can will countless things: there appears to be no reason why the willing of good should have a priority over willing of justice, or why a good will should be considered better than a just will.

Since neither good nor evil are necessary for rational willing or of any other act, they are said "to ride on the back" of any preferring act which *realizes* a higher or, in the case of evil, a lower value in the transverse order of values. That good and evil only "ride on the back" of value realizations not only explains why willing them alone does not make a person good or evil; the expression "to ride on the back" is also an index for the temporality of the person himself in that the person exists only in executing its existence by acting out its acts. The core of good or evil as pure personal values is seen in the person's *be-ing* good or *be-ing* evil, not in seeking good and evil as objects,— although Scheler does not object to the latter as a secondary form of realizing a good.

Good and evil are, first of all, moral-existential categories of the temporality of the person. At first sight, this seems to be a complex assertion because the terms "temporality" and "being" are used in the explication of good and evil. This complexity is able to be resolved, however, when the word being is taken as a verb, which was indicated by hyphenating the word. The verb *be-ing* is commensurate to the temporality itself of the person. It prevents the word from being taken as a noun that could lead to the implication that the person has a "substance," a conclusion to which Scheler strongly objects.

Let an illustration bring this state of affairs into focus. Imagine a child playing with toys in the backyard who spontaneously picks a daisy and brings it to his mother, saying, "Mom, here is a daisy for you." The root of the good in this example lies in spontaneously realizing the value of love of the mother over preferring the play with toys. By no means is it a case of a good deliberately realized for any specific purpose; nor is the good willed before the spontaneous picking of the daisy. The child does not "will" a good. Rather, the child simply picks the daisy and brings it to his mother. At the moment of picking the daisy, the child acts out of his *lived moral make-up which sets the stage* for the inception of the deed. It is in the emotive make-up of the child in that particular situation, or of any adult in any moral situation, that a degree of moral goodness *constitutes itself* while realizing a value higher than a given one. The goodness of the child rides on the back of the spontaneous preferring the daisy and the mother; the preferring flows from the child's heart, not from reason or will. The good attaches itself, so to speak, to the realization of a positive value. The good is an echo that resounds the prevolitional inception of emotively preferring a higher value. Of course, in this illustration of good riding on an act of realizing a positive value, the positive value realized is the love of the mother, which is not a non-moral value, but rather a moral value of her self-value. Hence a good does not only occur when a non-moral value is realized: it also occurs when the value realized is that of a person. This is always the case in the realization of the love of a person.

What has been referred to as the "lived moral make-up" of the child from which the inception of the act of value-realization was said to flow, can now be specified. The lived moral make-up refers to a term that is part and parcel of, and peculiar to, most systems of ethics enunciated by German ethicists, including Kant. The German term at issue is "*die Gesinnung*," which we have rendered elsewhere as "basic moral tenor." Translating *Gesinnung* as "state of mind" is misleading. Sometimes, "basic moral tenor" approximates the English "personality." The basic moral tenor of a person underlies human reason *and* will. It is the "direction" all acts have in a person, including volitional acts.

The direction of the will as one characteristic of the moral tenor is an important component of the ethics with which we are dealing because (1) *Formalism* is a *critique* of the formalism in ethics such as Kant's, and (2) because Scheler's ethics *does not set up an imperative* to be followed by the human race at all times. This follows because the existence and occurrence of good and evil only rides on the back of the realization of a value by a person. The quality of "riding" is a temporal manifestation of good and evil. Good and evil *temporalize* themselves while riding on the back of value-realizations.

In his own way, Kant also refers to the basic moral tenor (*Gesinnung*). For Kant, it cannot be "experienced" because it is no more than a "form" of intentions, whereas intentions are said to be able to be experienced. Kant's conception of the moral tenor consists only in "lawful," and never an unlawful arrangement of an intention of will-ing the good. In contrast to Kant, Scheler maintains that the basic moral tenor is (1) able to be experienced as a specific value-content, and (2) that it *suffuses* the will. The basic moral tenor gives the will a direction of when and how it should will.

This direction is essential to the nature of the basic moral tenor in the sense that the *direction* of willing, as well as of all other acts, is inseparable from the quality of the moral tenor. Therefore, the *Gesinnung*, or moral tenor, has the same function among all acts. In the illustration of the child picking a daisy for the mother, the child's moral tenor is not a Kantian "form" of intentions, nor is it the good realized by dint of such a form. Rather, the directive function of the child's moral tenor *precedes* the will's project, but in such a way as not to exclude a freedom of the will to do otherwise after a rational decision to do so.

The above discussion of the moral tenor of a person implies that each individual person possesses his own individual basic moral tenor. For this reason, no two persons are morally equal. There are count-less types of basic moral tenors: loving, distrusting, resentful, cold, lackadaisical, martial, stingy, heartless, and so on. No matter what the individual moral tenor may be, it also colors the *inception* of all acts. It sets the stage, as we put it above, for all acts and actions of an individual. The type of intentions and acts flowing from a loving and caring moral tenor must, therefore, be qualitatively different from a resentful, jealous or belligerent moral tenor. Let it be added that whole groups may share a moral tenor common to their group, a "group-tenor" (*Gruppengesinnung*). One can find various group tenors among religious, ethnic, political, and social groups, estates and classes. Plato may have had a moral group tenor in mind when we referred to the bronze, silver and golden character of groups in the *Republic*.

In stating that a person's basic moral tenor sets the stage, as it were, for the direction acts and deeds take, the moral tenor is taken to be an internal quality of personhood. But it also makes itself perceiv-able, for it permeates movements and expressions of a person's lived body. The literal meaning of person, coming from "*personare*," helps to demonstrate that the moral tenor "sounds through" the lived body's movements, gesticulations, appearance and expressions. It can infuse all levels of personal existence. A sorrowful moral tenor still permeates a feeling-state of joy, no matter how slightly; and joy can still permeate sorrow.

The levels of personal existence appear to have individual directions of respective moral tenors. In *Formalism* (II 158/F 144) they are listed along with their phenomenological correlatives as follows :

Person : World
Lived body : Environment (biological)
Ego : Exterior World
Object-body : Inanimate bodies
Soul : Lived-body-ego

These levels represent the basic phenomenological structure of being human. If the moral tenor is said to suffuse all levels of an individual, this is again saying that the possibility of good and evil as existential categories lies in the very "*be-ing*" of the person, i.e. the temporality of the person's existence. The *be-ing* of the person "exists," as was indicated earlier, (1) in the acting out of acts different in kind and nature and, (2) in the individually "qualitative direction" all acts have. This brings us one step closer to an understanding of the essence of *be-ing* a person. The temporality of the person must not be confused with measurable time or clock-time. Temporality properly speaking is, and must be, of quite a different character because the person itself cannot be measured—because the person is not an "object." The temporality at issue here will only come into full view later, as Scheler had not yet elaborated it during his first period of production. Nevertheless, he presented a sketch of it already in 1909 in a lecture on the "Foundations of the Historical Sciences" (*Grundlagen der Geschichtswissenschaft*) (XIII 167-238).

With regard to the practical and immediate relevance of what Scheler is telling us about the nature of the person is, we must stress, an often used expression of his, namely, the "sphere" of the person. The sphere of *be-ing* a person does not depend on gender and race. The sphere of the person is not only indifferent to them but is also above other phenomena such as the ego, lived-body or object-body.

The temporality of good and evil already discussed as occurring in every person in the act of realizing a value is also corroborated by the criterion of the *duration* of strictly personal values of the mind and of holiness. As pure value-*qualities*, these values cannot be divided, quantified, or artificially produced. They defy manipulatory management, in sharp contrast to the pragmatic and pleasure values.

Given the force of the argument of declaring the person to be the "bearer" of values including good and evil, one must admit that such a tenet must lead to consequential arguments concerning moral dilemmas especially familiar today, such as abortion, euthanasia, surrogate motherhood, genetic engineering and child abuse, to mention a few. In Scheler's own time, these problems were not as poignant as they are today, but he clearly saw them and occasionally addressed their moral implications on the basis of his value-ethics. Any ethics must contain guidance to these and other moral dilemmas even if it does not directly address them. It is in this that the viability of an ethics lies: it must be able to show how any moral dilemma now and *at any time* can be scrutinized from its very foundation. As Scheler puts it, "*Ethics is a damn bloody affair. If it cannot give me directives of how 'I' should be now, and 'ought' to be in my social and historical nexus, what, then, is it?*" (II 590)

We cannot show here how *Formalism* would shed light on virtually all of the major moral dilemmas of our time. Clearly, this would require a separate, but worthwhile, study. But let us look at least at one of the dilemmas, abortion, from a Schelerian perspective.

All sides in the above-mentioned moral problems are connected with an orientation toward the divisible values and their ranks, such as family planning, overpopulation, economic conditions, or societal shortcomings in general. The immensely divisive and litigious character of *society* shows strong propensities to solve moral dilemmas in terms of quantifiable and, therefore, more or less definable values. This in turn lends itself to legalistic delineations of right and wrong; this is a *sociological* reason why the very conception of the above problems and their possible solutions are charged with quantifiable values. The relationship between society and quantifiable values is discussed in *Formalism* (II 517-522/F 528-533) and in *Problems of a Sociology of Knowledge* (1924). This will be taken up later in more detail. The being of the person does not appear to be a moral base for solutions to the moral problems we are facing today.

On the basis of *Formalism*, abortion is killing, not murder because the embryo is not given as personality (II 319/F 315). Murder pertains to the extinction of an individual given as person and his self-value. Accordingly, capital punishment is murder, not killing, and should for this reason also be abolished (II 317/F 313). It also follows from this that one cannot murder an animal, but only kill one. An animal has no personality because it cannot think or will. In war, the enemy is not given as personal either and can, therefore, only be killed as an anonymous group.

According to the order of value-ranks, one must, nevertheless, also say that abortion sacrifices a living entity to lower quantifiable values, such as family-planning, pleasure-sex, or to one-parent family values, etc. Considered in this way, abortion is objectified as a rational choice, defying the evidential preference of the value of life over quantifiable values of lower ranks. In *Formalism*, the fetus is not a person, yet it must be regarded as a life value and its birth be emotively preferred over quantifiable values such as planning.

These moral consequences of abortion are certainly not enough to encompass all of its moral implications, but at least Scheler gave us a direction. He was one of the very few philosophers of his time who was concerned with such complex moral issues in his moral and political writings. As for other philosophers, we have only glimpses from a very few about what they would or could have said about abortion. For Aristotle, abortion can be seen in light of the potency that the fetus has for developing into the form of a rational animal. From this standpoint, it is hard to see how he could have promoted abortion. Christian thinkers from St. Augustine on could not allow it on the basis of faith. Kant does not seem to be concerned with it, probably because his categorical imperative could not allow abortion to be part of a "universal legislation" for obvious reasons. Perhaps Nietzsche would be *the* philosopher of today's "pro-life" movement. For him, the value of life is the highest value incorporated in the Will to Power as the essence of life which, in its purest form, possesses the value of the *innocence* of an infant, a value "beyond" good and evil and right and wrong, which are for him miscarriages of rational interpretations. Later thinkers like Husserl, Heidegger, Jaspers, Sartre and Merleau-Ponty, for example, seem to have regarded such moral issues as either not pertaining to philosophy or as a private matter of daily life, even though the issue of abortion is older than the Hippocratic Oath that embodies the duties of physicians. It would appear that foundational ethics, on the one hand, and present day legal and medical ethics, on the other, are still at odds in the matter of abortion. Because of the uniqueness of the person as bearer of all values, Scheler never abandoned the principle that the individual person represents the highest value. In his first period it is characteristic for him to place the person's dynamic existence in a position between God and Satan, between good and animality. God, on the one hand, can only be good; Satan can only be evil. But the human person can be a "bridge" between them both, as stated earlier.

Moral tenor cannot be separated from a person. It cannot be separated from a person's conscience. At this point we must open our discussion of conscience.

What has thus far been said about the moral tenor allows a critique at this point. In saying that the moral tenor amounts to a fixed cast determining the direction a person's acts, it could also be said that this direction cannot be changed because willing such change would have to remain within the same direction of the moral tenor: this would imply an encroachment on freedom in the moral tenor. This is a problem which has haunted representatives of German Idealism whenever the nature of the moral tenor has arisen. Scheler, however, admitted with good reason that at least one such change in the tenor is possible, namely in the religious experience of conversion. But even if a change in the moral tenor were seen as impossible, this would not preclude the possibility of the *freedom of conscience*, for which Scheler offered a new explication, very different from many traditional conceptualizations of it.

Thus far we have addressed the basic moral tenor as (1) a phenomenon of possibility of experience of the individual person, and (2) as a phenomenon experienced among groups identifying this or that group as also having specific value preferences and a "system" of value preferences (ethos).

Since the basic moral tenor occurs both in individuals and groups, and since there is no universal moral tenor of humankind, it cannot give rise to a universal voice that would morally bind all human beings to what ought to be done. Both the moral tenor and an ethos are always restricted to *particular* systems of value-preferences and individual groups.

Nevertheless, a moral tenor of one particular individual can at times exercise a fascinating historical power and influence of "exemplarity." It can assume the role of an indisputable, moral exemplarity providing many human beings with ineffable guidelines for their moral comportment. The exemplarity of one person may, of course, vary in degree of significance from age to age. During his first period, Scheler assigned such an exemplary moral tenor to St. Francis of Assisi. St. Francis' moral tenor was replete with peaceful and serene thankfulness to God for all nature and its creatures, down to the smallest; thankfulness for light, space and air that sustain nature, and for his own limbs and breath. In a rare moral tenor such as this one, the divine gift to man, nature, is, however, not for man to possess; rather, in receiving the gift freely from God, man embraces and feels God's love in it. It is in this Franciscan "spirit" of humility that the person can be rich without possessions; that is, he becomes rich in freeing himself from the materiality and profit of earthly goods for the sake of seeing every entity, large or small, significant or not, as a divine gift: "*Omnia habemus nil possidentes.*"

Individual richness in this case lies in a new moral tenor of giving everything away for others and thereby receiving the gifts of God. At the end of his first period, Scheler upheld such a rich moral tenor which truly receives in giving against the modern spirit of endless production, acquisition and profit, a spirit Scheler characterized as the "pleonexy" of material goods anchored in the modern "heart" disordered in its feelings by the strong sensitivity of lower value-ranks. According to Scheler, endless profit-seeking has lead political capitalism to be sharply distinguished (as we shall see) from historical capitalism. Scheler seems never have discarded the value of the exemplarity of Francis in order to show that a moral tenor can indeed be changed by a person of moral exemplarity.

Despite the significance a moral tenor has in a genuine religious experience, it does not provide an immediate moral direction for all. To put it somewhat simply: each religion seems to have its unique scope of moral tenor. In this regard, Scheler again carefully avoids establishing something like a universal moral principle. The question could be put to him why even conscience cannot provide a universally acceptable moral insight. This question offers itself because ever since conscience has become a key concept in modern ethics, ethicists have remained divided on the question of whether or not conscience reflects, at least in part, universally acceptable norms which would dictate to all what ought to be done in certain situations. In short, the issue is whether conscience is only relative to an existing ethos and, therefore, would lack universal validity.

The two seemingly irreconcilable alternatives of either individual subjective conscience or a conscience providing universally acceptable norms continues to play a surreptitious role in our society. One can refer to such conflict as one of "freedom of individual conscience" versus a "formal and universal conscience." While there is ground for the argument that a freedom of conscience potentially allows for moral pandemonium, it can also be argued that a universal conscience suppresses individual freedom. In our own time the issue simmers underneath various controversies. For instance, it is for the most part left to individual conscience of a conscientious objector to decide whether or not to avoid the draft. Similarly, it is left to the disposition of an individual conscience whether to consent to aborting a fetus.

Might there be a predominantly universal conscience telling us what ought to be done, or not done, in such cases? The controversy seems to flare up whenever an individual's moral tenor is not in tandem with a collective, overriding power, such as a state, government or long traditions. The collapse of dictatorial Communist states clearly shows that individual conscience did not succumb altogether to a state-conscience (*das Staatsgewissen*). Further, whenever a universal conscience is upheld over against the individual conscience, a dilemma is posed for religion. Whenever the faithful members are instructed to subordinate their conscience to that of a general faith, there always remain sheep running counter to the flock, whether openly or clandestinely. Additionally, there are also always individuals in a society who do not align themselves with society's rules of order. Finally, there are always people who refuse to follow directives of authority in any manifestation on the basis of a belief in the priority of individual conscience and value-feelings. In cases such as these, individual conscience can be very strong indeed, and in some cases such conscience is only evident to the particular individual.

Scheler's conception of conscience is immensely challenging insofar as the traditional alternatives just mentioned are discarded by him altogether. His description of the nature of conscience begins from a practical perspective and asks the question of how conscience is to function in a practical situation. Up to this point Scheler has told us that universality in ethics, such as formulated by Kant's categorical imperative, does not work in individual practice. It follows that the freedom of individual conscience must not be underestimated even by a formalist and rational ethicist. How, then, does individual conscience function?

We stated that any moral "ought" is based in the *value* of what ought to be done. In this sense moral oughtness is independent of an imperative which is devoid of articulating a value. The priority that value-feelings have pertains, therefore, to what is a "call" of conscience. The core of what we individually ought to be and to do is anchored in value-feelings, more precisely in feelings of one's self-value, because a call of conscience pertains to a comparison between what "I" am and what "I" ought to be or ought to be doing. In a way, there are always two I's: one that is present; the other that extends into a near or distant future. But how is the value of our oughtness situated in conscience?

First of all, in *Formalism*, conscience as such is not assigned a primary role in moral experience as one might expect. It is discussed explicitly in only ten places of the text, to be exact. There are two reasons for this: (1) *Formalism* recognizes the experience of values as the foundation of all facets of human morality—*including* conscience; (2) the role of conscience is restricted to only a negative function. When feelings of conscience well up, conscience speaks as a guilty conscience. The call of conscience first sets to work by telling us what we ought *not* to do. Only on this basis can conscience subsequently tell us what we *should* do. There cannot be conscience without its negating function. All wellings of conscience are rooted in negative experiences of guilt, of repentance, of regret or remorse. Therefore, conscience contributes at best only indirectly to what ought to be done. If it does lead us to a positive moral insight, it must have welled up from negating a negative value-experience of what ought not be or ought not to be done.

This argument purports, therefore, that conscience by itself does not point to a universally applicable insight of what is indisputably good for all human beings. What conscience can sometimes do positively, however, is this: conscience can sometimes reach a positive insight from the start that is acceptable to all. This happens whenever it accords with moral knowledge accumulated in traditions, history, or moral authority. But this knowledge that is accumulated in conscience through history may produce an appeal as a "moral insight" owing only to the privilege of one individual who is in a unique moral situation that is particular to an individual moral tenor and qualitative direction of acts. This leads us to an important and contentious aspect of conscience.

Since conscience is not a universal moral agency and since its evidential call rests in individual feelings of self-value, a person in a moral situation is in a situation that is not repeatable and is unique to one, and only one, individual. Conscience, in this case, can only provide a moral insight that is "good for me." The expression "for me" has nothing to do with selfishness; nor does conscience calculate what is good for me. (A calculating conscience would be like Pascal's "wager," saying that it is better to have faith than not to have faith in case God exists.)

The "for me" of conscience is only pre-rational and extends far beyond the alternatives of a universal or an individual conscience. The wellings of conscience occur independently of whether I am a moral universalist or an individual subjectivist. They are also independent of an individual's willing the good and finding satisfaction in obeying norms, imperatives, or complying to conventions and traditions. Indeed, conscience aims so far above any generally accepted moral standard that it speaks, as we shall see, in two or more than two persons *differently*, even if they could be in precisely the *same* moral situation.

The unconditional individuality of conscience follows from the *be-ing* of the person itself. This *be-ing* is act-being. It is acted out as the temporality of the qualitative direction of acts. It is at this juncture that the "principle of freedom of conscience" comes into play: every person must be "free" to listen to the call of his conscience. The call of conscience occurs *before* a rational attempt can be made to solve a moral dilemma. The call wells up by pre-rationally negating the negative value of what ought *not* to be done. The *pre-rational inception* of the freedom of conscience is also a moral device, says Scheler, that lends protection from all conceivably false rational claims that may be hidden in universal norms, laws and imperatives. Whatever such rational claims may morally do for the morality of humans, they can control neither the pre-rational inception of the freedom of conscience nor its simultaneous negating the disvalue of what ought *not* to be done. Scheler holds, therefore, that all statements of what ought to be and ought to be done are conditioned by the emotive insight of what ought not to be and ought not to be done.

Individual conscience can truly provide guidance and insight into the shortcomings of the moral tradition. (Clearly conscience has been at work in relation to tradition in the modern era when, for example, traditional forms of torture had been abolished.)

Granted, conscience can provide us with degrees of moral insight; granted also that it refers to what is morally good "for me" in a particular situation. Likewise let it be admitted that conscience may summon a person to act in a different manner from others in same situation. It is necessary, therefore, to provide an explanation of the interplay between the order of values and conscience.

c) The Call of Repentance

The interplay of values and the self-value of the person in the call of conscience appears to be most apparent in the act of repentance. Scheler's essay on this subject, "Repentance and Re-Birth" (V 27-59/ PV 33-65) is intrinsically tied up with his value-theory.

Phenomenologically, the inception of an act of repentance has two temporal dimensions: the past and the future. In this act, conscience can temporalize its feelings into (a) what was given in an earlier experience, and (b) into what would occur when a deed has been done. An example of the latter would be when a person weighs in his conscience whether to harm another in a unique opportunity in the future to make profit, or when a military leader weighs whether he should sacrifice the lives of his outnumbered soldiers before attacking the enemy. In such cases feelings of conscience well up *prior* to a deed.

If an act of repentance pertains to a deed done in the past it effectuates a present repentance. In this case, time flows from the *past* deed into the present repentance. The aforementioned cases of conscience, however, also show that time can flow from the *future* back onto the present, in terms of a projected profit or of expected sacrificing soldiers. This flow of time also occurs in repentance as we will see. First, however, it needs to be made clear that both cases of temporal flux lead to the present, one from behind toward the present, the other backward from the future onto the present.

There are two kinds of repentance: a) one can repent a past "deed," (*Tatreue*) and b) one can repent over one's "having been so" as to have committed the deed (*Seinsreue*). The first kind of repentance is a repentance of a deed, the other is a repentance of a past personal being. It is the latter kind of repentance over one's innermost moral level of "having been so" in the past which will provide us with a first clue for the cryptic and arcane nature of the moral, pre-rational *logos* that lies underneath both a person's moral tenor and his conscience, namely, the *ordo amoris*.

There is no act in a person's consciousness that reveals more to us what we ought to have been like in the past than the act of repenting, that is, repenting the moral level on which we lived during some period of our past. Scheler reminds us that every person always lives on varying higher and lower moral levels. In the present, the act of repentance speaks to us about a past moral level as if saying, "how could I ever have been so" as to have done such a thing. This experience of one's low moral level can be so strong that the person concerned may want to cover his face with his hands, weeping and wailing as if abandoned by all around him. In such a case, the feeling of moral insight into a past moral level gives rise to pangs of inexorable reproach. These pangs are not the menace of a universal imperative; rather, the pangs are *individual* and lay bare the lower moral level of the person's being. They are felt genuinely only when the person has the insight *by himself*, not mediated by someone else. Such moral insight can reach into the various levels of one's moral self-experience and, therefore, of one's own self-value. In such experience of one's own self-value, the act of repentance is always interwoven with the feeling of guilt.

Furthermore, the act of repentance is interwoven with another act: the act of comparing. In the repentance of one's past being, the person's past moral level is *comparingly* repented from a present, higher and different moral level. Emotive comparing in this case makes the person spontaneously feel what he has previously been and what he now is. The act of repentance bends backward onto the level where the guilt of a past deed resides. Repentance pinpoints from among the various possible moral levels the level on which a person ought to live.

According to Scheler what moral level we live on is contingent: one can always be on any other level of good or evil. Each level of good and evil has an infinite number of gradations and intensities. The pinpointing in repentance of a past low level and guilt does not follow causal laws. At its very roots and inceptions, repentance expresses an uncaused freedom of conscience to "dissolve" a past guilt. The act of repentance resembles a "mountain climber" who leaves the dark canyon below and behind him while pulling himself up to an invisible peak, making the canyon of a past bad deed gradually disappear. Repentance "extinguishes" guilt in light of the moral peak the act struggles to reach.

It is from the moral levels near the peak, its goal, that repentance arises. In a manner of speaking, Scheler says, the inception of repentance in this goal is earlier than the panging over the deeds of the past: the panging is evoked by the goal. Re-birth through repentance lies precisely in repentance's ascent, in its approaching a moral peak and the simultaneous disappearing of the canyon of guilt. This structure of repentance is similar to the process in certain animals whose various stages of aging and dying coincide with the gradual rebirth of a new organism. This would parallel Scheler's position that repentance is an act able to change the entire moral tenor of a person, a change of a person's "heart."

The general dwindling of the moral power of repentance in our society is as unfortunate as that of the aforementioned dwindling of shame. Their gradual disappearance has been replaced by a surreptitious *societal* attitude of morally levelling all persons. This diminishes moral respect of an individual's own introspection into his self-value. Persons who are not afraid of having subtle feelings of shame when it occurs and persons who can repent when a moral shortcoming prompts this feeling in them tend to be leveled in society with the increasing numbers of individuals who do not experience shame or repentance. Indeed, we will see that a large segment of society suffers from this inability to look into their moral selves and, instead, live extraverted lives and increasingly seek the enjoyment of public social reward and recognition.

Scheler accuses society of holding the attitude that repentance brings public embarrassment or loss of standing. Society promotes an image that is incompatible with the humiliation that can potentially accompany repentance. Society encourages one to give the *appearance* of feeling good even if this is not the case. Countless products are marketed to this end. Repentance in the form of confessing shortcomings can make one look like a failure to others. In short, repentance is at odds with the prevailing trend of society that encourages one to compete with one's fellow people and to strive always to be a winner.

Individual regrets are rare, Scheler says in his critique of prevailing societal attitudes, for moral or other shortcomings. From this societal perspective, shortcomings are to be blamed on an *external* cause: society is this external cause, a welcome and convenient scapegoat. Children at Scheler's time were taught simply to do better next time and not feel sorry for mistakes. Such instructions are already an external but false moral guideline for the improvement of a child's behavior. While such guidelines may accomplish something, they have little long-term effect. How many external guidelines exist in society's schools alone? They are countless. They numb the capacity to develop well-intended, genuine moral introspection into one's own life. According to Scheler the tendency of society to locate guilt in a source external to the individual contributes to an awesome moral deficit: moral extraversion is hounded by continuous, latent accumulation of evil from the past that individuals tend to emotively smooth over. By being overly preoccupied with its social and political present and future, society muffles the call of repentance.

With the disappearance of repentance, society, often unknowingly, pays a high price. By extinguishing guilt, repentance is the power of renewing the moral tenor of the person whenever the person ascends to the peak of goodness which reveals itself in this feeling. In the order of foundation—not in that of sequence—moral improvement is first an *individual*, not a collective affair. Without individual "*readiness*" to repent no new moral tenor can overtake the person's moral being. The same dynamic pertains to "collective repenting" (*Gesamtreue, Gesamtschuld*) as volumes II, V and XV show. Unfortunately, there is little discussion of collective repenting in Scheler's writings. Collective repentance is a collective call prompting repudiation of an immoral event of the past. This feeling is as subtle as it is rare, but occur it does. During the few hours after an assassination of a president, or after the death of a hero, of a holy man, a statesman or of any beloved person struck with the lightning of tragedy, this collective feeling among persons continues to accumulate. It engenders repentance in *solidarity*. Whether Scheler was right in saying that it spread among Germans after World War I, we cannot know. Whether it spread, to what degree of intensity, or where it spread after the holocaust we do not wish to speculate. Collective repentance is also a literary category. It can suffuse the hearts of an audience having witnessed the demise of a good human being.

It would appear that we can offer a first articulation to the answer of the question of how, in immediate practice, one can bring about a change of the moral tenor of an individual or a group. First, Scheler suggested that this happens when a person of moral exemplarity effectuates a moral "tug" onto his fellow men. Moral exemplarity acts as a vehicle to bring about a moral change of heart (which will be discussed in detail later).

A second vehicle for effectuating a change of heart is learning anew how to feel the significance of one's self-value. In this, the individual will recover from the apparent disappearance in society of the feeling of repentance and "un-deceive" himself (*ent-täuschen*) about the priorities of exterior social and political utopias of the divisible value-ranks of pleasure and utility.

The young Scheler gives this advice on the matter: "No utopianism but repentance is the most *revolutionary* power of the moral world" (V 50/PV 113). The readiness of accepting the pangs of repentance *can* truly "extinguish" them and at the same time give birth to a new person freed from those pangs.

3. The Quintessence of Imperative-Free Ethics of Values and the Person. The Order of Love (ordo amoris). The Call of the Hour (kairos) a) The Functionalization of Moral Experience

In the preceding presentation of Max Scheler's value-ethics, we discussed the following points:

1. The being of values
2. The relations between values and things
3. The ranks among values
4. The be-ing and temporality of the person, of good and evil
5. The moral tenor of the person
6. The freedom of conscience and repentance

We can now take a final step toward what was called the cryptic and arcane nature of the moral *logos* that underlies all of what has been said, namely the "order of love," the *ordo amoris*. The moral logos is cryptic and arcane because it has, as Pascal put it, "reasons of its own" that reason itself does not understand. Those "reasons" do not stand in the light of reason, and if moral reality takes its roots in "reasons" other than rational ones, there is little or no chance that ethics based in traditional rationality can grasp the moral reality of the heart. As William James put it in *The Will to Believe* (IX), "If your heart does not *want* a world of moral reality, your head will assuredly never make you believe in one."

Scheler published his essay "*Ordo Amoris*" in 1916 separately from *Formalism*. This is unfortunate; if he had included the text in *Formalism* it would no doubt have facilitated the reading of the demanding text. In the Preface to the first edition of *Formalism* he apologizes for the lack of organization in the text. Ortega y Gasset aptly commented that Scheler's writings are characterized by a contradiction: "disorganization and clarity."

In the Preface to the second edition (1921), he tells us something helpful to the understanding of his ethics. He states that Pascal's *ordre du coeur* has been revitalized in a time when there is rampant disorder of love among humans. He goes on to say that the "treason" committed in our age against the deepest sources of all moral reality and moral acting—namely, joy and love—is the result of Germany's post-Kantian phobia of a false heroism, of "duty" and of "work." In his essay on "Ressentiment" (1912) Scheler claims to have traced this treason to its den. This essay rather convincingly uncovers a number of the psychological roots of the treason against genuine and true joy and love, a treason characterizing our time. While the "*ordo amoris*" is mentioned in both the essay on "Ressentiment" and in *Formalism*, the first manuscripts we have of his "*Ordo Amoris*" date back only to 1916. Yet, as the references to "*ordo amoris*" indicate in *Formalism* (which was completed before 1913) the intuited essence of an *ordo amoris* in human beings was central to *Formalism* and not only amounts to the core of all writings on morality in the first period but also retains its significance later. There is a non-logical *a priori* that is distinct from the rational *a priori*, the latter one-sidedly having been regarded by Kant as the only *a priori*.

In the foregoing analysis we stressed that all moral oughtness is preceded by the *value* of that which ought to be done. But Scheler has not yet furnished us with an explanation of the factors *by and after which* conscience operates in its supposedly pre-logical functions that pinpoint the emotive level on which a particular evil is located in the moral experience of a person. The explanation of how conscience operates to achieve this end will lead us to the region of the very moral logos under discussion.

An explanation of how conscience operates in its pre-logical functions is embedded in yet another concept touched upon earlier. This concept forms part of the quintessence of Scheler's entire philosophy. It must now be afforded greater clarity before we examine the moral essence the *ordo amoris*.

The concept concerned is called by Scheler *Funktionalisierung*, or "functionalization." The failure in the past of not seeing, let alone discussing, the process of functionalization by luminaries of Scheler's lifetime contributed largely to the fact that the core of Scheler's critique of general formalism in ethics in favor of a non-formal ethics of values had largely been underestimated. Not only had the being of values been underestimated by both Husserl and Heidegger, for instance, but also the temporality of the person, as well as the dimensions of value ethics. Indeed, it appears that Husserl, Heidegger, Sartre, and other central figures of the phenomenological movement, had at best a cursory familiarity with *Formalism*. Husserl read it only in the early twenties; Heidegger once told me that Scheler's ethics did not have enough references to Aristotle. Had Heidegger read the *Preface* to Scheler's third edition of 1926 in which Scheler states that value ethics must not stand its test by casting new light on Aristotle, Heidegger would not have made such statement. Scheler states explicitly: "*Amicus Aristoteles, magis amicus veritas.*"

Why is "functionalization" significant in moral experience and what, precisely, is it when we look at it a second time in our context? What is its role in the processes of conscience?

Functionalization is a subliminal process of interaction between spirit and reality. The term spirit (*Geist*) includes all emotive value experience. The interaction concerned takes place between ideas, concepts, meanings, on the one hand, and *reality*, on the other, in which such spiritual phenomena may or may not realize themselves. Functionalization is significant not only because it plays an integral part in all of Scheler's works, but also because it plays a significant role in our everyday lives, much as we might remain largely unaware of it.

Functionalization is that conception which kept Scheler in connection with the exponents of Pragmatism. Functionalization is at work when an insight into a state of affairs occurs *while* making trials, probings, or experiments with things or states of affairs. The insight is said to occur initially without special awareness of its importance. In this sense, functionalizations infuse the ongoing work of craftsmen, artists, designers, inventors, planners of economics, politics, sports: in short in all walks of life. In *Formalism* (II 155, 565/F 141, 579) we are told that an artist is "controlled" by the aesthetic laws without consciously "applying" them.

It is only when the artist experiences something going astray "in" his artistic executions, that is, when his activity begins to be disturbed and veers from aesthetic laws, that he first becomes aware and gains such insight as to what should just have been done. The artist will then make appropriate emendations, improvements or corrections on the work he is creating. Perhaps geometry is a prototype of the roles that intertwine in functionalizations between ideas and reality. Scheler's theory would have it that geometric laws and axioms governing circles and triangles, for example, have *no* existence prior to their functionalization and discovery: they were not in a Platonic heaven.

Unbeknownst to Euclid, for example, who "found" them, axioms and laws are not preexisting data, but functionalize themselves *during* the sketching of geometrical figures in the sand. The axioms emerge *with* the things drawn in the sand. Again, they did not exist before; they entered into a function with reality. If they are unable to do this, they are soon abandoned and forgotten. Reality is, as it were, the fertile ground for the realization of ideas. If this ground in not sufficiently fertile to germinate ideas, ideas remain historically impotent. The formulation of axioms and ideas which follow upon their emergence in their testing and probing presupposes their dynamic functionalization *with* things. This functionalizing can be both complete or partial; that is, ideas may only partially realize themselves in a functionalization.

According to this brief description, functionalization implies that ideas, concepts and meanings are not static but dynamic: their mode of being is "becoming," because they realize themselves during a process deeply immersed in reality.

It appears that it has never been considered in European philosophy that the pragmatic methodology of functionalization is a viable alternative to the hitherto unresolved dilemma of whether the human soul possesses ideas prior to its entering the body at birth (Plato) or whether they are only "abstracted" from the soul's experience with reality (Aristotle). Max Scheler's sharp critique of both idealism and realism in his five-part essay "Idealism and Realism" (IX 183340/PE 288-356) of his second period, (which also takes issue with Martin Heidegger's *Being and Time*) is to be seen in the light of the concept of functionalization as initially articulated in his first period.

Functionalization is not, however, an academic affair. It occurs everywhere in daily life. In the blink of an eye, it may dawn on us that data which had long been incomprehensible to us suddenly becomes understood with clarity. This often leads to an "ah-ha" experience, expressing our own surprise of what suddenly happened to a long-standing puzzle. Not infrequently we try to retrace the lines of how the solution of the puzzle all of a sudden came to our mind. The peculiar self-emerging and "becoming" character of ideas functionalizing themselves with things shows itself most dramatically in designing, drawing, and outlining of *sketches*. (We will examine the nature of a sketch, a key aspect of Scheler's philosophy, in Chapter IX.)

The process of functionalizing also pertains to values. As we saw earlier, values as such do not exist unless they coexist, just as colors only exist against a background. A value must, therefore, enter into a function with its proper substrate, person or state of affairs. As persons of experience, the meanings of the rank of values summon us, no matter how silently, to attain a higher rank. A higher value calls for *real*-ization. If physical, psychological, mental, emotional or social incapacitations prevent higher value-realizations, such incapacitations as a rule turn into constant feelings of dissatisfaction, frustration or even resentment.

What pertains to values also pertains to the levels of the self-value of the person when the self-value is experienced in repentance. In a genuine act of repentance, a higher self-value of the person awaits realization: it beckons a higher personal being. It is through this beckoning that the previous lower level of self-value is felt. Although Scheler does not fully articulate it, good and evil likewise functionalize themselves *during* the realization of the respective positive or negative value. Good and evil emerge concomitantly within the act of realizing the higher or lower value. The realization issues forth from the height of the value which is not yet realized but nevertheless felt. In this sense, the value rides on the back of realization.

How does the functionalization of ideas, meanings and insights fit together with the moral category of conscience?

We stated earlier that conscience, too, works in such a way that it tells us when something has gone wrong and veered from the direction of ordinary moral experience. Conscience does not speak to us when there is no moral deviation. It wells up only when we have a feeling we ought *not* to have realized a negative value or particular state of affairs. In this, the functionalization of good and evil happens at the moment that is "fit" to wake us by the call of conscience. This is a conception of conscience quite different from formal ethics, according to which we are to follow a positive imperative. In contrast to formal ethics, non-formal ethics establishes that every "ought" has its foundation in what ought *not* to be: that is, whenever a human action runs counter to a moral reality, conscience evokes what ought to be and what ought to be done.

In the essay "Problems of Religion" (1918-1920), we are offered a description of the functionalization in moral experience which is more precise than what is offered on the subject in *Formalism*:

> It is only during the experience of mistakes and deviations from laws not present to our mind that it gradually dawns on us that an insight had all along been leading and guiding us, as it is also the case with all stirrings in conscience which object more to what is wrong than they would point by themselves to what is good. Nonetheless, in the background of the stirrings of conscience there is a *positive* insight into the good and into a positive ideal of both our own individual life and of human life in general. (V 198 translation mine)

Notwithstanding conscience's telling us what not to do, there must at the same time be a positive insight into the good that ought to be. What we ought not to do does indeed point to a good to be realized. This leads to the question of a positive moral insight of a good to be gained, a good that lies in the nature of the order of love, the *ordo amoris* and the functionalization of the good in time.

b) The Order of Love. Space. Time and Fate.

The following passage from "*Ordo Amoris*" encapsulates what has been said about the moral being of the person. In our discussion of the human being we should bear in mind that we are translating the German noun "*der Mensch*" as man (species). Its translation in English as "man" does not pertain to the male gender. Confusion may arise—particularly in a society overly sensitive to gender inclusive language—when *Mensch* is mistakenly rendered as "man" in the gender sense.

> Whoever has the *ordo amoris* of man, has man himself. He has for man as a moral subject what the crystallization formula is for crystal. He sees through him as far as one possibly can. He sees before him the constantly simple and basic lines of his heart running beneath all empirical many-sidedness and complexity. And heart deserves to be called the core of man as a spiritual being much more so than knowing and willing. He has a spiritual model of the primary source which secretly

nourishes everything issuing forth from this man. Even more, he possesses the primary determinant of what always keeps on settling itself around him: in space, his *moral milieu*; in time, his *fate*; that is, to become the quintessence of what possibly can happen to him and *to him alone*. (XI 348 translation mine)

There are three quintessential concepts contained in the quote, displaying the three facets of the *ordo amoris*, namely, love, space, and time. Love is seen in light of two aspects: of the moral milieu, that is, moral "space," and of time which is seen as the basis of human "fate." Space refers to one's moral world shared with others as well as to the values of the world around one. Time refers to fate; that is, to all that can uniquely happen to one and only one particular individual.

Time as fate must be seen in light of two points that had been established earlier: (1) the spectral value-ranks remain concealed behind all valuations and that the spectral order is given in pre-rational preferences. In the essay "*Ordo Amoris*," Scheler additionally shows us that what we had referred to as the "spectrality" of value-ranks is like a "shell" in which human existence is encased. We perceive the world around us through this shell's "windows" and we perceive no more than what its windows allow to show with regard to their ranked position or, figuratively, the "color" of their values. The value ranks remain translucent in the moral milieu around us, no matter how goods and things may change in this milieu, and "no matter how far man will travel into space." The *order* of the value-ranks remains the same as if man were incased in their "shell." It must also be recalled that (2) the three-faceted concept of the *ordo amoris* also substantiates a tacit claim made by Scheler that we referred to earlier: the moral values of good and evil have the character of temporality.

Except in the ethics before us, it appears that nowhere in the history of ethics since Socrates has the claim been made that good and evil are phenomena of temporality. But what is the temporal character of man's "*ordo amoris*" in whose value-ranks man's transverse value *a priori* is located and on whose realizations good and evil are supposed to be riding? What is a human being's fate in preferring values? How does moral space play an ingredient part in our moral lives? And what is "fate" in moral context? The common notion of fate must be set aside. It implies that our existence may be befallen with the unexpected and unwilled and with uncontrollable events. The traditional conception of fate has its roots in the Greek "*moira*" hovering above humans without mercy. Scheler's conception of human fate is an entirely new development. He defines fate as the unity of an "unvarying sense" that lingers throughout the nexus between a) the character of an individual and b) the sum total of events happening during the span of an individual life.

Let us illustrate this. If one could envision a person's entire life all at once, the countless sequences of events, situations and states of affairs, the countless intersubjective experiences with others, all of the personal experiences, both public and private; in short, look at all perceptions and thoughts: these might at first examination seem almost accidental because of the conspicuous absence of causalities among all series of events happening between his birth and death. But even *if* a person's whole life indeed consisted of only random happenings, the happenings would nevertheless mirror something about the very core of the individual person concerned.

This personal core of an individual Scheler calls the "uniform sense" running through the entire nexus of a person's life and world. This individual uniform sense is independent of the person's will and of any *de facto* random factors. For the will must, on the above premise, also be suffused by the uniform sense running through the individual's own life. How does this help to understand the meaning of "fate?" Fate befalls a person in a uniquely individual manner. Individual fate, that is, the temporal aspect of the *ordo amoris*, lies within the range of all experiences in the world in terms of the possibilities that are circumscribed by an individual's moral tenor and the qualitative direction of acts peculiar to such a person's character. Individual possibilities of experiences are *different* from person to person, and, on a larger scale, they are, as collective possibilities, also different from one people to another people.

It is Scheler's contention, therefore, that even if all of a person's experiences are identically circumstanced with regard to another person, the inner sense of both individuals would not permit the same "fatedness" between them. Indeed, the range of individual possibilities appears to be already prefigured in that it holds sway over the very beginning of a person's existence. Scheler states:

> In this more precise sense of the word "fate," it is the way a man's actual *ordo amoris* is formed—in accordance with definite rules for a gradual functionalization of primary love-objects in his early childhood—that governs the unfolding of the content of his fate. (X 350/PE 103)

How do time and environment, fate and the moral milieu relate to the phenomenon of love? Love has been described as the unceasing movement of the heart toward disclosing higher and higher values. A value that is loved "attracts." Love moves toward the light of the value that is loved. "Love at first sight" may be the prototype of the pre-

rational and pre-logical inception of the power of love as the disclosure of a value. In it, a value suddenly flashes out in a quality which
no one else could possibly feel: it is an indivisible moment shared by
two persons, or given only to one in case of the tragedy of love unrequited.

Love is no subjective movement toward an objective person. For
one thing, the person fallen in love with is no object. Nor is the
person a subject in the experience of values. On the contrary, the
person is neither a subject nor an object because of its dynamic temporal existence. The person, we were told, acts his existence out. Person is self-executory existence. Nor is a person a static substance. The
person "varies," Scheler stressed, at every indivisible moment in acting out the different nature that acts have. It is precisely the aforementioned "qualitative direction" of the person which functions as
the dynamic locus of the essence of the individual person's order of
love.

As we have seen, a self-executing existence cannot be subordinated
to a categorical imperative which would tell one how to act. This
would eclipse the very meaning of the self-execution of personal temporality and render it null and void. The dynamics of personal existence cannot be told by anything external what ought to be done in a
particular moral milieu and a particular point in time.

c.) The Refraction of the Order of Values in the Order of Love of the Individual Person

The dynamic existence of the person as the bearer of values allows
the voice of conscience to say what "ought not" to be done. This
experience occurs throughout all possible qualitative variations of the
person's executions of acts. The ought-not, which is, like positive
oughtness, based in and presupposed by the order of values, must therefore be different in every person because each person possesses a unique
qualitative direction to his own acts.

This point sets Scheler's critique of systems of formalism in ethics
apart from almost all other works of foundational ethics. He stresses
that there should *not* be "uniformity" in ethics itself. Scheler argues
that any claim as to what ought not to be in the moral world is a
misleading claim of uniformity of standards that encompasses all
humans (X 351/PE 104). With this statement, we are in a position
to formulate the result of what has been concluded about man's *ordo
amoris* as the quintessence of Scheler's *Formalism in Ethics and Non-
Formal Ethics of Values:*

The order of love—ordo amoris—has no fixed, immutable direction into the order of values. Rather, in each person the order of values is refracted in a manner different from any other person by virtue of the time aspect of the individual's ordo amoris: his fate. That is, the spectral value-ranks are refracted in the uniform sense prevailing throughout a person's life-time. The uniform sense runs through the entire series of experiences of events, tinged, however, by the qualitative direction unique to an individual person's acts throughout the nexus they have with all events that alone could have happened to one particular person in his own moral space.

Where, one must ask, is there a guide for what ought to be done or not be done at a particular moment? There is no such ordaining guidance. If there were one, say, attached to the individual from an outside authority, the freedom of human personhood and conscience would be affected.

What there is, however, is inner moral guidance. For Scheler this guidance is the quintessential category of ethics, namely, the "call of the hour" (*kairos*). The claim is made that at any significant moment in one's moral life, an individual's *moral intuition* can reveal the proper order of love and of values and may prompt to act accordingly. The individual is free to let this happen or not happen. The moral intuition must be strictly distinguished from a rational intuition. In moral intuition, man's heart, mind, love and will *merge* into one other and form *one* stream of moral experience (IV 544). In such cases, the person lives deeply within himself. The person is filled with thousands of calls coming from his personal past and future (II 417/F 420). He looks over his entire life in *one* act of moral "ingatheredness" (*Sammlung*).

We find close to perfect examples of a "call of the hour" in lives of holy men in various religions—Jesus at Gethsemane, at the foot of the Mount of Olives, being one of them. In such moments, a unique moral task and deed is evoked; this temporal moment is not repeatable. If we forgo the call, it will never present itself again or allow itself to be retrieved. Of course, the call of the hour is susceptible to various levels of intensities. It may go unnoticed while taking a walk; it may be experienced by a judge deliberating over a severe moral case; it may be experienced before marriage, whether to answer a draft, on the occasion of rescuing a child from drowning or shortly before death. The call is silent. As a rule, others do not share in it. The moral call may be the loneliest hour in a lifetime.

This *kairos* is imbued with both the moral issue occurring in an irreversible phase of the flowing uniform sense of the person concerned and also with the value-ranks as refracted by the particular uniform sense of a person. "*Kairos*" must, therefore, have a "background" consisting of the hidden spectrality of value-ranks whose order shines through all individual refractions of them in the particular moral situation.

But, since there is neither an articulated, external guideline in the call of the hour that would direct specific deeds and tasks, nor an imperative hovering above the personal moment of the call of the hour, Scheler's proposal appears to demand perhaps too much of an individual person's moral strength, perhaps even asks for the impossible in expecting the person to intuit what ought not to be done by dint of the hour's call. But this difficulty only lies on the surface of the phenomenon of the call. The call does not demand too much if it is listened to freely, that is, without reservation and apprehension. Scheler insists that no matter what the call of the hour will tell us, it will be accepted whenever the person's moral tenor is in the state of *readiness* to which we referred earlier, that is, the readiness freely to accept what ought not to be and what ought not to be done. Furthermore, the call is clearly pre-rational, it is not a call one works on, but a call which the person receives.

No matter what the extent of the order of values that is refracted in the individual—indeed, Scheler recognizes that the value-order can be twisted beyond recognition down to the levels or "organic mendacity" as in unrelenting feelings of hate and resentment—the order itself is maintained, no matter how unnoticeably, throughout any value deceptions. This is why when value-deceptions occur in feelings of resentment, the order of values is said to remain "translucent." The I, too, remains translucent throughout all forms of resentful "Turn-over of Values," (*Vom Umsturz der Werte*), which is the very title of the book containing these analyses.

Undiminished in his efforts, Scheler never gave up climbing the arduous road toward the essential residue of moral depth in human existence. All conceptions and definitions of man offered in the history of philosophy—as rational animal, as the product of evolution, as tool animal, as bearer of a transcendental ego, as Dasein, *Existenz*—remained unsatisfactory for him. This is because none of them contains what his own investigations had shown to be the essence of being human: love, the human being is an "*ens amans.*" Love, subliminal to reason and will, spans man's birth and death. Man participates in many forms of love: in the love of God, the love of being in the world, love of gender, love of country, love of fellow man, love of nature, love of the smallest and humblest. In all its forms, love discloses values and shines through thinking and willing, goodness, truth and beauty. This confers upon man, before anything else, his unique place in the universe as *ens amans*.

Love and the order of values with which it is imbued is as elusive to description as it is vulnerable to groundless interpretation. Love is a phenomenon more complex than everyday experience of it could tell. Like the filigree of the emotive processes we call the human "heart," love's very place in the constitution of man's being remains extremely contentious today. Undoubtedly there has been little or no room for the primacy of love and its hidden power in the philosophy of the twentieth century. Equally, there has likewise been little or no room for seeing that it is the call's *moment* that shapes our moral destiny, either individually or collectively.

The two graphs below should shed light on the nature of the *ordo amoris*, the quintessence of being human:

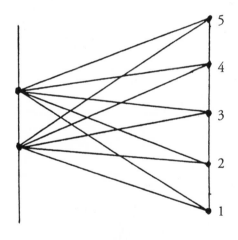

Graph A

The right side of graph A represents the moral "milieu" or *space* of the spectral value-ranks in their descending order, starting with No. 5, which is the value of holiness, down to the rank of sensible pleasure and entertainment.

The vertical line on the left side of graph A represents the dynamics of the uniform sense of a person's "fate" that runs through one's life's *time*. The two points on the line stand for the two moments referred to above:

1. They symbolize two moments of the unique moral demands in a single person (*kairos*). In each, the order of values is refracted differently as indicated by different angles with which the values intersect the moments.

2. The two points also may each stand for two persons. In this case they represent two persons in the same moral situation. Each person experiences the same situation, but the order of values is refracted differently according to their moral tenor, conscience, and individual *ordo amoris*. Graph A does not show value delusions. They are represented in graph B.

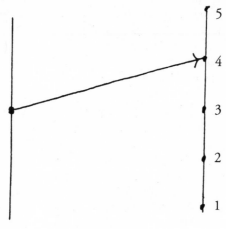

Graph B

Graph B illustrates that no individual can experience the ascending order of values at all times. The ascending order can easily be "turned over," or twisted. It is, for instance, turned over when the rank of the values of usefulness (No.2 in graph B) pertinent to technological exploration is preferred to life values (No.3 in graph B) pertinent to environment. Turn-overs of value-ranks form a myriad of (vertical) disorders in men as do all values (horizontally) on their ranks. They amount to disturbances in the transverse value *a priori:* they are "*désordre du coeur.*" Value distortions can reach such a point that they amount to "metaphysical aberrations" when they are felt to be on ranks where they do not belong on. Such is the case when the value of holiness is experienced with a thing (fetish) rather than with a person. In short, one can at least in theory conjecture many things as absolute. The "sphere of the absolute" in human consciousness and in conscience is open to countless possibilities of value-deceptions and to countless degrees of nuances of the feeling of absolute holiness.

4. The Vehicles of Moral Growth. Exemplars of Person.
Model Persons and Role Models.
a) Discussion of the General Problematic.

No systematic treatment of the foundations of ethics could be regarded as satisfactory unless it provided a means to enhance in practice the moral growth of individual persons, communities, societies, and the human race as a whole.

To claim that this objective can be accomplished is, in theory, much easier for an imperativist ethics (Kant), for an ethics of purposes (Aristotle), or for a utilitarian ethics aiming at the happiness among a maximum number of people (Bentham). These types of ethics systems are grounded in positive formulas of what ought to be done as well as in definitions of what the moral good itself is. Accordingly, these systems make it relatively easy to articulate guidelines for the moral comportment of individuals according to ordained formulae.

By comparison, it is much more difficult to enhance the moral conduct of human beings on the basis of an ethics anchored in pre-rational feelings of values as well as emotive intuitionism, like the one before us. The reason for this is obvious because ethics for Scheler is designed first to determine the *values* of what ought to be done and the nature of the being of values and that of the good in light of the being of values.

Scheler's value-ethics was shown to be a remarkable exception to the traditional assumption that the determination of what ought to be done has a priority over the determination of the being of the values of what ought to be done. In Scheler's ethics, all oughtness is based on the value of what oughtness refers to. Hence the center of his ethics first required a clarification of the nature of values as such. It is for this reason that the question of establishing a moral vehicle by which persons individually and collectively will or may enhance their moral growth in the future lies in a direction quite distinct from virtually all other systems in this respect.

It would appear that ethics itself cannot improve upon the moral status of humanity (II 88/F 69). During history, the human race has not improved morally (XI 69; XII 104). The reason why the discipline of ethics itself has not furthered moral improvement is that ethics has for the most part restricted its function to the "judgmental formulation" of what is given in moral cognition. It can at best only motivate, not compel, improvement of moral status. It is only a philosophical ethics—not professional or any other sort of ethics—that focuses on the moral *a priori* and cognition. Scheler intended to write another major work on this subject, but except for some notes on it (XI 54-71) the project remained unrealized. Nevertheless, the basics tenets of an ethics centered on the *a priori* of moral cognition are contained in *Formalism*, and we have referred already to several of them and we will return to the subject later.

The question of what can enhance the moral conduct of persons, that is, the question of what are the possible vehicles for moral growth of the individual—a question ever so significant for the education of our youth today—is dealt with at the end of *Formalism*. As we can expect, the question is seen in the light of the nature and value of the person: in particular, in terms of the personal exemplarity of individuals who can morally stir others.

An ancient Chinese saying has it that the first great gift we can bestow on others is that of a good example. Max Scheler's discussions of personal exemplarity may well also be the first gift to *contemporary* ethics, the education of children, and education in general.

In seeking to establish exemplars and set up models of persons— two distinct endeavors—Scheler anticipated by some eighty years the social, political and moral significance of what today is often referred to as "role models." We must keep in mind, however, that the "exemplars" of persons do not function like so-called role models who are set up by societal industries only to impart on humans certain values which must be adopted if one wants to be considered part of a "movement." Present-day political correctness has such an imposing character. By contrast, there is neither a rational nor dutiful compulsion to follow a moral exemplar. Therefore, the moral growth that follows from an exemplar arises from the freedom of the persons concerned and *not* from the obedience to moral prescriptions. Following exemplars is a *free* following. It is much akin to—nearly identical with— the "followship" of disciples engendered by the high moral value of a holy person. Such free following has nothing to do with a willful or conscious "imitation" of a moral exemplar.

Scheler's exposition of the role of personal exemplars sometimes gives the impression of having an unsatisfactory foundation. In fact, this is not infrequently the case with a number of aspects of Scheler's writings. It is often asked how Scheler could substantiate what he wrote about. Indeed the question is appropriate at this juncture. There are two reasons for posing this question. The first reason is that specific explanations of the foundation of Scheler's thought, while seemingly unsatisfactory, can be found in works other than the ones presently under consideration. We have already seen that the "*ordo amoris*" is only infrequently mentioned in *Formalism*, yet treated in detail in the essay bearing that very title. The same holds true for the subject of model persons which receives only mention in *Formalism*; detailed analyses, however, are found in a separate essay entitled: "Exemplars of Persons and Leaders" (X 255-344/PV 127-198).

A second reason for an apparent lack of foundation in some of Scheler's writings may be attributed to a genius-like personality—to which Ortega, Heidegger, Edith Stein and many others who knew him frequently referred—even if his way of writing was not systematic. Scheler worked on two books and various articles simultaneously all his life. He was a prolific writer, too prolific to lend more order to his writings which would have been of benefit to his readers. When he died, thousands of manuscripts lay piled up in disarray. It took almost thirty years for his widow Maria Scheler to codify and catalog them. Scheler was very generous in sharing his ideas with others, as Hans-Georg Gadamer aptly said: this too often caused confusion and misunderstandings. Scheler's mind was always "tossing and turning," as his close friend, Ernst Robert Curtius, the then renowned Romance philologist, had stated.

The essay "Exemplars of Person and Leaders" was originally planned to reach a book-form publication; but like many topics and projects that Scheler initiated, it too was never completed. What appears to have prevented the completion of this work was Scheler's intention to implement his value-ethics in practice. Accordingly, occupation with cultural, political and social issues of his time steadily increased. His essays and addresses on such subjects as "The Idea of Peace and Pacifism," "Politics and Morals," and "The World-Age of Adjustment" are political, social and practical perspectives on the status of contemporary humanity and its possibilities for the future. We have nothing comparable from any of Scheler's contemporaries.

In order to introduce the discussion on exemplary and model persons, let us cite a passage from *Formalism*::

> Nothing on earth allows a person to become good so originally, immediately, and necessarily, as the evidential and adequate intuition (*Anschauung*) of a good person *in* his goodness. This relation is *absolutely superior* to *any other* relation in terms of a possible becoming good and of which it can be considered its origin. (II 560/F 574)

This passage is expounded upon in detail in the essay just mentioned in which it is maintained that the moral exemplarity of a person is superior to two other, well known vehicles of moral growth: to "obedience" and to the "willing" of becoming good.

Obedience and will pertain to specific actions, not to the whole person. Their moral effect does not, as is the case with personal exemplars, infuse personal levels deeper than actions, namely, a person's moral tenor and individual directions of the person's loves and hates. A personal exemplar can, therefore, truly *transform* and even convert a moral tenor inasmuch as the moral exemplarity freely attracts and raises the person up to a higher level of self-value. All genuine conversions to be found in religious experience, for example, are not the result of "willing" to convert, say from non-belief to faith in God; nor are they the result of "obedience." Conversion occurs through the emotive attractiveness of the value of the moral exemplarity of that person whose self-value and direction of love suffuses the very core of the inception of a conversion. If a person just "wills" to be like another model person—as is often the contemporary case with followers of publicly fabricated role-models—there is always a possibility that a value-deception will unconsciously lead merely to wanting to "appear" like the role model.

The moral exemplarity of a person, however, touches the heart in an immediate, *a priori*, fashion; that is, the exemplary value of the person concerned is not transmitted by conscious reflections and judgments. A moral exemplar is linked with the emotive *a priori* of the *pre*rational order among value-ranks given in the *ordo amoris*. It is from this being-touched in the immediate, emotive intuition of the value exemplarity that the person "freely" *follows*, not obeys, moral exemplarity. It is in the free, undeliberate following that the texture of oughtness begins to shift toward the order of values. In this, the person experiences his own what "ought not to be." Moral exemplarity turns the inner core of the person away from what he ought not to be or be doing. Scheler wants to ground all possibilities for moral growth and change of the individual in the intuited experience of the value-exemplarity of a person.

There are, of course, many factual, moral model persons around us. In *Formalism* a number of them are mentioned. Those models that appear earliest in life have the most enduring effect, particularly parenthood. Scheler mentions many everyday models, such as the "chief" of a tribe. There are "good" and "honorable" models. There is the "wise" man or the "elder" in a community. There are models like "the man of the people," a "president." There are the models of "masters" in Eastern Cultures. There are models of historical "heroes," "poets," "statesmen," past and present. There are "business leaders" (or *the* "leader"). There are religious models like "founders," "reformers," "saints," and genuine preachers. In sum, every social unit and level may display entire systems of factual model persons, past or present, that at least tacitly attract people. Of course, for each model there are also negative counter-models.

As was indicated earlier every so often Scheler links up his theories with observations made in practical life. He tells us that in Germany the image of Bismarck was so strong that one could see everywhere "little Bismarcks" walking around wearing his style of beard imitating his imperial looks and style of language comparable in our own recent past with numerous little Karl Marx's wearing his kid of beard and imitating his often vulgar language in speech and writing. Even such imitations, which have nothing to do with free following, would indicate how even contrived models can become deeply seated and effectively penetrate the nature of a society at a particular time.

Factual model persons in everyday life are, in fact, short-lived: at best, they last a generation or two. The ephemeral character of everyday model persons is especially evident in contrived "role models," such as occur in personalities in the sports and entertainment industries. They are ephemeral because they represent only *divisible* value-ranks. They are artificially selected according to their accomplishments and celebrated in award ceremonies. These role models are esteemed and promoted on the basis of "achievement," and "success." Even though they are selected for their purported devotion, commitment or seniority, their moral tenor may not measure up to their quantifiable accomplishments. The moral tenor of the role models can even clash with their quantifiable accomplishments because of "unethical" standards hidden behind their public image.

An exemplary model person, on the other hand, possesses *indigenous* moral value associated with any phase of his acts and actions. A moral exemplar does not depend on quantifiable records and public acclaim. The very value of this person does not reside in such extraneous factors but in the "tug" that exercises an automatic effect: the same one that makes us pre-reflexively regard the exemplarity. This exemplarity is purely personal enduring: it is the characteristic of persons deemed "noble," "good," or "saintly." Whatever the attributes of the exemplar, these persons do not have a full awareness of the richness of their status, or at least do not use it for self-serving ends, as role models can do.

The human beings who freely follow a personal exemplarity compare themselves with it. It is intersubjective, interpersonal comparison, spontaneous, not deliberate. The act of spontaneous interpersonal comparing is one of the central acts in Scheler's phenomenology. This act is also at work in any experience of what one ought to do or ought to be. What ought not to be done is compared to what ought to be done. This comparing of what ought not to be done with what ought to be is also spontaneous comparing; that is, it is not yet rationally deliberated.

In feelings of what ought not to be done, a comparison is also made with something that does not exist. An ought-to-be that does not yet exist awaits realization. This happens also when we compare ourselves with an image we have of ourselves. We can even simulate comportment to such an image even if in practice we do not live up to it. Even in such daily experiences as looking at ourselves in a mirror, in comparing ourselves to an *image* of ourselves, we try to emulate and approximate this image in the mirror. Again, the image in this case does not in the strict sense exist. Indeed, this comparison has only one term: the existing person standing before the mirror. A term that does not yet exist is not, strictly speaking, a term.

Comparisons with one term only play an important role in our lives. A whole generation may continually be searching for a model person that does not exist; its non-existence can have an influential if only hidden role in the constitution of a generation. It could well be that the global restiveness of our own times is rooted in part in a strong, subliminal desire for a model person. It is the empirical power of an exemplary model person which alone can fulfill the dream of humans everywhere to obtain at least some moral balance and peace. It is not through the formulations of an ethics that makes humans better (II 88/F 69).

All of this would indicate that the average person's comparison of himself with a model person must be quintessential to an ethics that seeks to clarify the problem of how moral growth can be brought about in the human race.

b) Discussion of the Specific Problematic of Exemplars of Person

A sharp distinction must now be made between an "ideal" model person, on the one hand, and a factual historical model person, such as a leader, on the other hand. Scheler's term "ideal" is unfortunate and subject to easy misunderstanding. While the historical model person or leader has existed at some point in time, *ideal exemplars* of person do not exist "unless they drink the suitable blood from the wells of historical experience. It is only when they do this that they become *concrete models*" (X 269/PV 142).

This brings us full circle to the *functional* existence of values. "Ideal" exemplars are pure types of value-persons (*Wertpersonen*). Like the spectral ranks of values, these persons, too, are spectral, yet hidden in the myriad variations of concrete *types* of model persons. These spectral persons are "universally" valid, just as the spectral ranks of values are. By contrast, the existing model persons and leaders are only of individual validity. This is why one can "choose" among them and "will" to follow them. Such is not possible with regard to ideal exemplars of person because they provide the scope within which living models can occur, just as particular values are situated within the spectral scope of the value-ranks. Exemplars of person are "schemata" or outlines by which concrete models in the human race take on their forms.

How does Scheler establish these ideals and pure types of personal exemplarity? They are the result of the interconnection existing between the person as the bearer of values, on the one hand, and the order of value-ranks, on the other hand. Each rank must have its own personal prototype because each rank is borne by the person. This prototype is a rank's "exemplar." It must be stressed that the level of our consciousness of models, or "model-consciousness," is said to be entirely pre-logical and pre-volitional.

We can now list the exemplars of person. According to the five ranks among values, there are five ideal exemplars of personhood, one for each rank. Historical model persons and leaders are, without exception, embedded in them. In descending order of the value-ranks there are the following ideal exemplars of person:

5. The Saint
4. The Genius
3. The Hero
2. The Leading Mind of Civilization
1. The Master in the Art of Living

These pure schemata of exemplars are personal essences of each of the five value-modalities. The exemplars do not exist by themselves in the same sense that values do not exist by themselves. The exemplars exist only "in" the *functionalization* of the pure outlines of personhood with this or that particular person in this or that historical epoch. Their existence, too, is only functional existence. For this reason, the term "ideal" personal exemplarities must not be confused with a Platonic conception of a realm of ideas of perfect existence; Scheler stresses that they are not to be construed as empirically existing either. They only have functional existence when they "drink the suitable blood of history": in other words, when their outlines merge with the process of a person's life.

The existence of personal exemplars is operative in persons just as pure value-ranks are operative in things. As pure outlines exemplars are ideal. Pure exemplars of the person properly belong to the human mind itself. This may sound like an assertion with little foundation. But Scheler will present an unprecedented philosophy of the mind, which will dispel the impression that there is little foundation to his thought. As we shall see, what is called mind has no existence, strictly speaking, either, nor any productive power of its own.

By itself, the mind is said to be "impotent" unless it enters into individuated functions with things, states of affairs and reality in general. Mind exists "in" functionalizing itself only. The traditional notion of an existing "universal" mind, of "pure consciousness" or "pure spirit" was dismissed by Scheler as unacceptable already in 1913. With this he set himself off not only from the beginnings of the phenomenological movement centered around Husserl, but also from the systems of German Idealism of Fichte, Schelling and, in particular, Hegel, all of whom had assigned to the pure existence of mind or spirit a power of historical productivity.

Scheler's tenet that ideal exemplars of person or their "ideas" belong to the mind does not mean that the mind innately possesses them in a Platonic fashion: in fact, the opposite is the case. Ideal exemplars "possess us" (X 268/PV 141) because the mind on its own in no way produces them. They possess us as concrete persons in their functionalizations. From this we get a clue for understanding Scheler's concept of human historicity. Pure exemplars are its quintessence in that they are the sources of the outlines that circumscribe the many forms of how humans understand themselves historically in different ages and cultures. They are pure schemata in the dynamic act-being of the person and constitute the moral difference between real persons and ideal personhood.

In factual history, no living person is a pure exemplar unless recognized as such in a religion (for example, Buddha, Jesus, Mohammed). One cannot, Scheler says, "choose" such a religious exemplar. In the case of other exemplars one can choose. The personal exemplar called "genius" becomes real in various forms of art, such as music, sculpture and painting among which I can choose. Factual geniuses, for example, Beethoven, Michelangelo or Raphael, allow choices to be made among them. They tolerate other geniuses beside them. One can choose Bach over Beethoven, Rodin over Michelangelo, Rubens over Raphael. Choices between personal models representing the four lower ranks are always possible. But this is not possible with regard to a religious exemplar of holiness. This level of personal exemplarity is characterized by one motto: "If you are not for me, you are against me." Sacred exemplarity demands unconditional recognition: it exercises the strongest, the most lasting and, as Nietzsche held, the most historically enduring influence.

The discussion of exemplarity corresponds to what Scheler told us about the relationship between value-ranks and material. The original holy man needs no material for his message to be made manifest. He "is" the truth and the good. Jesus needed neither writing materials nor Aristotle's philosophy. (He wrote nothing as far as we can know.) A Christian philosophy based in Aristotle's thought was a useless twisting of a heathen's philosophy into incarnate love of Christ and the Creator. The necessity for materials and the importance of the role of the will increases, however, in the descending order of value-ranks. One can "will" to be a leader of civilization, to be a statesman or political leader. One cannot will to be saintly. The historical duration of a model also diminishes in the descending order of value-ranks. The number and variety of factual models and leaders also increases with the descending order.

We need not here go into the details of the relationship between an ideal exemplary person, his functionalization in historical reality as a model person and the ensuing classification of "occupations" resulting from the pentagram of exemplars and their correlative factual model-persons. While these classifications made by Scheler are of sociological import, they are not of an immediate ethical relevance.

It was stated that the moral example a person sets is more effective the earlier it is experienced in one's life. Hence, it is most effective with the child, or even with an infant. This also pertains to any negative counter-model that parents might set for the child. The counter-models can, as is well known, have the most pernicious effect in the development of children, teens and other impressionable stages of life.

This dynamic pertains also to groups and the development of cultures and civilizations. The model of the hero exemplified in the *Iliad* and *Odyssey* and throughout Nordic mythology has had a tremendous effect on Western literature, art, politics and morality. In Eastern culture a comparable model is the wise man, not the hero. As Scheler put it, Western man looks like a hunter; Eastern man is one of patience. The formative effects of model persons pertain to all subgroups and units of human society.

Scheler's educational psychology views the child as the bearer of value-directions of love and hate guided by model persons around him. Such guidance, even if unconscious, is part and parcel of Scheler's theory of the very subtlety and moral effectiveness that model persons have on human beings:

> Everything is highly important for this child. Whatever the adults in a family think to be significant—such as perhaps disagreements, love and harmony, a faked or well intended smile, or even look—all of this amounts to a tremendous drama in the child. This drama is all the more exemplary for the child's existence and development the more malleable the child's physiological-mental organism is, and the younger the child is in understanding this. It is not only the images of his mother and father, sisters and brothers, and relatives that determine the child's love or hatred toward these persons, but they determine *what the child loves and hates at all*. And they also determine the very scope of properties of any thing, of schemata of values within which the child's future loves and hates will have their play. Our recent psycho-analytical science will teach us more about the formation of the fate of a human being (experiences in childhood), despite exaggerations of it made, especially in its recent unnaturalist forms, by Adler, Maeder and Bergson, in contrast to Freud (X 272/PV 145).

No doubt Scheler challenges us to a thorough investigation into the role and function values play in our personal lives. There are two features of Scheler's "new attempt toward an ethical personalism" that bear heavily on his own formulation of the result of this complex work.

1. Each person comports himself differently from his fellow humans. Each person is different in his self-value from any other person. Every person's self-value is unique and irreplaceable. Even if an objection is raised that this interpersonal difference might not exist in fact, it nevertheless must hold before God.

2. The lower value-ranks are, the more they pertain to divisible values, relative to life and its respective material goods. These materials consist of all goods that are desired by drives and instinctive needs, among them the goods of nutrition and health. Access to goods and values relative to life *ought* to be *equal* for all.

Scheler summarizes the result of *Formalism in Ethics and Non-Formal Ethics of Values* as follows:

> To put it plainly, aristocracy "in heaven" does not preclude democracy "on earth." (II 500/F 509)

CHAPTER II

PHENOMENOLOGICAL INTERSUBJECTIVITY.

Prefatory Remark

Any system of ethics that does not furnish a full account of *how* other human beings are given and experienced within one's own self must remain deficient because an account of moral comportment must be given with regard to its relation to and bearing on other persons.

Throughout the previous chapter it had been implied that moral acts fall into two classes—just as all acts of consciousness, according to Scheler, must be divided.

The two classes of acts are solitary and social. Acts of consciousness are either solitary or social acts. Solitary acts pertain only to the individual who executes them. Acts of conscience such as those of repentance, for example, are often solitary when they point to what one ought not to have done with respect to *oneself*. This class of acts contains all acts of communion with oneself. By contrast, social acts are exclusively directed toward other persons. The act of comparing, for example, pertains to another self, whether present or absent, without which no comparing could take place. Of course, both classes of acts can also fall under their opposite classification. An act of conscience may also pertain to others which I have hurt; and an act of comparing can also pertain to my own self when I compare my present self to what I should have been but was not.

In what follows, we will clarify how others are given as others and therefore, how human communities and associations are the result of the phenomenological givenness of others in *social* acts. This account must be furnished because ethics, too, is rooted in moral intersubjective experiences. The account of how others are given to the self requires two clarifications: (a) a clarification of the matter as contained in Scheler's book: *The Nature of Sympathy*; and (b) a clarification of the phenomenological bases of sociology contained in *Formalism*.

The Primordiality of the Other in Emotive Experience
1) The Genesis of the Problem of the Other in Philosophical Literature

The first edition of Scheler's book on sympathy appeared in 1913, its title in translation being *Phenomenology of Sympathetic Feelings and of Love and Hate*. The details of the text were introduced in the United

States by Albert K. Weinberg in *The Phenomenological Method and its Application in Max Scheler* (1924).

In 1922 Scheler substantially extended the book and gave it a new title which literally translates as *Essence and Forms of Sympathy*. The excellent English translation by P. Heath appeared in 1954 as *The Nature of Sympathy*. Among other chapters Scheler added to the 1922 edition was one entitled "Other Minds." It is this text that contains the principles of Scheler's philosophy of intersubjectivity, commonly referred to as the problem of the "thou," or the "other."

Scheler's treatment of "the other" was the only one at the time to have a phenomenological basis. It was something quite new *vis à vis* commonly accepted theories in psychology holding that "the other" is given in terms of "associations," "assimilations," "analogical inferences," "transfers" and "empathy" of one's own ego "into" that of others. These theories, which Scheler quite successfully refuted, had been widely accepted at the time without serious critique. Scheler's text shows that he was very familiar with the arguments offered by the leading exponents in the vast literature on the matter. He held that the analogizing, assimilating, transferring and empathetic activity of the ego into others are laden with presuppositions.

Even Husserl's *Cartesian Meditations,* whose fifth part was a culmination of prevailing psychological theories, abounds, from a Schelerian view, with presuppositions. Husserl's typescript, which shows "ready to go into print" in 1929, appeared eight years after Scheler's second edition of his book on sympathy. The first printed text of Husserl's *Cartesian Meditations* appeared in French in 1931 (translated by Levinas and G. Pfeiffer), three years after Scheler's death. It was made available in German only in 1950.

Whether Scheler's account of other minds is a far more acceptable theory than the theories he criticizes may, of course, be questioned: at least he offered a distinct alternative for future research. He was apparently never credited for his pioneering phenomenological work. He was among the first, if not *the* first, to establish the evidence of the priority of the other over the self discussed in *Formalism* and to demand an incorporation of the sociology of the four *a priori* forms of human togetherness whenever the theme of "the other" arose. Scheler worked extensively in child psychology, mentioning M.W. Shinn in California who claimed, like William Stern and Koffka in Germany, that the infant shows reactions to expressions, especially that of the mother's face, much earlier than occurrences of "associations" and "transfers."

Scheler launched three major criticisms against those theories. (1) The problem of the other must incorporate a growing child's experience of the other for which such theories do not account. One must not address the problem of the other by only considering the adult. (2) Analogical inferences and apperceptions with regard to an other self presuppose that the other must be there already in the first place and that there must already be some acquaintance with another's expressive movements. Scheler contends, therefore, that these theories presuppose what they try to establish. (3) To know of the existence of another does not necessitate presence of his lived body: other minds can be given regardless of any physical presence.

2) The Argument for the Phenomenon of Communality and the Other Self

This basic critique of the traditional theories about the givenness of "the other" rests on a central argument of Scheler's which foreshadowed what Heidegger would later refer to as the With-World (*das Mitsein*) of "Dasein" in *Being and Time*. Let this argument be called the "Robinson Crusoe Model."

One can ask whether an absolute Robinson Crusoe, that is, one who never encountered beings of his own kind, could still have instinctive knowledge or a feeling of belonging to a community of fellow humans. In several of his works Scheler answers the question in the affirmative (II 511; VII 228-258; V 372/F 521;N 234-26;E 373). The possibility of experiencing human community cannot arise from calculation or abstraction. Such reflections can at best lead him to the assumption of a phantom community and could not prove communal experience to be a real one. Rather, Crusoe's communal experience lies in an *intuited a priori of communality* residual in the very *absence* of members. Briefly put, absolute seclusion is only possible through experience of communality.

Initially, humans find themselves ecstatically absorbed in a social world without having an ego experience of their own. Phenomenologically, the *a priori* of the "thou" functions as a "sphere" of consciousness. "Sphere," in this instance is just another word for what can be irreducibly given as a meaning in consciousness: communality is a "phenomenon." Crusoe experiences consciousness as lacking communality. Acts that require responses of others, that is, social acts, are paralysed for one who is isolated, like Crusoe. While Crusoe's experience in fact lacks individuals who might respond, his emotive and rational apparatus nevertheless does not lack the intentional referent of otherness as such. His social acts, such as loving, promising, thanking, obeying, serving, answering, etc., refer to a sphere of communality even without members being physically present.

Ironically, it is in the absence of members that the social *a priori* of communality lies. This is articulated in a passage 1924 from Scheler's *Problems of a Sociology of Knowledge*:

> Thou-ness (*Du-heit*) is the basic existential category of human thinking. Primitives, for example, see all natural phenomena in terms of the "thou"; all nature is for them a field of expression and a "language" of spirits and demons behind natural appearances" (VII 57/PR 71).

The "existential category of human thinking" clearly foreshadows Heidegger's later statement which was alluded to above:

> The Being-with-others determines Dasein existentially [*existenzial*] even if another is in fact not present or perceived. Also Dasein's being alone is being-with-others in the world. Another can only be *missing in* and *for* the being-with-others. (*Gesamtausgabe* 2, 161)

What are some of the specifics of Scheler's theory of the alter-ego, the "thou?"

As early as 1912 Scheler rejected the assumption that a transcendental intersubjectivity could account for the other as being constituted in such an ego. In fact, Scheler's rejection appears earlier than Husserl's later support of such an idea. Scheler showed in great detail that the thoughts of other minds are not necessarily second to our own, nor the contents of our own minds prior to those of others. Initial intersubjectivity of self and other is *undifferentiated*. The root of intersubjectivity is to be seen then, according to Scheler, in a "psychic stream" into which all are swept at birth even prior to experiential differentiation. This undifferentiation is even retained later in life in practical situations. We can share thoughts of the other as if they were truly our own, and vice versa, just as we can also experience anew feelings of others as our own, and vice versa. Intersubjective indistinction stems from the original psychic stream where mine and thine are still the same. Although Scheler does not explicitly articulate it, this initial point of indistinction between alterity and sameness in the constitution of human intersubjectivity also constitutes the origin of an *intersubjective time* which "runs off" prior to ordinary time in which mine and thine are distinct. (We shall discuss Scheler's philosophy of time later in Chapters VII, VIII, and IX.)

In intersubjectivity proper there is no clear boundary of mine and the others' mental contents. This situation manifests itself in the contents of a tradition. These contents come from others and the past even though we experience them as our own. Early in our lives, we accept the thoughts of parents, relatives, friends, teachers, etc., but only to reproduce them vicariously later without being aware of how they came to us. Scheler amasses abundant material to show how much an individual, while emerging from the initial psychic stream of indistinction, tends to live more in *other* persons. One lives more in a communal experience than in one's own individual self. Ideas and feelings that came to govern us when we were very young are initially those of the members of what is the basic form of the life-community into which we are born, namely, the family.

It is at this very early stage of the infant when one begins to experience the alterity of others that is highly important for the growing infant (as the quotation Scheler at the end of the previous chapter indicated). The community into which the child begins to live exercises the earliest and strongest determinations upon its future loves and hates; this amounts to the formation of an individual fate, his unique inner sense and moral tenor and his model-consciousness. An infant who is swept up in this initial psychic stream in which thine and mine are still undifferentiated only very slowly raises his head, as it were, above this stream flooding over it. The infant finds himself as a being who also at times has feelings, ideas and tendencies of his own.

The gradual detachment from the overwhelming domain of otherness occurs through gradual objectification of things of the child's immediate environment. That is, all indistinguishable contents that the child first absorbed with his "mothers milk" come gradually to emerge in bold relief. With this, a line comes to be drawn between himself and the community members around him. The child quickly becomes oblivious to the early indistinguishable contents and their communal origin which, nevertheless, continue to reside in the individual and all the while maintains a life of its own.

In this early stage of human life, the original self-other indistinction in the psychic stream forms ever more stable "vortices" that absorb ever more elements of the stream into their intersubjective "orbits." It is during this process that the stream unnoticeably differentiates into distinct individuals. It is here that the child's personhood emerges. The origin of the person is concomitant, therefore, with the first stirrings of his will. At first this is shown only in paltry self-assertions that are made possible through the intersubjective "distance" between the individual and the others who have been present all along. In this process the reality of the other person is seen. This is the reason why others, and the community as a whole, *resist* the emerging self in its distancing and alienation from what was initially for it a familiar, yet anonymous sphere of community in which the self had been immersed.

3) The Other, the Self, and the Role of the Lived Body

It is at this very early stage of the difference and resistance of others that the lived body also functions as a field of expression of psychic processes taking place in the body. Sorrow of the other may shine through his laughter; shame may be mingled with physical exhibition; blissfulness may show through a martyr's bodily pain; continued love may exhibit itself in unrequited love; relief may be expressed at the moment of death. These processes are understood as bodily expressions of psychic phenomena that are rooted in the self, phenomena that the self may have borrowed from others.

In *Formalism*, "lived body" (*Leib*) had been distinguished from the "object body" (*Körper*), as had the relation of both to the self. The lived body's constitution of a reference system of spatial regions such as right, left, up, down, front, back, had been articulated in *Formalism*, a theme later taken up in greater detail by Merleau-Ponty.

We are led to a question at this point that is almost as old as philosophy itself: how can one, given the genesis of the self-other relation, account for an "embodied" self and an embodied other? How does the self relate to its lived body? Clearly, both Plato's soul-body and Descartes' mind-body explanations fail to come to grips with the unity established in Scheler's lived body and self constitution. Let us consider Scheler's approach to these questions.

The self—always referred to by Scheler as "*das Ich*"—and the lived body possess two opposing characteristics. The self consists in "unextended," "interwoven" psychic experiences, whereas the lived body, when all its sensations are in phenomenological gaze, either bracketed or set aside, is a pure "expanse." We would have expanse-experience even if all our sensations had been completely suspended. This idea presaged the now common notion of the "lived body schema."

But how can the unextended self that exists only in the interwovenness of psychic experiences be reconciled with the pure, lived body expanse? The answer to this question is to be found in further analyses of the nature of the self and the body which Scheler presents. First, the self (*das Ich*) is an *object* of inner perception and does not, as Husserl asserted, constitute "world." The self has no "world" as an intentional referent. This point radically distinguishes Scheler from Husserl; for Scheler "world" is not the experiential content of the individual self or a transcendental self. A transcendental self (*das Ich*) necessarily leads to "solipsism." The phenomenon of "world" is over and above the self because of our "consciousness of transcendence." In this consciousness there is an immediate knowledge of the natural "independence" of the being of things from the very "*execution*" of any act of knowing including "this" present one pertaining to ourselves and the outer world (II 378-9/F 379).

The immediate correlate or intentional referent of the self is, therefore, the *thou*. The thou, not the world, is the instantaneous intentional referent of the self. Alone, the self is, paradoxically, intersubjectively *communal* because it is inseparably tied to the sphere of thou-ness. The immediate phenomenological correlate of the "world," however," is only the "person and vice versa," not the self. The self is nothing but the interwoven network of the unextended experiences of inner perception. In a manuscript note of Scheler's, the self is said to be seated between the eyebrows. This note gives us a clue that the traditional division between extended and unextended reality, that is, between mind "and" body, is not acceptable.

We have been using Scheler's term "psychic experiences" and must now determine what he means by it. Given as they are in inner perception, psychic experiences are part of the total (phenomenological) "consciousness-of" which, besides inner perception also encompasses all phenomena of outer perception belonging to the milieu and nature around us. While the ultimate referent of inner perception is given in consciousness-of, the ultimate phenomenon of outer perception is "materiality," which is to be understood as an irreducible "meaning" in consciousness.

What is the ultimate phenomenon of inner perception, properly speaking? Psychic experiences are complicated experiences (XV 9-38) and Scheler's use of the term *psychisch* is not always clear. Examples of psychic experiences are feelings, thoughts, pictorial representations, expectations, recollections, sensations and feeling-states (III 235-7/PE 28-30). This looks like a confusing list of terms. Scheler is clear, however, in explaining that psychic experiences exist within the "experiencing self" (*Erlebnis-Ich*) only, having a specific direction of "consciousness-of" (X 386). This direction is called "inner perception" and the realm in which instances of psychic experiences occur.

Strictly speaking, the self-body relation implies that the self must paradoxically have two sides: there is a lived-body-self and a pure self. Neither exists in complete detachment from the other. From this we may gain a clearer understanding that self and the lived body can perhaps reconcile the traditional opposition between mind and extended matter. But how can mind and extended matter be two sides of a self when they are not supposed to be heterogeneously detached from one another? We will try to answer this question from the writings of Scheler's first period. In his second period this question will emerge in the context of Scheler's novel philosophy of space and time.

The self, as an object of consciousness-of, possess a "locational bearing" (*Stellenwert*), dependent on the preponderance of its two sides. It reaches its purest form in the experience of all possible states of "in-gatheredness" (*Sammlung*). This is the human experience of the moral "call of the hour" in which humans live for a moment so deeply within themselves that their whole psychic life, including its past, is "one." In-gatheredness occurs during religious experiences, grave decision-making and when a human being must decide between two positive values, one of which must be sacrificed—as always happens in tragedy (III 149-169/T 3-18).

Such a grave situation portrays the fatedness of the person that was discussed earlier. The human being is not empty: its self is entirely "full." We are truly with and in our selves. Neither a specific event in our lives nor our very self is intended. Rather, a thousand "calls" are coming forth from our past and future which meet in the present of the call, a moment when we are all alone "in" our self, except for the possible glimpse of a divine Thou. In such in-gatheredness humans do also experience their lived-body-self, but only as something "belonging" to us, not as "being" us. The body is just present as a part of the "enduring existence" experienced in the pure self. According to Scheler's thought, Nietzsche entirely misjudges the role of the body in saying that "we are body." This cannot be a continuous existential mode of human existence.

Conversely, there can be a relationship of body and self such that we more or less completely live in our bodies. This is the case when there is a situation of intense fatigue, of being lost in physical diversions or of bodily exhaustion.

The two extreme opposite experiences of the self through the lived body, namely as a pure self and as a "spread" self, reveals that the self-body relation oscillates between an unextended pure self and a bodily spreading self. In the former, the body-self becomes insignificant; in the latter, the full self —with its unextended interwovenness of contents—begins to dissolve into the lived body.

Let us look at two illustrations for the argument of the two-sided nature of the self using for an image a dome in the shape of one half of a sphere.

(1) Let the highest points of the dome stand for the psychic contents of the pure self, and let all other points in the dome and its base represent the contents of the body-self. Depending on how the body-selves affect the highest points on top of the dome, the pure self will alternate its psychic contents. The pure self has "locational bearings" with the body-self. While ideally the highest points of the dome, that is, the psychic contents of the pure self, retain an identity that is not affected by a past and future, they are *de facto* affected by the body-self. It is only the extended experiences that move through the body-self which bestow on the pure self the impression that it is in a state of flux. Scheler insists that there is *no* sequence of the self's alterations of psychic contents. The pure self is *pre*-temporal variation only. In Scheler's phenomenological vocabulary, it is "*reiner Wechsel*," or pure variation: its contents are present. Its supposedly "past" and "future" content exist only as a present togetherness of the interwoven and intercontained psychic contents. From this follows the central phenomenon of inner perception: everything that is experienced in inner perception is experienced "against the *background* of this total givenness in which the *whole* of the individual ego is intended as temporally undivided." (II 422/F 427) The self appears against the backdrop of one's whole life, regardless of whether it is wholly or only partially given. The phenomenon concerned is, therefore, the totality of experiences of a unique individual's life.

In this sense all experiences in the self are, phenomenologically speaking, said to be "'*together and interwoven*' in the ego." (II 412/F 415) The contents have the appearance of moving sequentially only because human beings bestow on their own selves the misplaced and false impressions taken from outer perception. Languages—at least Indo-germanic languages—show this to be a case of an "idol" that is patterned after outer, not inner perception. If the self were patterned after inner perception, there would be completely different grammatical categories and syntactic formations. In his *Metaphysics*, for example, Scheler mentions that the word "in" belongs to inner perception rather than to the outer perception of a thing "in" which something is contained (XI 159).

In order to explain the deception of sequential appearances in the self, Scheler offers an illustration:

If a light is moved along a dark wall (the source of light unknown), various areas of the wall are successively illuminated; however, there is no sequence of the parts of the wall, but only the sequence of their illumination. One who is ignorant of the mechanism involved is led to believe that there is a sequence of parts. In this manner the factually sequential lived-body states illuminate interwoven determinations of the ego for inner perception according to specific laws of direction. It may seem that these determinations are *in themselves* sequential, but they are only coordinated to different, successively appearing lived- body states and are at the same time conditioned by them. (II 412/ F 214)

(2) Let the dome be pressed upon so that its top (the pure self) extends into the body-self, which is always the lived-body-self. In this situation, the pure self spreads into the body-self. But how can the unextended pure self spread? In cases such as fatigue, body pain or exhaustion we lose our pure self in favor of a "de-selfed" lived-body. But this is no answer to the question; indeed Scheler does not appear to offer any satisfactory answer. But the question is essential to the general problem called the mind-body problem. Within the first period of Scheler's philosophy, an answer to the question can, I believe, be formulated in terms of the paradox residual in the essence of a point. On the one hand, points like the one on top of the dome that represent the contents of the pure self are, by the definition of a "point," unextended. On the other hand, points also form an extended area on the top of the dome. The points featuring the body-self strangely enough imply extension precisely because they form an extended lived-body. Nevertheless, no point is by its definition extended. Hence, the two sides of the self, that is, its pure and its extended side, must, paradoxically have only one side, namely, that of the unextended self. This would then account for the states of fatigue and exhaustion as well as that of a dreamless sleep or a fainting fit in which "there is perhaps no consciousness at all." (II 424/F 428)

On the basis of what has been said about the genesis of the self who is surrounded by others and from whom it obtains its first mental contents "there is, at bottom, no very crucial difference between self-awareness and the perception of minds in others." (VII 245/N 251) Indeed, the theory implies that knowledge of the existence of an individual self does not require that of its body. In a work of art from the past, for example, we encounter the active self that produced it without its body being given to us; to know of an historical person and his influence on society does not require acquaintance with his bodily appearance. Conversely, we do not believe in the existence of the devil, much as many people have made the claim to have seen him in the flesh (VII 237/N 243).

4) The Four Levels of Sympathetic Feelings

The thesis that the existence of other selves is earlier and more originary than that of our own self and that others initially bestow on our selves the rudimentary contents which we gradually take to be our own may still be questioned phenomenologically at this point because we have thus far avoided the familiar notion of a "transcendental" ego or self, which is often held to constitute alterity "in" the ego. This position approximates the tenets of Fichte and Husserl and is a belief that Scheler did not share.

Scheler's thesis becomes more supportable when we apply his position to two other areas: (1) the realm of intersubjective emotive experiences, especially to *The Nature of Sympathy*, and (2) to the sociological forms of human togetherness as listed in Part II of *Formalism* that are discussed in the following chapter.

There are four types of emotive experiences in intersubjectivity. They are the basic forms of sympathy: joint feelings, fellow feelings, emotive contagion and emotive identification.

a) *Joint feeling with others* (*Miteinanderfühlen*) occurs, for example, when grief-ridden parents are standing side by side in front of their deceased, beloved only child. In this case the grief is felt "with one another" (*miteinander*) in *one* joint grief. Joint feelings of this kind do not presuppose any "knowing" of the other's individual feeling. Knowing another's feelings only occurs when we "share" them, such as expressions of sympathy. In joint feelings, however, one does not so share the other's feelings; they are not at all given externally to each person involved nor are they experienced as a shared object as would be the case in sympathy. Joint feelings are not observed by the persons who are conjoined in them because the joint feeling is one and the same in both persons.

We must also mention that a joint feeling is only possible with regard to the value-ranks of the person, not with regard to the lower values. Thus joint feelings with others occur in varied instances: while listening to the beauty of a musical work of art persons can become unified. Because joint feelings occur only in the sphere of the person, Scheler held that they can function as one of the most efficacious means of unification among persons of otherwise different orientations and beliefs.

By contrast, we learned that the values and feeling-states of lower value-ranks are never jointly experienced with others. Physical pain cannot be jointly felt "in" the body of another person: all physical feelings are extended locally on or in one's body. In contrast to higher

feeling-states of the person, the lower feeling-states are always subject to willful manipulation and control. They can be artificially produced and eliminated; this is not true of personal feeling-states such
as grief, spiritual joy and bliss.

Joint feelings can also occur with more than two people. They occur quite obviously in religious group experiences. They seem to be
present among members "following" an exemplar of a holy man. Indeed, in contradiction to recent rational theology's approach toward
an "historical" Christ, the New Testament teems with instances of
mutual feelings among groups gathered around Christ. A conjoined
feeling may occur in the presence of a miracle or an experience of
wonder, thankfulness, or humility that suffuses an entire group.

b) *Fellow feeling* (*Mitgefühl*) occurs in a friend of the grieving parents, in the example given, who enters into sympathy with those in
the room where the child lies in view. His feelings have an intentional referent *to* the parents' mutual grief. The grief of the parents,
however, is distinct from that of the friend because the friend "understands" their grief while the parents have no need of "understanding": they are conjoined in one grief. The friend, upon seeing the
parents in their joint grief, in effect reproduces the parents' suffering
in his own grief. He vicariously feels the parents' grief in order to co-
feel their suffering.

c) *Psychic contagion* (*Gefühlsansteckung*) as a sympathetic feeling
differs from the former two: it is an important if often unrecognized
feeling in all walks of life. Psychic contagion is different from joint
feelings in that there is no active participation of expression by someone else with this feeling. It is different from fellow feeling because it
lacks any intention towards someone else. In joint feeling there is
still the death of the child toward which or around which the feeling
of the parents is joined.

What then is psychic contagion? Psychic contagion can occur among
any number of people. Scheler provides many examples of it, among
them the scene of two old women lamenting and crying without
actually knowing what they are crying about. In this case, the psychic contagion is self-engendered by the two elderly women. A third
person looking at these two old women giving air to their woes with
tears might soon inadvertently be infected by the pathetic atmosphere,
even if this third person had earlier been in a jovial mood. The women's
state of feelings begins emotively to infect the third person and their
woes overtake the third person.

A more familiar experience of psychic contagion takes place when
one enters the cheerful atmosphere of a beer garden where a light-

hearted and care-free atmosphere prevails, sweeping up all those who join the happy crowd. While the atmosphere may for a while diminish owing to the frustrations and disappointments of the day, just even reading about or imagining a beer garden's care-free atmosphere can absorb one in the scene. Psychic contagion could also unknowingly settle with a person walking through a hospital who sees the patients' plight. In short, psychic contagion often sets in quietly when, for example, a person yawns and others do the same: even speaking or reading about yawning may infect an individual. Today "canned laughter" blended into TV advertizement, skits and especially situation comedies is a prime example of what is artificially induced through psychic contagion. Without canned laughter in the background, many viewers would not get a laugh from the scene. The same artificially induced psychic contagion pertains to eery background sounds surrounding detailed depictions of murder.

Non-artificially induced psychic contagion is quite apparent in mass movements. In cases such as a crowd chasing a bull through the streets of a Spanish town; people become aroused while looking at this and other sporting events, even if some people are killed and trodden in the enthusiasm. Revolution, public panic, a strike and violent demonstration are imbued with psychic contagion. This phenomenon is in many ways similar with that found among groups of animals that pack together or with migrating birds.

Psychic contagion has a particular difference from the other two sympathetic feelings. Extreme cases show that when this feeling permeates deeply seated anger of a group, the individuality of a person becomes almost completely indistinct. With this, psychic contagion annihilates the individual's self-value and the individual is overrun and trampled by the feelings of the group. Psychic contagion can play a critical role in society. A dictator who gives speeches to enthuse the masses for war or a stockbroker who rides the surges and drops of the stock market relies on an infectious irrational atmosphere.

No matter how unchecked contagion may seem, there are some trends that can be described. Psychic contagion is characterized by the domination of drives over thinking, a decrease of intelligence, the disappearance of moral responsibility and the readiness of the masses to submit to a leader—the mass, says Scheler, is like a "grown up child." The contagion is always, however, short lived. A dictator usually has an ability to use it to channel and maneuver psychic material to his own advantage. He postures like a vanguard or alpha-animal of a herd. He gives the air of being in ultimate possession of knowledge and leadership.

d) An extreme case of psychic contagion present in many people is *emotive identification* (*Einsgefühl*). It must not be confused with Husserl's notion of "*Einfühlung*," or empathy. Emotive identification occurs in two ways: either a human being's self merges with that of another; or a human being absorbs another's self wholly into his own. The former case is heteropathic, the latter an idiopathic emotive identification. In either case there is no "individual" consciousness.

Let us give some examples. Primitive man can identify with an ancestor, with a parrot or with a stone. In such cases, the primitive person *is* that with which he identifies emotionally. He "is" a parrot, a bird. Emotive identification occurs in ancient mysteries when the mystic turns into a state of ecstasy and becomes divine. It clearly occurs in hypnoses and in a child's playing mother to her doll-child. In the latter case the child "is" the mother to the doll while she herself "is" even the doll, suggesting "how" the child would like to be treated by her factual mother. In this particular case, the image of an exemplary "mother" is also present in the background of the child's emotive identification. Another case is one particular form of sexual intercourse. In his book *The Nature of Sympathy*, Scheler discerns four types of sexual intercourse: (1) "sensual" intercourse that aims at the pleasure of the flesh; (2) intercourse that only "uses" the partner; (3) purposeful intercourse directed toward offspring; (4) the type that is distinct from the previous three because it is the located in a positive emotive identification. By comparison to the first three, the occurrence of the fourth type is rare. There is *true loving* when the partners relapse into an impassioned suspension of their personality and merge during mutual climax into *one* life-stream at which moment their individual selves, too, become indistinct in "one" love.

In the second period of his productivity, Scheler will concretize this experience with metaphysical explications. In all emotive identification human beings express vitality because the awareness of individual personality is nearly dissolved so much so that there is complete emotive, not rational, identification between the people affected by it. A mother's glance at her infant's eyes is "one" with those eyes, and vice versa.

The possible roles of emotive identification as a psychic power have been largely ignored in modern sociological and political thought. But this power continues to have an enormous impact on various kinds of cultural ethos. While Scheler unfortunately did not pursue the historical function of emotive identification in detail, his references to it in a book on sympathy is sufficient to encourage investigations into the matter. As historical examples of this feeling, he refers to the ethos of ancient Indian jungle dwellers who identified with nature and suffering and to the ancient Greek ethos of a ubiquitous function of a "world-soul" uniting ideas and matter in Plato and Aristotle. One could add also the Stoicism that identified with and accepted nature in the state of apathy.

But we must make reference to a religious function this feeling manifested in a saint whom Scheler appeared to regard as most representative of the spirit of Christianity, namely, St. Francis Assisi, whose sainthood Scheler so masterfully described in a few pages in his book on sympathy. Unknown to Christianity prior to the thirteenth century, the emotive identification with the center and heart of every single and imaginable creature on earth, no matter how small or insignificant, whether animate or inanimate was embodied by St. Francis. His loving identification with creation also embraced the Divine presence in each of them. The emotive interfusion with God the Father and all entities, referred to by Francis as "sisters" and "brothers," became miraculous as the expressive field of Francis' lived body began to show the five wounds of the stigmata. So rare had the intoxication of the love of Christ and the identification with creation become for Francis that his own body became quite literally infused with it. No matter how much verity one may attach to Scheler's unique characterization of the Saint's emotive identification, it is phenomenologically and psychologically not impossible for emotive identification to exude on the skin of a body. An analogous interaction between psychic states and the body occurs in the experiences of sudden shame when cheeks redden and limbs weaken at the unexpected moment of a person looking at us.

We are now in the position to glean from our analysis of feelings certain laws holding in emotive experiences. Especially in regard to the four sympathetic feelings just discussed, Scheler was eventually able to put to rest the groundless assumption, long held in the history of philosophy, that feelings are nothing but bundles of chaos to be reined by reason and ordered by logic. As is the case for the laws that hold for values, the laws for sympathetic feelings do not pertain to laws of logic either. All lawfulness governing sympathetic feelings pertains to orders of foundations that hold among them, not to logical laws of inference and of antecedents and consequences.

There is a threefold order of foundation governing all sympathetic feelings.

The first foundational law states that fellow feeling is grounded in emotive identification. Grief and sorrow must have been experienced beforehand in order for a vicarious feeling to occur. Children and primitive people live first in variable states of emotive identifications before they develop vicarious feelings. The "oneness" of a primitive with an ancestor and the "oneness" of a child with her doll are instances of the foundation in which vicarious feelings are rooted.

In the foundation of fellow feelings the law pertains to joint feelings. We cannot have a fellow feeling with someone unless we reproduce the feeling occurring in him. This reproduction is not conscious but spontaneous. Scheler did not, however, mention that vicarious feelings that reproduce a feeling also presuppose this feeling in someone else in order for vicarious feelings to occur. It appears that this second foundation is reversible.

The third foundation concerns a relationship that extends beyond what has been explicitly said. This foundation indicates that both joint and fellow feelings are the foundation of "humanitarianism," understood as a general love of humankind which every one of us is supposed to have, no matter how undeveloped. The reason for this foundational order is that in the two forms of sympathy, self-hood and otherness are distinctly given as a reality equal to one's own self. In joint feelings the other's self is conjoined with my own. In fellow feeling the other self lies in my vicarious feeling of sympathizing with the other. A reality of selfhood must be there *before* any love of humankind can take place. But what is this love of humankind?

Love of humankind is not a deliberate or willful act but a spontaneous one directed towards what bears the unique facial features of a human being. As such, it is to be sharply distinguished from both the love of God and love of nature. Humanitarian love is genuine when it is directed toward all humanity stripped of national, racial, sexual, educational or moral differences: it is shared by friend and foe, slaves and the free. If such differences were retained, love of humankind could not possibly extend to enemies, slaves or any other group of allegedly less value. Thus, love of humankind embraces "all" human beings precisely because, and only because, they are *human* beings. As a spontaneous act, this love resides in the emotive spheres of all humans and may be analogous to the instinctive cohesion that binds animal species.

Genuine humanitarianism must not be confused, however, with the money oriented and well publicized humanitarianism of modern organized society. This kind was mercilessly attacked in Scheler's analysis of human resentment that stems from an inherent impotency to love. Scheler charged modern society with such impotency of love according to which the individual is replaced by a conveniently contrived understanding of humanitarian love buttressed by selfishly intended donations and awards masquerading as a love of humanity.

A final point should be added to the laws holding among feelings of other selves. In regard to laws holding among values, arithmetic and logical laws do not apply. This can be seen when a good that was realized twice would not make someone twice as good as realizing this good only once. Moral values are not additive. The same holds for sympathetic feelings. The joint feeling of the parents standing in front of the dead child will not be simply duplicated if they view the child a second time on the following day. As a matter of fact, their sorrow-with-one-another may diminish the more often they view the child. Clearly, then, this feeling does not comply with rules of addition either. Likewise, vicarious feelings, psychic contagion, and emotive identification, will not double in subsequent occurrences. These too might begin to wane rather than increase the more frequently they are felt. Feelings do indeed have the tendency to wane as the number of their occurrences increase.

Since values do not follow rules of addition (or subtraction) they are akin to the syntax of transfinite numbers (Cantor) in which $1+1=1$, etc.

CHAPTER III

THE FOUR SOCIAL FORMS OF TOGETHERNESS WITH OTHER PERSONS

Prefatory Remark

Any theory of the givenness of the other person and of values must make specific mention of the nexus they have with practical socio-logical conditions in which human beings live and without which we are unable to think of our lives with others. Theories of "the other" and of values must stand a test in regard to the *social forms* in which humans live. Such forms mirror and reflect (to some degree) or do not mirror and reflect the results issuing from theories of the other. If a correspondence between intersubjective experience and social prac-tice does exist, such theories will furnish a philosophical foundation for sociology. Sociological facts must, according to our thinker, play an ingredient part in any systematic theory of the other because:

> ...we have come to realize the full force and meaning of what can be briefly described as the question of *grounds of the nature, existence and knowledge of the ties of connection between spirits and souls of men*. Theodor Lipps has already done well to emphasize that only by a solution of this question can *sociology* be established on a philosophical basis (VII 209/N 213).

And concerning the connection ethics must have with sociology we read the following:

> One must fully develop a *theory of all possible essential social units* to be applied to the understanding of factual social units (marriage, family, people, nation, etc.). This is the basic problem of philosophical sociol-ogy and the presupposition of any social ethics (II 515/F 525).

Hardly any theory of intersubjectivity and values in contemporary philosophy appears to have accounted for this significant relation between ethics and sociology. Scheler's charge that the sociological relevance of theories of the other and of values have been neglected not only pertains to contemporaries of his, such as Husserl and Heidegger, but can even be extended to more recent studies on the subject of the "thou" by Buber, Marcel and Derrida, and to a certain extent to the thought of Foucault, Lacan, Levinas and Sartre.

The four social forms of human togetherness are: the mass; the life-community; society; and the encompassing person. All of the social forms are co-original. None of them exists by itself and none is prior to the others in time. However, all of them more or less overlap at certain times: accordingly, there is always among the human forms of being together one that predominates. As concerns the distinction between the two forms of "life-community" and "society," Scheler relied upon the sociologist Ferdinand Tönnies.

1) The Mass

The first social form, the "mass," has already been characterized in the discussion toward the end of the preceding chapter. During its short duration—at best of a few days—a mass is held together by psychic contagion. The contagion disintegrates as quickly as it arises. People caught up in it tend to imitate involuntarily the expressions and movements of their leaders or "alpha animals." Indeed, the mass has a striking resemblance to physical feelings because its unity can be explained by sensible stimuli (II 517/F 527). These stimuli are not transmittable from one body to another. This state of affairs accords with the relative absence of the other in all mass experiences. While the actions of a mass can, like sensible stimuli, sometimes be intentionally set in motion, as by a dictator, there is little or no will among the people that would ground their mutual contagion. There is neither co-responsibility nor self-responsibility. Masses do not have a relation to an objective value. There is no interpersonal sympathy felt and there is no mutual "understanding" of others. In a mass, the other is anonymous. Individual personhood is diluted in psychic contagion. The contagion of a mass propels its members forward, as can be seen, for example, in the mass of people running through the streets of Paris during the French Revolution; there is no deliberation as to which street to take while dragging royal corpses around the city. The forward trajectory of a mass can also be seen in instances of Japanese running forward in a formations of up to ten rows. Members of a mass do not stray or straggle. Since both consciousness and conscience are numbed in the stream of psychic contagion, the social unit constitutes only a border (II,515/E, 526) in relation to the next higher form of association, the life-community.

2) The Life-Community

What is called a life-community exists in various forms: family, clans, tribes, home communities and "people" in the nonpolitical sense. While in a mass there is little or no mutual understanding of individuals with one another because of psychic contagion, there is, nevertheless, a "natural understanding" among members of a life-community in which is found an amount of fellow feeling. Whereas there is no solidarity among individuals in a mass of people or mobs, there is lasting and proud solidarity among all members living in life-communities. Strictly speaking, there are no individuals in life-communities but only "members" of it who share in a particular stream of co-experience that has its own laws (II,515-16/F,526-7).

At this point, we can make another observation concerning the genesis and order of foundation of the various streams of intersubjective experience we have mentioned. It was stated that in early childhood there is a stream of experience, but one that is not yet differentiated as mine or thine. The child's early intersubjective experience does not distinguish others who surround him. In the intersubjective stream of psychic contagion which suffuses a "mass," mine and thine are likewise indistinct. But while the indistinction between mine and thine in early childhood is not willfully produced because we are born with it, it can be produced in a mass where it lasts only briefly. In early childhood it may last longer.

The stream of experience among members of a life-community, is called "natural understanding." Natural understanding among members is distinct from and on a higher level than that of the anonymity of contagion. In the life-community there is not yet a fully objective understanding of the other. Such objective understanding is only gained when individuals live in a society.

In the life-community there are three social characteristics. (1) The self becomes distinct from others in the child's experience. (2) The givenness of the other becomes distinct from the stream of psychic contagion once a mass has dissolved. (3) There occurs a natural understanding in the stream of life-communal experience among its members. One cannot say that the intersubjective stream prevailing in a life-community stems from psychic contagion but only that it emerges with communal joint-feeling and fellow-feeling. But what is this natural understanding in a life-community, and what precisely is a life-community? We will answer this question in terms of a number of characteristics of the life-community as they come to bear on its prevailing fellow feelings.

Natural understanding is distinct from deliberate and objective understanding. Through it others are given as fellow-members of the "whole" of a community in a way analogous to the relation organs have to an organism (VI 335). Being born into and belonging to a life-community makes all members familiar with one another: there are no strangers. All values and actions are experienced within communal solidarity and serve the well-being of the whole. For this reason, members of life-communities show constant, natural co-thinking, co-living, co-hearing, co-seeing, co-hearing, co-loving and co-hating with each other. There remains little to be found of logical reasoning in tribes, nomads and sparsely populated home-communities such as the Amish or native Americans.

Of course, the members are given to each other "as" others, and have different roles to play in their respective territories. Fathers, mothers, youths and elders respectively care for arable land, hearth, hunt, education, etc. Nevertheless, the other "as" other continues to be experienced *within the whole* of the community in which there is widespread and spontaneous mutual *trust* along with natural loyalty. A further characteristic of the life-community is that it has no need of criteria for truth. Truth, first and foremost, has the character of being *received* (II 197/F 189), not of being rationally constructed or disclosed. It is only secondarily that truth can be discovered, sought after or found through activities of the mind, as is the case with individuals living in society.

Natural understanding is expressed more through dialectical language than abstract or artificial terminology. The predominant character of all forms of communal life is that it requires neither contract or promise in order to hold the members together. They grow together, if you will, and are held together by bonds of blood, kinship, and, most fundamentally, the "family" which is the original seat of the member's immediate sympathy (VI 335). For this reason the family is also the social seat of religious experience. Older life-communities have family and tribe gods. These gods or God are present to life-communities as experienced *among and with* its members. God or a holy man are not objects of knowledge. They are experienced in the *life* of the community. The life-community is, therefore, the social territory of original founders of religions. Buddha, Christ and Mohammed were born in a life-communal family, but were born with no societal ties. The life-community makes possible the emergence of a "holy family." The life-communal religious values must be clearly distinguished from those of societal theology which tries to explain that God is accessible to human knowledge (*der Wissensgott*). A life community has neither need of nor interest in what constitutes criteria for religious truths or an interest in proofs for God's existence.

Since all fellow-members in the life-community serve its whole, both the will of members and individual self-responsibility are dependent on the whole and its values: there is a moral *coresponsibility* with others but only limited self-responsibility. As a consequence, members lack a purely individual will and self-responsibility. The sphere of the person of a life-communal member is said, therefore, to be still undeveloped or *not of age* (X 265/PV 138). The constant awareness of the whole and solidarity of the community incorporates even domesticated animals and the home-ground (*die Scholle*) or territory the life-community occupies. In short, *all* members are bound in solidarity and fellow-feeling to such an extent that intersubjective experience is fittingly described according to the motto: "*one for all and all for one.*"

The solidarity of a life-community, while in one sense may be said to encroach upon individual responsibility for one's actions, in another sense is essential for a life-community inasmuch as the solidary co-responsibility is constitutive of the whole. Again this contrasts with a mass of people whose psychic contagion suppresses both co- and self-responsibility and lacks direction that aims toward its own whole. In the aftermath of an experience such as a revolt no one is willing to bear responsibility for what has happened.

It should be added that the solidarity of a life-community is no "representable" solidarity. A representable solidarity at best pertains to the critical understanding held among people in society. Rather, the life-communal mutual solidarity is guided by care for the commonweal of the whole. No member can be artificially represented or replaced in this task. Anyone who damages the ties of solidarity is seen as a traitor and defector. In a manner of speaking, the form of togetherness is sustained by a psychic glue which maintains its survival in every generation, just as a tree survives the growth and death of its leaves over the years (VI, 335).

Another facet of the life-community is its experience of time as *duration*, not succession. It is for this reason that its members are tethered to the feelings of ancestors, are circumspective of their fellows and mindful of subsequent generations of the community. Thus life-communities are genuinely anchored in *tradition*.

Let us examine the nature of communal tradition and the experience of time in life-communities.

Life-communal tradition is a lived tradition. It must be distinguished from traditions that are observed and attended. Life-communal traditions are the foundation for societal traditions. Societal traditions, such as birthday celebrations, festivals, feast-days, holidays, etc., are listed on calendars as a means of reminding one of them. In cases of political traditions like flag day, thanksgiving or parades they are willfully instituted. They can be discontinued at any time, for example, when a new political era begins. Societal traditions are, in short, similar to conventions, customs, habits and rituals.

Life-communal tradition is not, however, a tradition that is willful and calculable. Rather, traditional contents and values are *unreflectively* experienced as being alive and *in* the present: it is lived tradition. By contrast, societal tradition can artificially reenact what happened *in* the past by consciously retrieving a past event. Human history has been imbued with a greater degree of life-communal character, albeit unconsciously, than is usually assumed. This character even extends back to the mythological ages.

Two observations are appropriate concerning the global prevalence of the life-community. 1) Life-communities do not only live on their own individual territories but, taken collectively, share in one territory: the earth. This is, as we will see, very different from a society which does not have a territory. The territory of a life-community is not staked out like real estate or geopolitical borders. It reaches as far as the feet of its members who walk on it. This territory is, therefore, dynamic and always subject to lived changes.

2) The characters of life-communities helps us to understand why present day societal intersubjective experiences continually clash with the structures of life-communities. Today most of these structures of them are referred to as developing countries. The structures of these developing countries are replete with organismic world-views that stress life-values such as honor, organic growth, pride in heritage, natural well-being, strength and solidarity and a sensitiveness to offense, all of which are distinct from the quantifying values of utilitarianism, such as compromise, pleasure and entertainment.

For example, the military forces of industrialized countries that are stationed in predominantly life-communal countries such as Saudi Arabia are regarded as taboo by the indigenous population. Diplomatic efforts made by industrial nations with the so-called underdeveloped countries conspicuously lack a familiarity with the traditional structures of these life-communities. The international relations that are pursued by industrial nations lack the philosophic comprehension of the importance of lived traditions and the experience of time. Even among the industrialized nations themselves there is lack of comprehension of the communal tradition which is occurring unbeknownst among them. One only needs to look at the organic and life-communal management of Japanese corporations. There is a communal bond of solidarity between management and workers for the sake of the well-being of the corporate whole. By comparison, the internal structure of American and European corporations, while it may be highly effective, is in fact a game of competition for power between managers and workers. There is a high price for such an entrenched mechanical mind-set which lacks a lived solidarity.

Let us now turn to the experience of time among members of a life-community.

We can begin to draw a conclusion about the nature of communal time-experience from what has already been said about tradition. Life-communal tradition is not a consciousness of a tradition that is artificially maintained in the present; rather, its contents flow from the past into a present which is "filled" by the contents of the past. If, for example, I let a person of high office walk to my right side out of respect, I may not be aware that I am unconsciously following a tradition of the distant past when knights wore daggers on their left side ready to be pulled out with the right hand and to be held up in defense of the person walking to their right. The tradition flows unbeknownst *from the past into the present*: but the direction of the flow of time is not realized during the act.

The same phenomenon holds true for the future. Life-communal experiences of the future are filled with anticipations that are linked to cyclic events that touch the present, just as the cycle of seasons do. The future is not a box into which plans are made. Rather, the future bends backward into the lived present: the present is a meeting point for both past and future. The contents and values of the past continually shift into the present and fill it. The contents of the future, for example, pre-visions offspring and generations yet to come, bend back onto the present. Life-communities are not progressive as societies might be said to be progressive. Life-communities tend to be conservative and protective of the present. Thus their articulation of life-values are frequently praised by political conservatives in society.

The time flux that comes from the past and future into the present is already filled with contents and gives meaning to the present as their point of meeting. This stands in strict contrast to the societal experience of time according to which people living in a society experience the past as irretrievable, as a box containing countless historical facts. In this societal experience, the past is seen from and through the present. It is the present that makes the past alive: the past lies in back of what is present. This allows society always to reinterpret or reassign the dates of past events, whereas the life-community is anchored in the past and lives from *out of* its contents and values without the need deliberately to re-interpret them because they "are" present, no matter how unconsciously.

The nature of life-communal time-consciousness as flowing from the past into the present—in contrast to the objective flux of time according to which individuals in society run from the present to the past—can now be seen as a sociological confirmation of what Scheler told us about the stream of indistinction between mine and thine of early childhood. It was stated that when the child grows up, he becomes oblivious to the many experiences that come from past human beings. As one grows, these experiences and contents become "one's own." The child absorbs them even though their sources become obscured.

A final character of the life-community must be mentioned in order for it to be seen as essentially different from a mass and a society. This character is what Scheler referred to from 1909 on as "natural view of the world" or "natural worldview" (X 463-74; XIV 293/PE 202/87). Its sociological subject is the life-community and its forms (X 404/PE 168).

The term "worldview" was ill-chosen by Scheler because of its overall philosophical and theoretical connotation, which Scheler had not considered. It should be stressed that what Scheler meant by the natural worldview is the same as what Husserl later referred to as the "life-world" (*Lebenswelt*) and what Heidegger referred to as "everydayness" (*Alltäglichkeit*). Both these thinkers are indebted to Scheler because he stressed that the pre-theoretical, natural givenness of the world is distinct from the world or universe as understood by science. In the natural worldview, the sun sets and rises: in the scientific view, the earth rotates around the sun.

There are, however, some distinctions to be made between Scheler's natural view of the world and Husserl's life-world.

The natural worldview is, from the standpoint of the sociology of knowledge, not a constant and unchanging one that embraces all humanity as if all its cultures are based upon only one natural worldview. A constant natural worldview is only the theoretical result of a philosophical description peeling off, as it were, the living and genuine traditions of groups (VIII,60-1/PR,74-5). Scheler gave no details about this "peeling off." His emphasis was restricted to the relativity of natural worldviews.

Natural worldviews are relative to various cultures and groups. This contrasts with Husserl's and Heidegger's constant life-world and everydayness. Neither Husserl nor Heidegger considered such socio-logical group factors. If, according to Scheler, man is a *social* being living in thou-I relations, then the essence of the human being can-not be stripped of sociological facts, as seems to occur in Husserlian phenomenology and Heideggerian ontology. In fairness to Husserl and Heidegger, we must ask why a natural, non-theoretical view of the world should be relative to life-communities, families, clans, tribes, indigenous home communities as well as races in the genealogical, not political sense of this term. The response will depend on how the natural view of the world is defined. Scheler's states:

> We define this concept as follows: to the relative natural world-view of a group subject (primarily a genealogical unit) belongs whatever is gen-erally "given" to this group *without question* and every object and con-tent of meaning within the structural forms "given" without specific spontaneous acts, a givenness which is universally held and felt to be *unneedy and incapable of justification.* But precisely such objects and contents can be *entirely different* for different groups and for the same groups during various developmental stages (VIII 61/PR 74).

In the natural world view, no state of affairs needs a justification of proof. While the sun is setting behind the horizon, I am not in need of a proof for the setting. A scientific proof *destroys* the givenness, the "without question" of the sun's setting when I am enjoying the beauty of its color. Just as the existence of demons is accepted by primitives "without question," so also is the givenness of tools taken for granted while they are being used. Indeed, we have to learn from primitives how to use their natural tools. But the relative world-view spans even wider circles of human units. In Asia and India, Scheler says, the souls' afterlife belongs to the natural worldview. Its continuation is given here without question, whereas in other cultures, such as in the West, it is not (VI 16).

The social group factor which is referred to occasionally in Scheler's first period will come to play a decisive role in the philosophy of mind developed in his second period.

Throughout Scheler's analyses of an alleged disarray of emotive experiences, he appears to be quite perspicacious in showing that their presuppositions are beset with shortcomings, as was shown al-ready in regard to the order of values, feelings and their lawfulness. There are, in fact, also laws which do tie the human thou-self experience to the social forms in which humans live. This leads us to a description of the social form of human togetherness, called "society."

3) Society

What has been said provides obvious indications that there are basic differences between a life-community and a society. In order for us to bring into view what will later be referred to as the highest form of togetherness in which humans can live, namely, the "encompassing person" (*die Gesamtperson*), it is necessary to focus on the differences between the life-community and society and their respective origins.

We saw that the difference between a mass and the life-community exists in their duration. Masses are ephemeral. The human material of the mass soon finds itself living again in life-communal conditions. It cannot escape being restored and retrieved by the life-community's natural way of looking at the world. The collapse of a mass is analogous to the disintegration of life-communities (X 266/ PV 138).

Living in a society as we do, the differences concerned will be of interest to us because while actually living in a society we are often unaware of these differences and thus Scheler's descriptions of them will not be immediately convincing. In society one takes for granted, for instance, that the historical role of society is almost completely irreplaceable. As Scheler tells us, human beings are not aware that they are haunted by a customary deception: a general prejudice that they can live only in one particular social form, one society at a time, rather than living simultaneously in a plurality of social forms. This implies that for Scheler all social forms are "co-original" in man's constitution and do not develop sequentially (IV 379).

The use of the term "society" requires that we render explicit the meaning of its essence. For the sake of the work *Formalism* and for the discussion of intersubjectivity one must clarify the term "society" as taken in the substantive sense. Today the word "society" is used with a myriad of cultural, journalist, political and social nuances. The term can be used with emotionally charged, negative and obscure meanings, such as identifying it with immoral aspects of technology, with a conservative ideology that stands in need of repair or with a social arena of degenerating human conditions. A clarification of the essence of society must be given sociological relevance and freed from obscure usages. One aspect of the essence of society must consist, therefore, in a clarification of how human beings live with one another in it, that is, its form of togetherness.

This social form has no reality of its own, as the life-community does (VI 336; II 518,551/F 529,564). Society is, nevertheless, co-original with the other three social forms of togetherness: the mass, the life-community and the collective personality discussed below. All of these exist in various degrees of proportions and "mixtures" (II 529/F 541). Society, too, rests on permanent constituents of consciousness. But there is a discrepancy here: on the one hand, society is said to have no reality; on the other hand, it is supposed to be co-original with the other social forms. This discrepancy can be explained, however, inasmuch as society is also concomitant with the decline and collapse of life-communities replaced by a social *artifact* which is called a society by humans. In contrast to natural life-communities that are based in drive-conditioned factors, societies arise rationally from man. But society cannot exist without the life-communities, in particular it cannot exists without the family:

> There can be *no society without life-community* (though there can be a life-community without society). (II 520/F 531)

This fundamental axiom has many consequences. Society does not survive the generations of its people, as is the case with the life-community that survives its members like a tree its changing leaves. A society depends on people sustaining, fixing and amending it constantly through new laws. Scheler's contention, and that of others from the school of the sociology of knowledge, however, who hold that society does not survive its generations, seems to run counter to practical experience. Has society not survived past generations since the thirteenth century when, according to Scheler, it began gradually to supersede life-communal conditions and to develop into its highly sophisticated present state? Why should present day society not survive the present generation?

The essence of the four social forms of togetherness is circumscribed in each by "how" human beings live and relate to each other. In this regard, societal relations are substantially distinct from 1) a mass within which individuals do not relate; 2) sympathetic feelings of living-with-one-another in the life-community; and 3) the collective personality. Scheler chooses to focus on the moral experience of solidarity in order to set the nature of society off from the other social forms. There is no solidarity in society that is comparable to that in a life-community. At best there can be something like a proclaimed and resolved solidarity in society that is instituted and defined by one of its groups, perhaps one with representation in government. Before solidarity occurs in society, individuals must *will* to relate to one another in terms of *conceptual agreement*. Because there is no emotive solidarity, one must *choose* to join a solidarity . In society, the individual possesses much more freedom than members living in life-communities.

A society that is open to freedom of choice, to conceptual relations and rational reflection, is a society that is highly dependent on *criteria for what is true and what is right*. Such criteria are many and depend on the status of laws. In contrast to a life-community, it is the individual who, in society, is responsible for their application. Objective thinking comes from the individual which is now self-responsible. The individual relates to someone else *as* an other, not *with* another as in the life-community. In the latter, willfully established relations among members are of minor importance to the community.

The other in a life-community is first experienced as "lived with." He is an organ among other organs that forms a whole social organism. Self and other are mutually inclusive. A high degree of co-responsibility is found among the members including ancestry.

Before making a moral decision, an Indian might first seek seclusion in order to experience the strong fellow-feelings of his ancestry in order to be told what to do. In the artifact of society the other is not at first experienced as co-lived but as an alien-other precisely because he is an element separating him first from his self so that he can will or not will to relate to another. According to Scheler, it is the individual *will* in society that makes its individuals "of age," while the subordination of the will under the solidarity of the whole of the life-community makes its members not quite of age. No act of a societal person is subordinated to the whole of a society. All are in full possession of their volitional self with a capacity for decision-making and conceptualization.

It is because of the discrepancy between the experience of freedom and individual self-responsibility, on the one hand, and the lack of natural co-responsibility, on the other hand, that societal individuals "size each other up" prior to the possibility of becoming partners or friends. The individual must reach out and relate to others. The individual must first make the acquaintance of the alien-other; only then can relations be established. Hence, societal individuals from the beginning are suffused with a degree of original "*distrust*" (II 518/F 529). This social distrust cannot function, however, without the intersubjective life-communal trust. One can, therefore, say that the quotation above that described the foundation of society in the life-community implies that the foundation of distrust is, in fact, communal trust. If this is the case, what could a society that is laden with pervasive distrust possibly hold together?

Society overcomes its lack of internal trust through willing the establishment of artificial and negotiated contracts. The act which serves this purpose is the obliging act of promising. If two mutually alien individuals decide to live together, they must give reciprocal promises to that effect. The act of promising amounts to the formulation of a "willing-with-one-another." Both individuals must will the mutual understanding of their promise (II 520/F 528).

It is because of this promise and despite the artificial nature of it being made that society is co-original with all other social forms of togetherness. A mutual will to live together must have its roots in something other than prior acts of such willing. If there were such an infinite regress of previous promises, it would yield the same result. This is why Scheler argues that the establishment of inter-human relations by will and intention that are designed to sustain at least an apparent accord among persons must have its roots in the solidarity of the life-community from which the conscious acts of a promising and volitional consensus to live together issues. But a society must be held together by artificial terms of contracts that can pertain to anything like agreements, bargains, constitutions, pacts, vows, etc. They are a part of legal systems in common, Roman, and, especially, private law. The litigious nature of society itself dictates that it "consist" in contract-making (II 546/F 559).

The foundation that contracts have in life-communal solidarity does not imply that societal groups held together by contracts must always first form life-communal relationships before they can draw up contracts. Societal individuals are free to enter a contract with anyone, even with men on Mars. In practice, however, there is the law that all societal individuals must at one time have lived in a life-community in order to be able to fully understand the very difference between natural solidarity and rationally agreed upon contracts (II 521/F 532). For in all types of mutual accord, individuals relate to one another only through a "mediate" understanding, not by a natural or immediate one. The lack of co-living and co-feeling among societal persons also allows for the drawing up contracts with someone who is neither liked nor trusted, as in marriages of convenience, something quite unfeasible in a life-community. Contracts can even be drawn up for the sake of sheer political expedience which does not affect mutual disdain among co-signing partners, as was the case between Hitler and Stalin on the international scene. Societal contracts rest only on this kind of mediate understanding; that is, on acts of deliberate reflection that allows for high levels of distrust. Partners in a contract need not have any factual communal relation with one another at the time of exchanging contractual signatures.

Nevertheless, all contract relations do presuppose a wider community than the one in which the individuals happen to live. All nations belonging to the cultural unit "Europe," for instance, form a community *vis à vis* those of the cultural unit of "Asia," says Scheler. In each, all members are co-responsible for the whole of their particular cultural unit. Nevertheless, within Europe and within Asia, nations entertain societal relations among one another. But these relations exist under the wider whole of the "people" of Europe and of Asia. In this non-political sense of "people," people also form a community. Scheler's argument is, therefore, that any contractual relations presuppose a wider life-communal context: Asia and Europe are such wider communal wholes. Although society is, in contrast to the organismic life-community, only an artifact characterized by conceptualized rather than natural thinking and therefore a social unit separate from life-communities, all societal human beings continue to belong to a higher communality of life.

The distinctions made between society and life-community are perhaps even sharper than has been indicated. For one thing, a societal individual can seek and establish only relations to others, rather than consider others as terms of relations. One can chose what kinds of intersubjective relations one wishes to establish. In this regard, societal relations *themselves* can be used, manipulated, exploited, terminated, revived or instituted. For example, a person can plan to wheedle himself to sit at a corporate president's luncheon table and establish and use the relation with the aim of gaining a promotion. In this case, the term of the relation, that is, the corporate president as such, does not matter. It could be anyone in such a position. It is a relation sought which serves a goal: in general, relations themselves can turn into a commodity serving other ambitions by, say, introducing another person into the relations established for further deals.

In this regard, the artificial nature of society cannot have duration as the life community has. For society does not only just "consist" in contractual relations as we stated earlier (II 546/ F 559), it *dies and is reborn every second* by the drawing up of ever new contracts (VI 336). One reason why society has no comparable duration is that contracts can only be made among individuals "living at the same time." Strangely enough, a contract is said neither to pertain to deceased nor to the future people for two reasons. First, if a partner of a contract dies, the contract ceases to be valid "between" the survivor and the deceased, although it may stipulate that something be done on the part of the survivor. The same provision can hold for future people also. Secondly, a living person can neither make a contract with a deceased person nor with a person not yet born. In the latter case, there can only be a contractual stipulation about what will be the case should a projected person be born. But such a contract is only potential and, therefore, has no validity in the present.

The principle of contract now gives us a clue as to why society does not only encompass people living "at the same time" but also international contracts which also undergo alterations. The artifact of society tends to spread increasingly into different peoples that are predominantly characterized by life-communities. It intrudes into life-communities that still have original natural territories and lack political borders. The natural territory of an American Indian tribe, for example, originally had no political borders: its territory spread as far as tribe members could move and walk. In a manner of speaking, a life-community has a natural habitat as long as societal people do not intrude; if they do, life-communal land turns into objective and negotiable political real estate. Since societal relations are not bound by a natural territory, it is *non-spatial*, as well as having no duration. That is, whatever "residences" it establishes are transient and have no lasting natural territory.

At first glance, the absence of duration and spatiality of society seems to contradict the order of value-ranks and their relations to space and time because society is said to consist only in terms of contracts made by persons living at the same time and lacking an indigenous territory. One could argue that if society is independent of a spatio-temporal dimension, it cannot have any proper relations with the order of values in which these dimensions play a part with regard to the different ranks of values. It was stated, on the one hand, that the higher value-ranks are, the less spatial, extended, manageable and controllable they are, but the more lasting they are. On the other hand, the lower the value-ranks are, the less duration they have, but the more spatial, extended and manageable they are. Societal persons who are said to live in a form of togetherness having neither space nor duration would have at best a very peculiar, if not perverted, relation to the experience of value-ranks. This is indeed the case because society on the whole manifests a predominantly objective, not an emotive relation to value-ranks. Values, including all higher ones, are or can be treated like manipulable objects.

This lies in the nature of a society itself. In contrast to the life-community, society not only tends artificially to establish human relations by contract-making, it also tends to bring such relations under manageable controls. The other self is not only an alien, an alien-other, but also the object of a controllable, observable relation to the self. The other is experienced amidst controllable things. Not only is the universe an objective, controllable world but so is the human world with others, i.e., a "societal" with-world. The life-communal organismic worldview is replaced by a mechanical one. True, society cannot exist without life-communities: it cannot exist without the life and blood of their families. But this does not preclude its unusual social mind-set that is ever so different from that of a life-community. While life-communities share predominantly in feelings of life-values, society is characterized by those value-ranks which are the most controllable ones: *these are the divisible values of usefulness and pleasure* (II 546/F 559). The values of usefulness and pleasure are the "stars" of society (X 266/PV 138). All the values that are higher than these, the values of the mind and of the holy, are not given in their respective feelings of the person but are given in a predominantly objectified way. They appear in critical and reflexive attitudes of consciousness. They become objects of scrutiny, proof, scientific and theoretical investigation and round table discussions.

We can now provide an inventory of the differences of inter-human experiences occurring in the life-community and the society as well as characterize their relations to space, time and values:

Life-Community	Society
1. Natural Thinking	1. Conceptual thinking
2. Immediate membership. Co-living	2. Contract relations. The alien-other
3. Members not of age	3. Individuals of age
4. Trust, solidarity	4. Distrust
5. No criteria for truth	5. Criteria for truth
6. Life-values	6. Divisible values
7. Duration	7. No duration
8. Territory	8. Non-spatial relations

With this in mind, we can now describe the forth form of human togetherness, the "encompassing person."

4) The Encompassing Person

The term "encompassing person" is an approximation of the German *Gesamtperson*. This cannot be adequately rendered in English.

Various translations have been suggested such as "collective personality" and "totality person."

The part of the German word consisting of the adjective *gesamt* means "all-inclusive." Literally the *Gesamtperson* is all-inclusive. It encompasses the three forms of togetherness already discussed: the life-community, society and the ephemeral mass. This encompassing, all-inclusive and highest form of togetherness among human beings has both similarities with and differences from life-communities and society.

There are three types of the all-encompassing person: a religious, a cultural and a national encompassing person. Each of them does not only encompass all the social forms but likewise encompasses all types of sympathetic experiences among humans as life-communal co-feelings and societal reflexive and objective understanding of being with others. The term encompassing "person" refers to a collective person but also to an individual person, in the manner as each encompassing person possesses an individuality of its own. Examples of the religious encompassing person would be Buddhism, Christianity and Islam. Examples of cultural encompassing persons would be the Western and Eastern Cultures or ancient Latin American ones such as the Maya. National encompassing persons are France, Spain or the United States, etc.

Encompassing persons do not necessarily have geographical borders: they sometimes overlap. There are elements of Christianity in Islam; there are elements of Western culture—which for Scheler comprises the Americas, Europe, and parts of Russia—in Eastern cultures, and vice versa; there are traces of Mayan mythology among present Christian practices of the Mayans. A nation might encompass citizens living far outside their own political borders, such as French people living in Quebec or Germans living in Poland.

In the context of Scheler's first period, however, it is not quite accurate to describe the encompassing person in this way. Such a description would be more representative of the distinct philosophy of Scheler's second period that came after 1922.

In his first period Scheler did not mention any particular religion by name when discussing encompassing persons. Rather, he states that it was historical Christianity that first realized the highest form of togetherness in which humans can live, namely, in terms of the historical inception of *love*, unknown to preceding encompassing persons. Instead of mentioning any religion by name, Scheler considered "the church" to be the highest encompassing person. The reason for this was that during Scheler's first period he thought that ultimately there could be only one ultimate religious encompassing person because there can be only one God. The "church" apparently satisfied Scheler's argument at that time.

Yet what Scheler meant by "the church" is not fully articulated. We can be sure, however, that he did not identify "church" with a rational, legal and administrative organization. This is largely because he rejected the Aristotelian bases of Catholic theology. Aristotelianism does not do justice to the eminent role of *love* in Christian religion. Aristotle lived three centuries before Christ lived. Christ had no interest in Aristotle or Greek philosophy. The Greek influence on theological Christianity, especially that found in the Middle Ages, is deplorable because it tarnished both the essence of love of the person and the pure exemplarity of the holy and of Christ with rationality. According to St. Thomas one must first know something in order to love it. According to Scheler, however, one can only know something by first having been drawn to the *value* of what is to be known. On this account Scheler wrote an essay with the characteristic title placing the word love before cognition or knowledge: "*Liebe und Erkenntnis*" (Love and Knowledge) (VI 77-98/L 147-165). The ancient Greek orientation of Christian theology also had deplorable sociological effects on the structure of the church. Popes, bishops, priests and public servants are portrayed like "Roman rulers" (VI 92). They even hold an "office" and observe "legal" stipulations in contrast to the essence of love. Redemption must be believed in according to "dogma." The essence of the human person is supposed to be a "substance" (Aristotle) rather than *the* bearer of love. Charity and love tend to be observed as part of a Divine will, rather than in a free, selfless Samaritan way. In all of this there is a confusion, says Scheler, of Christian love and Aristotle's teleological system, culminating in a theological confusion of Aristotle's god as the "thought of thoughts" or "unmoved mover," on the one hand, and God as seat of love, on the other.

Similar to Heidegger's saying that a Christian philosophy is a "square circle," Scheler tells us that Christian theology is an error of "Greek philosophy with Christian ornaments." The Church officially recognizes the authority of St. Thomas's reading of Aristotle as infused into theology. Scheler's Catholic orientations in his first period was strongly oriented by those who were, like he himself, in disagreement with Thomistic Christian philosophy. He studied intensely the writings and lives of Augustine, Francis, Bonaventure, Bernard of Clairveaux and Pascal. No matter whether one takes the highest form of encompassing persons to be the church, or various religions, Scheler's general explanation of it pertains. What then is the nature of the person encompassing life-communities and societies?

All three types of encompassing persons are spiritual spheres held together either by a faith or by basic worldviews which are held among people and which are or can be formulated in theologies, philosophies or laws. Encompassing persons are trans-generational; in this they possess a peculiar lawfulness of their own. This lawfulness consists in their having a collective consciousness of their own (II 512/F 522-23). But such collective consciousness does not have an idealist meaning: a church, culture or nation requires living individuals on which it is dependent for its own existence.

The dependency on living persons for the existence of the encompassing person is only one side of its nature. The encompassing person is also independent of living members because it is not dependent on *this* or *that* member in it. Its members are not only variable and free; persons can forsake the encompassing person and new persons can join. One person can even be a member of two encompassing persons at the same time, for example, of a religion and a nation, while both are not necessarily compatible in their beliefs. Such was the case in France at the time of Napoleon and in Russia during Soviet domination: a Frenchman could still be catholic-christian and a Russian an orthodox.

In the encompassing person there must also be an experience it has itself of its own as "above" all finite member-persons. The twofold character of dependence and independence in the encompassing person makes it neither absolute nor universal nor transcendent as it could be regarded through the eye of German Idealism. Rather, the encompassing consciousness itself is experienced and contained "in" every individual member-person as a part of the latter's encompassing qualitative direction of acts. There is only a part of an individual's own qualitative direction of acts that contains the qualitative direction of the encompassing person because no individual can ever be in full possession of the entire collective content of the encompassing consciousness. Likewise, no one can be in possession of the entire meaning-content of a nation's encompassing person. No one can be in possession of the entire historical roles and effects a nation historically had or will have in the future. Therefore, the encompassing person is always experienced by the individual as something "beyond." It outlasts its member-persons in terms of its overwhelming historical duration, in terms of its encompassing content and in terms of its encompassing historical effectuations.

The order of sequence of encompassing persons—namely, the church, culture and nation—corresponds to the order of values of the person. The highest form, the church (or of religions) corresponds to the value of holiness. The corresponding values of cultural encompassing persons are the mental values. The corresponding values of a nation pertain to the personal, not biological part of life values. All encompassing persons have, in descending order, two characteristics. (1) A church (religion) can or does encompass both nations and cultures. It is above them or "supranational and supracultural." (2) It is immanent in both culture and nations: it lives in them.

Each nation must be above a social form that is not an encompassing person. It is above the "state" in the sense of a politically unified people with defined borders. The nation is above the state. It is "supra-state." Yet, a nation is immanent in a state. While Scheler sometimes remained ambiguous in regard to whether the state is a collective personality, it must be denied that it can be one because any state is anchored in divisible, controllable and quantifiable values of the lower value-ranks. Any individual living in a state always experiences the background of the nation and the culture to which he belongs. A culture is not dependent on the existence of any state.

The order among encompassing persons also implies that the "one" highest religious encompassing person comprises various cultures and that the number of cultures encompass even more nations.

While the three types of encompassing persons comprise both life-communities and society, they also comprise the very different experiences in the togetherness of church members and individuals of a society. Members of a church are unified in communal solidarity. They are responsible for and to their religion and their religion is responsible for and to them. This mutual responsibility also pertains to culture and nation. Scheler emphasizes the corresponsibility among church members because it is expressive of the solidarity of its members in their common goal of attaining salvation.

Society cannot, however, be an encompassing person because it has no duration in that it rests on individuals living only at the same time who form a countable sum (census). They live by their variable contractual relations during their life time. Each individual has "interests" in his own well-being and, therefore, has little coresponsibility for others. All of this sharply differs from a life-community and the encompassing person of the holy.

While the individual of society is self-responsible and while in the life-community all members are corresponsible in solidarity, people experiencing their encompassing persons possess both moral self- and coresponsibilty for and to their encompassing person. The encompassing person itself, say a nation, must be considered corresponsible for its members. But the mutual responsibility between the encompassing person and the individual is not an ultimate responsibility; nor is the responsibility which each encompassing person has in respect to other coexisting encompassing persons. Ultimate responsibility is only before God to Whom both self- and coresponsibility pertains. This responsibility before God is the highest degree of responsible "solidarity" possible for humans. Solidarity among humans, therefore, is a "fundamental article of the cosmos of finite persons" (II 523/F 534). Through it, the totality of the moral world becomes *one* encompassing whole—no matter how far the cosmos of moral persons may extend in space and time, on earth or on undiscovered planets (II 522-4/F 533-5).

CHAPTER IV

PHENOMENOLOGY OF RELIGIOUS EXPERIENCE

Prefatory Remark

In the preceding chapters, occasional references have been made to religion, God and the Holy in various contexts, but have been largely unclarified. References were made in the context of value-ethics, the thou-I relation and the forms of human sociation.

One could expect that these references could lead us to a so-called "philosophy of God." Scheler, however, explicitly rejected a philosophy of God, maintaining that philosophy should deal only with religion *per se* and pursue a philosophical investigation into the essence of religious experience. Scheler regarded such an investigation as being possible only through phenomenological investigation; that is, a phenomenological investigation into religious experience must decipher the contents of consciousness in religious acts and the nature of religious acts *per se*.

Scheler shares with almost all of his contemporaries the position that "phenomenological experience" is an experience immanent in consciousness rather than an experience of something outside us. But in strict contrast to his contemporaries he holds that phenomenological experience does *not* rest on sensory experience.

This second point is important with regard to understanding Scheler's place within the early phenomenological movement; he often set himself off from other phenomenologists, including Husserl. Scheler challenged Husserl's, "categorial intuition" (*kategoriale Anschauung*) in 1913/14, saying that it, too, is falsely associated with the presupposition of and alleged foundation in sensory experience (X 448/PE 221-2) This point may cast some further light on his description of the discussion he had with Husserl when they met the first time in 1901 (VII 307-8).

The general significance assigned to sensory experience by phenomenologists may well explain the reason why only very few of those who associated themselves with the beginnings of phenomenological movement showed no interest at all in the immanent experience of religious objects. This lack of interest is manifested by Herbert Spiegelberg in his monumental work, *The Phenomenological Movement*. Spiegelberg does not pose the question as to whether an immanent object, such as the phenomenon of the Divine, or an experience of the eternal "in" human beings, can be associated with sensory experience.

The title of one of Scheler's basic texts on religion which appeared in 1921, *Vom Ewigen im Menschen* (*On the Eternal in Man*) reveals the two aspects of the phenomenological experience of religious objects: the experience is, in a nutshell, immanent and non-sensory. On the basis of this understanding of phenomenological experience we can set out to delineate religious phenomenological experience and the givenness of its respective objects.

1) Controversial Aspects of Phenomenology

As is the case with all areas of phenomenology, the self-givenness of a so-called phenomenon in consciousness can never be satisfactorily explained. Much of the secondary literature of phenomenology refers to phenomena extensively but is somewhat disappointing to readers not familiar with the goals of what is called phenomenological science. Wilhelm Wundt (1832-1920), renowned German philosopher of his time and contemporary of Husserl, once remarked that Husserl's 1900/01 *Logische Untersuchungen* (*Logical Investigations*) only tell us what phenomena are not, never what they are. Indeed, Wundt's critique foreshadowed immense criticism of phenomenology during this century: it does nothing more, says Wundt, than tell us tautologies, such as "a judgment is a judgment" (X 391/PE 152). This is undoubtedly true in more than one respect.

There is, however, also another side to this kind of critique. First of all, a book concentrating on phenomenology *per se* is written with the intention of making the reader "see" for himself, and only for himself, what a phenomenon *qua* essence of a state of affairs in fact is. The phenomenologist can only *point* to the X he is talking about because the object to be brought into view relies on the insufficient means of language and concepts. Let us take an example. Scheler is clear on this matter:

> We cannot observe "that something is color," "that something is spatial," "that something is alive"; we can observe that *this* colored surface is triangular, that this body is oval-shaped, that this living organism has four legs. If I try to observe "that something is color," I find that in order to circumscribe a circle of possible objects for observation I must look to everything which is of this *essence*, which consequently is already seen. If, on the other hand, it is a question of distinguishing essences from mere concepts, then an essence is everything which inevitably and intrinsically becomes entangled in a *circular* definition

whenever we attempt to define it. Thus, an essence as such, as a pure whatness, is itself neither universal nor individual; both universality and individuality are concepts which first make sense in relation to objects depending on whether the essence comes to light in several objects or only once (X 395/PE 157-8).

There are two points to be made here which returns the ball of critique to Wundt's court and of others. First, if an essence or phenomenon is neither universal nor individual, it stands to reason that it cannot positively be defined with logical means as "genus" and "specific differences." Second, while all other sciences at least allow descriptions of their objects on the basis of observation, in the science of phenomenology something that is "meant" is not observable and is brought into mental view in terms of a phenomenological attitude. In such attitude nothing is empirically observable.

Let us illustrate this by a practical example that Scheler supplied, namely the phenomenon of "color."

Color has many functional meanings in various disciplines of knowledge. In the natural sciences colors are signs of motion and waves. In physiology they are signs of chemical processes in the optical nerve. In psychology they function as signs of sensations. But what is "meant" by color as a meaning that consciousness has an awareness "of"? "Color as meant," "itself," as a content in consciousness, is not contained in any of the sciences dealing with colors. Nor is there any need for the various sciences to ask the question what "color" is independently of them. Nevertheless, color as a pure content is "*there,*" as Scheler puts it. Color is a basic datum in the mind, as it were, an X underlying the disciplines in their dealings with colors. True, "red" is an X that may refer to motion, a nervous process or to a sensation. But this is so without being given *as* a thing in itself, as "red." Thus draft after draft—that is, a bank draft or check—is drawn on "red" and so long as one remains within science they are negotiated in infinitely varied ways against other drafts drawn on "red." But they are never absolutely redeemed.

Phenomenology claims to redeem all the drafts on red, including those of extra-scientific nature found in symbolic expression of various civilizations. A goal of phenomenology is realized whenever the "self-givenness" of red—freed from all non-essential characters that red has in the sciences and elsewhere—turns into an immanent experience of the phenomenon. Scheler calls this phenomenological intuition.

The experience of a phenomenon (the essence of a meaning in consciousness) is *that* experience in which the *self-givenness* of an immanent object coincides with its *meaning*. Phenomenological intuition means that the self-givenness and the meaning of an immanent object are *congruent*. But how does one "see" such congruence of self-evidence and meaning in practice? It is not seen by reflective description or methodological steps, but by the *attitude* proper to intuition itself.

The congruence of self-evidence and meaning is advanced by Scheler in 1911 and reveals his rejection of a role of sensory experience in the phenomenological "method" and his radically distinct conceptions of phenomenology. This pertains to the very starting point in the phenomenological enterprize. In contrast to Husserl and his disciples, a self-given phenomenon must, for Scheler, be located at the *beginning* of a phenomenological experience and be grasped through immediate *intuition*, rather than occur at the end as an outcome of a series of phenomenological methodological steps. A method is a goal-directed procedure, says Scheler, of "thinking about" something, as in methods of induction and deduction, for example. If this something thought about is "there" in the first place, one must ask what a phenomenological method is supposed to do. Indeed, in his second period Scheler tells us in no uncertain terms that Husserl's method which consists in (a non-phenomenological) withholding of judgments, amounts to no more than child's play (IX 207/PE 316). As we will see below, Scheler's phenomenology is characterized not by "method" but by intuitional *attitude* (*"Einstellung—nicht Methode"*) (X 380/PE 137).

Scheler's insistence on intuition is, however, sometimes confusing. In fact he frequently uses the terms "method" and "bracketing" (*absehen*) in such a way as to leave one at a loss as to whether his "viewing of the essence" (*Wesensschau*) or a phenomenon is the center of his conception of phenomenology. Nonetheless, his intuitive viewing does represent the nucleus of his concept of phenomenology. This is corroborated in a number of key essays for which he is better known than for his acrid critique of the phenomenological method. Such essays in questions are those on "Feelings of Shame and Modesty, " "On the Tragic" and on "Ressentiment." In these essays the phenomenon under discussion is first grasped, seen and described as much as is possible within their intuitional view. It is only after the intuitional view of the internal object—which is plainly "there"—that practical, observable, historical or empirical data can fill out or redeem the "drafts" of what is under discussion. The unnecessary shells covering the phenomenon in practical experience are not first bracketed by a method in order gradually to lay bare a phenomenon concerned; rather, they are "bracketed" *in*, not by, the intuition. That is, they do not appear as such in intuition. There are no judgmental steps as required by a method.

A quintessential question emerges here: do intuitions of internal objects given in a phenomenological attitude have an order of foundation among them? The elucidation of this question will sharpen our focus on a "phenomenon." The problem concerned pertains to Scheler's detailed analyses of the "regions" of consciousness and of the unique nature of a religious act.

2) The Immanent Regions of Consciousness and the Region of the Absolute

The German word for "regions" in consciousness is "*die Sphäre*," "sphere." Neither "region" nor "sphere" suffice to describe their phenomenological meaning. In fact, this writer holds that nouns of any language obstruct phenomenological description because both structure and vocabulary of spoken languages have their roots in the outer perception that is operative in the "natural worldview." In everyday parlance, the connotations of words like region or sphere, for example, are patterned after the extension given in outer sensory perception. They are not patterned after temporal dimensions that are operative in interior perception. The word "region," therefore, has a specific meaning when applied to consciousness that is different from the spatial orientation of human languages.

It is well known that the restrictive character of language as concerns descriptions makes for a complicated states of affairs. While this is true of the sciences, it perhaps pertains more to phenomenology. No matter how one describes the happenings in the world of atoms in the science of physics—for example, the Heisenberg uncertainty relation—we are always restricted by the use of words like space and time, even when the state of affairs clearly indicates that their use is insufficient. Thus the introduction of words like "space-time" exceed the structures of languages that are based in the natural view of the world where space "and" time are articulated as separate and not according to their rudimentary unity. The transcending of ordinary language will play an immense role in Scheler's later elaborations on metaphysics; for the time being, however, we will restrict our analysis to the notion of "regions" in consciousness.

Since such regions cannot clearly be defined, we chose earlier to introduce such extra-sensory meanings indirectly. We discussed the regions of "aliveness" and of the thou-I relation. Concerning the latter, we availed ourselves of Scheler's illustration of Robinson Crusoe saying that the social relation of "thou-I" is most apparent for the absolutely isolated Crusoe who in practice would never have seen any other fellow human. We also articulated the pure region of the "thou-I" or with-world as experienceable only by dint of the *absence* of any living people. In the illustration of the thou-I region, Crusoe experiences a maximum of loneliness by the absence of what could fill the region out. But although he is totally alone, the existence of the unfulfilled region in the structure of consciousness does *not* itself make him "alone." Any region of consciousness is always "there," as Scheler puts it, open to be filled or fulfilled, unfilled or unfulfilled by whatever belongs to it.

In this particular case, it is the phenomenon of the thou-I, that is of alterity, that also already emerges in the young child who does not yet distinguish between his self and that of others, even though others like his mother are pre-given anonymously, if you will, to the child. Hence a "region" of consciousness is a phenomenon of first order even if it remains unfulfilled. Whatever appropriate meanings fill out a region, we refer to them as a phenomena of the second order. Scheler says that all propositions pertaining to phenomena of the second order are also *a priori* if they follow from their respective first region.

From this it follows that phenomena of the second order cannot be present without the region to which they belong. The phenomena of first order are many and may even allow of combinations. Among them we also find those that are essential for all philosophical investigation: inanimate materiality, aliveness, relationality, spatiality, temporality, mechanical motion, self-motion and even method itself. For some of these, the region and its phenomena of second order can remain indistinct: this is not, however, material to our present discussion.

The regions of consciousness within which phenomena occur resemble a pre-given framework. Scheler mentions the regions in various places, but only distinguishes them in detail in his *Problems of a Sociology of Knowledge* (1924) where he lists them in a specific foundational order (VIII 57/PR 70-1). Let it be added that, according to what we have said, there must also be orders of foundation in a number of the phenomena of second order. These foundations have the form such that "A" cannot be without "B." We are already familiar with one such foundational order, namely that the self cannot be without the thou. In what follows, we will arrange Scheler's enumeration of the regions somewhat differently by organizing them in twelve units in order to achieve maximum clarification:

1. The region of the Absolute.
2. The Thou-I relation or the "with-world."
   The Thou is pre-given to the I.
3. The region of the outer world.
   It is pre-given to the following region of the inner world.
4. The region of the inner world.
5. The region of aliveness. It is pre-given to the following region of inanimate or non-living nature (the child playing with her "live" (but plastic) doll, etc.).
6. The region of inanimate matter.
7. The region of the outer world of our co-subjects belonging to the with-world. It is pre-given to the following region of what "I" can know of the outer world.
8. The region of what "I" know of the outer world.
9. The region of the outer world of my own particular with-world. It is pre-given to the following region of the inner world of my own with-world.
10. The region of the inner world of my own with-world, including its past and future. It is pre-given to the following region of my own inner world.
11. The region of my own inner world.
12. The lived-body as field of expression is pre-given to corporeality or the object-body.

None of these regions can be reduced to the others (XI,103). Taken by themselves and without any meaning specific to their appropriate object, they possess only an amorphous, intuitive content. In no sense do they form a (Kantian) synthesis of their respective phenomena of second order that fill them out. Regions are passive and purely *a priori* "there" without the activity or productivity of a synthesizing mind. They simply passively constitute all directions of experience and knowledge. One object can suffice to fill out the region in order for them to be at least partially fulfilled. The phenomenon of "aliveness" is already fulfilled in one organism or one organ.

The factual objective contents of the regions are, of course, variable. The variability is the reason for the controversies between the sciences and philosophy. For example, one can assign an inanimate atom with a kind of "will" in order to explain its statistical motion (Erwin Schrödinger); one can conceive the entire universe as being "alive" as in all organismic world-view (Aristotle) in contrast to our usage of the word "matter" since Descartes. The ancient Greek word for matter, *hyle*, refers to the growth of wood and animate matter; *hyle* does not refer to inanimate matter as Descartes would have it. Inanimate matter as we know and perceive it was not a concept for the ancients, not even for the atomist Democritus. The variability of objects in the region of the Absolute allows that anything under the sun can be filled with it (IX 76/P 2).

In aberrated or false absolutizations of "finite" objects in the region of the Absolute there is only one requirement in order for the person to be able to hold something that is finite to be absolute: "You may take away from me everything, but not this" (XI 106). An example of a finite absolutization could be a nation that experiences itself as sanctioned, as an extreme nationalist country might, or as a culture that maintains extreme isolation or a religion characterized by fanaticism. One can even absolutize ideologies and certain individual philosophies and philosophers. Even "nothingness" can fill the region of the Absolute as was the case with Gorgias in ancient Greece, just as "Being" can fill out the region of the Absolute as was the case with Parmenides or other subsequent thinkers.

The content of this region can be felt as "Nirvana" devoid of desire (Buddha) or as "unknowability" (Agnosticism). Of course, one can also absolutize specific finite things, such as money and possessions (Capitalism), sex (Don Juan) or Satan (black mass). In these cases of aberrations, the person "identifies" a finite or worldly idol with the absolute sphere. The large number of such displacements of phenomena of the second order *into* the region of the absolute are for Scheler aberrations or "idols."

All displacements of finite contents into the region of the absolute can reveal deep-seated psychological or rational value-deceptions. The reason for this is because they all lack a phenomenologically genuine religious experience of the *value* of holiness, of an "*ens a se*" or of a "universal efficaciousness" (V 169/E 172-173). But the large number of possible absolutizations of these and other "metaphysical aberrations" also have a positive side which reveal that: "Every finite spirit believes either in God or in idols" (V 261/E 267; IX 76/P 2).

From this it follows that every consciousness has a peculiar "metaphysical penchant" toward absolutizations, which is the source of all religions (X 208). This penchant is even operative in any nihilism or atheism that denies the absolute: such a person is a "nihilist *of* the Absolute" because the experience of phenomena of first order in consciousness, the "regions,"—in this case that of the Absolute—cannot be annihilated.

The metaphysical penchant toward absolutizations gives rise to two distinctions to be made in the experience of the Absolute itself. First, the penchant can lead to all kinds of "farcical obsessions" (*Vergaffungen*), referring to the filling out of the region of the Absolute with finite objects. Secondly, the metaphysical penchant makes possible all myth and mythology and leads to metaphysics as a discipline of philosophy.

Every finite consciousness has of necessity a metaphysics -*insofar* as it exists without God's factual self-disclosure. (X 207)

From this follow two practical results: (a) Religious education must not function as a pilot that would lead human beings on the right paths toward God. Rather, all personal and historical idols, displacements and aberrations that accumulated in the region of the absolute must first be "demolished" (this development made Scheler a precursor of modern negative theology); (b) while one can always argue what may or may not fill out the region of the Absolute, one can *never* be in doubt *that* it is constituent of every finite consciousness because no matter what the contents are that fills it out, it is implicit *that* this region "is" (*bestehe*) (X 201). No farcical obsession, aberration or idol experienced in it can change the facticity of the sphere of the Absolute in finite consciousness.

The irrefutable existence of this region, postulated by Scheler's analyses of human consciousness, represents the footing for his analyses of 1) the special place religious acts have in phenomenology, and 2) the distinction between "faith" and "belief" in particular. His phenomenological view of the content proper to the region of the Absolute results from these analyses and represents the culmination of his philosophical investigations of religion of his first period.

3) The Special Place of Religious Acts in Consciousness
a) The general Character of Religious Acts

We made a number of references to the differences that exist between the conception and function of Scheler's and Husserl's phenomenology. (We will focus on these differences more later.) If we were to isolate only one disparity between Husserl and Scheler, it would have to be Scheler's particular assessment of the nature of the religious act in consciousness.

Husserl gave little attention to this particular stream of intentionality or flux of consciousness. For Husserl, the center of all "consciousness-of- something" is the human ego. Its intentional referent, "world," is an ultimate horizon in consciousness, holding together and unifying all phenomena. The phenomenon of "world" had been accepted as ultimate by the entire phenomenological movement at the time Husserl was lecturing in Göttingen. The point was expressly elaborated by Husserl's student, Heidegger, whose 1927 analyses of Dasein's "world" identified Dasein with "being-in-the-world."

Scheler held fast to this ultimate phenomenon in consciousness called "world." In contrast to Husserl, however, it is seen in Scheler's *Formalism* as the ultimate correlate of the person, not as an impersonal or transcendental ego because for Scheler there was no ego unless it was that of a person. Throughout his writings, there is not one essay, let alone a book, that deals in particular with the phenomenological meaning of "world" as an irreducible intentional referent of every consciousness.

The reason why Scheler refrained from looking at the "world" in this fashion is seen in his analyses of the nature of the religious act; no one else at this time in the phenomenological movement had dealt with this issue.

In looking at the peculiar nature of religious acts, we first describe their general character and then we will look into their center, the act of faith. What makes religious acts, which occur among thousands of acts of consciousness, so special? We must first realize that there are many kinds of religious acts: praying, worship, self-communion, communion with something Divine and specific calls of conscience, emotive identification with the Divine, acts of thanksgiving, repentance, awe, love of God and forgiveness in light of faith. These acts and many others are the common stock of religious experience. But even though they can, religious acts do not necessarily occur in all human beings.

There are three peculiarities that set religious acts off from all other acts of the consciousness.

1. Religious acts transcend contingent objects of the world. In this, religious acts unify all meanings of entities of the world into one whole. When a religious act is acted out, such as imploring God for a turn of events "in" the world, all other worldly objects slowly fade into obscurity. The "world" recedes from consciousness and is gradually replaced by the region of the Absolute in which no worldly thing has a place. In a religious act the phenomenon of "world" is transcended. In this stream of religious experience consciousness moves from the "hither" of the world to its "yon" to succumb to a special kind of response which the ultimate phenomenon of the "world" can never provide. Religious acts are therefore distinct from all other acts that have as their ultimate referent the meaning of "world." Hence, transcendence of world into a "yon" is the first peculiarity of the experience of any religious act.

This peculiarity of religious acts by which consciousness moves thitherward to the region of the Absolute rather than staying in the hither world reveals an abyss between a phenomenology of religious acts and that of mundane acts of consciousness. This abyss can be articulated by referring to Paragraphs 51 and 58 of Husserl's *Ideas I*. Husserl maintains the opposite of what has just been said, namely, that the ultimate correlate of consciousness, "world," must be retained and that God's transcendence understood to be His existence prior to and beyond the world, too, must be suspended in the phenomenological reduction. Husserl never abandoned nor fully developed a theology based in human rationality and transcendental subjectivity. He maintained that something like a World-God, without transcendence, is an unacceptable conception.

2. The second peculiarity of the religious act implies that its "possible fulfillment" can only come from something extra-worldly, perhaps something Divine which, in the experience of the act, excludes the possibility of finite entities having such a function. Because of this, the "world," which contains nothing but indistinct finite objects, cannot be effectual in religious acts. It follows from this that, phenomenologically, religious experience is to be distinguished sharply from all other phenomenological experiences of consciousness: no other act of consciousness correlates to possible extra-worldly "fulfillment." Religious acts refuse to accept or respond to any finite thing unless that finite entity—such as a fetish—has been falsely placed into the region of the Absolute and been falsely absolutized in it.

There can be only *one* kind of "holiness" that can possibly fulfill the religious act like the one of petition mentioned above: Augustine's "*inquietum cor nostrum, donec requiescat in te*" ("our hearts are restless until they rest in Thee") pertains only to the religious act. In this regard, Scheler shared with the German theologian Rudolf Otto the idea that the value of holiness is never exhausted merely in the perfection of moral goodness, but that it represents a totally new value-quality (V 301/E 306).

3. The third distinction to be made between religious acts and all other acts is seen in the negativity of religious acts. They have no earthly foundation or goal even though they can be empirically motivated. The negative character of religious acts is linked to the ancient Greek distinction made between the "existence" of an entity, on the one hand, and its "whatness," on the other hand: the distinction between existence and essence. In religious experience these metaphysical principles are entirely different.

Religious acts are not directed to "what" something that "exists" is; rather they are correlated with that which is "totally different" from the world and its explanation. Especially, religious acts correlate to the ineffable. This not only implies that it is possible that religious

acts are able to be fulfilled (for example, an act of repentance is fulfilled by the experience of Divine forgiveness) but also that the "totally different" *bends down* and reaches *into* religious experience. This
bending-down is experienced as a spontaneous and sometimes miraculous response: but it is not willed.

Even if all religious acts were illusions, the response from the "totally different" in them cannot be found in any other act of consciousness. This is especially true for acts of questioning and asking
because the experience of anticipating a response does not stem from
something which is "totally different" but from the world. Asking a
question presupposes a context of meaning *into* which we inquire.
The answer to a question presupposes that the question pertains solely
to a mundane domain.

The reason why rational questions about the existence or non-existence of God are futile is because the act of questioning is restricted
to the world, not to the religious experience of the sphere of the
Absolute. Scheler holds that the experience of the "totally different"
that bends down into the religious experience of the person gives rise
to a religious act that provides a hint that something like a Godhead
does or can infuse Himself into human consciousness. Although the
felt response from the "totally different" must be experienced differently by each person—because the "*ordo amoris*" and values are, as
we saw, refracted differently in each person—all religious response
intimates that the "totally different" must also be personal if it is to
be experienced. The religious act is, paradoxically, a "receiving act"
and also because of this is distinct from all other acts. In the receiving
character of the religious act the person simultaneously unfolds
thitherward into the "totally different" and the person experiences
the response in his own hitherness. According to this phenomenon,
something "eternal in man" occurs.

It must be asked whether or not the three peculiarities of transcendence, fulfillment and of negativity characterizing religious acts beg
the question: is it not the case that in speaking about religious acts,
we already presuppose something like absolute Holiness or a Divinity of an X right from the beginning? Could it not be the case that
the religious act is a deception and an error *par excellence* to which
humans fall victim? For the sake of argument we will briefly consider
a position that opposes that of the religious act, namely, meaning-
lessness, as articulated by Nietzsche's well known motto "God is dead."

For Nietzsche the "totally different" is an illusion, just as good, evil
and truth are. All of these are perspectival and erroneous "interpretations" of the world concocted by humans who live in a small corner

(*die Ecke*) of the universe and are endowed with an unfortunate faculty of reason which interprets the meaning of the text of the world.

The unflagging history of rational interpretation of the world is beset with shortcomings, owing to the very nature of interpretation. The status of interpretations as erroneous will require, according to Nietzsche, that all interpretation be discarded. Nevertheless, there is a human need for interpretation. The interpretation arises when the earthling, who occupies in the universe but a small corner whose angles distort thinking, creates idols which permit him to sustain his condition in the cosmos. Reason acts as blinders which encourage man to absolutize. But man will eventually bring about a "twilight of the idols" through which all the absolutizations that have occurred since Plato will be smashed beyond recognition. In this smashing of the idols of interpretation the "Overman" comes to be. He is not "over" all falsely absolutized idols, nor "beyond" them. He is the incarnation of the will to replace them through the pulsating power of life in him, not through the influence of reason. Only "will to power," not mind, can decapitate the "error of truth." For truth is interpretation. In the future, when all absolutized idols have been replaced, a full view of existence will open before life: namely, the "eternal recurrence" that peaks at "noon" when the zenith of the sun is directly above Zarathustra, a moment when there are no shadows of absolutes, including that of God. At that moment, human reason's obfuscating blinders that concoct such idols as God, Satan, truth, falsity, good, evil, unity and being are shattered by the Sun's beam of light. The death of all illusionary absolutes entails the death of man's obscuring region of transcendence. What is left after the smashing of idols and their realm is "innocence." Overman's innocence that knows no absolutes makes him look like a clown, or as Nietzsche chose to say, a "madman," to baffled onlookers. Early one morning the madman yells, "God is dead." Not any particular god, as Heidegger showed, but transcendence itself is dead (*Gesamtausgabe* 48 8-10).

The annihilation of transcendence is the zenith of Nietzsche's "Metamorphosis" that traces its beginning to the belief in absolutes initiated with Plato and comes to completion with the annihilation of absolutes and the sphere of the Absolute through the will of will, namely, will to power. For Nietzsche, this inevitable historical transformation, which he calls "nihilism," consists of three phases. The transformation begins with humankind's initial existential state and is symbolized by "*das Kamel*" (camel), which in German is used as an image of ignorance and stupidity. This phase leads to a state of belligerence among humanity, called the "lion." Finally there is the state of innocence symbolized by the infant who cannot practice interpretation and posits no absolutes and represents the noontime of humanity. This happens, in fact, when Zarathustra is sleeping and speechless. Thus at noon he lives "half an eternity," like an innocent, speechless infant. (One should be mindful that the word infant derives from ancient Latin *in-fans*, *infari*, meaning "not speaking.") Fine. But why has Nietzsche's powerful proclamation of God's death slipped into our discussion of the religious act and its correlation to the sphere of the Absolute?

The very region of the absolute and the transcendence experienced in the religious acts, while negated by Nietzsche, is affirmed by Scheler. Thus there is a juxtaposition of the two extremes of faith and nihilism—neither of which is subject to rational proof or disproof—in the confrontation of these two thinkers.

Nietzsche's proclamation "God is dead" is a judgment made on future human history. Scheler holds that as a judgment one can neither prove nor disprove the existence of a transcendent region in consciousness because such a region is *a priori*, like any other region in consciousness. Likewise, one can neither prove nor disprove Nietzsche's prophetic view of the Overman because the Overman does not as yet exist. For Scheler, sheer "existence" of anything, even God's, is not provable. Nietzsche would undoubtedly concur. Yet, if it is the case that the absolute sphere is a priori, then Scheler may appear to have a phenomenological point over Nietzsche inasmuch as any consciousness is endowed with the region of the Absolute, *no matter which* absolute may be experienced in it.

If we are to grant Scheler this phenomenological point, we could argue that Nietzsche's "noon," his reversal of Platonism and the death of God, are absolutizations in consciousness. The sphere of the Absolute becomes filled with just another idol: an Overman freed from beliefs in God, Satan, reason and truth. Does not Zarathustra preach the absolutization of the "earth" to which his soul is tethered during his noon time nap? He feels too heavy to get up and loosen himself from this tether. If Zarathustra is to follow the inexorable wheel of life *qua* being, that is, the eternal recurrence, he must untie the knots that connect him to the earth. From Scheler's perspective, Nietzsche's "Twilights of the Idols" and the "noon" do not abolish the region of the Absolute but just endow it with another content: nihilism.

While proofs for the existence of God are phenomenologically impossible owing to the *a priori* of the region of transcendence, Scheler nevertheless offers a rational argument that God's existence cannot be proven. He outlines three concepts that relate to all endeavors for such a proof.

First, there are customary "proofs" (*Beweise*) as used in the sciences and mathematics. In their stead there are two procedures for mounting a proof in religion: *Aufweis* and *Nachweis*. Scheler's use of these words is very difficult to render in English. These two German words belong to an entire set of nouns relating to the German verb *weisen*, which means to point to something, as, for example, in a direction whose end point is *not* really known. (German nouns etymologically stemming from *weisen* are commonly used. Examples include *Erweis*, *Zuweis*, *Hinweis*, *Vorweis*, *Verweis*, and, of course, *Beweis*, *Aufweis* and *Nachweis*, along with their respective verbs.)

If "pointing to" refers to something that is yet unknown, there is an *Aufweis* to be done. The *Aufweis* points to something not yet found and can, therefore, show us something for the first time. It corresponds roughly to the English verb "to show," in the sense that one says "show me what you mean" or "show me what happened," which indicates that there was no prior knowledge of the object concerned.

On the other hand, if "pointing to" refers to something which had already been found earlier but was lost and is to be recovered, there is a *Nachweis* to be done. This procedure is typical of detective stories, criminal investigations and the like. It plays a substantive role in determining juridical circumstances and evidence. *Nachweis*, therefore, comes close to the "demonstration" of something already known—at least to a certain degree—but which is yet to be recovered. Both *Aufweis* (referring to something yet unknown) and *Nachweis* (referring to what was originally known but lost and to be recovered) play an important role in the affirmation of religious experience, whereas a proof (*Beweis*) does not.

Scheler's reasoning on this matter runs as follows. Only "propositions" which have already been found, are able to be proven (V,253/ E,259). The object of a "proof" does not originate in deductive methods used in proofs. The object must be there first in order to be proven. It is only in mathematics that the origin of an object comes forth simultaneously with the steps of the proof. The steps of deduction coincide with the steps of the construction in which the X of an object comes forth. The coincidence of proof and deductive steps is unique to mathematics, however, and plays virtually no role in the affirming of something like religious objects.

God cannot be constructed while being proven. If the concept of God allows that God as object coincide with the deductive steps of the proof—as it is with objects in mathematics—it would be a proof of God in the absence of faith. But God does not disclose himself in the fashion of a proof because the value of the "holiness" of God precludes the possibility of having access by deductive or rational means. Indeed, the more the powers of constructive proofs hold sway as in mathematics, the more such proofs are removed from giving access to God.

Deductive proofs are applied by consciousness as long as consciousness does *not* intend to access the region of the absolute (V 252-3/E 258). Thus such proofs are justified only within the limits of propositional assertions pertaining to what is already given. Clearly this excludes religious experience in which no "reality" of God is given as a reality, that is, as something that could be proven by propositions. Therefore, it is "finding" God in terms of *Aufweis* or *Nachweis* that comes closest to telling us rationally what might be a belief about God's reality, but in Whom there can only be faith (V 254/E 260). This brings us to an analysis of the act of faith that is at the core of all religious acts.

b) Faith and Belief.

It is material for an understanding of what follows that a distinction be made between "faith" and "belief." The German language has only one word for the two which are linguistically distinct in English: *Glaube*. To preserve clarity, Scheler in fact used the two English words "faith" and "belief" in order to make the distinction. The English verb "to believe," like the German equivalent *glauben*, can have two meanings, depending on whether it pertains to faith or belief. One can believe *in* something and one can believe *that* something is.

In both cases, belief *in* or belief *that* something is, the belief attends to reality. If I say "I believe in God," something is given in consciousness as real "in" the act of believing. This reality lies beyond a proof; indeed, it does not require one. Believing *in* something links the whole person with what he believes in. More precisely, the center and innermost self of the person is linked with the value of that which is believed. Believing in something is personal. By contrast, believing *that* something is is not necessarily accompanied by such a personal commitment. A person can remain unaffected by and indifferent to the fact *that* something is—for example, that there are more or less billions galaxies. Believing *that* something is pertains primarily to worldly goods, states of affairs and finite entities. The "belief-that" is contingent.

Nonetheless, one can also believe *in* finite objects. These finite objects, too, are subject to change. One can, for example, change one's belief *in* a nation or a cause. Yet, even believing-in finite objects "fulfills" the person to some degree in relation to the finite object in question. For example, a person may feel "patriotic" and cannot be detached from the fulfillment that accompanies patriotism. However, believing *that* something is does not necessarily give me fulfillment; for example, one can believe *that* something is despicable, but this gives no fulfillment. Likewise, we can believe *that* logic is the foundation of the humanities, but this too would give no fulfillment. The belief-*that* which refers to finite and contingent objects does not by itself lead to personal fulfillment. Nor does belief-*in* which refers to finite and contingent objects.

The situation is quite different when belief-in occurs in matters of faith. The believing act is quite different when its internal correlate refers to faith. Only then is belief replete with *personal* fulfillment: that is, belief *is* faith. Within faith, the person, prior to judgment and willful intention, is spontaneously drawn toward the highest *value* of the "totally different." When the belief-in finite objects occurs, then this value is not experienced. The value of the "totally different" exercises a tug in the religious act of belief-in.

There must be a fundamental difference between the religious act and all other acts. What, phenomenologically, makes the religious act even more different from any other act of consciousness?

No other act can be substituted for the religious act because it is unbending: it does not allow other acts to be intertwined with it. All other acts allow of admixtures with others. We can, for example, "think" while we "dislike" what we think, or doubt while we are "recalling" what we doubt, etc. But the religious act is inviolable. The topology of its direction is the reverse of all other acts: the end point of the experienced value of the Divine in the region of the Absolute is at the same time its cause in the person (V 255/ E 261). This is a general character of the religious act that we had mentioned earlier with regard to an act of repentance. This makes religious acts singular. The person who is replete with love of God through faith experiences this love coming *from* the Divine. The uncompromised bond between Divine Love and faith precludes that bond being constituted by rational acts.

The act of faith reveals the most central category of the self-execution of personal existence (both human and Divine): it unfolds and conceals in personal silence. Just as the person must be in a state of unfolding while communicating with others, God, too, unfolds himself in an act of a person's faith but still remains concealed, just as finite persons remain concealed to certain degrees from other persons with whom they communicate.

What does this tell us about the reality of God? The reality of God can only be experienced through God's "self-disclosure" (*Selbstmitteilung*) in faith. Personal self-disclosure, in both humans and in the Divine, has an ontological, not a rational or cognitive significance. Divine self-disclosure is not experienced by reason but only evidentially in the core of the person or the heart (*Gemüt*); that is, in the *ordo amoris* (X 184).

In order for us to fully grasp Scheler's understanding of the reality of God, we must again be mindful of the executionary status of the existence of personhood: the person is not an object. A person acts out its existence. It is a being of acts. For this reason all inter-personal "understanding" implies a pre-rational self-disclosure and self-concealing of a person. The dynamics of personal existence allows for the "unfolding" oneself to others and for quiescence and silence (*das Schweigen*), which is markedly different from any simple not speaking.

A person can "let" another person understand or not understand himself. He can block his self-disclosure (*Selbsterschliessung*) and therefore conceal himself. The term, "self-disclosure" and "self-unfolding" are of as subtle a connotative distinction in English as their German equivalents, *Selbstmitteilung* and *Selbsterschiessung*. Self-disclosure and self-unfolding belong to the person of God, as does self-concealing. These categories of personhood do not hold for the expressive field of a lived body of a person. Certainly the embodied person standing before me "exists" as such a person and I understand the embodied person as he is. But this understanding of the embodied person is very different from the understanding of pure personhood, the disclosure and concealing of the person. Disclosure and concealing are the foundations of all inter-personal communication that do not depend on the lived body. The categories of self-disclosure and concealing lie in the very essence of self-executionary being of the person. Self-disclosure and self-concealing (quiescence) are purely *temporal* phenomena within the execution of the person's existence.

Since God is exclusively "Person," the question of God's reality can be addressed only through the *self-disclosure and self-concealment in the act of faith*. This establishes the only condition for the possibility of knowledge of God (theology).

God's self-disclosure is the *a priori* grasping of the value of holiness experienced in the region of the Absolute in an act of faith or any other religious act. Earlier we mentioned that the object of the religious act coincides with its inception in the finite person. This was to point out that a religious act opens doors, as it were, for God to enter us and for Him to disclosed Himself. Thus the topology of the religious act *defies any sequence* of origin and endpoint in this act. There is neither a *terminus a quo* nor a *terminus ad quem*.

c) The Dwindling of Faith and the Therapist of the Age

Scheler's incisive discussion of the apriority of the region of the Absolute, of the determination of its proper content as self-disclosure and unfolding, his exposition of the "totally different" personality of God and his analyses of the peculiarity of religious act as a receiving act are not aspects of his thought that were simply put forward in order to arouse research among scholars of religion. Scheler was one of the very few philosophers in the twentieth century who insisted that philosophical ideas and insights should reach the uninitiated and be tested in the practical lives of ordinary people.

Ideas alone, valuable as they may be, do not suffice to disclose the human and personal being of God. Scheler never ceased to maintain close contact with practical, everyday life. Accordingly, we are in the fortunate position of being continuously presented in his ceaseless writings with analyses and critiques of our age. Scheler was not only able to observe but also to envision what was to come: his prognostications are remarkably pertinent even today.

One such critical observation of our age is Scheler's astute characterization of the "type" of human being that has emerged in the wake of the rise and spread of modern capitalism since the thirteenth century. In his 1913/14 essay "Death and Afterlife" (X,11-64) he tells us that the modern man has come to avoid facing death and has ceased to be interested in what may come after life. In addition to his many more social, cultural and political critiques, Scheler observed that public inertia *vis à vis* death and afterlife is motivated by the contemporary *moral tenor* in the human race.

There are, according to Scheler, two factors that contribute to the general dwindling of faith in our time. 1) Thinking has increasingly been turned into and identified with "calculative" thinking (*das Rechnen*). 2) Modern man's lived body is increasingly experienced as a corporeal object, rather than as a lived body. It functions as a body-object amidst a realm of thing-objects. The body is more an individual "possession" than a member of a community. For such thinking life and its value are ephemeral.

The predominance of calculative thinking in society implies that vital values are readily subordinated to those of management, utility, success and expedience. Since quality, forms, values and knowledge proper are not calculable, modern man tends to replace them with what he only holds to be a real phenomenon, namely, objects which *are* calculable. It is because of this kind of thinking that modern man has no dwelling place, no home (*Heimat*): it has been transformed into a cold and stony object of relations that can be calculated within the context of an unceasing work. Endless work, the modern work-*ethos*, allows little room for individual contemplation, care, love or faith. The ethos of work and profit has settled over humanity. Competitive networks of business calculations for their own sake—something that Pascal deemed modern man's questionable medicine—have begun to numb both thought of and respect for death and faith.

Having in mind what has been said about the nature of religious experience, there must be a vast discrepancy between this experience and the general moral tenor of present-day humanity. This discrepancy requires steps to be taken toward further understanding the nature of the human being: An investigation of the nature of the morality of our time.

To take an unprejudiced look at the moral, social, political and cultural fabric of our time is, next to the moral role of the individual exemplary person that was discussed above, the presupposition for the possibility of improving a moral tenor flawed by contorted societal values. It is in this regard that Scheler came to speak of the "therapist of the age" (*Der Arzt der Zeit*). This therapist is a person seeking to find curative psychic techniques for the purpose of stripping man's absolute region of all its idols.

At first glance the notion of the therapist of the age looks like a hopeless, if not a fantastic one. Yet, the search for practice of curative psychic techniques, designed to purify and cleanse the human soul, is as old as humanity itself. In every age and culture we find such techniques with their promise for better life. Practices of psychic techniques are especially rampant in our own age, some of which have developed into lucrative business. Among some of the recent techniques found in Western culture are exorcism, faith healing, sorcery, the practice of various forms of superstition, the staging of televangelist phantom miracles, and the application of psychology and psychiatry. Fads with mass appeal such as physical fitness, autogenetic self-training, the imitation in the West of buddhist techniques of acquiring a nirvana and the wish to introduce various techniques for a better individual life all have something in common: the desire to chase away any negativity from the body and mind and to cleanse or redeem them from some evil.

Scheler's therapist of the age, however, does not seek to divulge in individuals' concerns as much as to cure an age and its people—who have been deceived by myths from the beginnings of history—of its "metaphysical penchant" for absolutes. While there is no absolute definition of the therapist of the age, he can be said to be the highest form of a "physician" (X 220). His goal is the purification of the spirit of an age and the liberation of it from the deception of idols. This is accomplished by psychic techniques, not rational instruction.

Scheler did not develop the apogee of all techniques to be used by the psychic therapist of the age. He thought that a foundation for their details had to be explored. Such a work on these foundations was to consist in a systematic study of not only the more common psychic techniques just mentioned, but also in an inventory of the techniques of other cultures and past history.

Scheler suggested that the phases of life in which falsely absolutized idols occur should likewise be first identified, but he himself only provided insights into the genesis of the consciousness of exemplarity (*Vorbildbewusstsein*) for a cure of the age.

We must add, therefore, that both individual and collective life pass through five phases: birth, growth, maturity, decline and death. These phases are not separate from each another but reach into one another because life is a continuous process of "becoming-unbecoming" (*Werden und Entwerden*) of temporal phases. In growing, life also declines and dies; in declining, it also grows. The entire process called "aging," indicates that life begins at birth and through aging extends itself into its *own* ending. Inanimate things, by contrast, neither age nor die.

The five phases of life are not to be taken only in a biological sense. In humans they are accompanied with respective contents of "how" experience flows in them. The contents of what is experienced is affected by the five phases. It is not only the contents of experiences that undergo changes during the five phases but also the functioning of these contents in the phases changes (X 223-225). *How* we experience contents is accompanied by a change in the foci of contents. This holds for both the individual and for the community. For the young child, his father and mother still provide a touch of holiness or, in case of child abuse, a touch of evil. As childhood progresses many things are experienced in terms of higher value-qualities than are experienced later in life. A tree, a toy, or the sight of the backyard of our birthplace may initially have been experienced with a high value-quality only later to become less important. They lose higher

valuation which they earlier had. People do, in fact, sometimes remark that they cannot understand why a particular event or experience had such significance for them when they were young. This
points to a developmental law according to which the valueness
(*Wertwesen*) through which we first experienced things and persons
around us gradually shifts into the more relative regions of belief.
The same developmental state of affairs holds for myths which are
first popularized expressions of man's "metaphysical penchant" to interpret the finite, natural world around him.

It is only philosophy and religion that are competent to surpass
man's metaphysical penchant and to come to grips with the accessi-
bility or inaccessibility of the essence of the Absolute. Present day
humanity is in dire need of a catharsis leading to the "salvation of our
age" (X 229). Humanity must work toward abolishing its idols. The
moral tenor of the age is largely marked by a controversial "spirit of
capitalism." Many of Scheler's contemporaries, such as Max Weber,
Werner Sombart, Ernst Troeltsch and Karl Mannheim were concerned
about this matter. While Scheler was familiar with most of the writings of these thinkers, the bulk of his own corpus, which could only
be published since 1982, were not known to the readers of his life-
time.

Scheler dealt with the issue of the fundamental need of present day
humanity for salvation by investigating the insidious poison in the
human soul that keeps spreading surreptitiously through the masses,
that is the phenomenon of "ressentiment." This psychic poison plagues
the very soul of contemporary humanity. Its significance had already
been seen by Nietzsche; but Scheler penetrated to its very core, namely
in terms of modern value deceptions.

CHAPTER V

RESSENTIMENT

Prefatory Remark

Scheler regarded World War I (1914-1918) as an historical event of the first order because it set in motion for the first time a global intercultural and international experience of humankind as a whole. This did not occur only because of the war. For the first time in history, technology began to link all corners of the earth through fast growing communication systems that bridged the continents and cultures with a flow of almost instant information.

With the technological and cultural interpenetration of diverse peoples of our planet there came the first signs of the growth of a second migration of peoples, as it were, consisting of millions of refugees, migrant and foreign workers and wide spread resettlement. This contributed to numerous instances of unrest, discontent and anxiety that persist until today and will stretch into the future. Unlike the first migration of peoples sixteen hundred years ago which was motivated by desires of conquest, racial and ethnic hate and war, present day migrations were and continue to be primarily economically conditioned.

The global interpenetrations among peoples manifested hitherto unknown aspects of what phenomenologists refer to as intersubjective experience. The political implications of overpopulation augurs poorly for the earth. Not only does it create the tragic phenomenon of new kinds of migrations. It also leads to mass starvation and a lack of basic care for millions of people, especially children for whom it creates frightening inadequacies of education in many parts of the world.

Under the shadow of these and other more visible predicaments that have appeared since World War I are equally alarming problems associated with uncontrollable rise in awareness of the differences that exist among nations, races and groups: differences between East and West, differences of religious beliefs and convictions and of course the emotional differences between social classes. Persistent friction among these groups often contribute to international misunderstandings born of ignorance, misjudgment and distrust. Neither diplomacy, the international press nor governments and telecommunication seem to be able to reduce the intolerance toward such differences despite the efforts even in the United Nations to do so.

In his 1921 essay "Problems of Populations as Questions of World-Views" Scheler confronted the problems associated with population growth and density. This particular essay is the result of a speech he gave on the occasion of a congress convened at Cologne University that same year. The conference highlighted the problems of population from various aspects, such as sociology, medical and political science and law. For his introductory address, Scheler braced himself to cast a philosophical light on the problems of abortion, contraception, prostitution, venereal diseases and sexual morality. We must bear in mind that at the time such themes were not exactly open for public discussion as they are today. Scheler was far ahead of his time in raising these issues because they threatened to undermine the future that he envisioned in his 1926 essay "Man in the Era of Adjustment" (IX 145-170/P 94-125). Scheler showed his gift of foresight as early as 1912 when he published an essay "Concerning the Feminist Movement" in which he described the irreplaceable roles of womanhood in history (III 193-223/CM 42-54).

Scheler's active engagement in what was going on at his time only confirms what was stated earlier, namely, that despite his sometimes abstruse insights that challenge comprehension, he did not let the practical facts of the day escape him. The facts of daily life were not easy to face in a defeated Germany which was restrained by the provision of the 1918 Treaty of Versailles. As a result, the twenties in Germany were roaring with political turmoil, unemployment and inflation, mixed with a considerable loss of national pride that so often characterizes the vanquished. It was this loss of national feelings, coupled with political rumblings and economic weakness that conveniently played into Hitler's revenge against the world and against its non-Teutonic population and ethnic groups, such as Gypsies.

In marked contrast to many of his contemporary philosophers, Max Scheler did not write books on the times by sitting in an intellectual observation tower. He did not just bemoan the miserable lot of his fellow men and women but wanted to face the problems of the times. As was mentioned, he published a lengthy essay on the causes of the hatred of Germans by others (IV 283-372) and scanned the shortcomings and weaknesses at the bottom of the human soul in general from which, in fact, the psychological, social and political roots of future disasters were growing and which spurred the poisonous hates and ills to come. To be sure, he foresaw the outlines of the future as with the eyes of a prophet, as his wife Maria once said. This side of him is not only attested to in the 1926 essay, "Man in the Era of Adjustment," but also by his premonitions of impending Fascism and National Socialism during the twenties in his essay on the idea of peace (XIII 77-121/IP 154-166; 36-50; IV 598-9,655-6,668-9).

Commensurate with his foresight, Scheler did not show any fatalism; his was not a gloomy mind-set. He would not have subscribed, for example, to Heidegger's statement, made after World War II, that "only a god can help us." On the contrary, Scheler for his part also faced the rising perils of technology and social strife and turmoil—precisely as Sartre did a generation later. No doubt, Scheler would have emphatically rebutted the view that only a god can help us with the response that "it is only we that can help us." And this he endeavored to do with all his powers.

At the center of Scheler's confrontation with the shortcomings and weakness of the collective soul of present day society and its value-illusions is his investigation of "ressentiment," which was contained in an article first entitled *"Das Ressentiment und moralisches Werturteil"* (Ressentiment and Moral Value-Judgment) that appeared in 1912. This lengthy essay was republished in a considerably extended form in 1915 under the new title *"Das Ressentiment im Aufbau der Moralen"* (Ressentiment in the Structure of Morals, III 33-147/R 23-172). This investigation can neither be separated chronologically nor thematically from his Value-Ethics or from the essay *"Ordo Amoris."*

In German, the French word *"Ressentiment"* was introduced by Nietzsche, retaining its spelling and pronunciation. In German, the word "Ressentiment" is in common usage. Scheler rightly states that there is no German equivalent to the French word. The same holds true for English. Ressentiment expresses in ordinary discourse a much stronger nuance of hate than the English words "resentment" or "rancor" would. Therefore, we also will retain the French spelling of the word—and its pronunciation—in order to indicate the peculiar nuances that serve Scheler's penetrating study into this kind of human hate.

1) The Emotive Structure of Ressentiment

The feeling of ressentiment is an incurably persistent hate that occurs in certain human beings. Ressentiment is rooted in equally incurable impotencies concealed in subconscious levels of emotive experience. This is why such feelings well up without awareness and haunts humans. This particular feeling of hate not only occurs in certain individuals but also collectively among groups, classes and perhaps whole cultures. It is still an open question as to whether ressentiment has a role in the origins of religions and denominations and whether they can generate corrupt moral judgments under the facade of positive truths.

There are various kinds of feelings of impotencies and weaknesses in certain human beings from which strong ressentiment and hate feelings well up. Ressentiment is, therefore, a contradictory feeling: its relentless strength and occasional violence wells up in a weakness of the human being that cannot be overcome. Ressentiment is the prototype of a disordered heart, a "*désordre du coeur*." Such weaknesses and impotencies can be psychic, physical, mental or social in nature. Examples of these weaknesses reveal a blockage in the ability to communicate with others. The root of ressentiment, impotency, is concomitant with feelings of one's own disvalue. From this we can already draw a preliminary conclusion of the entire nature of ressentiment when we recall our analyses of value-feelings. When a value-feeling stems from a particular impotency, this feeling, too, must be feeble and must *miss* its proper value-correlate. Ressentiment is a disorder at the center of value-feelings. It is the cause of a disorder in value-preferences. That is, it is a deviation from the order of values constituted in the prism of the *ordo amoris* and thus amounts to an anomaly of the moral tenor of a person. We can thus discern three overriding structures in ressentiment feelings:

1. They are "detractions" of those positive values that the ressentiment-subject is powerless to attain. But the ressentiment-subject is continuously "plagued" by those detractions of unattainable values in that he emotionally replaces them with disvalues issuing forth from his impotence. In the background of such an illusory and self-deceiving turn-over of positive values and negative values according to Scheler, there still remains transparency of the order of values and their ranks.

2. There are "initial forms" of ressentiment leading to ressentiment proper.

3. All ressentiment feelings necessitate "comparisons" with other persons who have no ressentiment feelings. For this reason, ressentiment feelings form a profound factor in all emotive intersubjectivity. Phenomenologically both passive and active comparing with others must belong to the very root of all intersubjectivity, a point not always seen in its full significance in the respective literature. Kant already saw the importance of comparisons leading to original sin and the well-spring of reason in his essay "*Mutmasslicher Anfang der Menschengeschichte*" (Conjectural Beginning of Human History).

We must now take a closer look into the threefold structures in ressentiment.

a) Ressentiment feelings stem from the unattainablility of positive values. Unattainable values are emotively detracted and belittled while negative values situated in incurable physical, psychological, mental or social impotencies are subconsciously elevated onto higher unattainable value-rankings where they do not belong. More precisely, they are delusively felt in the location of the unattainable positive value that in turn is simultaneously belittled. In all ressentiment there are passive disturbances in the lower levels of feelings that make the subject helpless.

All human beings at some time or another experience such a simultaneous lowering and elevating of values, although a ressentiment feeling is not necessarily at hand. Because of an absence of ressentiment feelings, one can actively negotiate the values concerned; such a negotiation is not possible in ressentiment. We may, for example, want to buy a ring and are presented with an option of a cheaper or more expensive one while both look to have the same quality. One may tend to inveigle oneself rationally into buying the cheaper one because "it just serves the same purpose anyway." We thus belittle the higher quality of the more expensive ring a bit and let it be where it is.

Aesop's well-known fable of "The Fox and the Grapes" captures this tendency. The grapes, out of reach to the fox's numerous jumps at them, gradually lose their juicy looks and finally, tired of jumping in vain, the fox thinks "they are sour anyway."

If, however, a value-detraction does not stem from such more or less rational self-persuasion but passively grows from a continuously experienced impotency, a negative judgement on positive values is, before it is even made, already blended with the bad odor of hate. Such passive tendencies of value detractions can express themselves already in disparaging gestures, ridicule, snide remarks or ostentatious neglect of another, all of which is imbued with the incurable, emotive rebuff of an unattainable value that is represented in someone else.

This passive, concomitant value detraction and value elevation can be illustrated by way of a graph. "V" stands for an unattainable value and "I" for impotence. The arrow on the left side illustrates the detractive function of feelings of ressentiment. The arrow on the right side serves to illustrate the self-deluding, emotive elevation of a disvalue generated by an impotency into the location of the unattainable higher value V.

What this graph does not show, however, is the pre-rational emotive tussle of the value delusion and the transparent order of values which

Scheler says persist in the background of the entire emotive process. While the fox convinces himself that the grapes are sour, they can only be so "through" the transparency of their unattainable sweetness.

All subjects of ressentiment *per se* suffer from a continuous "tragic conflict" between value-delusion and the translucency of the order of values. One of the most urgent but perhaps insurmountable tasks in society for Scheler is to "un-deceive" (*ent-täuschen*) humans in order to restore the order of the heart.

b) There are specific initial forms that lead to the formation of ressentiment proper. These are revenge, malice, envy, spite, as well as "*Scheelsucht*" and "*Schadenfreude*" which have no adequate English equivalents.

The German *Scheelsucht*, rare in German parlance, refers to an uninterrupted obsession that seeks to detract from positive values in general, even when there is no immediate value-object at hand. A more common German adjective form of the noun *Scheelsucht* is *scheel* which means "cross-eyed." The German *scheelsüchtig* means to have a continued urge to look askance at someone and disparage him. In our context here the word has the meaning of "cross-valued" in the sense of the above converse value detraction and elevation. *Schadenfreude* refers to the revelling in someone's misfortune and bad luck. In sports, the fans of the losing team may revel over a winning team's sudden series of bad luck leading to the latter's unexpected defeat. The fans enjoy such bad luck.

The initial forms that lead to ressentiment proper only do so inasmuch as they remain unsatisfied. If it is the case that sweet revenge for dissatisfaction is dealt an object of ressentiment completely, as in Edgar Allan Poe's short story "The Cask of Amontillado," then there would be no proper ressentiment in the person who revenges himself because the desire for revenge disappears. In Poe's story the main character walled up his offender, a drinking companion who had badly insulted him, brick by brick. The last brick that closed the offender up forever terminated the revenge. Nevertheless, even after having been freed from the feeling of revenge, he continued to rejoice over the companion's death. Such vindication does not happen in genuine ressentiment. In true ressentiment there is no emotive satisfaction but only life-long anger and anguish in feelings that are compared with others.

The impulses from the initial forms of ressentiment can lead to two directions of ressentiment: ressentiment can be directed to specific individuals or to indeterminate individuals. This latter direction is group ressentiment. Members of a group can become random targets of hate, born out of an impotence, that seeks to level the group. Scheler mentions a crime characterized by unusual ressentiment that took place in 1912 in Berlin. A person who harbored ressentiment against the rich who possessed convertibles tied a rope around trees on either side of the road so that *any* person who owned such a car would have his head shorn off. Serial killers, too, often suffer from an inability to identify individuals and display such group ressentiment. This is especially evident in ressentiment directed toward a gender. The hate, which springs from physical and psychic impotencies, seeks to level the values of the group. A pimp, for example, may show signs of ressentiment against the potency of the male clients that he lures into his territory in order to revenge himself by cashing in on their lust.

Scheler mentions the mother-in-law as a tragic figure in situational ressentiment (III 55/R 45). The son she loved and cared for turns to another woman who did nothing for him, yet demands everything. The mother-in-law is powerless and must even accept with affection the intrusive young woman. Similar cases of situational ressentiment pertain to the envy younger children may feel toward their elder and first born brother or sister.

One of the most intense impulses of ressentiment is found in crimes committed out of pure spite which does not involve any effort to find relief for the feeling. The 1912 Berlin crime is a case in point. The ressentiment-subject "enjoys" anew every head whirling in the air and hitting the ground.

c) All feelings of ressentiment are accompanied by acts of "comparison" with others. Indeed, acts of comparison run through all feelings of ressentiment. The desire to compare oneself with others is generated out of the feelings of impotency that the subject of ressentiment suffers from by simply looking at certain others.

There are two important aspects of this feeling. Ressentiment is not likely to well up among individuals living in a social group where there is little or no felt social difference; likewise, ressentiment will not arise when individuals freely accept the social levels into which they are born.

Intersubjective comparisons of jealousy and envy, therefore, are not likely to occur where comparisons with others are minimal. The pervasive slavery in ancient Greece and Rome, for example, did not develop into ressentiment against those in power because to be born a slave was felt to be a natural state. Neither the Aristotle of the *Ethics* nor the Plato of the *Republic* mention social upheavals when they discuss social classes. They presuppose the predominant way of ancient society that accepted unquestioningly the social station meted out at birth.

By contrast, any group in which individuals neither freely accept their social level nor freely accept persons of higher social or moral station will—as is the case in a competitive society—be fraught with ressentiment that germinates in initial forms of comparing, such as envy and jealousy. This situation arises because the individual is born into a situation of comparison and may lack those qualities that others have or which society has set as role models and goals for success.

By contrast, a person of outstanding moral exemplarity, a noble human being, is the extreme opposite of a ressentiment subject because the noble one has no need to compare himself to others. He has the strength to admit his own shortcomings without losing his personality and integrity.

The comparing frame of mind found with individuals of a society is also the occasion for intense and sometimes reckless competition. The distribution of countless awards is all but a competitive obsession. Awards for practically anything that can be achieved make the awardees objects of comparing. Yet, such competition makes others less comfortable. For the most part, people in society follow competitive patterns of behavior and look with admiration to successful models. Such patterns of behavior are similar to those found in herds that follow and seek to imitate their alpha animals.

Societal individuals are incessantly endeavoring to outdo one another through active and passive comparing. Excessive awards for things like the worst movie or ugliest face of the year are some grotesquely competitive examples. Passionate acts of both inadvertent and intentional comparing are the phenomenological foundation for competition. Ressentiment, therefore, is always prone to occur in a comparing society.

A clear example for competitive ressentiment based in a psychic impotency is the overachiever or "arrivist" (*Streber*). "Arrivist" is the word used in the English translation of the Ressentiment essay. It is no common word, yet its Latin root (arripare, to seek to come to land) comes very close to the German word *Streber* that Scheler uses. He is a person unable to love, to give and forgive, who is unable to suffer defeat, to make friends or to be content with his own self; he is also impotent to enjoy life. The arrivist is much better at smirking at people than at having a natural smile with them. Living mostly in psychological isolation, his excessive work and cravings for perfection and success are not motivated by contributing to a common good; rather, his impotency of character and limited self-value generates a constant urge to make up for his deficiencies by winning over others and garnering their esteem. Such measures as high marks and to be first and a winner at everything cover up his inferiority as a person.

The value-delusion of the arrivist is an almost obvious one: over-accomplishment is more important than benevolence, reward is more valued than giving. Business ethics is sometimes tinged with delusive value comparisons based on professional achievement and success over persons who possess a high but not always visible moral self-value because they lack public success. Success as a visible but spurious societal criterion in judgments made on values of a person can betray the concealed strains of a ressentiment against the unsuccessful but morally good.

Having explained the three components of the structure of ressentiment, namely, delusive value detractions and elevations, the initial forms of ressentiment and the role of comparisons with others, there is no need for us to analyze further the number of instances of ressentiment that Scheler offers in his investigation. We are now in the position to look more closely into the crucial function of moral value-judgments in society that stem from ressentiment. Scheler passes over those that can be found in the historical past. His focus lies on modern society.

2) Delusions of Value-Judgments in the Ethos of Society. a) Ressentiment and Humanitarianism.

While cases of ressentiment found in individuals are most revealing for the functions it has in their lives, the thrust of Scheler's investigation lies in tracing ressentiment in the structure of systems of morality. His arguments seem sometimes debatable when seen from the present status of the society in which we live. However, he may very well be right in stressing that the modern delusive preferences among value-ranks are so entrenched in our souls that the order of ranks among values, that is, the *ordo amoris*, has in large part been obscured in feelings and judgments of society.

Modern man conveniently eludes the mirror that Scheler holds up to society's fallacious moral tenor that is imbued with the venom of societal ressentiment structures. Modern man tricks himself into the firm belief that his perverted feelings and experience of values, that is, the disorder of the heart, are true—before God or without God.

The massive assault launched by Scheler, especially against modern humanitarianism, had been shared by Nietzsche. Nietzsche and Scheler are among the few philosophers that took issue with the illusions of humanitarianism. It is not always clear whether Nietzsche's and Scheler's understanding of "humanitarianism" is the same as what the term is used for today, yet it seems that there is no apparent substantial difference. Let us see what "humanitarianism" means and what its aims are.

Humanitarianism is not a movement: it rests on a feeling-state of pleasure and pain attached to sensible feelings. It spread during the eighteenth and nineteenth centuries and has its historical sources with what Scheler refers to as "great English thinkers" with whom he was familiar: Hutchinson, Smith, Hume and Bain. Rousseau was its French representative.

More implicitly than expressly, and likely unintended by its founders, humanitarianism spread throughout the masses by dint of psychic contagion, (III 97/R 93). It does not appear to have started from a single person who was responsible for its authorship. Even up till now, we think it quite acceptable to praise someone as a "humanitarian," or for his "humanity" without being aware that grains of ressentiment might be contained in such public, formal praising. An indication of this may be seen in the fact that humanitarian tributes are effective only for the moment and not as a lasting value.

In more particular terms, humanitarianism supports a rationale according to which humans have a principal obligation to be predominantly concerned with the welfare and well-being of the whole human race, rather than individuals. It rests on the assumption that humankind can indeed approximate a state of social perfection, if it would only concern itself with itself, thereby renouncing divine intercession. This aspect of humanitarianism easily lends itself to atheism which is sometimes noticeable in humanitarian politicians.

Scheler sees in the humanitarian mind-set a kind of love that is directed exclusively to humanity, namely, "humanitarian love." The humanitarian is a special kind of a philanthropist. However, while he generally abdicates the idea of God, a philanthropist does allow for faith in and love of a highest Being. This is testified in all philanthropy found in Buddhism, Christianity, Islam, ancient China, Egypt, Greece and Rome. But for the modern humanitarian it is precisely an all-embracing love of humanity alone that comes first and that cannot and should not be surpassed by any other love. All other loves, such as love of God, of country, of home, of family, are loves to be subordinated to the love of the human species. Indeed, humanity represents the widest domain that human love can cover, whereas all other loves are less extensive and less significant. Protagoras's famous epigram: "Man is the Measure of all Things" is probably the best—although unwitting—formulation of modern humanitarianism's message.

While humanitarianism must not be confused with philanthropy it must also not be confused with "humanism" of the Florentine Renaissance. Admittedly the latter drew heavily on ideas from antiquity in its endeavors to reinstate the value of man and his freedom in protest against the Medieval Ages. Nevertheless, the Florentine humanists did not expunge the notion of love of God from the human mind in order to replace it with an exclusive love of humanity based in ancient values.

The ressentiment of modern humanitarianism has infiltrated many walks of life. Even theology in its more recent "political" forms (III,112/R,107) has been affected by it. Part of contemporary Christian theology manifests humanitarian dimensions. For example, it tends to strip Christ of holiness and sanctity and replace it with an "historical" Christ, claiming he appears more as a human than as a holy man. He appears as a farmer or carpenter; in more extreme cases He is homosexual or a social revolutionary. In short, He is almost completely stripped of the sphere of holiness and thus humanized.

Demythologizing Christ in this fashion goes hand in hand with a detraction of values as was practiced by numbers of "missionaries" the world over who considered Christian love to consist first in providing for the needs of the poor. As a political mission it was supposed to prove that faith rests on social conditions. In short, poverty is supposed to impede faith, notwithstanding the fact that the Holy Family was itself homeless, yet apparently not in need for improved social conditions in order to attain its value of Holiness. In more recent times, churches are increasingly perceived more as human institutions rather than in terms of their pristine function of being in communion with God. These humanitarian perceptions would already indicate that its implicit ressentiment lies in the idolization of the "whole of humanity" at the expense of the love between individuals and for the individual.

Indeed for Scheler the love of humanity arises from the impotence to love the individual, family and community. More specifically, humanitarian ressentiment is almost surely present when human beings are so extraverted that they see in any one part the whole of humanity and, therefore, constantly desire to cling to other humans. This ressentiment of excessive social concern springs from the emptiness the humanitarian betrays in his burning, extraverted behavior. He is impotent to look into the core of his own impoverishment. Extraverted humanitarians are usually unhappy when they are alone. They have a compulsion to socialize others and to extend their assistance to them.

One specific form of a humanitarianism, altruism, can often be confused with the pristine, spontaneous Christian love of the individual. Within the context of ressentiment altruism is not "love" of others but can become a malicious social disposition riveted in self-hatred (VII 154/N 151). It is a psychic device designed to cover the self's feeling of nothingness so that social approbation for altruist devotion to others can be gained, preferably in public. This kind of altruist, Scheler says, can frequently be found among socialists or those people who praise "social conscience" while at the same time blaming others for not having a conscience and instructing them on how to care for others. Here again altruism is a surreptitious inability to tend to one's self and one's own shortcomings. The low value of emptiness of self is projected as love of others; while this invites social esteem, it is a false esteem. The love of others is only a vehicle, not a moral act, and is thereby devalued from its moral status.

Altruistic ressentiment can take on various other forms that Pascal had already noted (*Pensées* 141,143). Human beings, Pascal says, spend precious time in following and playing with a ball and escape their inner vacuum by constantly enmeshing themselves in others' business and in community work. Altruistic ressentiment can cover up inner individual nullity in many ways. It can even develop to the extent that the individual deliberately draws others' attention by inflicting painful harm on himself, by intentionally losing his business, by feigning physical pain, as in sports, or even by refusing to eat because one supposedly does not feel well. All this is done in an effort to gain others' empathy and attention.

b) The Inversion of Life-Values and Values of Sensible Pleasures, Usefulness, and Values of Technology

There are even more rampant and alarming phenomena of ressentiment in modern society than altruistic humanitarian love. These serve Scheler as illustrations of severe value-delusions that haunt society. They stem from a wider range of psychic and emotive impotencies than the societal individual is willing to admit.

A ressentiment subject not only inveigles himself into the belief that his value-delusions are "true" but he also engenders the belief that only he, suffering from toxic emotions, knows how to distinguish right from wrong. He does not acknowledge the poisonous hate that flows from his subconscious impotence. This is particularly true in the societal obsession with quantifiable and manageable values, with the value of what is self-earned and with making values subjective.

The chief manifestation of the "ressentiment slave revolt," Scheler writes, is the fact that the order among value-ranks—itself determined, as we have seen, by the distinctive content in each of them and by the distinctive levels of feelings in which ranks are given—is reversed in society (III 126/R 121). This reversal can be seen in the fact that societal individuals are overly sensitive to the lowest ranks of pleasure and utility values as well as the biological and environmental part of vital values of the third rank. This reversal also pertains to their feeling-states, such as body sensations, sensitivity for illness, health, etc. The other higher values of personal life values, such as heroism situated in the third rank as well as the mental and sacred values that are given in personal feelings, as well as feeling states of spiritual joy, bliss, salvation, etc., are felt to be of little if any effect in the functioning of society.

While Scheler does not discuss the subordination of mental and sacred values in particular, that is, the subordination of the values of the person to the lower ranks, his focus lies on the ressentiment found in the societal subordination of life values to those of the lower ranks of the values of pleasure and of usefulness. While he does not explicitly discuss the present worldwide problem of value-deceptions that prefers technological progress rooted in values of usefulness over environmental and other life values, this tendency is unmistakably implied.

We learned earlier that the main value-orientation of society is centered on the lowest ranks or society's "polar star" which, in turn, make the sociological structure of society discussed in Chapter III responsible for the toxic, emotional inversion of the order of values and the human *ordo amoris*. No matter whether one accepts the sociological analyses of society that Scheler advanced at the end of his first period and which he deepened in a much more detailed analysis in his second, one cannot fail to admit that these analyses reveal a high degree of consistency. Already in *Formalism* society had been conceived of as an artifact constructed by contracts, constitutions, stipulated conventions and legal systems that are designed to regulate inter-human behavior and relations. In this, society appears to resemble a grid spread over humans that live in it. It consists of green lights warranting individual freedoms, red lights guarding over checks and balances and yellow lights for grey areas, so to speak, indicating undefined and undefinable states of affairs in this artifact and that allows for various interpretations of contracts, constitutions and laws on which society has been built. This man-made grid is, of course, subject to constant reform, amendments, and repairs.

Prior to its first publication in 1924 the essential message of the *Sociology of Knowledge* had already been developed in terms of the inseparability of the styles, patterns, types and ways of thinking from the sociological fabric in which humans live. It was stated that the type of thinking and experience of values of members living in a life community is different from that of a society. Underneath this functional relationship between thinking, on the one hand, and a social structure, on the other, lies Scheler's later metaphysical conceptualization of the "interpenetration" of life and mind which made him reject any dualism that can be seen in philosophy from Plato to Descartes. Descartes' dualistic error, by which he declared the body and mind to be heterogeneous, still haunts contemporary models of the mind in physiology, neurology, psychology and in what is left of artificial intelligence. The human mind is identified with a physiological or even highly complicated computer-like "brain," devoid of functions of motivation, emotion, intonation of speech or any novel intuition and insight. But one can argue that any philosophical clue found to be supportive of the idea of an interpenetration between life and mind, emotion and reason, silence and language, dooms as futile any mechanical models of the mind-body relation even though mechanical models invite interesting work. The predominantly mechanical view held in the post-Cartesian era implies the belief not only that organisms are complicated mechanisms but also that all social problems are at least in principle repairable. These problems themselves are the products of a society which is itself an artifact.

It stands to reason that the two lower value-ranks preferred over life values in society must, because of the interdependence of thinking and social structure, be held as a prevailing but unfortunate necessity. There are four reasons for this. 1) Both ranks contain exclusively quantifiable and manageable values and goods including those of technology. 2) Both ranks pertain, like any mechanism, to divisible materials and goods. 3) Both allow humans to make use of a maximum will to realize projects in them with success. 4) Both value-ranks and their goods are subject to artificial improvement, abolishment and re-institution at any time. That is, societal value-ranks and goods predominantly occur in the mode of clock-time; hence, they must be measurable, calculable and divisible, as Scheler had demonstrated in his ethics. Utility values of the stock-market, for example, last only for the time of their usefulness in terms of quantifiable profit: they may last only a second.

Throughout society the values of business and technology function in all walks of life as generally valid moral values. This is why cleverness, quick adaptability, calculative thinking, steadiness and success in work are cardinal values in society. Life-communal valuations of martial courage, readiness to sacrifice, faith, relative indifference to material goods, patriotism, family, tribe and humility, have—admitting exceptions—begun to be subordinated to such cardinal societal values (III 132/R 127).

In order fully to appreciate Scheler's concept of the inversion in society of life-values and utility-pleasure values, one must keep in mind two forms of wholes that life values, on the one hand, and pleasure-utility values, on the other, represent: namely, organic wholes and mechanical wholes. All mechanical wholes pertain to technology; technology and its application forms a huge collection of mechanical wholes.

A difference between the organic and mechanical wholes was unacceptable to Descartes. By contrast, Scheler and modern biologists claim that an organic whole is, like an organism, "more" than the sum-total of its parts, in contrast to a mechanical whole like any engine. In fact, any living organism possesses three characters that set it off from a mechanical whole:

1. It possesses a "vital" energy propelling its growth and all of its functions.

2. It possesses the capacity of self-motion like that of beats of the heart.

3. It ages and it dies.

By contrast, a mechanical whole possesses no vital energy but rather the six forms of physical energy (heat energy is in both organic and inorganic nature); it is neither endowed with self-motion (except in atoms) nor does it age and die.

The societal value-inversion of utility and pleasure values over the values of life can now be described as a stratum in the ethos of society in which mechanical and technological wholes are preferred over organismic ones. The mentality of societal populations betrays an increasing sensitivity for quantifiable and manageable values and a simultaneous dwindling of the feeling for life-values. Since life-values are only in limited cases controllable in the way mechanical and technical values are, it is what is useful and promises success that becomes the dominant trait in the societal ethos. Something is pleasurable when it enhances sensuous and sensible body-feelings. Whatever is useful can also be a means for pleasures. From this law, Scheler draws the familiar conclusion (II 347/F 345-6) that both enhancement of pleasure-values and unlimited production is at the root of societal, utilitarian civilization. This conclusion, which he also based on a recognition of the practical experience of the world around him, accords with his revelations of ressentiment in society.

Any form of enjoyment is dependent on the "capacity" a person has to enjoy. Society has not retained much of this basic human capacity. Indeed, society is increasingly becoming incapable of enjoyment. Proof of this can be seen in the endless production of gadgets, psychological and cosmetic contraptions and devices designed to enhance enjoyment of life and to "feel better," as a common expression goes. But enjoyment imposed through technical, artificial means, including those of marketing which are applied to organic wholes such as families and other "targeted" groups, only betrays the inner unhappiness and dissatisfaction of those who are dependent on them for enjoyment.

The endless production of enjoyable things actually numbs the capacity to enjoy to the degree that the human will keeps the individual chasing in vain after ever more satisfaction to the point of brinkmanship with compulsory buying. Even if the will to acquire enjoyable things is almost exhausted, as in periods of economic recession, advertizement designed to counter unwillingness to purchase is an applied psychology that makes use of mechanical wholes. Examples of these are polls, measures of population density, racial statistics and trends of tastes and fashion patterns, all of which are quantified in mechanical wholes. Scheler maintains that, in the end, the excessive production of enjoyable things is detrimental and will not serve to enhance genuine enjoyment; as Thoreau put it, it will serve unimproved ends.

The endless productions that stem from work-ethics and that arise from the mind-set of endless production is an outcome of the delusive preferences for the lower rank values. This tendency of production forgets that happiness and true enjoyment are not dependent on ever new options and supplies of things through marketing situations. True enjoyment is what it says it is: an experience of a minimum of agreeable things (III 130/R 125). In this regard we think of, for example, the flower that the child picks for his mother simply for her happiness and without any excessive emphasis on expecting something in return. Even the "minimum" of a word of love, of recognition or approbation easily surpasses any and all awards or values of the production of enjoyable things.

It is within this context of the impotency of genuine enjoyment stimulated by supplies of concocted means that serve business ends that Scheler saw a strong ressentiment in his own country, especially in Berlin and the industrial cities of northern Germany. His argument seems to fit with the fabric of present day urban population whose capacity for enjoyment appears to be numbed by floods of daily advertizement that promises a more enjoyable life. The capacity for urban enjoyment has dwindled to the lowest levels owing to the profusion of pleasurable things and countless forms of entertainment to the point where one cannot absorb such profusion. The metropolitan noise, glare and glitter furthers urban joylessness. The abundance of stimuli for pleasure and entertainment literally deadens the genuine enjoyment capacity: "that is the 'meaning' of our metropolitan 'culture' of entertainment" (III 130-1/R 126).

No matter what harm will ensue from this, what matters for us is the root for this aberration: the preference of utility values, of technological practicalities, serviceabilities, efficacious marketing techniques, and endless invention-values and pleasure-values over the value of life. All clashes between the two lower ranks and the rank of life-values betray the inversion in societal value-feeling. Incessant technological pollution of the environment that should be accorded life-value such as water, earth, air, and stratosphere, reveal a toxic emotion generated by the societal diminution in feeling such values in their proper rank-position. Life-values, including birth and death, are becoming objects of a kind of thinking that is predominantly calculative and mechanical. Scheler is not saying that such calculative thinking should be entirely abandoned but that it should be held within the boundary of moral limits; that is, within the boundary formed by the value-ranks themselves over against higher ones so that the criteria of the two lower ranks are not carried over into higher value-ranks.

According to the authentic order among ranks of values, Scheler stresses that agriculture, as among the foremost domains of values of life, must be reinstated as a value that is higher than technology, business and commerce, whenever the latter exceed their proper compass of being at the service of life. Agriculture should be supported as a higher value even when industrial progress yields a greater economic profit. The order of value-ranks commands the preservation and cultivation of both plant and animal life, of forest and landscape, against the "devastating tendencies of industrialism" (III 147/R 174).

c) The Value of What is Self-Earned and the Absence of Moral Solidarity

The societal thinking pattern within mechanical wholes also underlies other delusive value-preferences. This occurs in the spurious but firm belief that whatever is "self-earned" determines at least part of the moral value of the individual. According to this delusion, the self-value of the individual is seen in those qualities that have been acquired by labor and work (III 115/R 138). Labor and work, however, are quantifiable in terms of the "self-earned." Someone with a self-earned accumulation of value serves as a role model for those who lack such a value. This implies that non-quantifiable values of labor, such as those of research, composition, sketches of art designs, as we find them in the humanities, or the earthly labors offered for the grace of God by a holy man and his followers, as we find in religion, are of lesser value because they are not deemed useful or do not improve upon everyday pleasures.

Another aspect of ressentiment follows from this. It occurs in the use of vocabulary. Throughout the strategy in societal ethos of elevating the value of what has been visibly self-earned and self-accomplished, there is little need for expressions of non-quantifiable values such as "natural grace," "talent" or "virtue," among others. They are prone to generate ressentiment in others who feel they lack these values. In everyday discourse, already beset with terms of quantity—among them "computerese," officialese" and "legalese"—one avoids terms that refer to qualities that human beings may have. Natural grace, talent, and virtue, for example, are obsolete in everyday discourse and displaced by "having had a "fluke," by having "skills," or a high "moral level." Indeed, contemporary vocabulary reveals a ressentiment similar to that of the German vocabulary of Scheler's own time (III 133-4/R 128-9).

Vocabulary that reveals the dimension of weakness in ressentiment may not be as important as the tendency to exalt what is "self-earned" such as it is judged in terms of moral approbation. The entire sphere of virtues characterized among others by values of sacrifice, honesty, giving, forgiving, charity, magnanimity and love is imperiled by public approbation and praise of the measure and quantity of what has been visibly self-earned. Given this egregious individualism, Scheler deplores the absence in society of even a glimmer of the first social principle of Value-Ethics, namely, *moral solidarity*. It has become almost "incomprehensible" in modern society (III 120/R 142; see also II 522-3/F 534). According to this social principle all mankind ought to be bound by shared coresponsibility, which, as Scheler maintained concerning the life-community (II 517-19/F 529-31) has been superseded in society by self-responsibility.

Historically, moral solidarity stems only in part from the Christian idea that "all sinned in Adam" and that all should participate in guilt and share in the merits of saints. But in essence the principle is expressive of four moral axioms:

1. The very "omission" of an act of love caused by excessive attachments to sensible values is itself sinful.
2. The rise and decline of moral values is not bound to their visible manifestation (III 119/R 114-151).
3. Communality, and with it collective guilt and merit, belongs to the essence of personhood as being social in terms of its Thou-I relation.
4. All moral comportment, borne by social acts as love, esteem, consideration etc., is in essence reciprocal (II 524/F 535).
5. A collective guilt and a collective moral merit exists (II 488,523; VII 167/F 596-7,534-5; N 165).

The social principle of moral solidarity posits that any individual person is coresponsible for any other individual's deeds (II 488-9/F 496). But how can Scheler say this? Do I bear guilt for the child dying today in Somalia?

First of all, contrary to moral solidarity, the routine of societal life contains deplorable amounts of negligence of moral coresponsibility, including coresponsibility for the guilt of others. Routine patterns of societal behavior reveal appalling negligence in sanctioning omissions of love for one another. Instead of a caring society, society is litigious. This defect is rooted in the intersubjective distrust, as we saw, that characterizes the moral tenor of a society in sharp contrast to a life-community's overriding trust expressed in "all for one and one for all." For this reason alone, moral solidarity is a principle of life-communities and, especially, of a global, moral community of human beings (II 522-3/F 533-4). Moral solidarity is the foundation of societal contractual relations just as the life-community is the foundation of society. For the latter, however, moral solidarity is "incomprehensible" to its individuals. To share in any other's individual guilt automatically sounds indeed far fetched. But in society guilt has turned almost exclusively into an individual affair of self-responsibility all but blinding it, so to speak, from solidary coresponsibilty. Guilt shifts into the social sphere on which society is fixed (III 309/PC 142-3).

This blindness to the principle of moral solidarity explains Scheler's promotion of it as an enormous up-hill fight against the fabric of society's moral tenor. Let us demonstrate this point by way of recalling recent events.

The blindness expresses itself, for example, in the rampant yet unnoticed lack of moral solidarity surrounding the enthusiasm about the global entertainment during the 1992 Olympic Summer Games that cost the host of the games some eighty million dollars. At the same time, according to recent estimates by the late Audrey Hepburn and relief organizations, thousands of children starved to death during the time in Somali, southern Sudan, and other poverty stricken

parts of our planet. During the same summer, the entertainment industry finalized contracts for top rock-concert stars surpassing a one
billion dollar figure while the figure for only the top five entertainers
ran up even to more than twice this amount.

As seen from a Schelerian view, the planet itself is being obscured
by a mental experiment that results in one seeing only its earthlings'
interests and activities. There is very little collective guilt for such a gro-
tesque prostitution of the value of life that is deprived of its dignity by
the delusive value-preference of entertainment and pleasure. Despite the
long overdue relief aid that is now trickling down to these children, there
appears no more evidence now of a global moral solidarity than there
may have been for the life-value of the victims of the holocaust.

What argument can Scheler advance for implicit and hidden collective guilt? His argument is both transcendental and phenomenological, as can easily be seen.

The principle of moral solidarity of living individuals is itself independent of him who bears or does not bear guilt or moral merit. This
transcendental argument is seen in light of the basic social act, love.
Love implies an act of answering in the very act of loving itself, as
much as any social act implies an act of answering. This can be best
seen in the social act of asking which always implies an act of answering. Indeed, the answer may not come; but in the failure of an answer to come one can notice the very absence of that which belongs
to any question. In this sense, as Heidegger showed, any question
asks for its own response. The response, paradoxically, has to come
"earlier" than the question. But Heidegger failed to account for the
entire range of social acts themselves, including the act of loving others, as they bear on what he calls "being with others." Love implies
answering love. Even if an answering act does not occur, as is the case
in unrequited love, its absence or denial is experienced. The nature
of the reciprocity of social acts was shown in Scheler's model of an
absolute Robinson Crusoe who is constantly experiencing the absence of the thou, or others.

More convincingly, however, Scheler's transcendental argument for
moral solidarity among all is rooted in the analyses of the "Thou" as
pregiven to the "I" as discussed above in Chapter II. The "social bed"
into which the I is born must bear coresponsibility for the I because
of the sociality of the act of love in the Thou. Coresponsibility, therefore, grounds self-responsibility, just as the solidary life-community
grounds the artifact of contracts of society.

Any lack of coresponsibility amounts, in this transcendental reciprocity, to guilt, that is, to a collective guilt of all members of the

social bed. The love of B toward A, because of the reciprocal nature of the social act of love itself, arouses A's love into answering that of B. This answering component spreads into the communality with others, to C,D,E, as a "stream" (V 376/E 377) flowing into eternity, including even subjects living on other planets, as Scheler says. Therefore, guilt and moral merit come close to being a transcendental effect that bridges the whole of a life-community with a global community that ultimately reaches into the answering love of God.

Moral solidarity also pertains to the intersubjective aspect of personal exemplars and to their being followed. The more the community loves its exemplar, the more it is united in and with the exemplars' moral merit. Whoever fails or ceases to love the exemplar, solidary guilt permeates among the followers. Christ and his disciples or the early Christianity are, perhaps, appropriate examples for clarifying the almost impenetrable principle Scheler envisioned.

The argument for the first social principle in ethics has yet another foundation. It rests on the fact that, like individual moral good and evil, both collective moral merit and collective guilt are not objects to be pursued. One cannot love a universal good as an object of love (as Plato holds) if it is the case that Scheler correctly demonstrated in *Formalism* that good and evil ride on the back of the realization of a value or disvalue, like an echo, as it were, of a value-preference at hand. Because persons are pure act-beings, their loves and hates, too, must constitute a solidary collective merit or guilt. The moral cosmos, therefore, does not contain a law of conservation of an equal amount of goodness and an equal amount of evil. Rather, moral solidarity in humanity can both decline and increase, rise or fall in any historical epoch (II 523/F 534).

In the present age it would appear that by showing the characters that make up the social form of togetherness called "society," moral solidarity has fallen to such low levels to the extent that this principle has become almost imperceptible. But this does not preclude a rebirth of moral solidarity in an other age marked by a different mind-set.

d) Egalitarianism. Subjectivation of Values

It is at this juncture that we can best bring into relief the ressentiment spreading beneath egalitarian endeavors.

This ressentiment follows from a morality that approves the individual's moral value on the basis of what has been self-earned. As we saw, there is no activity that is supposed to account for the distinctions among persons other than this criterion. For Scheler, how-

ever, the distinction among persons are moral distinctions constituted by the "qualitative direction" of a person's acts. We learned that
moral distinctions are neither constituted by intentions and willing
nor by established purposes. The qualitative direction of acts can
always be changed for the better by the passive attraction of moral
exemplars.

In sharp contrast to what alone distinguishes individuals in egalitarianism are unequal work conditions, institutions and other traditional social factors. The amount of success accomplished through
work actually makes people different from one another. In egalitarianism, the so-called deplorable distinctions among humans are clearly
made on a judgmental level, as was the case in the other societal
movements we have discussed. A person of superior nature, it was
stated, and one who does not suffer from impotencies of personality
neither needs to make judgmental comparisons with others nor to
accumulate work hours in order to improve upon his moral station.
He "is" his person, fully.

It is not difficult to follow the argument that ressentiment underlies modern political, social, moral and ecclesiastical inclinations that
seek to make human beings equal. And it is not difficult to see in
egalitarianism a hidden, resentful disparagement and degradation of
persons of some value higher than those who are craving for equality
(III 121/R 117). All proclivities toward establishing inter-human
equality seek to amend the very impotencies that cry for equality and
the emotive need for constant comparisons with their fellow men.
Scheler argues that only he who is afraid of losing adjures to the
principle of equality among all. But according to this principle of
equating all members of the human race with each other, all people
can never be equal unless those who are bearers of the least and lowest values are also calculated into the equation. Hence, egalitarian
ressentiment feelings cannot tolerate the bearers of exceptional values and accordingly "decapitates" them. Ressentiment seeks to locate
existing reasons for inequalities in unequal work conditions and opportunities. If this cannot be shown to be the case, egalitarianism
easily shifts the blame for the existence of differences among people
onto unjust institutions, "which the pathos of our era now does its
best to destroy" (III 122/R 117).

Scheler's charge that egalitarianism is rooted in the ressentiment of
disadvantaged persons who seek a level of equality with those of higher
qualities implies that the level of ressentiment must be the lowest
level possible anywhere, in education, art, religion, craftsmanship,
etc., precisely because "all" must be equal and no one should be or is

more than any other. Scheler's analysis of this form of ressentiment suggests that he might also have challenged the belief that all are equal before the law. It seems as if he indirectly takes issue with the American Constitution inasmuch as it claims that all people are born without differences among them and are, therefore, equal.

I do not know whether Scheler read the Constitution. But on the basis of his lifelong interest in American pragmatism and his eagerness to learn about the United States, one can assume that he had an understanding of it. The reason why he does not mention the equality of humans from birth under the law, which is a political matter, is because Scheler is concerned with the moral implications of egalitarianism.

In egalitarianism all people are equal regardless of age, gender and interests. Differences of social standing and individual morality are decapitated in this manifestation of ressentiment. According to egalitarianism equality is supposed to hold during the entirety of the individual's life-time. (If egalitarianism is taken to be political, it would fulfill the requirements of nowadays's so-called "political correctness.") That people are born equal is, however, not important to egalitarianism as a political movement. What speaks against the principle of egalitarianism, therefore, is that political equality under the law does not in fact make men morally equal. Indeed one can argue that if all people were morally equal there would be no need for the law. Clearly, what Scheler had in mind is the subconscious comparing that goes on according the egalitarian tendencies of humans who cannot stand the differences that they feel from others who are on a level different from their's.

One could anticipate that in the future both the growth of the masses and the slow but steady increase of population will lead to a steady increase of egalitarianism and ressentiment. If human beings are morally different as persons, there will always be persons of above average and extraordinary quality upon whom the egalitarian principle can amply feed itself. In society's tendency of moral leveling, deviants of moral norms tend to be falsely upgraded, almost to the point of normalcy, and what is normal is sometimes degraded to the point of deviancy. This value reversal is a key issue for those trying to restore societal "family values."

We can now turn to the last manifestation of modern ressentiment and value judgements. If the ethos of a society is characterized by the preference of the value-ranks of pleasure and usefulness, this must have its origins in the impotence and weakness to feel the order of values as a whole in which societal values are given as lowest ranks.

That is, man's heart is too weak to feel higher values in their objectivity of the emotive *a priori*. There must be resentful feelings of those values that appear in the translucency of the order of values but which are unattainable because of weak value-feelings. At the bottom of the subjectivation of values and valuations is the impotency to feel the objective order of values and their ranks.

Modern value-subjectivation leads to the conclusion that higher values are delusions and that a substitute must be found for them so that a general recognition, or general validity, will be found to judge something as "good." This endeavor is meant to compensate for the absence of objective values and their ranks. But judgments do not erase the transparency of the order of values. Likewise, people do not erase the order of values by whatever they do or do not do. By emphasizing what "one" does (to follow a Heideggerian phrase pertinent to "*das Man*") one fails to confront the value preference inherent in the *ordo amoris*.

The modern subjectivation of values is precisely that: it can even lead to the denial of all values as being relative and fundamentally chaotic. Nietzsche may himself have suffered from a ressentiment of the subjectivation of values in denying the *a priori* of value-feelings and their properly felt correlates, namely, values.

CHAPTER VI

CAPITALISM AND ETHICS
THE WARPED MORAL TENOR OF SOCIETY

Prefatory Remark

In what has preceded thus far we have investigated four points that gradually prepared us for a presentation of Max Scheler's understanding of the essence of present day capitalism. These four factors need to be reviewed in order to provide a basis for our present discussion.

1) One cannot expect from ethics an advancement, betterment or refinement of the moral status of the human race unless ethics is in living touch with the society and the era of history in which it has been formulated.

2) Any ethics written for the purpose of establishing universal rules, norms or imperatives acceptable in theory to all, is unlikely in practice to bear on the general moral condition of a society.

3) Without such a living touch with the reality of life, ethics is unlikely to motivate people to look into the order of values and of their preferences in order to accomplish a renewal of their moral tenor. A renewal of the perception of values will not arise from political, economic or competitive endeavors, which pass by the priority of value-experience; nor will solutions to human problems come from a universal imperative or categorical ethics. These problems will only be solved by the individual person's listening to the moral call of the order of values seated in one's heart.

It is the deeply seated direction of the moral power of individuals (*ordo amoris*), and not sweeping calculative advice contrived by figures of authority, that is the primary vehicle that determines the moral current in a society. But this individual moral power appears to have little noticeable effect in a society in which moral ills and violence are almost the order of the day. A "*désordre du coeur*" appears to be spreading like a weed along the road of endless competition which is coupled with a frightening neglect of emotive perceptions of values. Descartes' claim that truth must be given rationally, clearly and distinctly still prevails over Pascal's claim that the perception of truth lying in the human heart is totally different from the logic of reason.

4) Unless the individual and collective moral tenor prefers or "leans toward" the zenith of the Divine in his moral compass, all decision making processes in matters political and economical run the danger

of a perilous miscalculation of the hidden powers of emotive preferences among values. Neglecting the moral power in the feeling hearts
of individual humans and substituting it with moral generalizations
is likely surreptitiously to produce the spread of moral decline and
decadence.

In 1914 Max Scheler began to write a lengthy treatise entitled
"The Future of Capitalism" that was followed up in 1919 with "Christian Socialism as Anti-Capitalism" (III 382-395;IV 615-675). A number of the conclusions of his Value-Ethics are reflected in these essays. For example, in *Formalism* he argued that (1) all material goods
ought to be equally distributed among men, but that (2) no individual person is an object and that he possesses his own irreplaceable
self-value. Persons, Scheler stated, are not morally equivalent. Hence
"democracy" ought not to imply that persons are morally equal. Although laws must uphold equal rights for all persons, the claim of
ethics for the moral inequality of the self-values of individuals must
remain intact. The unequal moral "aristocracy in heaven" amounts
to a meta-legal, that is, moral dimension of human personhood. A
person's self-value, conscience, and moral tenor and readiness to accept the order of values is not accountable to law but only to God.

In applying these and other principles of his value-ethics to society,
Scheler also presented a frightening vista of the moral tenor of the
age of capitalism that he showed stems from a specific "frame of mind"
of modern humans. (The German terms Scheler uses for the capitalist "frame-of-mind" or "mind-set" is *"der kapitalistische Geist," "die
kapitalistische Einstellung,"* or *"die kapitalistische Bewusstseinseinstellung."*)

Scheler continued to be strongly occupied with applying his value-
ethics to society in order to uncover society's ills and propose possible remedies. In a speech given in Berlin in the winter of 1926-27
he expressed in a nutshell all his work by saying that both politics
and morals have their foundation in the order of values (XIII 43).

In order to realize the full impact of this theory we must clarify
Scheler's conception of capitalism before we can grasp the morality
that underlies it.

1) The Origin of Capitalism: the Modern Mind-Set

To be sure, the concept of capitalism is as much obfuscated as the
term "socialism" (the latter is not infrequently confused with social
legislation). It is equally confusing, Scheler holds, to look at capitalism as something fostered only by the rich, causing social unrest among

the underprivileged. For Scheler, neither capitalism nor socialism holds eternal solutions to the social problems at hand. He would have subscribed to Winston Churchill's characterization, made in a speech delivered before the House of Commons in 1952: "The inherent vice of capitalism is the unequal sharing of blessings; the inherent virtue of socialism is the equal sharing of miseries."

Present day usage of "capitalism" is rather slovenly. In journalism and politics in general, for instance, it appears like an admixture of either political, economic or ideological connotations or as the antipode of socialism. Usages of this kind are not shared by Scheler. Rather, he wants to focus on the phenomenon of capitalism as gained through phenomenological intuition and thus discard such connotations and opinion of it.

As an historical movement manifest primarily in politics and economics, capitalism has occurred not only in modern times but took root already at the end of the Middle Ages. It is a frame of mind or a mind-set characterized by specific value-preferences tied to the capitalization of quantifiable things. This mind-set lets things, objects, commodities, articles, tools, utensils or gadgets appear as if saying, "Look at us and see what you can do with us. Perhaps you can find us useful, no matter how little we can serve you. And if you find us useless and not promising some success or profit through us just discard."

The range of things experienced in this mind-set is as vast as the technology behind it, yet it is perspectival. In a way, the world is framed to be an immeasurable marketplace full of potential to realize the pragmatic values contained in the second lowest value-rank of utility. The essence of capitalism, however, must not be elucidated by a critique of the times but only by an elucidation of the concept of a mind-set. This can be achieved by furnishing some examples.

What is the capitalist mind-set? What is *der "kapitalistische Geist,"* *"die kapitalistische Einstellung"* or *"Bewusstseinseinstellung"* to which Scheler refers?

A mind-set is an *attitude* of consciousness that determines "how" things appear in the human milieu. Depending on the nature of a specific attitude of consciousness, things around us appear in a specific light. But most of the time we are not aware of this or that attitude of our consciousness and we presuppose that the way things are appearing amounts to their objective reality.

Let us illustrate this by way of four examples showing how things in the human milieu can undergo perspectival alterations. We choose a table to show how it can appear in four different attitudes of consciousness or mind-sets.

a) For a carpenter making a table, the table appears in light of the craftsmanship and construction he puts into it; its value is largely felt in the work he put into it. The table addresses the carpenter's mind-set under the aspect of a crafted quantity and time of labor.

b) An artist looks a table with the attitude that makes it appear in light of its artistic and aesthetic values and not so much in terms of the work put into it. Even if he himself created a table, he did so by aesthetic design. Of course, the carpenter, too, might use a design before building it. But his design is one of what a "real" table ought to be. This differs substantially from the artist's mind-set. When the artist designs a table or paints it, the table appears to an aesthetic frame of mind such that "this, too, could be a table," but it is much different from the tables you see out there.

The painted table is more than the real table because the artist's attitude toward the table is what should or could be a table, while in reality it cannot be found. This attitude also pertains to photography. Certainly photography is a more mechanical art than painting, but it, too, tends to represent the table in such a fashion that its image shows it to be more than a real table standing before the camera. In movies, too, things are often shot in a way that is not actually real. But in painting the table, the artist creates it as if from nothing—unless he uses a table as a real model, which he does not have to do. His attitude is not a pragmatic one; it is mostly designed to bring forth the essence, rather than the specific material details of the table. As Scheler aptly put it in this context, "the artist is a small god" (XI 35/ MA 109). While the carpenter builds the table from real materials, his table is a mechanical whole. An artist's table is created and transcends real tables.

c) To a businessman the table may appear as something to be sold. His mind-set makes the table an object of usefulness and profit. For the most part, it appears neither as something crafted nor created. In fact, he may never actually *see* the table except as computerized data. The table may even come to be replaced by more profitable merchandise. To such a calculating attitude of consciousness, which to a large extent characterizes a capitalist mind-set, the table may anonymously fade away and be reduced to nothing but numbers on a balance sheet.

d) In sharp contrast to these examples, according to a religious attitude, the table is also more or less anonymous but not because of its relation to sales but because of an overwhelming presence of God who created all forms and materials in which the table may partake. The table functions as a God-willed creation with the goal of experiencing God's presence. In saying grace at the table, the table is anonymous, but still holds bread and wine for us to realize that we must thank God for everything.

These four examples of mind-sets refer, of course, to only four particular kinds of individuals. What about mind-sets prevailing over an entire civilization for an extended period of time? The various art forms of past civilizations appear to give testimony of the collective mind-sets in and through which all entities of the world presented themselves to these mind-sets in a particular way. In retrospect, art historians can frequently only guess at what kind of mind-set disclosed diverse styles, subjects, executions of works of art, architecture and the particular values related to them.

A capitalist mind-set is only one among many succeeding or concurrent mind-sets in history. People born into the particular frame of mind of the era in which they often live believe that their era possess an edge over other eras, particularly those of the past. A present mind-set effects humans to such a degree that they adopt it even when they harbor serious objections to it. Even staunch Marxists may object to capitalist institutions such as banks but still take up their practices. No matter how strongly one dislikes a prevailing mind-set, and even protests against it, it inevitably has some effect because there is no way to escape it. This holds for the capitalist or any other mind-set.

In the capitalist mind-set, things and entities of the world are experienced under aspects of profitability, capitalization and usefulness that pervade our technological civilization. This may be an acceptable theory, if not a new one. In German philosophy the discussion of a "*Weltanschauung*," a view of the world as it occurs throughout the ages, only roughly corresponds to what has been said concerning a mind-set. A *Weltanschauung* is an objective view of the world while a mind-set is a subjective pattern of thinking and perceiving that promotes a particular world view.

What is novel to Scheler's theory is that the mind-sets remain independent of social classes. Not only the rich are said to be capitalists, but also the large majority of all people of present day Western civilization, including the poor and socialists who disagree with the tenets of capitalism. Scheler claims that spiraling wage demands are as much a part of the capitalist mind-set as are material ambitions and the insatiable hunger for success found in any class of individuals. By themselves, wage demands and the desire for success are not negative values. But when a general mind-set recklessly propels individuals toward endless demands, material acquisitions and ever greater success, it becomes clear that there is an insatiable void situated at the core of the soul of such a civilization.

In such a mind-set where everything, even human beings themselves, are automatically assessed according to their quantity of accumulated successes achieved on the social battle field of competition, we are confronted with a rampant, rapacious disposition that underlies such an era, and not merely with political capitalism alone. This proposition may be graphed as follows, whereby the mind-set of capitalism is distinguished from political and economic socialism and capitalism. This distinction is rendered henceforth by capitalizing the mind-set under discussion:

Capitalism

capitalism   socialism

2) Arguments for and against Capitalism as a Mind-Set

To argue that both capitalism and socialism are but two different historical manifestations of an overriding mind-set of Western civilization is an impressive account of these phenomena and distinguishes them from other non-capitalist civilizations, such as that of China or India. Scheler contends that the shortcomings of modern Western civilization, comprised of the Americas, Europe and Western Asia to the Ural mountains (the bulk of the populations of which is Christian) do not stem from shortcomings of political and economic capitalism or socialism but from the very mind-set in which the world appears. In short, Western man is a "*homo capitalisticus*" (IV 632). His world is a universe appearing as a marketplace and theater on which he can capitalize.

If Scheler's understanding of capitalism is correct then the tenor of modern society is one with an insatiable appetite for values of useful things, for the endless accumulation and acquisitions of goods and for efficiency and success gained at the expense of higher value-ranks of the person: in short, a prostitution of the higher values of the person. Scheler could easily show this by referring to the increasingly pitiful role life-values play in the mind-set of modern society. Artificial insemination, surrogate motherhood, prostitution and adoption business are but a few loathsome instances of the cheapening of life-values in society.

No question, he could argue that these and other examples make evident the preference of use and profit over the value of life. By the same token, Scheler could argue that the decrease in the feeling of life's value—a decrease expressive of excessive sex and subsequent abortion rates as well as of a lack of respect of sex and subsequent commensurate abstinence—holds in both capitalism and socialism and would therefore point to the common root of the Capitalist mind-set. Samaritan, selfless love of one's neighbor, is neither useful nor profitable in society. It dissolves in the profusion and management of humanitarian love that gives priority to *quantifiable* values. Society offers little opportunity for practicing selfless samaritarian love of the other. People choose to meet their own needs at the expense of others, leading to widespread greed and lack of responsibility.

The idea that contemporary capitalism and socialism are offspring of Capitalism cannot be supported without reservation. A capitalist can easily argue that many of the goods produced out of the Capitalism mind-set save the lives of millions of people, pointing to progress that space technology, plant and animal research have made to medicine. But a socialist might argue that the positive aspects of competitiveness of capitalism are often accompanied by inhuman and merciless activities. Moreover, the socialist position that seeks equal distribution of vital goods among people might be argued as preferable to capitalist competition.

Scheler's thesis that Capitalism stems from a mind-set that has increasingly been spreading in the West since the thirteenth century, might, however, gain more weight if we consider for a moment an alternative mind-set Scheler mentions in support of his theory that plays in the constitution of an era at any time in history.

Let us first look at mind-sets of the past. A theophantic mind-set dominated the age of mythology according to which earthly things and events bespoke the divine. The celestial bodies, the seasons, animals, mountains and oceans appeared according to a mind-set that attributed their existence to the divine. By contrast in our time it is difficult for a Capitalist to imagine, for example, the fury of Zeus manifest in a thunderbolt.

Yet the mythic age was a "world" appearing according to a human mind-set. Such a mind-set lingers on among American Indians, African and other tribal peoples and in Chinese cultures. The theophantic mind-set is still alive in many logotypes and names for technological products of Capitalism, such as "Pegasus" and "Apollo." But Capitalism has blinded us to a retrieval of the theophantic mind-set that actually occurs. Who would believe in the power of the flying horse Pegasus to provide for the horsepower in a certain gasoline? Who would give credence to the image of Apollo's splendor shining through the fires of a rocket lifting off? To the Capitalist mind-set there is no theophantic world. There is neither a god (*theos*) nor an appearance (*phainestai*) of a god in things surrounding him. Conversely, it would be very hard for a theo-phantic human of the past to imagine that he could live as an example of a profit-making world.

Dissatisfied with the mind-set of Capitalism because it runs counter to the order of ranks among values established in *Formalism*, Scheler suggested as an alternative, namely, a "Christian Socialism" (IV,615-674) to replace the frame-of-mind from which capitalism and socialism developed. Christian Socialism was envisioned by Scheler as a global "solidarity" that morally binds all humans. Its spirit draws from the charism of St. Francis. This mind-set would be "anti-capitalist" inasmuch as it would experience things not as pragmatic, but as gifts from God. Such a Franciscan mind-set is characterized by widespread gratitude for all there is, including the light of our own existence that illuminates the world between our birth and death. In such a mind-set, all things are "with" man and God rather than being estranged, manageable objects before man. This mind-set would also institute a correction in man's present emotive confusion: Franciscan joy in, and despite poverty is the greatest joy of all joys because it allows God's presence to transpire in all things around us, as Scheler wrote in his book on *The Nature of Sympathy*. This joy arouses humility in an act as simple as looking at the smallest objects in nature, such as contemplating a blade of grass and identifying it with a cosmic Creator.

Such a non-economical and non-political mind-set and moral tenor is certainly conceivable. But in the mind-set of Capitalism it is simply counter-productive and non-profitable. The spirit of Francis looks like wishful, utopic thinking. That is to say, the Capitalist's *judgment* on another mind-set is *already* steered by those values that are preferred by Capitalism, namely, the values of utility and pleasure.

For this reason it seems impossible to change Capitalism into another frame-of-mind by way of persuasion or instruction. What alone can have a moral effect on the prevailing mind-set is the exemplarity of a special person who can effectuate a change of heart. The role of an exemplary person is the only vehicle, it was said, for such change of heart.

A metaphysical question is implied in this discussion: throughout history, mind-sets and world-views associated with them seem to come and go rather randomly. We do not know why a mind-set, say that of Mayan culture, is so different from the Asian Indian. Nor do we know why Christ's moral exemplarity shook the Roman *ethos* at its time. In the course of history, this could have happened sooner or later than it did. There is no sufficient reason for the birth and the end of a new mind-set. This also holds for Capitalism. We are at a loss to answer the question why there is Capitalism in the first place and not some other set. Capitalism seems inexorably to set the stages for a robotic future in which humanity, in line with the two lowest value-ranks of divisible pleasure and usefulness, will be increasingly divided and yet tend to be egalitarian. This humanity will be one living with a mechanical world-view that spans atoms and the depths of outer space.

3) Homo Capitalisticus

Scheler's proposition that individuals of modern society are largely determined by the two lowest value-ranks has been repeatedly articulated. In sum, it was argued that society, in contrast to a life-community, is man-made and, therefore, in constant structural change depending what improvement humans seek. In this sense we were told that society is reborn every second by new situations, laws, projects, goals and interests.

Scheler's ever-present sociological penchant, seen from his early writings on, becomes a major component of his philosophy after 1921. Indeed, he told us that his new *Problems of a Sociology of Knowledge* (VIII 15-190/PR 33-239) is one of two introductions leading to his metaphysics that was to be fully articulated in Japan during his second, final period of production.

For the moment, however, Scheler needs to provide additional explanation of the peculiar type of individual that lives in a capitalist mind-set. To be sure, on the basis of his ethics and later writings, every age is characterized by a specific "type" of human being who bestows on his age various value-preferences, for example, those of art-styles, governmental constitutions and goals of science, agriculture and technology. The peculiar system of value preferences of an age, we were told in Scheler's value-ethics, is an *ethos*.

We are presently in a better position than Scheler was in his own time to see whether his assessment and characterization of the type of human being concerned are accurate. Although Scheler's comments on these issues are sparse, they are quite interesting. They can be found in *Formalism*, in his 1914 essay "Der Bourgeois;" (III 334-382) in the 1919 essay "Christian Socialism as Anti-Capitalism" (IV 615-675) and in his 1921/22 lecture, entitled "Sozialphilosophie" (XIVFor our purposes, we summarize these characterizations in what follows.

The expression *homo capitalisticus* appears in the essay on Christian Socialism (IV 632). This type of human being is said to be brimming with an inexhaustible drive for material appropriation and acquisition of capital and materials (*Erwerbstrieb*). The modern concept of "capital" is not restricted to money, be it paper or coin currency, but, as we saw earlier, to every thing that can contribute to profit. In the limitless drive for acquisition and profit, every individual thing can be valued as "capital," be it the energy of the sun or the prostitution of a girl's virginity. While Scheler holds that there have always been instruments used as a means of exchange, Capitalism has not always existed. For example, Capitalism did not necessarily exist in the ancient institution of barter. There was little or no Capitalism in that time because the drive for "limitless" acquisition and profit was not prominent (IV, 621).

What makes the new type of human being enter the scene of modern times? It is his perceptual focus on the ability to capitalize on the usefulness and marketability of entities. This is spurred by the coincidence of the impatient "drive" for acquisition and his mind-set. Scheler tells us that the structure of this drive of man has undergone a shift in that it is the *entities themselves* which, in their appearance to sensory perception, either "lure" or "deflect" modern man from seeking unlimited capital (IV 623). The entities themselves are those of the human environment or "milieu" (IV 622-3) which, in our natural view of the world, have an immediate effect on us (II 153-156/F 139-142).

Scheler's critique of the modern preference of the second rank of pragmatic values must not, however, be understood as a general critique of those values *per se*. On the contrary, he will tell us later that pragmatism is correct in stating that the human attitude toward things is ingeniously pragmatic and practical, not theoretical. He expressly states that all milieu-things are given to us first in light of their usefulness to us (IX 198-9/PE 306). This position, too, foreshadowed Heidegger who was to stress the pragmatic givenness of things in terms of their at-handedness (*Zuhandenheit*).

What Scheler does heavily criticize, however, is the over-inflation of this rank by dint of (1) the capitalist mind-set at the expense of appropriate approbation and feelings for higher value-ranks, and (2) by dint of an eccentric structure of drives in modern humanity. This puts into relief a peculiar feature of all of Scheler's philosophy. His position is that *perception is conditioned by drives*. This position sets him apart from virtually all modern European philosophers.

The nearly epidemic drive of acquisition spreads like a weed into the three main drives: propagation, power (*Machttrieb*) and nutrition. This explains why "anything under the sun" can be an object of capitalization and profit-making, be it human beings, political, economic or other powers, and all earthly and cosmic goods.

In this eccentric capitalization of objects, the objects themselves do not have to be present in order for their values to be capitalized or negotiated; they only have to be present at some time in perception. The drive of acquisition is the driving force beneath the present complexion of the market. According to this mentality, objects of capitalization are counted by their "head," if you will, as the etymology of the term "capitalism" suggests; the word, in English usage since the thirteenth century, stems from the Latin *caput* meaning head. The English expression, "how many head" and its German equivalent, for example, of cattle, illustrates the Schelerian stance toward Capitalism: namely that the value or the usefulness of an object is at every moment decapitated for the sake of the greater pragmatic value of another object. From this perspective capitalization amounts to uninterrupted value-decapitation.

The rampant drive for acquisition is, therefore, at the root of the emotive value-structure of the *ethos* of Capitalism. Like the *ethos* of any other era in history, Capitalism too possesses theoretical underpinnings. The analysis of Capitalism shows that there is an ethical underpinning to Capitalism.

The ethics of Capitalism is utilitarianism. Scheler recognized utilitarianism as the only appropriate ethics for the sociological form of togetherness called society. But his critique of utility can be easily anticipated: the value of utility is not and should not be the highest value of a society. Neither society's own value nor that of its individuals should be assessed by values of utility. While the utility value-rank lies like the other value ranks in the pristine human condition, this does not make it a moral value. For Scheler, the utilitarian stance that morality is equated with utility in fact does not assure morality. In society, utilitarianism is based in the "interests" of numerous political, economic, ecclesiastical and social groups, each of which lobbies for what is most useful to itself.

The profusion of ever emerging and waning interests in a society sets the stage for the apparent dilemma of determining what is morally blameworthy or praiseworthy. Blame and praise stem largely from the interests of those who do the blaming or praising: what is praiseworthy is good or useful for the interests of the one who praises while the blameworthy fails the test of usefulness. Thus, says Scheler, the utilitarian often uses the term good when he is speaking of the useful.

What then characterizes *homo capitalisticus*? Scheler does not give a comprehensive answer to this question. But there appear to be four major characteristics to which he alludes.

First, the *homo capitalisticus* is a type of human being fascinated by the realization of values of the two lower ranks and is, according to what has been established about the criteria of the five value-ranks, divisive and lacks a natural tendency toward communality.

Second, he is a type of human being fascinated by the manageability of values. He is thus characterized by strong inclinations to control both milieu-things and inter-personal relationships. *Homo capitalisticus* looks continuously for technical means for satisfying his need for athletic, cosmetic and pleasure yielding cults of the body that cover his deep-seated alienation from natural communalization.

Thirdly, it must be recognized that the relentless quest for technological control over nature in the sciences, such as medicine, meteorology and other areas, has been remarkably successful in bettering mankind. But the passionate fascination of controlling ever more of the phenomena around us runs the danger of misplacing the value of the person under that of mechanical control. Scheler would certainly agree with today's common perception that many lives are already victimized by technological data.

Fourthly, Scheler subscribes to Adam Smith's statement that every group of humans experiences both nature and the world by way of its predominant structure of interests and activities (XIV 375). Anyone captivated with work on and with things will become mentally absorbed by inanimate material. Such an individual will regard the world as though it furthers the activity and structure of his work. In this, things are the point of departure for all daily activities. Everything that crosses his path is looked at as an analogue to a material thing: the world, the state, church or groups of people. These objects are seen "from below," that is in terms of their assumed materiality and manageability. For this type of individual the nature of the world can only be known as tangible, mechanical, measurable and causally determined. Indeed, the world appears to be the sum total of manageable parts.

When this view is transferred to human groups, they are regarded more as individual *objects* than as living persons. The possibility for reaching out for higher values is only necessary to satisfy basic needs of life. This type of individual seems to subscribe to "I live therefore I am," or, as Scheler put it, by "*primum vivere deinde philosophari.*" If these four characteristics are accurate, even if only in part, then they are the main reasons for selfishness and ego-centrism that accompany the fascination with the two lower value-ranks relating to the body.

It may not be a fortuitous phenomenon in modern philosophy that the issue of the separation and the possibility of mutual understanding between the "I and thou" has so often been raised. It is not surprising because an acceptable explanation of the priority of the I over the thou enhances the chances for an adequate perception of the nature of a society as a whole as it is held together by those types of individuals that construct inter-subjective artifacts and rules by which to live with one another, such as contracts and constitutions. The pre-occupation with the "I and thou" issue also gives testimony to a high degree of a deep-seated alienation among such individuals—an "alienation" in society about which Scheler had already voiced strong concerns as early as 1914 (III 343-4).

In particular, the alienation stems from the above stated effectuation of things in the perception of modern individuals. The perceptual focus on the usefulness of things either lures or deflects the sensory perception from the other. At first sight, to maintain that things effect human perception seems to be a far fetched proposition. How can things have a particular effect on the perception of an individual living in a certain era?

The answer lies in the fabric of the modern mind-set through which things appear in their utility. The present mind-set must, for *homo capitalisticus*, roughly be that of the business man for whom the table is either useful or not useful, profitable or not profitable, in contrast to the carpenter, the artist let alone the holy man.

The perspectival perception of the business man is one among many that structures all entities of the milieu according to his mind-set. In his discussion of Capitalism, Scheler maintains the position on "milieu" as presented in *Formalism*. In it, there obtains an order of foundation. Every species has its own particular milieu. Milieu is the foundation of the structure of sensory perception of a species. Among humans, the perception, and all possible perspectives of it, is the foundation of interests. This is founded on the drive-structure of living beings. It must therefore be the case that the "milieu" of human individuals makes possible the peculiar perspectival perception of human beings living at a certain age.

The human milieu is different from that of animals in that for humans the milieu is open to such perspectives as those mentioned in the discussion of variable "mind-sets."

The ultimate reason, however, why the apprehension of entities has particular perspectives lies in the functional role that drives play in and for perception. Human development has undergone a shift to the predomination of one of the three main drives over the other two. In our era it is the nutritive drive, manifest in the growing role of economics in all walks of human life, that has begun to prevail over the power drive and procreative drive and their respective historical manifestations. The laws of drive predominations in man's drive-structure will be discussed later in detail.

CHAPTER VII

SUBLIMINAL PHENOMENOLOGY

Prefatory Remark

The phenomenology of Max Scheler has remained largely in the background of the phenomenological movement since World War II. Even today, no detailed study is available. There are two reasons for this. (1) The German Collected Edition of his works progressed slowly from 1954 while the fast growing phenomenological movement in Europe concentrated on Heidegger, Husserl, Merleau-Ponty and Sartre. International availability of their works had been promoted by the second generation of phenomenologists who had known them in person. This is especially true of the phenomenology of Husserl whose work was promoted by Van Breda and Cairns and, in their wake, by Gadamer, Gurwitsch, Spiegelberg, Landgrebe, Strauss, and other American and European scholars. (2) Scheler never offered a detailed presentation of his phenomenology, except in two essays from 1911 and 1914, "*Lehre von den drei Tatsachen*" and "*Phänomenologie und Erkenntnistheorie*" (X 377-502/PE 136-287).

Throughout his works, however, Scheler made numerous references to phenomenology and to the fledgling phenomenological movement in Göttingen and the part he played in it before and during World War I. A first discussion with Husserl (VII, 307-11) who is often referred to as the "father" of phenomenology, occurred in 1901. It centered on the concepts of intuition (*Anschauung*) and perception. Scheler, who was fifteen years younger than Husserl, outlined to him his own novel concept of intuition. Scheler's explanation was that the scope of intuition extended beyond its possible sensible components and logical forms. Husserl in turn remarked that he too had come up with an analogous extension of intuition, probably referring to his categorial intuition of his *Logische Untersuchungen* (1900/01). Between 1910 and 1916 Husserl strongly recommended Scheler on various career opportunities. But by the end of World War I, the relationship had cooled remarkably and it remained that way. As a free lance-writer from 1910 to 1919, Scheler had an astonishing record of publications that spread his name quickly throughout Europe.

Although Scheler harbored severe reservations about Husserl's phenomenology, he acknowledged and praised him on occasion. This might be explained by Scheler's dependence on Husserl's recommendations and by the deference common at that time in Germany to the office of a senior, full professor.

Scheler, like other phenomenologists in Germany at the time, was not only critical of Husserl's *Ideen I* (1913), charging it with egological Cartesianism and methodological shortcomings. Scheler was also critical of the *Logische Untersuchungen*. The critique of the latter had already been formulated by 1904 and is contained in his posthumous *Logik I* (XIV 9-256). It provides incontrovertible evidence of Scheler's independence in matters phenomenological on what he called the "loose circle" of phenomenologists with which he was acquainted. These included Geiger, Hildebrand, Daubert, Lipps (who founded the phenomenological circle in Munich 1911), Pfänder, Reinach and Edith Stein.

Scheler specifically charged Husserl with "platonizing" phenomenology in the *Logische Untersuchungen* because Husserl had (1) admitted truth in itself as separate from objects and thinking, and (2) regarded truth as existing prior to judgment making. This was, of course, incompatible with Scheler's contention that thinking must be conceived as being in function with (*Denkfunktion*) entities.

Scheler's express independence of the early phenomenological movement came fully to light, however, in a lecture held in 1908/09 on the foundations of biology in Munich (XIV 257-361). It contained the central themes of his phenomenology at the time when he was about to publish them in the two aforementioned essays. Unfortunately, his other comments on this subject are scattered throughout his works, including *Formalism*.

1) Specifics of Scheler's Phenomenology

The phenomenology of Scheler is distinct from all others by its wide *subliminal* range and aims. Scheler does not confine himself to logical rigor because he emphasizes the emotive aspects of consciousness or the subliminal "reasons" of the heart. A number of factors must be seen within this range which will be discussed below in the following order:

(1) Phenomenology is not to be based in a method.
(2) In intuition, phenomenology must suspend sensory data.
(3) The origin of time is in the self-activation of life.
(4) Consciousness presupposes the being of the person.
(5) Emotive intentionality is pre-given to all other acts.

(6) The ego is an object of internal perception.

(7) Reality is resistance.

(1) It must first be pointed out that the noetic-noematic bipolarity of act-consciousness and the consciousness of noematic meaning-contents, conjoined with the former, allows two approaches to lay bare the structure of consciousness per se. It is possible to investigate the *noetic* act-intentionality and it is possible to make the *noematic* meaning-contents of consciousness conjoined with its noetic component. Scheler refers to the noetic approach as "act-phenomenology" and the noematic approach as "phenomenology of facts." The former shows "how" phenomena are given, the latter "that" they are given. When using either approach it is not possible to exclude entirely its correlative opposite.

In general, phenomenologists claim that whatever their starting point it must be without presuppositions. Scheler's presuppositionless starting point is *that* being (and the sphere of the absolute), as the ultimate background of all meaning-contents, are pre-given to any cognition (*Erkenntnis*) and knowledge (*Wissen*). There is no cognition and knowledge, including phenomenological cognition, without the pre-givenness of a form of the meaning of being, including the meaning of the incomprehensibility of being. This pre-givenness of being must not be understood as a first fact that is followed by cognition. Rather, the presuppositionless givenness of being is the foundation in the *order* of all facts in consciousness. From this it follows that a phenomenon is a fact of consciousness or that consciousness is "of" facts whose foundation is their being in consciousness. These points had to be made for understanding Scheler's general negative assessment of methodology.

(2) Facts are given as contents of immediate intuition. Such phenomena are, for instance, spatiality, temporality, materiality, relationality, thingness, aliveness and the Divine. Methods, observations, and definitions, *presuppose* that which is to be uncovered by them. This is why the *that* which is spatial, temporal, material or alive is neither observable nor definable as "something" that can be uncovered by a method. Phenomena are therefore "pure" facts and are not arrived at by method. The fact of spatiality would allow observations or methods only when a particular extended configuration of a thing, such as something triangular or an organism, is in question. But the "fact" of the spatiality of something triangular, or the "fact" of the aliveness of something, is already *intuited* and, in this sense, *a priori*. Facts are meaning-contents without presupposi-

tions. They are *devoid* of sense experience. They are, as Scheler puts it: "there" (*da*) (X 380/1/PE 138). This "there" does not exclude the presence of illusions in intuition.

A phenomenological illusion occurs when something is apprehended as residual in consciousness where, in fact, it does not belong. For example, something may be given in the phenomenon-form of "aliveness" when in reality it is not alive. This might happen, as we saw in Chapter IV, when one believes one is looking at a person only to discover that the person is a dummy. In Paragraphs 8 and 13 of his *Analysen zur passiven Synthesis* Husserl also pointed to this dummy experience but saw it only under the aspect of a mode of a "doubting" consciousness, that is, of a judgment. For Scheler, however, such illusions are not "judged" as being true or false. Intuitions are not simply true or false; rather, they are deemed true or false after the occurrence of an intuition. Whether pure phenomena in intuition can be described or explained is a point of controversy among critics of phenomenology. This critique asks how we can meaningfully talk about a phenomenon that cannot be sufficiently explained or described. Scheler answered this criticism in two ways.

A distinction must first be made between intuition and discursive thinking. The word "discursive" comes from the Latin *discurrere* meaning to run through. Scheler gives five characteristics to discursive thinking. a) Discursive thinking requires various steps to be made in measurable time toward a final cognition, result or truth. b) Discursive thinking focuses on what is here and now and the relations between them. c) Discursive thinking presupposes space and time in which the steps occur. d) Discursive thinking can be inductive or deductive. e) Discursive thinking is "symbolic" and proceeds from parts to wholes.

By contrast, the intuitional grasp of a fact or phenomenon is different from discursive thinking in two ways. a) The parts of intuition are embedded in a pre-given structural whole. b) There is need for only one example of an entity in order to see it as a universal fact *without* going through discursive steps. That is, intuition of a fact is "supra-discursive."

Let us try to "explicate" what cannot be explained because explanations themselves are discursive according to definitions given above. The phenomenon "aliveness" is *there* in our consciousness, no matter whether I perceive an animate or an inanimate entity through this phenomenon. Mistaking a dummy for a live person is first seen as alive. In the inception of its occurrence in consciousness the fact-meaning "aliveness" is, therefore, indifferent to the truth or falsity of whether there is a dummy standing there. Such awareness is also in-different to the spatio-temporal determinations of the dummy, or of a living person standing in the window. The phenomenon of "alive-ness" as intuited *precedes* space and time. In a cartoon of Popeye for example, Popeye is experienced as if "alive" on the screen. Without this phenomenon one could *not make sense* of what he is doing. Pre-given, intuited aliveness can subsequently be analyzed in a series of steps of discursive arguments, including phenomenological argu-ments.

That a phenomenon is indifferent to space and time is significant for Scheler's phenomenology and, as we will see, for his *Philosophische Anthropologie*. No matter the degree to which a phenomenon can be approximated in Scheler's "phenomenological reduction," space and time, too, must be bracketed. That is, their phenomenological origin in the self-motion of the center of a living being must be suspended. Without the self-motion of life, there would be no space and time. "Phenomenological reduction" means, therefore, that there is a sus-pension of the vital life center or "impulsion" in which reality is given as "resistance" (IX 208-215/PE 313-317; IX 245-253). This point will occupy us later in detail in Chapters XIII and IX.

There is one more clarification necessary for understanding Scheler's phenomenology in this regard. What has been called "fact," or "phe-nomenon" are *Urphänomenone*, that is, "primal phenomena." When-ever a primal phenomenon such as "aliveness" *coincides* with an "idea" of, for example, the "idea of life," then the mind attains an intuition (*Wesensschau*) or knowledge of an essence (*Wesenserkenntnis*).

In order to understand the triad of primal phenomenon, an idea, and knowledge of essence, it will be necessary for us to look into Scheler's unique comprehension of what an "idea" is. For reasons of facility, this will be postponed until Chapter IX.

Because of the status of *Wesensschau*, as a rule Scheler's writings begin with general descriptions of intuited facts as much as this is possible, as is the case with shame, the tragic, repentance and resent-ment. Concerning the intuited fact of the Divine in consciousness, he developed an entire *Wesensphänomeologie der Religion* (V 157-328/ E 161-332; X 179-253), as we tried to show.

All pure facts have in common that they cannot be observed or subjected to methods. They are also indifferent to the categories of truth or falsity. This contrasts with the external facts held by science and the natural world-view. In the former, we stated, the earth turns around the sun; in the latter, it rises and sets. Intuited facts are inter-nal and "seen" only in a phenomenological attitude, not according to one that is mundane or historical. Scheler reached his phenomeno-logical attitude by "psychic techniques" similar to those in Buddhism. He was aware of a relationship between his own psychic technics and Buddhism.

Granted that phenomena are pure facts in the inception of intuition rather than the result of a method, the question of whether the senses play a part in intuition must be addressed.

Scheler's independence from the early phenomenological movement is further evidenced by the role that he assigns to sense-data. Because intuition is exceedingly richer than sense experience, it cannot be readily maintained that sense experience is primordial, let alone that it is the only experience a person can have. This also holds for what phenomenoloigsts call the "life-world," a concept arising only late in Husserl's posthumous writings. The term *Lebenswelt* was first used in 1885 by Scheler's teacher, Rudolf Eucken, although not quite in a phenomenological way. Its phenomenological use first occurs with Scheler in 1908, slightly changed in German as *die Lebewelt*. Although Scheler also used this term in his later writings, he preferred the expression "natural way of looking at the world" or "natural world-view" (*die natürliche Weltanschauung*). He detailed its phenomenological role throughout his writings. The natural world-view is given prior to all functions of the senses. Only those sensible data enter into play that the natural world-view "allows" to be. This also pertains to the "*milieu*" of animals. The role of sense-data is primarily a vehicle of an organism's *reactions* to its environment for the preservation of its life. Sense experience is not a condition, however, for facts of human intuition. On the contrary, to assign to sense experience a foundational role in and for intuition itself would defy phenomenology.

(3) The phenomena of spatiality and temporality must not be confined to human beings alone. Rather, they are generated by two powers any living beings has: *self-movement and self-modification*. Both spatiality and temporality have a metaphysical origin. In this respect, phenomenology, Scheler says, cannot be divorced from metaphysics or from theory of knowledge.

Neither spatiality nor temporality take their roots in the lived body or a time-consciousness. They stem, like reality itself, from a four-dimensional manifold of vital energy called "*Drang*," meaning impulsion. But they are not yet separated from each other in impulsion. The state of impulsion is pure, irregular fluctuating "variation" or *Wechsel*. Impulsion has no substance as a bearer of its existence. It can be compared to wave patterns in atomic energy whose reality, according to Scheler, also rests on vital impulsion. Four-dimensional impulsion suffuses all entities. It even reaches into the visual field of humans where the four-dimensional vital energy still holds. When one looks at parallel railroad tracks, they appear to "meet" in the horizon. Likewise, in four-dimensional geometry there are no parallels because there are no straight lines.

Impulsion is both individual and universal. In all of its phases of fluctuating variations, it is simultaneously "becoming" and "un-becoming" (*Werden und Entwerden*), a characteristic translucent in the continuous, simultaneous decline and growth of living beings. The following two laws obtain: (1) All *movement* issues forth from impulsion and is, in principle, reversible; (2) all *modification* issues from impulsion and is in principle irreversible.

The phenomenon of irregular, fluctuating variation is a pivotal one throughout Scheler's philosophy. An illustration will be helpful inasmuch as the German word *Wechsel* as Scheler employs it has no precise English equivalent. It should not be taken to mean "reciprocity" in the sense of the term as used in Kant's table of categories.

The examples of fluctuating variation that Scheler supplies are taken from sensory perception. They help to illumine his sense of the term. Examples of fluctuating variation is the sight of a large school of fish that appear to be swimming in random directions, or the random movements of ants in their colony, or the fluctuation of light and shadows beneath a tree that is exposed to the sun and wind.

In the last example, one could interpret the fluctuations of each shadow and patch of light either as the reversibility of shadows and light or as the irreversible modifications of the surface itself. The individual elements of these quivering appearances lend themselves to either interpretation. Moreover, each shadow's movement is theoretically and really a reversible movement. There is nothing that could make one believe that the shadow would not sometimes return to where its movement started. Nevertheless, all shadows do undergo an irreversible variation in time, even if they were all to return to their original places. The whole of the irregular variation would have modified in light of the time elapsed. One could also mention here the irregular activity of the snow on a television screen. Any one point of the snow of such shimmering activity is interpretable in both said ways. Hence, irregular variation lies at the bottom of both objective space and time also.

In summary, irregular, fluctuating variation can be interpreted as either reversible movement or irreversible modification. As reversible, it turns into spatiality and ensuing objective space. As irreversible modification it turns into temporality and ensuing objective time. But what holds for outer perception also holds for inner perception and metaphysics. It must be stressed that impulsion propels life into a continuous self-moving and self-modifying process of becoming-unbecoming at any of its phases. It is also admitted that space and time are not yet separated in impulsion and that the phenomenological constitution of time-consciousness must take its root in a metaphysical impulsion.

The impulsion energizing all processes of life ramifies in humans into three main drives: those of propagation, power, and nutrition. The fluctuating variation of impulsion now begins to bifurcate in the drives into reversible movement (spatiality) and irreversible modification (temporality). What in drive-life is less urgent becomes "distant" and "later" and what is more "urgent" to a drive becomes "near" and "first." The main drives are conjoined with three germ layers of vertebrate organisms (ectoderm, mesoderm, entoderm) in the gastrocele stages of an embryo. By dint of complex ramifications with other drives, this plays a basic role in the temporalization of passions, needs and interests as well as perception. In Scheler's philosophy all perception is, as had been mentioned earlier, conditioned by drives but in turn all drives by impulsion.

The first phenomenological experience of spatialization as detached from temporalization is a vague "about-awareness" (*das Herumbewusstsein*). The first phenomenological experience of temporalization detached from spatialization consists in pre-conscious run-offs of phases "filled" with phantasmic images (*Bilder*) flowing from impulsion. This implies that originally living beings do not live "in" an objective space or time. First and foremost, they spatialize and temporalize *themselves* out of the vital energy of impulsion.

The passage of impulsion into irreversible modification reaches human consciousness in form of "absolute," not objective time. Absolute time is characterized by three qualities: 1) simultaneous congruence of meanings and their phases; 2) continuous becoming-unbecoming; 3) The run off of absolute time "in" transitions between any A turning into a B. The latter includes also the transition between one meaning and another in consciousness or between potency and actualization. The absolute time of transition also applies to "protentions" turning over into "retentions" in Husserl's terminology. For Scheler, then, time-consciousness may be described as the *absolute self-temporalization of transitions in the flux of becoming and unbecoming of meanings locked in their individual phases, all of which is propelled by impulsion.*

Absolute time permeates all phases of life and the entire act-being of the human person. It is also latent in the continuous transitions in aging toward death. This holds, *a fortiori*, for the shifting in consciousness of the *horizons* of past, present and future. In its younger stages, consciousness has an endless horizon of the future. A small horizon of the past begins to grow and grow until both past and future horizons are in relative balance. In mid-life they begin increasingly and inexorably to squeeze the present between them. That is, the future-horizon retracts by closing in in a reverse direction, as it were, on the present from its front, while the horizon of the past gets wider and wider, pressing against *both* present and future from behind until the resistance of the latter collapse and are, at it were, swallowed up. The shifting dynamics of the three horizons is a fact of time-consciousness and imply Husserl's "leaning toward death" (*der Hang zum Tode*). The shifting dynamics is also at work in the process of aging. Aging itself is a manifestation of *absolute* time. Dying is the *self-ending* of *absolute* time. Death is secondarily an occurrence in objective time when observed by another.

Most aspects of the role of personhood in phenomenology and the following aspect of emotive intentionality had been discussed earlier. We wish to reiterate the points discussed nevertheless for the sake of covering the above essential points of Scheler's distinct phenomenology.

(4) Scheler had told us already in 1913 in *Formalism* (published then in Husserl's *Jahrbuch)*, that the being of the person is the foundation of all intentional acts. As we showed, this implied that the sphere of the person is not in objective time. Rather, the person is "supra-temporal." As such, it is the "person," not the ego, that is the foundation of consciousness. Each act of consciousness is different in essence from any other act. Scheler declared that especially feelings, but also volitions and religious acts, must not fall victim to the traditional privileging of rational acts and reason in the wake of René Descartes' cogito. For this and other reasons Scheler branded the concepts of a "consciousness in general" and a "transcendental ego" as "evident non-sense" (II 378/F 378 sic). Both concepts overlook the being and the self-value of the *person* that permeates all acts. What is called person, we had been informed, exists solely in the "execution" of any possible acts. The execution of acts is different, we saw, in each person by virtue of the "qualitative direction" the acts take.

(5) All perception, willing and thinking are borne by the emotive experience of values. That every act is suffused by the person and that the person varies in each different act by virtue of the qualitative

direction of its acts encompasses, *a fortiori*, emotive intentionality, that is, acts of feeling and their correlates, values. Values are the pre-rational, intentional referents or *noemata* of emotive intentionality. Its essence is the act of love. Like colors, values are independent of their substrates. The value of beauty may pertain to a landscape or a musical work of art, just as the sky or a cloth can be blue. All values possess the spectral order of five ascending ranks: the values of what is bodily agreeable; pragmatic values of what is useful; the life values ranging from noble (*edel*) to faulty (*schlecht*); the rank of the mental values of beauty, justice, cognition of truth; and the rank of the Holy and unholy.

Emotive intentionality consists in the act of preferring higher (or lower) values to the values given. Preferring is not choosing these values; rather, it is a spontaneous leaning toward something. This "leaning toward" is not founded upon reason. Its seat is the heart, the *ordo amoris*, whose "reasons" have a logic of their own. Good and evil do not belong to the five value-ranks. They are not intentional referents, that is, correlates of emotive intentionality. They emerge during the realizations in the preferring of higher (or lower) values and "ride on the back" of these acts. Good and evil are purely temporal phenomena and emotive instances of what phenomenological vocabulary calls passive synthesis. As such, the essences of good and evil are not objects.

(6) Because Scheler's phenomenology of consciousness rests on the being of the person, it also follows that consciousness, be it human, Divine, or fictional, must be "in-person," that is, have the form of a person. The ego is not, therefore, the foundation for the constitution of the human being as a conscious being, nor is the ego a point of departure for consciousness and its acts. This Schelerian assessment of the ego, also made in the 1913 *Jahrbuch*, appears to be the very opposite of the foundational role the ego plays in Husserl's *Ideas I* that was contained in the same *Jahrbuch*.

First. Scheler locates the ego in terms of five descending steps. First. In his 1913 book on *The Phenomenology and Theory of Feelings of Sympathy* the ego is shown to emerge in a human being around the age of two when it begins to distance itself from "pre-given" alter-egos.

Second. Pure intuition that is only given in a person encompasses both internal and external intuition. It is independent of the lived-body.

Third. In reality, however, the ego does belong to a lived-body. This generates three separate act-qualities: sense perception, remembering and expecting, all of which are encompassed by pure intuition.

Fourth. These three act-qualities generated in the linkage between ego and lived-body have as intentional referents "being-present" (*hic et nunc*), "being-past," and "being-future." Like protention, retention and the fleeting present of time consciousness, these referents do not occur in experiences of objective time or clock-time. This is because they are not given in reflective acts. The being-present as intertwined with retention and protention yields perception in its division between external and internal perception.

Fifth. It is internal perception in which the ego is constituted as its "object" in this perception. Although Scheler does not say so, it follows that egological phenomenology, such as that of Husserl, must be one of internal perception. Yet, the ego, as an object of internal perception, is not extended in that perception nor is it sequential because experiences of past, present and expectations of future are "interwoven" in the ego. The ego's interwovenness (*das Ineinandersein*) is the ultimate object of internal perception. The ultimate object of external perception is "pure expanse" (*das Auseinandersein*).

Scheler's theories would suggest that the traditional Cartesian dualism between mind and extension does not hold. While the ego can be a pure object, as in states of personal ingatherness as in a "call of the hour," and while it renders in such cases the lived body less important, the ego can also "spread" through the lived-body and undergo a transition of itself from pure to a "lived-body-ego" (*das Leibich*). The ego can thus spread as is the case in extreme physical exhaustion, intoxication, gluttony, etc. It may be, Scheler says, that in a dreamless sleep the ego disappears altogether until it begins to resuffuse the lived-body when awake (II 424/F 428).

(7) While the concept of reality bears heavily on Scheler's later *Philosophical Anthropology*, it should be mentioned that the concept of reality is, in part, a result of Scheler's sharp critique of Husserl's phenomenological reduction. This reduction must not center in a method, Scheler charges, but in a "technique" of nullifying (*aufheben*) the factor of the reality in the life-world itself so that pure phenomena can appear in consciousness. Husserl's reductive method simply takes real being as having a place in time to be bracketed by a *judgment* (*Daseinsurteil*). In a judgmental method, therefore, phenomena remain tied, no matter how slightly, to the *reality* of the life-world that is to be nullified in the first place. Because of the sensory linkage the method has, which stems from the "thought-procedure" of the phenomenological reduction itself, phenomena do not yet

appear as they should, that is, as *pure* facts alone. Hence the reduction is not radical enough. For this reason Scheler proposes to eliminate the very root that posits reality. This root, however, lies in the capacity that posits reality: impulsion. While consciousness or "mind" in general can only posit the whatness of something, it is "impotent" (*ohnmächtig*) to posit the reality of something. A temporary nullification of impulsion is necessary, therefore, and it can be achieved only by a psychic technique to accomplish the "phenomenological attitude" necessary to reach a pure fact. This technique alone promises a momentary access to what is in "pure intuition" as facts, severed from the realities of the natural world view or life-world and that of the world of science.

2) A Glimpse at the Dionysian Reduction

Toward the end of his life Scheler also envisioned an opposite direction of the psychic technique by momentarily suspending the sphere of the person, instead of impulsion. He thought it to be possible to "see" the essence of impulsion by placing oneself in it and becoming united with it. He called this technique "Dionysian reduction."

Throughout his work Scheler applied his very own phenomenology of intuition with the express aim of uncovering the *essence of being human* and of approximating the meaning of what we as humans are. This essence, as we saw in Part I, was designated as *ens amans*. Being human means to be a loving being, no matter how distorted the order of love may be in individuals and groups.

The tendency in the past of judging Scheler's subliminal phenomenology to be an "application" of Husserl's methods for a long time prevented the recognition due to the brilliant insights into what it phenomenologically (and as we shall see metaphysically and anthropologically) means to be a *person*.

CHAPTER VIII

THE FORMS OF KNOWLEDGE AND SOCIETY

Prefatory Remark

Scheler wanted his investigation, *Die Wissensformen und die Gesellschaft* (*The Forms of Knowledge and Society*) published in 1924 to be understood as containing two introductions to the major writings of his second period of productivity.

There has been ample speculation as to what precisely precipitated the change of direction of his thought in this second period in which he rejected the traditional religious conceptions, such as that of a perfect God Who created the universe. This rejection is imbedded in his notion that spirit by itself, whether human or Divine, cannot bring anything into existence unless their ideas are in joint functional process with impulsion (*Drang*) that only is able to realize them in history. The change in direction of thought consists in the recognition that metaphysically spirit is seen as impotent to account for reality and that for this reason the traditional Creator-God is an impossible assumption. The Deity, too, must possess *both* spirit and impulsion through which only Its reality can be made plausible, no matter in which novel way this will have to be done. The theme of the last work of Scheler's first period, *On the Eternal in Man*, now takes on a new direction which may be retitled as "On the Becoming of the Eternal in Man." In the 1925 Preface of *The Forms of Knowledge and Society* Scheler tells us that the two treatises contained therein "Problems of a Sociology of Knowledge" and "Cognition and Work: An Investigation into the Value and the Limits of the Role of the Pragmatic Motive in the Cognition of the World," are the result of years of research covering the areas of (1) sociology of knowledge and (2) theory of knowledge. One may not immediately see the connections between these areas according to Scheler himself, but they hover over most of his later philosophy. During his research, both the sociology of knowledge and theory of knowledge turned out to be complementary to one another, leading to converging results that are not imposed on the two areas but emerge by themselves. Both "Problems of a Sociology of Knowledge" and "Cognition and Work" are the aforementioned "introduction" to two major works that were still in the making at the time. The "Sociology of Knowledge" is said to lead into his projected *Philosophical Anthropology* (XII 5-341) and "Cognition and Work" is said to be an introduction to his metaphysics (XI 11-267). Both his *Metaphysics* and *Philosophical Anthropology* remained fragments that were published posthumously in 1979 and 1981 respectively. Sketches of a "Philosophy of Work," are scattered throughout these and other treatises written between 1914 and 1925.

Scheler recognized three essential types of knowledge: knowledge of salvation (religion), knowledge of essences (metaphysics) and knowledge of controlling nature (science). Both "Problems of a Sociology of Knowledge" and "Cognition and Work" focus largely on the last type of knowledge in the sense that Scheler repudiates the presuppositions of the mechanical view of the world as it still effects society to this day. In his 1911/12 essay "Theory of the Three Facts" and also in "Cognition and Work," which he continued to work on since 1909, a number of facets also foreshadow Husserl's *Crisis of the European Sciences* (1936) concerning the order of foundation between science and the natural view of the world, that is, Husserl's *Lebenswelt*. For example, what Husserl refers to as a "subjective-relative" status of science with regard to the *Lebenswelt* corresponds to Scheler's expression of its "vital-relative" status with regard to the natural world-view. Instead of German *vital-relativ* Scheler mostly uses a misleading German term, *daseinsrelatativ*, or "existentially relative." Its meaning, however, is the same as *vital-relative* throughout his works. A comparative study between Husserl's and Scheler's works concerning the foundation of the life world or the natural world-view with regard to science has not been furnished and thus Scheler's pioneering perception in this regard has remained unnoticed.

The title, *Die Wissensformen und die Gesellschaft* indicates that forms of knowledge are or can be relegated to the social status of society. But in this work, society is not only seen as an "artifact" as it was in *Formalism* and especially in "Cognition and Work"; it is also the sociological domain of work and labor seen in light of pragmatism. Forms of knowledge and work are two interrelated facets of a society. In "Cognition and Work" it is the interconnections between processes which can lead to knowledge, called "cognition" (*Erkenntnis*) and work leading to changes to be made in the human condition and the world that are the central issue. "Problems of a Sociology of Knowledge" investigates the sociological bases of knowledge. *Die Wissensformen und die Gesellschaft* therefore establishes a relationship between knowledge and society and between cognition and work. Of the five types of this relationship, Scheler addressed only three. The first relation pertains to the *social-historical* domain of human existence. It is covered in "Problems of a Sociology of Knowledge."

The second, psychological, and third, physiological, aspect of the relation are covered in "Cognition and Work." A fourth relation between knowledge and society was projected to cover a newly conceived "physiology of work," and a fifth relation was to cover education, in particular Dewey and the German *Arbeitsschule* or "Learn-Through-Work-School," initiated by Kerschensteiner.

Throughout the book, there is a common theme in both treatises. It is the metaphysical and anthropological, i.e., "meta-anthropological" self-moving vital ground of impulsion, *Drang*, without which no mind—or as Scheler prefers spirit (*Geist*)—can function. *Drang* is the condition for *Geist*. This backdrop foreshadows the historical drama between humankind and an unfinished Deity envisioned by Scheler at the end of his life. Phenomenological aspects of Scheler's thinking increasingly recede in favor of the intuition of the historical becoming of a unity between man, world and God in absolute time.

A) Problems of a Sociology of Knowledge.
1) The Structure of Scheler's Investigation.

"Problems of a Sociology of Knowledge" is divided into two parts. Part One is an investigation into a sociology of culture in relation to a sociology of reality. Its main theme consists in the disclosure of relations existing between "ideal factors" and "real factors."

Ideal factors are art, ethos, law, metaphysics, religion, science, technology and *Weltanschauung*—all understood in a broad sense. Real factors are all those factors that stem from the three major drives, of propagation, power and nutrition. Real factors are race, population, but also the geographic make-up of the earth, geo- and national-political distribution of power and economics. All of these possess indigenous laws of their own that do not allow scientific or other controls (IV 627).

Part Two deals with sociology of knowledge proper. As he will do later in the treatise "Cognition and Work," Scheler distinguishes between basic types of knowledge: the "formal problems," on the one hand, and "material problems" of sociological conditions, on the other. In both "Problems of a Sociology of Knowledge" and the treatise "Cognition and Work," he is highly critical of the mechanical world view whenever it is taken to be the only dependable or correct view of the world. For this reason, Scheler's repeated challenges to mechanistic systems and models as they are still resident in our own time, occupy large parts of *Die Wissensformen und die Gesellschaft*.

2) Sociology of Culture

The overriding themes of Part One of "Problems of a Sociology of Knowledge" are: 1) the interactions taking place among ideal factors; 2) the interaction taking place among real factors; and (3) the interactions taking place among ideal *and* real factors. Insofar as real factors have their roots in drives, a theory of drives is required. Insofar as ideal factors occur throughout culture, a theory of spirit is indispensable.

Scheler furnishes a number of instances of the interplay among all ideal and real factors. The ideal factor of art, for example, can interrelate with an other ideal factor, such as religion during the Medieval Ages. The interplay can also tie in with technological progress as it does today with the concern for materials used in the creation or production of art-works. Art can be influenced by a real factors like politics and political ideology, or by those of specific styles inherent among various races or populations, as it does, for instance, in Chinese or Indian art. Beneath such multiple, historical interactions lies Scheler's theory that these interactions comprise a significant part of the content of human life. Scheler now offers outlines of a general law that permeates these interactions among ideal and real factors. As we will see, these outlines are, however, more detailed in his published posthumous works.

At this point, we must be aware of a difficulty running through Scheler's sociology of knowledge. On the one hand, spirit is again said to be "impotent" by itself to bring anything into existence. On the other hand, the essence and contents of spirit as they occur among cultures are said to be a free and autonomous creation of spirit. And yet, the existence of cultural factors is entirely dependent on the drive-conditioned real factors. Luther, Scheler says, needed the political interests of territorial barons as well as a rising bourgeoisie and population for his ideas to become real. Raphael needed political patrons and markets of handcrafted art tools for his paintings to become real. Without a drive-conditioned support of real factors *no* ideal factor can by itself bring anything of the kind into existence.

This state of affairs becomes a rather complex one, however, when the real factors are shown to have a lawfulness of their own which, as such, spirit cannot essentially change. That is, spirit is fated by a lawfulness inherent in the course of real factors without which spirit cannot realize anything. But spirit can become effective *within* the respective scopes of real factors. When this conjunction occurs, spirit can more or less *direct* (*leiten*) the structure of such a scope and it can then put it to its use. Spirit can modify the indigenous flux of real factors but not their course as such. To make this point Scheler uses Comte's well-known expression, *"fatalité modifiable"*: that is, the fatality of real factors is only to a certain extent modifiable by spirit. If the drive-conditioned real factors do not allow development of spiritual processes, spirit remains ineffectual. For example, if a program designed to reduce unemployment fails to be supported by the given conditions of real factors, the program is a futile endeavor and would be described as outmoded in a political dictionary. As such, the program hits the "granite" of real factors. The peculiar *contents* and products of human spirit themselves, however, are, as the example shows, free and independent of real factors; at least they are never completely determined by them. Spirit determines only *whatness*, not the existence of what something is.

The real factors have an edge, so to speak, over spirit because they function like "sluice-gates" which open and close to varying degrees, allowing spiritual contents to flow. Taking unemployment as an example, this would be a condition in which the gates are obviously closed or at best half-open. During all unfavorable conditions of real factors of economics, the sluice-gates narrow or close the flow of economic ideas and projections for modifying such conditions, while favorable conditions open the gates and invite, as it were, ideas in abundance. The economic conditions of today do not tell us what theses conditions will be tomorrow. One can make short term projections, while long-term projections are more vulnerable to miscalculation and often used as a political ploy to instill economic hope among people during an election; but people are not infrequently disappointed later by what had been promised by candidates. The invisible sluice-gates in real factors can also impede the development of cultural factors such as education and the arts much as they can foster and nurture them.

3) Some Formal Problems

Scheler now proposes laws inherent in the historical strides of real factors. They bear on individual cultures and history itself. These are four meta-historical laws by which one can bring into relief any given period of history in terms of its respective *Weltanschauung*. The first of these laws can be described as follows.

The first law pertains to three shifts in the predominant major drives in three macro-phases of history. The first phase is characterized by the predominance of the oldest and strongest real factor based on the drive of propagation, blood and the preservation of the species. It marks the bond among groups. This phase occurred in that part of history preceding societal structures and the state. It occurred when tribes and ethnic factors formed communities, as during the age of mythology, its social form whenever blood bonds are predominant is the life-community.

The second shift of drives occurred in a second phase when the power drive becomes predominant. In this shift one group seeks to form power over other groups. Wars in this phase are usually those of extermination of racial or ethnic groups ("ethnic cleansing" is the present-day euphemism in Bosnia for such tragedy). Such wars easily lead to the formation of states and to even grater political aspirations. We still live in this phase according to Scheler but it will come to an end in a still distant future because of the law inherent in the progressions among the three main drives.

The third shift of drive-importance takes place in the age of economics. The nutritive drive will predominate over the other drives or the procreative and power drives lose their intensity. These drive-shifts occur within history as a whole, within a cultural unit, but also during a person's life: youth, adulthood and old age. Scheler refers to the predominance that characterizes each drive as "primary causation" or *Wirkprimat* that is at work during interactions between ideal and real factors.

The second meta-historical law pertains to alterations of subliminal drive-objects. In each of the above shifts, the power drive alters the objects in these drives. During the procreative phase the power drive determines the drive-object as "power over humans"; in the second phase it extends to "power over humans and things"; in the third phase the power drive seeks control only over things in nature.

This law implies that the drive-object of "power over humans" *decreases* while that over things in nature *increases* in the direction of mechanical and technological mastery of nature. It should be added that each phase is characterized by a specific social form: 1) the Life-community, 2) society and 3) in the future "Era of Adjustment" of confluence among cultures, in which the drive conditioned aspirations of power over humans, including the domination of men over women (XIII 132) will be virtually nil. But Scheler died before articulating the social form of this future era. We have good reason to assume, however, that he had a social form of an international, inter-racial, intercultural *planetary solidarity* in mind in which humanity actively participates in the becoming of the Deity.

Hence, the law of shifts among the primacy of drives throughout the three eras of history, and ages among cultural units and within individual growth, is simultaneously accompanied by the shift in the role the power drive plays in the procreative and nutritive drive. This shifting likewise affects both the kind of objects *inherent* in the drives as well as the "material" for spiritual order (XIII 131).

The following graph illustrates the point.

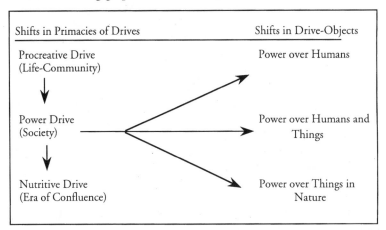

Shifts in Primacies of Drives	Shifts in Drive-Objects
Procreative Drive (Life-Community)	Power over Humans
Power Drive (Society)	Power over Humans and Things
Nutritive Drive (Era of Confluence)	Power over Things in Nature

The third meta-historical law brings to completion the move of history away from power over humans and toward power over things in nature. However it must be observed that the shift of drive-objects, which is largely generated by the role of the power drive, is not identical with periods of objective history. The process is a manifestation of *Richtungsschrittgesetze*, "pace-laws" or "phase-laws" in the "direction" that the shift takes place. These laws lie beneath the factual historical development. Scheler defines them as follows. They are neither quantifiable nor measurable but only qualitative, a phase B follows a phase A if and only if a phase A occurs. Whether a phase A occurs, however, is unpredictable. If A does occur, it does not determine either when or even if B will occur. There is only a "tendency" for B to occur. The occurrence of B can be obstructed by the freedom of the person. It is important to note that Scheler also speaks of laws of "blind" real factors working beneath human history.

These explanations of laws inherent in drives must not be construed as a linear view of historical development progressing from one age to the next. In Scheler's macro-vision of human history and the history of life, there is no such uniform, linear development. Rather, history and life are polyphasic. His conception of the origins of the human race holds, for instacne, that there are different origins of the human race and of its groups at different time-phases. Scheler thought that the Asian-Chinese race was older than the white and the latter older than the black race (XIII 137). The more we travel into the past, he tells us, the more we find separate groups and separate cultures that were originally peaceful. War is not originally natural to humans. Furthermore, it is questionable whether humanity is borne by a "unity of blood." The multi-faceted polyphasic history of humanity has entered into a phase of a slow convergence of its parts in 1914 when it for the first time had a global experience of itself with the outbreak of World War I. Such convergence pertains to history and seemingly does not pertain to life. While life is said to be an ongoing history of continuous successful or unsuccessful attempts to create individual forms, it resembles a huge set of hieroglyphs of which only a number can be decoded, many of which have been lost. Life does not seem to tend toward a final forming stage. Scheler believed that a biological polygenesis comes closer to the truth than the notion of a uniform direction of evolution just as phase laws do by comparison to a notion of a linear progress of history. He was led to such conclusions because there is as we saw no "constancy" of the human being (XII 93) and no constant apparatus of human reason (VIII 9) as Kant had presupposed in his three *Critiques*.

This leads us to a fourth meta-historical law which is twofold. It pertains to the influence spirit has on real factors and to the growth of spirit during this influence. These two laws work against one another, so to speak, but at the same time compensate for this dynamic. Spirit, Scheler reminds us, occurs separately among different groups; there is not *one* universal spirit. Given this perception of spirit scattered among groups, the influence spirit has on real factors increases with the sequence of the drive-shifts; the fatedness of the development of real factors decreases in that sequence. Race and blood factors give way to powers of rising states; these and other powers, in turn, give way to economic, drive-conditioned interests of capitalism. During this process there is growth of spirit during the directional shifts that drives and drive-objects take.

When the procreative drive is predominant there is a minimum of discharge of spiritual potential and a maximum of obstructions against those potentials by the real factor concerned. The sluice-gate of the real factor is partially closed for spirit's growth and activity. The second and subsequent shift toward the predominance of the power drive occupies a middle position. During ages of power-seeking, the ideal factor of culture becomes rich and the role of work is accompanied by increasing discharges of spiritual potential. Finally, in the forthcoming age of economy that only now begins to blossom, there will be a maximum of spiritual potential and simultaneously a minimum of obstruction by the real factor riveted in the nutritive drive. This means that the future economic age will be characterized (1) by a maximum of spiritual potential and (2) by a minimum of the role of historic and social reality. But this leads also to the sociological effect of growing formations of masses and an isolation of spiritual life, as is revealed by growing numbers of isolated specialists, virtuosos, exceptional talents, secluded scholars, esoteric circles, or the sprouting of clandestine sects and subgroups. This is as much elaboration that Scheler provided on these two laws (VIII 50-1/PR 62-3).

One point remains clear in Scheler's line of thinking: drive-phases and their corresponding real factors, on the one hand, and spirit with its realm of ideal factors, on the other hand, are in a *functional* relationship as long as spiritual potentials more or less coalesce with courses that real factors take. We have come full circle again to see that there is *growth* in the plurality of spirit of groups rather than in one, static universal human reason. This growth is now perceived as conjoined with drives and the course of real factors riveted in them. It must be added that the growth of pluralities of spirit is not a simultaneous one. There are still group spirits tied to tribes and isolated communities; there are still wars of extermination often conjoined with such groups; there are, at the same time, developed and industrialized groups for whom peace is an ideal factor guiding the present and the future economic era.

In his essay *"Zur Idee des Ewigen Friedens und der Pazifismus"* ("The Idea of Eternal Peace and Pacifism") Scheler leads us back to his ethics and to the person of the role model as seen in light of these laws:

> Whatever happens in historical time happens by way of ideas and drive-life *simultaneously*. Just as interests, no matter how strong, powerful and widely spread they are, remain ineffective when they do not meet with conscious apprehension of their unity by the wills of great individuals, so also ideas and ideals of value remain ineffective when they, in turn, do not meet with interests of groups and masses which developed according to their own laws and which, as it were, vigorously 'snap up' those ideas and thus make them powerful in the end (XIII 80/ID 155).

With this quote we can now bring together five essential components in the relationship between ideal and real factors. These components are part of every historical event occurring in the interplay of ideal and real factors. They are also components of every action of the individual. These elements are:

1) The role of a great individual (a model)
2) directing (*Leitung*)
3) Steering (*Lenkung*)
4) The obstruction of real factors (*Hemmung*)
5) The releasing of real factors (*Enthemmung*)

We have discussed the role of great individuals, of exemplary persons and moral model persons in Chapter I. We can now concentrate on the four other components between ideal and real factors and illustrate them in terms of a model: that of a skipper steering his boat over rough seas. One could also use as a model a wind-surfer or a pilot flying through turbulent conditions or any other model having the five components of controllable and uncontrollable activities. Let us take the example of a skipper.

The skipper struggles with real currents and high tides but is guided by an idea, say of his destination, of a plan, or of a fixed star that serves to keep him on course. Scheler argues that spirit holds ideas out before itself (*hält vor*). At this point we wish to defer an explanation of "idea" to facilitate matters for a moment. An idea, in turn, determines how the boat is to be steered. Steering, therefore, is the second function of spirit (VIII, 40/ PR 197). But spirit does not realize anything unless it is in touch with the real factors. In our model the real factor is a geographic one: currents and waves of the water carry the boat. These are not, however, under the skipper's control. Their movements have a lawfulness of their own with which the skipper can only reckon. His boat is either obstructed by the currents and waves or the currents and waves release their forces in favor of the direction the skipper is then able to keep. The ancient Romans capsuled this state of affairs in an adage translated in a more acceptable plural form, saying "Waves carry us but we cannot control them" (*Unda fert, nec regitur*).

The background that these formal problems provide for the second part of the sociology of knowledge, that is, the material problems of religion, metaphysics and science, comes to a close when Scheler introduces "knowledge" in the broad sense, by which he means that knowledge is constitutive for society. Society consists of groups having their own individual group-consciousness. A group-consciousness determines knowledge of objects that are more or less common to one such group. Knowledge, in the general sense, determines structures of a society just as conversely the structures of society co-determine the knowledge that occurs in society. Thus all knowledge has a sociological character.

But society does not determine contents of knowledge so much as it *selects* the objects of societal knowledge. This happens in two ways: in terms of social "perspectives of interests" prevailing in the group and in the ways knowledge is communicated, for example, in schools, academies, universities, or learned societies and institutions. In this process, knowledge first "functionalizes" itself in particular social groups and respective outstanding persons. In the domain of religion the religious group, such as a sect or a church, the members follow its charismatic founder (*Stifter*). In all metaphysical knowledge the social group is a school with its central figure of the sage. Scientific knowledge has for its social group a learned society, such as the university or academy, with the scholar being its leading figure. Knowledge will then gradually filter into the group concerned. The role of the outstanding persons is reminiscent of the "Exemplars of Person and Leaders."

Given the assumption that society consists of various groups, Scheler holds that there is no one universal "natural view of the world" or *Lebenswelt* among all groups as Husserl thought. There are only natural views of the world *relative* to individual groups which, originally living in the social form of the life-community, have a "group-soul" that develops into the social form of society having a "group-spirit."

Relative natural world-views are characterized by the manner in which nature is given to its members. Everything that is given "without question"—that is, what is not doubted—belongs to a relative natural world-view. It is true, for example, that in the natural world-view the experience of a setting and rising sun is without question; it does so always in terms of different values. Throughout the Maya culture, for example, every sunrise and even every day is a new god; this is not the case in ancient Greece culture. The differences among such natural world-views can also be seen throughout Western and Eastern mythologies, even among modern nations. While some things are taken for granted in one nation, they are not in others, an experience every traveler soon comes to realize.

But Scheler himself did not elaborate this line of argument. He simply states that the concept of one general natural world-view, or one life-world for all, is untenable because religion, metaphysics and science build upon relative natural world-views. These three types of knowledge—religious, metaphysical and scientific—are formally characterized by their historical movement that accelerates with the degrees of their artificiality. Religions move at a much slower pace than metaphysical systems which, in turn, move and change much slower than scientific constructions of systems. These differences stem from the origins of knowledge. Every group possesses an unbending urge for its preservation and salvage (*Heil*); this urge merges with an instinctive curiosity and belief in something holy and powerful. Therein lies the root of the search for religious knowledge. The root of metaphysical knowledge is "astonishment" (drawn from Aristotle) at there being something rather than nothing which lends itself to continuous modifications and interpretation. The root of scientific knowledge is an active eagerness to gain knowledge of every action and type of work in order to increase control over nature.

Because initially knowledge is often communicated by outstanding persons, and because knowledge is subject to intersubjective experience in general, all knowledge is situated in the "thou-I" relationship. Knowledge is communicated and shared with others. This participation is the principle ontological component of knowledge that will be discussed in *Erkenntnis und Arbeit*.

Scheler at this point stresses, however, that the primordiality of "the other," the "thou," the "with-world" precedes the "I" as had been established in *Wesen und Formen der Sympathie*. He uses the argument of the primordiality of the other here in preparation for what will be said about knowledge in *Erkenntnis und Arbeit*. He wants to show that knowledge arises from the entire societal body of knowledge. This cognitive participation in society has various forms, some of which had been discussed in the work on sympathy. All of these forms are encompassed by two outermost terms: feelings of "identification," such as that between mother and child, and by "inferences" or analogies typically made by societal individuals between bodily expression and internal experience. An example of the latter is a person's cheeks reddening while being ashamed.

The region of the "thou" or the "social sphere of the with-world" is pregiven to all other spheres of consciousness (as we saw in the Chapter on "Phenomenological Intersubjectivity"). The "Sociology of Knowledge" now tells us that because the thou is the "basic existential category of human thinking," one can at the same time

> ...see clearly how much more deeply the conviction of the *reality of society* is rooted in us than is the reality of all other objects belonging to the other spheres of being and knowledge. We can 'doubt' all other realities or leave them as they are. But we can *no* longer doubt this reality (VIII 57/PR 72).

A critical observation is in order at this point because there is a contradiction as to how society had been described in *Formalism*. In *Formalism* and elsewhere during the first period, Scheler explicitly describes society as an artificial unit and a fabric of relations that individuals deliberately set up for themselves; that is, there are ever new contractual relations, customs and conventions that continually surface and disappear. Society, we were told, has no duration in con-trast to the life-community. Instead of an unbroken solidarity pre-vailing among members of a life-community, societal individuals were said to live in a mutual understanding of each other by way of bodily gestures that express internal experiences all of which is always im-bued with "distrust" of another (II 517-18/F 528; VI 336). In the first period then, society has no reality for Scheler whereas in his second period it is emphatically stated that it does. Why this change of position?

One answer could be that the unshakable conviction of the reality of society implies degrees of society's non-reality. This is supported when Scheler qualifies the non-reality of society in *Formalism* as be-ing "not a special" reality (II 518/F 529). The "thou" must be pregiven in one way or another in all of the four social forms: in the mass, in the life-community, collective personality as well as in society. Scheler illustrated the pregivenness of the thou with the Robinson-Crusoe-model in *Formalism*. If society is held to have no special reality, as Scheler maintains, then this situation can only pertain to the moral and legal context in which society is seen in *Formalism*.

Sudden changes of contractual relations, mores, and laws in soci-ety can indeed make the reality of society dissipate. This would not negate, however, the sociological facticity embedded in the all-en-compassing pre-givenness of the other. Even the absolute, solitary Robinson has no special reality as such. Another's reality must be attributed to the sphere of a consciousness that has no "special" real-ity in the absolute Robinson. It is in the *absence* of others, who like-wise have no special reality, that others are in fact given. The analysis of Robinson holds for both an absolute Robinson who has no reality and for another who has no special reality with regard to Robinson. The phenomenon of "loneliness" always presupposes that one can be lonely only in relation others.

The very region or sphere of otherness, therefore, makes the reality of society *formally* possible although this reality was denied in terms of society's legal and moral continuously innovating aspects. Never-theless, Scheler's emphasis on the reality of society in the "Sociology of Knowledge" leaves one with an impression of contradiction. This contradiction may ultimately have its source in the overall change in the direction of Scheler's philosophy during the second period. Even so, the impression of contradiction is countered by Scheler's con-

vincing argumentation that there are *parallelisms* between social structure and patterns of thinking (VIII 62/PR 201-02) against the backdrop of the interdependence of real and ideal factors.

4) Some Material Problems

In the portion of "Sociology of Knowledge" called "Formal Problems" Scheler had already enumerated a number of cases of parallelism between levels of development. He sees much evidence of such
parallelism: between particularism of cities and the polytheism of
ancient Greece; between the graded feudal structure and the teleological view of the world in the Middle Ages; between the seventeen
century concept of absolute monarchy and the Cartesian *cogito sum*;
between political liberalism, free trade, balance of power and the word-
engineer-God of deism; between social individualism and Leibniz's
monadology; between the development of the Prussian state and
Kant's philosophy of imposing rational order on the chaos of drives
and sensations; between competition and class struggle and the
"struggle for life" concept of nature; between czarism and orthodoxy.

There are also parallelisms between social structures and patterns
of thinking, for example, those between forms of constitutions and
theist, materialist and monist thinking. Let it be added that Scheler
also mentions parallelisms pertinent to developmental psychology,
for instance, the one holding between the behavior of masses of people
and children (VIII 62/PR 201-2).

One may ask whether it is true that our own increasingly machine-
driven society also begets patterns of thinking such as rule-following,
coordinating, arranging in segments, structuring, assorting, impersonal and unfeeling routine thinking, and blind computer-obedi-
ence. Is it not true that a stroke of a key retrieves past information in
a fraction of a second numbing both imagination and memory and
replacing them with mechanical "creativity," if such thing exists? Is it
not true that the value of talent has given way to public recognition
of technical skills? Is there not a widespread tendency to rely on quantification and statistics rather than evidence of quality? Is it not true
that we increasingly organize our lives in terms of experiences of *separate* situations by keeping apart work time, pleasure time, quality
time, retirement time, etc., until there is no time left? Could it be
that what one calls "god" when referring to a perfect artificial intelligence machine indicates a process of thinking that mechanizes the
Absolute in the modern ethos? Could it be that such patterns of thinking are a by-product of the powerful sensitivity for *divisible values* in

the ethos and mind-set of Capitalism, now seen in its parallelism with the artifact-structure of society?

If these analyses hold true, then the interdependence between real and ideal factors would justify Scheler's stress on the "reality" of society in that society is the bearer of real factors such as politics and economy. Our critical observations on the "reality" of society may indeed point to the significance that the material problems of the "Sociology of Knowledge" have when seen in today's light.

However, the bulk of the material problems, as distinguished from the formal ones, is devoted to the sociology of science, the relationship between science, techniques and technology and to the real factor of economy, all of which are representative of the structure of society. First, the origin of modern science is seen in the particular type of humans who disassociated themselves from contemplative thinking and who, in turn, preferred technical work and crafts. This type of human characterizes Western humanity as the product of a belief according to which God is maker and *creator*. In the East there is no such notion and hence no such technologies and incentives to work on the world to such degrees. Eastern techniques apply predominantly to the internal experiences in the individual's soul and to the control of individual's way of being. Western motivation to sanctify and continue God's work by contrast is motivated by a strong will to increase controls over the forces of the universe and the atom. But the bulk of this work ethic was shouldered by lower, non-contemplative classes who grew in numbers only to join the higher social orders of the bourgeoisie. This bourgeoisie has therefore two social characteristics: it is composed of 1) working people and 2) of people who have the freedom and leisure to engage in speculative thinking. Concerning working people, Scheler offered an observation in his 1921-2 lecture, *Sozialphilosophie,* that bears on his theory of the cognitive and social interdependence of real and ideal factors. This observation provides clarification on the interdependence offered throughout *Die Wissensformen und die Gesellschaft.* We wish therefore to give a lengthy quotation from the lecture. It clarifies much of the material problems of the "Sociology of Knowledge" and of the essay, *Erkenntnis und Arbeit.*

> Every group looks at nature and the world according to the prevailing structure of its interests and activities (Adam Smith). A worker engaged in manual labor who has no leisure for meditation, contemplation and for procuring a general view of life and world, experiences himself entirely entangled with inanimate material. For this reason, he tends to disavow freedom of the will and of the person. He feels as if

tossed around in all directions. He develops for himself a world-view commensurate to his work's goals in such a fashion that the given phenomena of the world appear in such an order allowing them to be points of departure for his work. He looks at everything in an analogy with the "corporeal, material thing" that concerns him first. He keeps looking at the world, at the state, at a church, at groups and also at himself "from below," not "from above" ("serving function of mechanisms"): In practice, the world is determined for him only as long as it is (1) mechanical, (2) tangible, has handles to hold it by, and measurable, (3) as long as the world has causes and effects in the sense of laws holding in space-time contacts and as long as there is recurrence of the "same." What is concrete and tangible are the individuals living in the groups. Since the worker's internal experiences are for him only of "passing and concomitant" nature by comparison to the states of his lived body (which as their bearer appears to him unvaried), a socio-psychological disposition for epiphenomenalism of the soul is at hand. This is because most pressing needs must first be satisfied so that the human being can raise his eyes toward spiritual projects. *Primum vivere deinde philosophari.*

The mechanical view of the soul, of the world, and of society "belongs" to individualism: both as a way to live by and as a theory; and because the mechanical view is the form of perception and of the thinking of the world and of groups living in the social form, called "society." (XIV 375-376)

The interdependence of real and ideal factors is not addressed as such. It is only illustrated with a particular case of interdependence of cognition and labor, i.e. of *Erkenntnis und Arbeit.* Nevertheless, the illustration of this interdependence can be expanded into other areas also. The significance of the passage can be tailored to any other type of work, for example, to computer work, to art work or the work of a businessman. In all cases of work involving manual skills, Scheler's argument would *mutatis mutandis* hold: the world view among different groups that are bound together by the same type of work is *commensurate* to that work in which they are involved. In turn, the things and entities of their particular world view are "points of departure" that themselves stimulate the kind of interest for the type of work in which people are engaging. "Work" pertains not only to manual labor, to which the above quotation refers; it refers to any *pragmatic* type of work related to things.

Since the end of the Middle Ages and the beginning of the Reformation the rise of society brought with it increasingly complex issues. Pragmatic work became increasingly complex. It called for "division of labor" in order to achieve control and mastery of nature's forces that are to be utilized for society's purposes. In this process, cognitive patterns of religious experience and contemplation were bound to give way to scientific, methodological thinking. But the rise of science is not the actual reason for the waning of religious faith that occurred. It is religion itself that must be held accountable for its own decline as an ideal factor. (One such reason given by Scheler is that "organization" of churches have been modelled after structures of states.)

On the other hand, as for the future of metaphysical knowledge in society Scheler voices daring optimism. He gives three reasons for such optimism. First, the smaller European nations that have less technological interests than the larger ones provide an atmosphere for the cultivation of meditation rather than technical thinking. Second, Russia promises, in the long run, more meditation than scientific sophistication because of its deep ties with contemplative orthodoxy. Thirdly, the mixing of races and cultures, socialist tendencies (as propagated by Upton Sinclair and known to Scheler) as well as the gradual diminution of Anglo-Saxon leadership in the United States would give rise to a more contemplative and warmer types of person. This would supplant Puritanism, technocracy and formal-mechanical thinking. Further, the United States, says Scheler, shows that we need not be concerned about spiritual culture in an economic age, nor that the industrial wealth and controls over basic production of goods and energy will replace what the state has done for culture. America has set an example with achievements outside its borders, especially in China. The disadvantages of capitalism are, therefore, only "temporary and will be offset by well defined economics" (VIII 186/PR 183). In a somewhat surprising contrast to such laudations, Scheler was not only critical of Europe on occasion but also of his own country, especially its moral status. His arguments, often implicit, run through his social and political writings. They began with his 1916 essay *"Die Ursachen des Deutschenhasses"* (*"The Causes of the Hatred of Germans by others"*). This was published only two years after his book *Der Genius des Krieges* (*The Genius of War*), in which he shared the enthusiasm for the outbreak of World War I. He shared with the vast majority of Germans a stinging critique of the Allies, singling out England, with arguments that bordered on the absurd. He softened his position in the 1916 edition of the book.

In 1917 he backed up the moral critique of Germany that had been advanced by his friend and statesman-industrialist Walter Rathenau, who had referred to ubiquitous sensuousness, vanity, lust, uncontrollable desires for possession, greed, passion for unlimited security, hunger for criticism, lack of moral mutuality, and prostitution in Berlin that was tolerated by people belonging to top levels of the socio-mechanical order. Such depravities contributed, Scheler argued, to the very cultivation of mechanical-scientific thinking (IV 557).

Scheler offered another set of examples to show how his theory of the interaction and parallelism between real and ideal factors bears on the sociological development of science. 1) The disintegration of ecclesiastical hierarchy since the Reformation coincides with the disintegration of thinking restrained by doctrine, canons and other regulations. 2) During the Reformation the human soul loses its function of procuring self-redemption and instead directs itself toward a new purpose of working in the world. 3) The growing gap between church and state allows "freedom" of science to develop. 4) A new valuation of nature is the result of a new direction of love toward nature. 5) The new direction of love of nature spawns a will to control nature. 6) The growing gap between emotions and intellect is mirrored in Descartes' "*cogito ergo sum*" in tandem with the dissolution of the organismic life-community and the rise of society in which emotions are suspect (Kant).

Scheler does not stop here. He also unveiled structural identities between the real factor of domestic politics and types of knowledge. He does so by referring to history and to a "logic of classes" following the findings of his friend the sociologist Werner Sombart. Why is it, Scheler asks, that metaphysics made a resurgence on the European scene after the disturbing ties metaphysics had with the old Church? Why were the bourgeois democracy, science and technology, simultaneously victorious by the middle of the eighteenth century? Conversely, why were the political powers, the estate hierarchy and traditions of the feudal era mirrored in a contemplative, biomorphic metaphysics represented largely by monasteries according to which metaphysics inhibited rather than fostered the rise of science?

The answer to the last question can be seen in the political privileges of the class of feudal leaders that accrued its wealth not by its own work but through that of others working for them. In this way the privileges of the feudal class maintained contemplative classes that were economically unproductive, especially inasmuch as the feudal lords worked together with ecclesiastical offices that engaged in politics. But the chances of survival of contemplative metaphysics diminished as the bourgeoisie began to work for itself and produce its own wealth. In this political context, metaphysics became deprived of its necessary economic basis. It is the economic unproductiveness of the metaphysical contemplative classes that caused the collapse of the metaphysics of forms, purposes and of substances and that reduced its existence to "lonely thinkers" and "schools." These causes are "eminently political." Institutional metaphysics fell victim to the lower revolutionary classes of the "fourth estate" and their leaders who replaced both religious and metaphysical thinking increasingly with the mechanical and logical thinking of science.

Scheler tells us in this regard that the stress on "induction" and "method" in society rests on the volitional direction of those groups who are convinced of equal rights for voters and the necessity of having a principle of majority rule. He argues that scientism, induction and the division of labor work together within the framework of the ideology of proletarian socialism. Beneath this sometimes cloudy perception is, however, the idea that is at the heart of Scheler's philosophy of history: the understanding of an historical period rests first and foremost on how human beings of that period understand themselves. In the age of science and technology this self-understanding centers around the idea of the *homo faber* according to which humans perceive themselves predominantly as persons living among utensils and equipment, among machines and technical contraptions: in short, as "tool-people."

A clarification of the term "proletarian" as used above is needed. In identifying lower class orders with "proletarians" Scheler does not intend the Marxist use of the term that refers to a class that must sell its labor in order to survive because it has no property of their own. This Marxist meaning is closer to the ancient Roman usage of the term that refers to the lowest class order whose contributions to the state consists mainly of providing blood to keep the community going—the Latin *proles* meaning "offspring"—whereas Scheler's usage of the term pertains to lower class orders that work for profit and possessions and are, as we saw, mini-capitalists themselves represented by unions who manage their material interests. It can easily be seen that the proletarian class order in Scheler's sense is the one that tends to "absolutize" positive science and to obliterate both religion and metaphysics because these kinds of knowledge are not progressive. Hence, at the beginning of "*Erkenntnis und Arbeit*" "work" (*Arbeit*) is the name given for the "pathos" of modern humanity that is controlled and, perhaps, haunted by knowledge of practical and pragmatic achievement, progress and success. The motives for this pro-science-ethos of lower class orders are said to the following:

1. Science addresses "all the people."
2. Thinking and truths in the sciences are subject to the people's approval. The "masses" make the decisions as to what the true and false facts are. Thinking is to be grounded in sense data of experience.
3. Science fulfills a basic character of society: distrust. Distrust and doubt are the foundation of science and allow of public criticism. Therefore, science also fulfills a basic requirement of democracy.
4. Science upholds the motto of proletarianism and egalitarianism: "a speck of dust is as important as the stars in the skies."
5. Science is rebellious. Wherever the "Baconian spirit" takes a root, a revolution will grow. The proletariat hopes that this quality of science will destroy existing orders.

These pro-science motives are not, however, systematically treated in *Erkenntnis und Arbeit*; rather they underlie the treatise. Scheler wavered on the title of this essay; he cited it many times in the reverse order of the nouns as "*Arbeit und Erkenntnis*" and he also spoke in the 1926 edition of "principles" rather than "motives" of the pragmatic cognition of the world. One should not put too much importance on the title changes because he had been working on subjects of this treatise since 1909. But the enumeration of the pro-science motives must by implication be kept in mind as underlying *Erkenntnis und Arbeit*.

B) Cognition and Work
1) Outline of the Relationship between Cognition and Work and the Concept of Pragmatism

What follows is an attempt to appraise the second introduction to Scheler's *Metaphysics and Philosophical Anthropology*, entitled, *Erkenntnis und Arbeit: Eine Studie über den Wert und die Grenzen des pragmatischen Motivs in der Erkenntnis der Welt*. (*Cognition and Work: An Investigation into the Value and the Limits of the Pragmatic Motive in the Cognition of the World*).

The use of the word "cognition" must be clarified because its usage in English philosophical vocabulary does not have the philosophical sense as it does in German. "Cognition" must be distinguished from "Knowledge": instead of speaking about "theory of knowledge," we will speak about "theory of cognition." In German usage, the word for cognition, *Erkenntnis*, can have two meanings: it can signify the process that leads to knowledge or possessing the knowledge of something as that which it is (IX 111/P 39). The title "Cognition and Work" relates to this second sense of cognition.

The German word for "knowledge" is *Wissen* which can mean either the various forms of knowledge or knowledge *per se*. A form of knowledge, such as that of science, leads to a particular kind of knowledge and to a theory of cognition belonging to that knowledge. On the other hand, *knowledge per se* (*das Wissen*) does not permit a theory of cognition of itself because a "theory" of cognition presupposes some knowledge in that theory. A convincing argument to show that theories of cognition imply some knowledge would be that they presuppose that cognition is a process of forming judgments. Scheler means by this that all judgments are subject to the criteria of truth or falsity whereas it is senseless to assign these criteria of judgmental thinking to cognition, as if cognition *itself* could be true or false. To say that 2 + 2 = 5 would be a false judgment but the cognition *itself* is not false.

Knowledge *per se*, however, is nothing but an "ontological relation" to be investigated only with "purely ontological," not epistemological, terms (VIII 203; IX 111/P 39). The title, "Cognition and Work" refers, therefore, to the interconnections existing between a knowing possession of something as something (*Erkenntnis*), on the one hand, and work (*Arbeit*), on the other hand. This point is central to Scheler's understanding of the concepts of "work," "cognition" and "pragmatism." Our task must first be, therefore, to outline these concepts in more detail.

By "work" is understood any psychic and bodily activity leading to the change and transformation of the material being used. "Cognition, on the other hand, has nothing to do with such changes and transformation. For, he who wants to gain cognition of something does not want to bring about a change of what he wants to have a cognition. All acts which may accompany cognition and imply changes such as acts of observation or attention, are not themselves acts of cognition but are only in the service of the latter.

There is a threefold relation between cognition and work.

1. The relation of temporal sequence. Must there first be a theoretical cognition before work can take place or does cognition grow in time along with the increasing intensity of work devoted to change in given materials? Or, does a child learn through working at a project, or must the child first be equipped with theoretical concepts in order to do so? (VIII 450). In Germany this question still underlies the education system today as it did in Scheler's time. It splits educators into two camps: one that promotes the aforementioned "*Arbeitsschule*" the other the "*Bildungsschule*" or cultural education.

2. The question of origin. What are the specific acts that yield cognition? Can these acts be reduced to those acts that play a central

role in the pragmatic work activities? Or are acts of cognition irreducible to such activity? Is there pure thinking? If the latter is the case, metaphysics is possible. If the former is the case, cognition has one function only: it is only a "lantern" shedding its light on human needs and practical environment. Its acts always yield to such activities that serve useful changes of materials. That is, these acts are intermixed with the activity of work.

3. The value and purpose of cognition and work. If there are pure acts of cognition there must also be a culture of the mind (*geistige Kultur*) to be enhanced in its self-value. Work must then be conceived as a means toward this end in this case. If there are no pure acts and culture of the mind, the practical advancement of work is the alpha and omega of our existence and all those who assert that there is an overriding value of the culture of the mind are in practice "unproductive drones of society which have concocted an attractive name for their laziness" (VIII 452). Since pragmatism deals with "what works" we look into Scheler's understanding of this.

The concept of pragmatism, Schiller's "humanism" and as a small movement of the same name in continental Europe has its origins in the United States. Scheler's thoughts on the concept of pragmatism arise from his reading of William James's *Pragmatism*. Pragmatism responds to the threefold relationship between work and cognition in the following way: cognition has its origins in work; cognition has only one purpose: to guide processes of work; and the human world is a man-made world and the practical result of human reactions to it.

One of the most deplorable mistakes of philosophy has been to try to define "world" as being independent of what we make out of it. This error stems from the ancient Greeks whose disregard for work led, sociologically, to the institution of slavery. But why such concern about cognition and work today? The answer lies in the Western mind-set that suffers from an obsession with work that dominates the social fabric. This point was glorified in the Communist Manifesto of 1848 in which work is held to be the sole creator of civilization. The pathos modern man connects with work, Scheler writes, has intensified ever since Christianity lost its influence and ever since the Western roots in ancient Greece had been forgotten. In particular, it is the *interconnections* between the natural sciences and technology that have created the peculiar Western mentality in our era, in which the human being understands himself more as a working "tool man" rather than as a rational being, let alone as *ens amans*. This mentality is very distinct from Chinese, Indian, Ancient Greek and Medieval culture, all of which emphasize wisdom more than work. The adulation of work in the West is also based in the Western capitalist mind-set (VIII 193) that affords economics, priority over politics, cultural and educational activities. The interconnections between natural sciences and technology are therefore also grounded in the very *ethos* of the West, characterized, as we saw, by the preoccupation with those values that largely relate to work: usefulness and comfort, technology and the productions of goods (*Güterproduktion*).

In showing the significance of the problem of the relation between cognition and work, Scheler poses the following question to be pondered for the sake of focusing on what continues to occur in the West: Is modern technology and the production of goods an application *subsequent* to the theoretical *cognition* man has of nature? Or, is modern technology spawned by a conscious or subconscious *drive and will to dominate nature*? There are two consequences that will follow if the second alternative is true:

1) If the latter is true the natural sciences would merely consist of formulations made subsequent to what has been gleaned from experience, actions and practical conduct. Science would amount to a systematization of the successful or unsuccessful reactions that humans have when they deal with nature in practice.

(2) If this was the case, the very forms of human intuition and thinking as well as the methods and goals that the natural sciences apply to nature would have to be spawned by a *pre-logical* "will to power to dominate nature." That is, the forms of scientific thinking, its methods and goals would have grown over a long period of time by way of adaptations of this will. In this case the possibility of a pure cognition of entities is not excluded. A researcher does not first have to look into experience to gain an insight. In this respect, Scheler mentions what he considers to be the final refutation of Bacon's method of induction that was launched by the German chemist Liebig (1803-1873). When scientific discoveries of technological import had been made, Scheler argues, these discoveries were not necessarily made for technological progress but often for the sake of gaining pure cognition. Gauss (1777-1855) in Göttingen, for instance, used a wire connecting his institute with the observatory to measure electromagnetic waves but did not have in mind the consequences of this for modern telecommunication systems. Scheler holds, therefore, that the role of experience in natural science is a limited one.

The answer to the question of whether the technological age developed subsequent to cognition or whether it has been spawned by a drive and will to dominate nature is the overriding theme of "Cognition and Work." But Scheler does not give an exhaustive answer because the question should be confronted in five ways mentioned above. Instead he addressed this issue in only three ways: 1) historically and sociologically; 2) epistemologically, 3) in terms of developmental physiology and psychology, and he left open discussion of a "physiology of work and of the *Arbeitschule* (Learn-through-work-school).

The general outline of the relationship between cognition and work asks what is the specific relationship that cognition has to knowledge, on the one hand, and to work and practice, on the other hand. In his general description of pragmatism, Scheler states that pragmatism takes all knowledge to be a genetic result of conduct and "inner actions" and that this knowledge has the goal of bringing about changes in the world in which we live. In this project, all knowledge has to serve human actions. Scheler will develop an elaborate *theory of perception* in distinction from those theories affiliated with pragmatism. He will argue, as was stated earlier, that all perception is *conditioned by drives*. To understand this, the distinction between cognition and knowledge must now be freed from the obfuscations implicit in it.

2) The Nature of Knowledge and Cognition

Scheler describes the essence of knowledge in two lengthy passages: one in "Cognition and Work" (VIII 202-210) the other in his 1925 lecture "The Forms of Knowledge and Culture" (IX 111-119/P 39-49). In the latter, Scheler complains that his philosophy is still unclear to many because he had not yet formulated his theory of cognition, which he expected to do in the forthcoming *Metaphysics*. But he does give a detailed analysis on the subject in the 1925 lecture, an analysis of which will serve our presentation.

Knowledge is not an object of epistemology. It is an "ontological relation" (*das Seinsverhältnis*) which all forms of being presuppose. As such an ontological relation, it consists in an entity's *partaking* in the whatness (*Sosein*) of another entity or that of the partaking entity itself. This relation does not effect the whatness of either term: the whatness remains the same. Partaking means that what is known of the whatness of another entity becomes part of the knowing relation. As purely ontological, the relation is neither causal, spatial nor temporal.

But in this sense, what is the condition by which knowledge occurs? Scheler responds that partaking in whatness is made possible through "spirit" (*Geist*) as an X that "knows." This answer, however, is not satisfactory. Spirit itself, therefore, needs to be defined as clearly as possible. A being that knows must have an inherent tendency of evolving from out of itself and of going beyond itself. Without this tendency there cannot be knowledge:

> I can think of no other name for this tendency than "love," devotion and, so to speak, a bursting of the confines of one's own being and whatness through love (IX 113/P 40) (translation slightly changed).

In Scheler's second period of production, it is love that is again the hub of human existence. Love, however, is no longer seen in its phenomenological-ethical relevance but in its ontological role. But during the few remaining years of his life Scheler did not fully develop an ontology of love. Despite the sparse references to love's ontological meaning, Scheler laid fertile ground to continue this line of thinking.

Given the ontological relation a knowing X has to either an interior or exterior whatness, one must be careful not to extend it and its bearer, spirit, to the reality that a whatness may have. Spirit cannot,, as we saw, account for the givenness of reality of something.

The origin of reality is different. As noted earlier, reality comes about in the resistance that is experienced over against entities and the entire world. An entity that does not have the capacity to resist does not, strictly speaking, by itself exist.

It should be noted that Scheler's "ontological relation" foreshadows Heidegger's *Dasein*. Scheler subordinates "consciousness" to an "ontological relation" (*Seinsverhältnis*. Heidegger uses the same word.) while Heidegger subordinates consciousness to *Dasein*. For Scheler, "consciousness" is only a particular kind of the ontological relation.

What has been said about knowledge certainly does not illuminate the concept of "cognition." First of all, as mentioned earlier, there are various types of cognition. There are cognitions in the natural sciences, in metaphysics, religion and art. The confusing array of modern theories of cognition could be arranged into some order were it not the case that one kind of cognition is, in the present state of society, *the* cognition applied directly or indirectly to all other kinds of cognition. This privileged type of cognition is that of the natural sciences. Accordingly, object areas of other types of cognition, such as that of cognition in art, become affected by a cognition that is not proper to it.

This point leads Scheler to an elaborate system of criteria that each type of cognition possesses. Criteria belonging to a particular kind of cognition do not belong to other kinds of cognition unless they are intentionally or subconsciously shifted into those others. Scheler maintained that the determination of such criteria in different types of cognition is extremely important for eradicating misunderstand-ings that occur when such criteria are confused. For example, scien-tific cognition has the indispensable criteria of logical truth and fal-sity, whereas there are no such criteria in art appreciation. There ex-ists an entire array of "criteria of cognition" among which true-false is only one, but one which dominates all societal thinking based largely on the practice of forming judgments.

There is a system of criteria or "measures of cognition" (*Erkenntnis-masstäbe*). Each measure occupies a different level of cognition. In the sequence of levels given below, the measures follow one another or, to put it differently, the preceding measure is the presupposition for the one that follows (X 413/ PE 179). These measures are:

1. Self-givenness or evidential cognition.
2. Adequate or inadequate cognition.
3. The relative level of existence of objects.
4. Straightforward truth (*schlichte Wahrheit*).
5. Non-formal true or false.
6. Correct-incorrect.

Self-givenness (1) is "coincidence" (*Deckung*) between what is meant and what is simultaneously given. In other words, the first measure of cognition is between an immanent intuition of an essence and its unmediated givenness. This in turn means that the most immediate contact with the world is in the phenomenological "being-*there*-it-self" of what is meant and given while this is being lived out (*"er-leben"*). This measure in turn is the presupposition for (2) the ad-equate or inadequate cognition. The relative level of the existence of an object (3) is the presupposition for the occurrence of a straight-forward truth; the latter consists in the coincidence between the mean-ings, judgments and existence of facts of that level. The fifth and sixth measures pertain to non-formal value-meanings as the presup-position of the formal relations holding among values, which Scheler does not mentioned here.

Furthermore, cognition of something is the result of only the con-sciousness *of* something that emerges from that consciousness and reveals the self-given facts of intuition (1). There is no cognition of something without cognizance (*Kenntnis*) and no cognizance with-out the self-givenness of subject matters (*Sachen*).

Cognition is relative with regard to a particular bearer. Relative cognition, forms of perception and observation as well as causal and logical laws are always expressive of the human being as their bearer, the human being. This relativity does not, however, quite pertain to self-givenness or an absolute cognition. Self-givenness can only be "intuited" (*erschaut*) and is therefore indifferent to individuality and universality. The intuition of a self-givenness is not tied to perception, observation, symbols, proof or a language. It is "*die Sache selbst*," "the thing in itself."

There are five instances of the relativity of human cognition:

1. to life as a whole, including mechanical objects (II 421-469/F 424-476),
2. to human life only and its "natural world-view,"
3. to races, for example, their different ideas of the world,
4. to male and female with regard to their different experiences and feelings of certain objects,
5. to only one individual, for example, an object hallucinated by that one individual.

In all of these levels of relative cognition, the aforementioned measures of cognition allow a multitude of possible combinations. This multitude of combinations can in turn be regarded as a precarious ground in the human soul for all kinds of misunderstanding among humans. Such misunderstandings occur, for example, among the young and old and among those of different races and cultures. The latter can lead to serious misunderstandings in international diplomacy.

The ancient Greeks, for instance, had a more adequate cognition of Zeus than we could possibly have today. Ancient cultural traditions preserve themselves in the present when those living in the present live on another measure of cognition. Scheler implies that the Western scientific and calculative world-view does not have a monopoly over other world-views. In fact, the relative cognition of the scientific world-view can cover over the first measure of cognition of self-givenness.

This point would support justification of Heidegger's life-long struggle of retrieving the adequate and self-given cognition of the Greeks, for example their Heraclitian "flux," of truth as adequation or self-givenness in "unconcealment." Heidegger's retrieval of Greek thinking would also be supported by Scheler's insistence that adequate cognition is not dependent on "true" and "false," even though "true" and "false" are applicable to objects relative to human life.

This independence of adequate cognition is possible because adequate cognition itself is anchored in self-givenness. Scheler also tells us, however, that judgmental "true" and "false" do in fact have universal applicability throughout all relative cognition. Again, this does not pertain only to the common notions of logical or scientific "true" and "false." The fact that he who says that the sun has not risen although it has, makes of course a false judgment while he who says it did makes a true judgment. This shows that "true" and "false" are relative to human beings. But on the level of science it is another matter because *per se* there is no rising or setting of the sun. Therefore, if there are two contradictory statements of the form A = B, and another A = non B, one is false but *only* on the condition that in both propositions the A is on the *same* level of cognition; if not, they can be both true and false. In this example, therefore, the A possesses a different relativity of existence (*Daseinsrelativität*).

3) The Three Types of Knowledge

Granted that knowledge is an ontological relation, there is a coincidence between specific classes of acts and the regions of being given in such acts. It is this point that leads Scheler to distinguish three fundamental types of human knowledge: The three classes of acts, which are embedded in the experience of the value of the holy, of mental values and of values relative to life, relate to three "spheres" or regions of being: the region of the divine (discussed in Chapter IV), the region of the essential and the region of the fortuitous existence of entities. In these regions that are given in respective acts, the ontological relation of knowledge is displayed historically: (1) in religion; (2) in the wider sense of metaphysics; (3) in science. Each of these rest on their own specific sociological factors.

Scheler addresses the question of the goals that knowledge must have. Knowledge always serves the "becoming" of something because the *goal* of knowledge cannot itself *be* knowledge. Knowledge must have a "final" and "ontic" meaning (VIII, 204; IX, 113). There are three such goals. Knowledge serves (1) the becoming of the world and its ground; (2) the becoming of the person; (3) it serves man's practical mastery of nature. There is an order of foundation among the three types of knowledge that can easily be gleaned from *Formalism*. The highest knowledge is the knowledge of *salvation* (*Erlösungswissen*); the second highest knowledge is that of *essence and cultural edification* (*Bildungswissen*); and the third highest knowledge is that of *control* over nature (*Leistungswissen*).

Knowledge of salvation aims at absolute being. In this knowledge the person seeks to participate in the ultimate ground or source of entities. This may sound like abstract speculation. But Scheler wishes to say that, in practice, man is a microcosm in which all forms of being converge: the physical, chemical, vital, mental and the spiritual. In this, Scheler's speculation seems indeed to be an insight according to which the study of being human is the first possible access to the Deity (IX 83).

Knowledge of essence and cultural edification aims at the essence of entities. It approaches such essences in the absence of space and time. The question either "what" life is or what a "number" is cannot be answered by the disciplines of biology or mathematics. The answer to such questions lies on the level of metaphysical insight. This insight is a "transcendental prolongation" of and above the limited realm of real things in objective time and space. It precedes real and practical experiences and for this reason is *a priori*.

Knowledge of control, finally, aims at determining laws that hold among entities in space-time.

4) Pragmatism
a) Critique of Pragmatism

Given this threefold division of knowledge as reflected in human history, pragmatism represents the third kind of knowledge in the division. As such, it cannot therefore be an entirely mistaken philosophy as is sometimes contended by European thinkers (VIII 206).

Pragmatism's shortcomings become an issue when it one-sidedly takes this knowledge of control to be the sole base for all knowledge. It universalizes its own theory of scientific cognition. Scheler does not single out only the pragmatism of Peirce, James and Schiller as being responsible for the unscrutinized acceptance of one particular knowledge and cognition. There are many indications that Scheler charged other philosophers along the same lines, particularly his contemporaries Heidegger and Husserl who treated only the second, wider metaphysical type of knowledge (IX 254-340/RR 288-356; III 171-197/IM 138-156). What distinguishes Scheler *in nuce* from his renowned contemporaries is that his entire philosophy deals with all three branches of knowledge, not only one.

As we shall see, Scheler's critique of pragmatism appears to have a number of solid grounds, besides revealing a vast knowledge of British and American pragmatism. He is quite aware of the difference and partial compatibility pragmatism has with British empiricism, as well as with the differences of views held by Peirce and James. Through his reading of current research he was also aware that in the heydays of pragmatism there existed as many different interpretations of what "pragmatism" precisely meant, just as there were numerous interpretations of what "phenomenology" meant in its zenith. In fact, Scheler points to German variations of pragmatism as found in the works of Dilthey, Fichte, Nietzsche, Schopenhauer, v. Sigwart, Vaihinger. There are also affinities with Bergson and pragmatism (VIII 223-6).

There are some incidental yet perhaps interesting parallels between James and Max Scheler, who both had their mentors, Peirce and Husserl respectively. In their own times (and perhaps even still) James and Scheler were not infrequently considered by some to be renegade disciples of their mentors. But in their cases, James and Scheler broke the dependence on their mentors and developed their own thought. One can grant that both James and Scheler started along some lines of their mentors but took distinct direction in their development of them. Scheler's starting point, intuition, is a departure from the position at which Husserl began. Scheler and James shared an early interest in *moral life*, in contrast to Peirce's and Husserl's early preoccupation with logic and mathematics. The former were over-generous in the acknowledgment of their mentors while the latter underestimated the potential of Scheler and James.

Let us now take up the primary arguments Scheler advances against a number of misconceptions to be found in pragmatism. Already in *Formalism* Scheler had referred to pragmatism on various occasions, mainly with regard to the implicit consequences it must concede in regard to an ethics of values. With respect to moral deeds, the moral tenor of a person is entirely indifferent to both such deeds and the conception of the success of their workability (II 127/F 111). Scheler argued that the moral tenor permeates all deeds, even if this permeation is influenced by willed deceptions. True, a moral tenor can be "confirmed" in deeds and proven to be true, but such confirmation cannot supplant the *evidence* of a moral tenor that already exists prior to any deed being done. Confirmation is neither the basis for the cognition of a moral tenor nor a starting point to evaluate the moral value of a person. If confirmation is used in this fashion, a moral tenor will cease to be a moral category because it will be dependent on all the judgments and conclusions of such confirmation. Scheler clearly implies that the very relationship between the antecedent and consequent—that is, between moral tenor and confirmation—that is so central to pragmatism is distorted by pragmatism. In showing the nature of this relationship as he sees it, Scheler employs his analysis of the ontology of knowledge, and the logic implicit in the relation of antecedent and consequent.

Adhering to his tenet that knowledge is an ontological relation that consists of a knowing being partaking in the whatness of another knowing or non-knowing being and that all knowledge refers to whatness only and never to the existence of something, Scheler can, indeed, say that pragmatism falsifies the concept of knowledge itself. The concept knowledge does not involve a relation to actions and deeds. But according to pragmatism this is assumed to be the case inasmuch as pragmatism falsely takes the meaning of a sentence to be identical with practical consequences. Pragmatism takes the truth of a conception to be nothing but its "useful" consequences (VIII 228-229). In other words, Scheler refutes Peirce's argument that "in order to ascertain the meaning of an intellectual conception one should consider what practical consequences might conceivably result by necessity from the truth of that conception; and the sum of these consequences will constitute the entire meaning of the conception." (Collected Papers, Vol. V, #9)

Pragmatism misinterprets the relationship between precedent and consequent. While it correctly teaches us that sensory perception is conjoined with "psycho-kinematic behavior," (*praktisch-motorische Haltung*) or self-motion, it is wrong in assuming that psycho-kinematic behavior is the condition for sensory perception to occur. Rather, as Scheler holds, the condition for perceptions to occur is the spontaneous *impulse* in a vital center of the organism, whether it is a subconscious drive-activity or an arbitrary one. Consistent with his having established the primacy of value experience in *Formalism*, Scheler identifies this impulse with rules of a *subconscious preferring in drives* that are themselves guided by "attention" and "directions of interests." The impulse is the condition for and guide of sensory perception. This is a preliminary point to his metaphysics: the impulse is the vital energy of impulsion that propels all activity of an organism.

A more stringent argument for the disabusing of pragmatic misconceptions pertains to its mistaking the notion of the difference between knowledge of essence and inductive knowledge. The assumption of a parallelism between knowledge, on the one hand, and deeds, on the other, does not pertain to all knowledge and all deeds but only to a limited domain. The domain where the parallelism holds is within the knowledge of fortuitous reality, not in that of essence or salvation which are forms of knowledge beyond that with which pragmatism deals. This knowledge does not change the world, as knowledge of control does, because it remains evidential throughout all perceptions. It is *a priori* for all conceivable worlds. It follows that the knowledge of essence does not come under the criteria of truth and falsity. Its criterion of cognition is, as we mentioned earlier, evidentiality. Only when a judgment enters this knowledge does the criterion of "true" or "false" come into play.

Pragmatism is also mistaken in its assessment of the possibilities of changes that can be made in the world. This possibility that is open to human beings had already been discussed by Scheler in *Formalism* where he distinguished divisible and indivisible values. We recall that things are more prone to bring about changes in practice the more they are relative to life or vital values and the more they appertain to the human species. The farther such divisible values are from indivisible values, the more they can be managed in practice and calculated for success: one can reckon with them. Conversely, we recall, the less divisible values are, the less they become manageable and "useful." Since pragmatism only allows knowledge of control, that is, those values that can be reckoned with and are manageable and have useful consequences, it misconceives the threefold nature of knowledge itself.

The misconceptions of pragmatism stem largely from the Kantian leanings that Peirce's pragmatism reveals. That Peirce knew almost by heart Kant's *Critique of Pure Reason* is well known. For Scheler, the Kantian notion of reason as a static grid of twelve categories unchanging in history also underlies the pragmatic systems. This conception of reason is only one example prevalent within European thinking, Scheler said. On this point Scheler's critique of pragmatism is mixed with his metaphysics: all *a priori* forms of thinking are grounded in the *functionalization* between objective thinking and ontological knowledge of essence (VIII 232). Human spirit itself *grows and develops*. Growth and development do not exclusively pertain to new compilations of the results of cognition of fortuitous reality. That is, the "*evolutio*" of human spirit is a value higher than the applications of "accumulation" of cognitions for practical ends. Scheler emphasizes that not to see this point is as great a shortcoming in pragmatism as it is in Kantianism.

There is also a misconception pervading pragmatism pertaining to logic. George Boole (1815-1864), the first logician of pragmatism, as Scheler calls him, furnished two logical principles that seem to be false: (1) that two propositions are supposed to have identical meanings when they lead to the same actions; and (2) that a sentence is true if it determines an action having useful consequences (VIII 233).

The first principle is refuted by the "inviolable" logical rule that consequent and effect never univocally determine the antecedent and cause. That is, the meaning of a proposition or a question is not given with its logical consequences. It is equally unacceptable to identify the meaning of a conception with the practical bearings it is supposed to have. The latter cannot hold because different theoretical presuppositions can, in fact, determine the same practical behavior, and the same presupposition can in turn lead to quite different practical ways of behavior. While Scheler refrains from developing his logical arguments, he is quick to show that science and its criterion of cognition has the eminent significance of demarcating its limits over against metaphysics. All questions in science whose answer is outside verifiability and measurement can nevertheless have meaning, even if not for science. The "unanswerability" of questions does not imply that they are redundant and that they require that science replace metaphysics and religion altogether. So called meaningless questions, in other words, do have a "meaning" even if their answers slip through the networks of logical criteria and scientific methods.

Scientifically unanswerable questions pertain to what Scheler calls "meta-physical" and "meta-biological" questions. They belong to a domain of meta-science that is located between individual sciences and metaphysics. It forms a gateway to metaphysics proper. A metaphysical question, would be "What is space?" and a meta-biological question would be "What is life?" Neither the science of physics nor biology can provide an answer to these questions by means of their respective criteria and theories of cognition. But the absence of scientific answers does not imply that these are meaningless questions. As to the two questions mentioned, both the evidence of the meaning of the *phenomena* of "spatiality" and of "aliveness" can be approximated according to the various degrees of adequation. Beneath Scheler's critique of pragmatism unmistakably runs his phenomenology of the intuition of meanings.

Scheler also finds fault with the pragmatist conception that the thinking of meanings is supposed to *consist* in the application of a word-sign, or a sign of a sign. He argues that when we say "this lawn is green" pragmatism neither assigns "lawn" nor "green" an independent meaning that could be fulfilled in the perception of a green lawn. Pragmatism holds rather that in perceiving things resembling "green" we produce a word as a sound-complex of "green" and that we produce the sound-complex "lawn" when we perceive things resembling lawns. Taken in this form, the theory does not hold. A perceived content "green lawn" can find perceptual fulfillment in an infinite number of contents of judgments and different meanings such as "a green plain" or "grass."

Scheler's interest in cases of the kind reveal the avid interest he also maintained in psychology. In the case just mentioned, he refers to the extensive experimental research done by Gelb and Goldstein that shows that with two persons who lost the perception of colors resulting from an accident can after a while reproduce a color, for example, "green" when they vocalize the correct word "green" in an experiment. They do not reproduce "green" in visual perception when they vocalize "blue" or any other color except green. Gelb and Goldstein showed, however, that it is *not* in "vocalizing" green that green is retrieved, but by dint of the "category" to which the color belongs. We do not wish to follow further these arguments, interesting though they may be to the Schelerian assessment of pragmatism's shortcomings.

We now turn to Scheler's arguments for the justification of pragmatism in philosophy and of positive elements of pragmatism.

b) The Justification of Pragmatism

The major positive element of pragmatism is to be seen in its determining the relationship that human beings have to the world: It is not a theoretical but a practical relationship:

> Pragmatism correctly holds that the primary relation human beings—
> and for that matter all organisms—have with the world is a *practical*,
> not a theoretical relation; for this reason, the '*natural view of the world*'
> is guided, and borne by, practical motives. (VIII 239)

The primary relationship between man and world as a practical one, we saw, had already been articulated in *Formalism* with regard to the "milieu" or lived immediate environment. In this milieu human beings "reckon practically" with things:

> A sailor, for example, is able to 'reckon' with an oncoming storm from
> the changes in his milieu without being able to say which *specific* change
> (e.g., in the formation of clouds, in temperature, etc.) serves as a sign.
> (II 154/F 140)

Scheler shared the determination of the nature of man's primary relationship to the world as practical with pragmatism from early on to his latest writings. It is forcefully articulated in his 1927/8 treatise, "Idealism-Realism," saying:

> On a certain level called the 'natural view of the world' whatever is
> before us is given to us *exclusively* as a world of usabilities
> (*Brauchbarkeiten*) or, as Heidegger recently has appropriately charac-
> terized it as 'the stuff at hand' around us. [*das Zeug*](IX 198-199/PR
> 306. Translation slightly modified)

It is well known that Heidegger also explicated the relationship between man and world as a practical one. He explained the at-handedness of things, "*das Zeug,*" (the stuff at hand around us) in detail in the third chapter of *Being and Time*. There is no doubt that pragmatism, Scheler and Heidegger addressed the same phenomenon. Heidegger, and most of his disciples did not give due historical recognition to pragmatism with regard to the determination of the practical relationship between humans and things. As such, both pragmatism and Scheler as early as 1913 see it as *primary* in human existence.

Scheler too departs, however, from the pragmatic view. He states that his own view is "relatively pragmatic." This is because he thinks the ontological status of the human being to be a "vital being endowed with spirit" (VIII 242) for which earthly human beings are only an "example." He hastens to state that the natural sciences cannot claim to suspend life in general when they establish formal-mechanical laws. They can rightfully claim only that they suspend specifically human titillations (*Reize*) and sensitivity, but not "life" in general. Science, therefore is vital-relative to life and the natural view of the world with its sociological base of the life-community. Throughout the history of modern science, the nature of its vital-relativity in the sense described has been misunderstood in four areas: materialism, rationalism, Kantianism and positivism. Scheler seeks to uncover now the misunderstanding of formal-mechanical laws in some detail in order to show that his own "relatively pragmatic" view (VIII 242) and that of pragmatism itself can claim a justification of their own.

Since Scheler will refer quite often to the branch of physics called "mechanics," let us briefly recall the elements of mechanics. Mechanics deals with (a) the motion of bodies (kinematics) and its causes, called "forces" (dynamics) and (b) the conditions for an equilibrium of forces and when no accelerations do occur (statics). The basic concepts of motion, velocity and acceleration are meaningful only when assigned to a system of reference, say a fixed star. Simplifying as much as possible, when employing mechanical laws, physicists sometimes resort to idealizations of conditions, such as the concepts of a "mass point" or of "frictionless motion." Scheler singles out four cases where formal mechanics has been misunderstood.

1. Concerning materialism he furnishes seven shortcomings: a) materialism fails to see that all physical mechanisms are relative to a knowing subject; b) materialism recognizes that all mechanism is relative to pure logic, but it fails to see that the laws of logic cannot be

explained by mechanical laws; c) materialism fails to see that there is, besides sensory perception and intuition, also non-sensory perception and intuition like that of a "*gestalt*" or of structures that are the condition for sensory perception and for intuition; d) materialism does not recognize that mechanism is relative to empty space, time and motion. The latter are "fictional" and do not exist without human reason and general life. In this, Scheler will present to us his own philosophy of time and space that turns out to be compatible with Einstein's theory of relativity; e) materialism fails to recognize that organic life cannot be reduced to mechanisms; f) materialism fails to see that mechanisms are relative to the technical goals set by living beings who want to dominate nature in ways that are at least minimally pragmatic; g) materialism fails to see that every formal-mechanical representation has only one value: a symbolic interpretation of nature by way of signs. Symbolic interpretation as little determines "what" the states of affairs holding among things are as an address book would tell me anything about the character of people listed. The sevenfold relativity of formal-mechanical nature leads one to one conclusion: materialism elevates the status of formal-mechanical laws to be a "thing in itself." It therefore overestimates such laws (VIII 242-4).

2. Concerning his critique of the value of formal-mechanical laws, Scheler refers to the philosophies of Descartes, Spinoza, Hobbes, Herbart, Wundt and Schlick and the Marburg School of Kantianism saying that if one in fact does admit science to be vital-relative to a knowing subject, contrary to materialism, one can also be easily led to assume that "to think about the world" and "to think mechanically about the world" are one and the same. But such identity is unlikely to be the case. For laws of pure logic are compatible with both a formal-mechanical and a non-mechanical universe. Indeed, pure logic would be compatible even with an absolutely chaotic and ever changing concept of being. The assumption of a coincidence of thinking about the world, and of mechanically thinking about it, for Scheler contradicts the findings also of H. Driesch: that it is *not* the concept of a formal-mechanical world that coincides with thinking it, but a "monistic ideal of order" that coincides with thinking about the world. This disproves that the world is ultimately formal-mechanical in principle.

3) The stated view is different from Kant's because of the theory of apriority, subjectivity, and the forms of intuition of space and time in Kant's philosophy. True, Kant lead the way in seeing that pure logic also applies to worlds other than a mechanical one and recognized

that "things in themselves" have no cognitional value because space, time and motion are only inherent in the respective forms of human intuition. But in this, Kant and Kantianism at the same time obstructed the emergence of a true theory of space and time and the foundation of theoretical physics; that is, a theory that shows that space and time are vital-relative to general life, and drives, before they can possibly be forms of intuition. From the very beginning, Kant assumed that the formal-mechanical view of the world was universally valid, including being valid in empirical psychological life.

4. An evaluation of the formal-mechanical conception of nature is offered with regard to Mach (1838-1916) whose theories had already been scrutinized in *Formalism*. Because Scheler's critique of Mach is mostly of historical interest and because Mach's theory had already been subject to criticism in his own time, we can for our purposes summarize Scheler's position.

Whereas the relativism of formal-mechanism had largely been inflated in the theories of (1) materialism; (2) the assumption of a coincidence between it and thinking; and (3) Kantianism, Mach's assessment of it largely underestimates the significance of relativism of formal mechanism. This is because the true positivists of the time did not only explain formal mechanism as relative to the biological science and practical tasks designed to gain control over nature but also saw it as merely historically relative in that they considered it to be a transient phenomenon in the history of science. This is one reason why Mach rejected any ideal of a formal-mechanical explanation of nature and sought to replace it with purely mathematical and geometrical descriptions.

In this, Mach even went so far as to question the reality outside sensations, including atoms and metaphysics, because they fail to obtain in the principle of verification. In his *Analyses of Sensation* (1886) he regarded matter, including the self, as a complex of sensations. All concepts are nothing but shorthand symbols for classes of sensations. These explanations are nothing but the reduction of something unknown to something relatively known, such as measurable data of sensation, by way of a minimum of steps in thinking, or by way of parsimony, an economic way of thinking.

Scheler's critique of this is based on Max Planck's (1858-1938) quantum theory, that says that the magnitude of a quantum of radiant energy of a given frequency is equal to the product of the frequency multiplied by the constant "h." This "h" is the smallest effect in nature and, as such, must be essential in a philosophy of nature. The principle of the smallest effect, however, not only pertains to the mechanics in inanimate nature but also to animate nature and life (VIII 255). In this, natural science shows itself again as vital-relative, or relative to life in general. The Mach critique also restates Scheler's phenomenological position that there is also non-sensory intuition besides sensory intuition. This brings us full circle to the place science has in the order of foundation with the natural world-view: the formal-mechanical structure of objects is nothing but an idealization of what is given in the natural view of the world on which mechanical objects rest (VIII 259).

Regarding the concept of sensation to which Scheler alludes often in his writings, he tells us that both Kant and Mach were mistaken in their assumption that sensations are purely receptive and primary in all experience. They supposed that sensations occur without a factor called "subliminal attention in drives" (*triebhafte Aufmerksamkeit*). Scheler's theory of sensation claims that sensations are not primary but *subsequent* to this subliminal attention of drives. He also calls it "pre-love" and "pre-interest." This pre-love or pre-interest is a schema that is *devoid* of sensation but not devoid of meaning. Sensations are subsequent to this subliminal attention that is at work in the drives because sensations are a "means" that "fill out" the schema (VIII 259).

A mechanical conception of nature gains significance for philosophy when new aspects of mechanical laws have been introduced by "methodic pragmatists" in specific areas. In theoretical physics they are Maxwell, Boltzmann, Lord Kelvin and the young Einstein. What characterizes methodic pragmatists is the reduction of formal mechanical natural phenomena to phenomena that are necessary, and in contrast to older rationalism, never univocal.

This means that in modern theoretical physics there is an infinite number of mechanical models possible that offer equivalent explanations. In this, the methodic pragmatists share the viewpoint of philosophical pragmatists that the axioms and principles in formal mechanics are neither univocal within their contexts nor do the propositions that formulate them contain truth by and in themselves. Axioms and principles are carefully selected "implicit definitions" that do not allow for logically contradictory propositions.

This line of thinking also pertains to matter and forces: they are relative to the explanation given of them in a particular field. There are no absolute building blocks of matter for the scientific theory of cognition. But there are three questions that Scheler addresses in order to uncover the philosophical implications in the reduction of necessity, possibility and absence of univocity:

1. Why must there be a formal mechanical reduction of nature?
2. Why must this reduction always be possible?
3. Why can it never be univocal?

His answers to these questions hinge on two points: (a) he intends to provide common ground between his wide knowledge of theoretical physics and the base of his metaphysics, that is, the concept of vital energy or "impulsion"; (b) His answers rest on the concept of motion.

1. If it is true that sense perception and thinking cannot take place without a vital energy of impulsion and drives that account for the ongoing activity of perception and thinking, one must come to the following conclusion: no object can be perceived unless it stimulates movement in an organism which in turn exercises a *counter*-movement or a "motoric conduct" against objects and thereby resisting objects.

In this circle of movements that come upon us and are countered by our organic capacity to move against and resist them, all initial perception and its contents is embedded: the contact with nature first takes place in a direct or indirect stimulant (*Reiz*) that affects our motoric conduct. Phenomenologically, however, there is not an "intentional" relation but only one of causation between motoric conduct and objects moving toward the organism. Whether or not a perception fits a thought that is formulated about reality, does not matter at this point. Scheler wants first to establish the initial biological function of motion taking place between the two terms of contact. The answer to the first question can therefore be formulated like this: the necessity of formal mechanic explanations of nature lies in the consequence of the fact that no perceptions and conceptions are possible unless there is a capacity for moving within us that goes against a movement coming from the outside. Scheler's motoric theory necessitates the conclusion that the devising of a mechanical model based on motion allows us to conceive of phenomena as either produced directly by us or as having been produced indirectly by objects. Scheler also believes that this motoric theory underlies the physical theories of Maxwell and Boltzmann. Boltzmann developed a method, among others, that states that there can be arbitrary presuppositions in mechanics from which we choose in such a fashion that theories and scientific facts already known to us can be deduced from arbitrary propositions that such models contain. That is, these models are neither *a priori* nor evident. Boltzmann formulated this state of affairs by saying that it is neither logic nor metaphysics that decides what is true or false: only a scientific fact can do so. In looking at technological accomplishments, Boltzmann says, we must not consider them to be just by-products of science but as being logical proofs. Without technical accomplishments we would have no means to practice scientific deductions. And only deductions made from technological accomplishments are correct and promise practical success, which neither pure logic nor metaphysics can guarantee.

Most important for philosophy is the implication that the motoric theory of perception and thinking processes has with regard to space, time and motion: it reverses their relationship and order of foundation. Whereas for Newton space and time were infinite, extant containers in which motion was said to occur; and whereas for Kant space and time were subjective forms of intuition making motion possible, in contemporary theoretical physics it is *motion* that determines space and time. All statements about space and time must be anchored in motion and the experience of it in order to avoid false conclusions.

2. This implies the answer to the second question: on the basis of the motoric theory of perception and thinking, a formal-mechanical reduction is "always possible" because of the new order of foundation. A mechanical model is always possible because during thinking and conceiving of the relations in formal mechanical models the phenomenon of motion is the presupposition of space and time. It is therefore the experience of the meta-biological motility in us and of exterior motion that warrants the possibility of formal-mechanical reductions and models.

3. But motility also implies that an infinite number of mechanical models can always be designed for a particular state of affairs and that none of them is ideal or absolute. For models are not copies that are congruent with the part of reality to which they pertain but only constructions that establish a coincidence between what we can expect from them and future perceptions. One may think, for instance, of the "corpuscular" and "wave" models of the atom. In their own right, each model has the role of coinciding with perceptions made during and after the different arrangements of the experiments.

But the opposite of what has been said also turns out to be acceptable: if there were indeed one ideal and univocal model one could still think of types of nature entirely different from the nature in which we live while the ideal model could also hold in each of them. There is no one-to-one relation between models and their objects. In either case—that is, one ideal model and different natures or one state of affairs and an infinite number of models for it—the models as such are equivalent. Choosing among them depends only on criteria such as simplicity, purposefulness, advantage of logical explanation or economic expediency.

Scheler asks, however: is the philosophical conception implicit in this lack of univocity among formal-mechanical reductions any different from Einstein's general theory of relativity? The relativity of the magnitudes of space, time, and motion with regard to the motion or standpoint of an observer in a four-dimensional space-time continuum amounts to saying that every phenomenon in nature can be explained by way of an infinite number of mechanisms. It is only the *Lorenz transformation* that describes how, in the special theory of relativity, mathematical measurements of space, time, motion and other physical quantities differ for two observers who are in a uniform relative motion. It combines different conceptions of the world into a *logical* unity; only in this way must it be regarded as absolute.

The new formal mechanical conception of nature as based on both Planck's quantum theory and Einstein's theory of relativity solicits a philosophical rethinking of nature (VIII 147/PR 148-149; VIII 267-282). Scheler's arguments are fragmentary because a complete coverage of this topic was planned to be part of his metaphysics, which was not completed before he died. Nevertheless, he provides us with clues for his projection of a "new metaphysics" which in his sociological thought cannot be dissociated from the two major cultural units of East and West. Let us here remain with his philosophy of science.

All philosophical theory of a corporeal world and extended substance has entered a new stage with the arrival of non-Newtonian science. If an extended substance turns out or is proven to be an "objective appearance" that stems from physical forces, the traditional distinction made between primary and secondary qualities will no longer be a valid one. And if reality is given first as *resistance against* acts of *vital movement* and if reality is given *prior* to corporeity and its qualities of duration, color, *gestalt*, etc., then such a theory of reality *qua* resistance coincides with the findings of modern theoretical physics and the formulations of its ultimate subject areas. But there are two possible directions metaphysical thought can take:

(1) One can take a subjective position that the changeability of extensive magnitudes of bodies as well as relations among magnitudes, such as those of "before-after," are relative to the standpoint of an observer and have, therefore, subjective meaning.

(2) One can take an objective view that, for example, secondary qualities—long thought to be residual in the human body—are also

as independent of the biological organization of humans as are the primary qualities, such as mathematical qualities. This view allows an equivalence between primary and secondary qualities: both are the result of *force centers* and reveal themselves to us as "objective appearances" or, as Scheler more often puts it, as "*Bilder,*" that I render as "phantasmic images" stemming from physical force centers. Physical force centers, along with "vital forces," are unextended constituents of impulsion in which primary and secondary qualities are still indistinguishable. Further, space and time cannot be subjective forms of intuition or existing forms of the physical universe but must be riveted in the force of impulsion or "*Drang.*"

This was Scheler's view. He was consistent enough to draw the conclusion that it is not only humans that fall under this pattern of thought but also animals and plants that must share in the phantasmic images that emanate from the forces of impulsion that underlie all life—no matter how different the images of space and time in them may be from our own. His metaphysical argument is rooted in meta-physics and meta-biology that lead to a pure metaphysics. We can also see that despite Scheler's involvement in the new theoretical, non-Newtonian physics, which summarizes his own view, his position is nevertheless more meta-biological than meta-physical.

Scheler argued that his position must be an acceptable one if one agrees that there is a universal agent of life, namely impulsion. Increasingly, Scheler's philosophy will foreshadow the present-day relative distinction made between inanimate and animate matter as evident in the area of virology or in regard to the limited validity of causality in the restricted field of human perception by comparison to the universal base of statistical lawfulness that holds throughout the atomic sub-world that is beyond human perception. In short, the traditional distinction between inanimate and animate matter is becoming blurred.

While the idea of a universal agent of life, impulsion, is not, however, the result of speculative thinking, in "Cognition and Work" Scheler shows that without the idea of a universal life-agent one gets into conflict with certain modern theories of physics. Much as he tells us that his point will be presented later in his *Metaphysics,* he does give us two interesting arguments here in its support. If there is not believed to be a universal impulsion (1) all formal mechanism in science is "*subjective, human* construction" that serves human purposes, and (2) "laws in nature" would be even less meaningful. In this case, there must be "*subjective restrictions*" of expectations of practical principles of "*work*" to investigate nature in certain perceptions so that certain new perceptions can be gained and come within the realm of experience.

If, however, there is assumed to be a universal life agent of impulsion then formal mechanical systems turn out to be *relative* to impulsion in comparison with physical systems of functions and of organs relative to the whole of the organism. Formal mechanical systems, in this case, would have an intermediate "*sense*" with which impulsion and drives "construct" phantasmic images whenever the inorganic forces are in the process of stimulating universal impulsion. Accordingly, laws of nature as expressed in formal mechanical systems would only be *statistical* or laws of the greatest number (VIII 271-273).

Pragmatism proves to be correct in all of this: our belief in formal mechanical laws of nature has neither a deductive nor any inductive foundation; nor is this belief a condition for experiencing the measurable sequences of objective time. The belief is only a consequence of "*selections made in the uniformity of time*" and, as such, co-determined by the needs of *living* beings and their drive-structure. Within the human milieu or environment, forms of things emerge (*herausgestalten*) according to this selection and uniformity of time and, consequently, are there for human perception. Most important is the fact that formal mechanical laws of nature have no ontic significance. They are not "in" nature but are precisely laws whose validity is relative to biological and practical factors.

There are also laws of nature that are not relative to life. They are the laws of pure logic, analysis, topology and (phenomenological) interconnections of essences as well as *gestalt*-laws. It is only they that are the proper object of a "philosophy of nature." After having discussed the relativity of formal mechanical systems as relative to life, Scheler briefly suggests that other types of knowledge with which humans can comprehend nature must at least be mentioned. These types have unfortunately been more or less overlooked in favor of scientific knowledge and its goal of control over nature which is prevalent in Western civilization. Despite its accomplishments, this knowledge also contributed to a formidable "*alienation from nature*" (VIII 278).

There are four other types of knowledge that do not relate to nature as an object of exploration and control but which allow humans to be "one with nature." First, there is philosophy of nature itself in the sense of dealing with purely logical laws, analysis, topology, intuition of interconnections of essences and *gestalt*-laws. Second, there is the history of nature (*Naturkunde*) that sufficiently describes cognition of phantasmic images of nature that ultimately stem from impulsion. Thirdly, there is knowledge of nature in the emotive understanding in which nature is a field of expression with which the human unites. Scheler familiarized us earlier with this knowledge in his treatment of *sympathy*, in particular, his analyses of "emotive identification." Fourthly, a metaphysics of nature would have to combine and seek common ground in all knowledge of nature, including Asian ways of thinking, among them the Indian techniques of becoming one with nature. These must be studied in order to approximate a globally acceptable knowledge of nature.

5) Theory of Perception:
Transconscious Phantasmic Images (Bilder). Perception, Sensation

At this point in the treatment of "Cognition and Work" it is obvious that Scheler's thinking on the subject is obfuscated by numerous digressions and the use of concepts that were not given clear explanation. Among them there are those of impulsion, of space, time and his own conception of pragmatism *per se* which is interspersed with a number of metaphysical arguments of his own that lack direct references to Peirce and James. Indeed, the German text makes for difficult reading; this must be compounded when the account is rendered in English.

The reason for this lies in the fact that Scheler *presupposes* that the reader will have a familiarity with a number of conceptions in the essay he had begun dealing with while working on *Metaphysics* and *Philosophical Anthropology*. At times it appears that he was not aware of this and, knowing that he was always working on several books or essays at the same time as his second wife Maerit wrote me, he failed to pay attention to his readers' situation and provide them with appropriate help. Among those terms relatively unexplained is that of "phantasmic images," equally ambiguous in English, to be sure, as its German counterpart, *Bilder*.

Within the context of the theory of perception, we are in the position to obtain clarification of these terms with the aid of some texts that we examined earlier, as well as a few manuscripts of the posthumous *Metaphysics* and *Philosophical Anthropology*.

Before embarking on his challenging theory of human perception, Scheler tells us that up to this point knowledge of nature has been shown to be productive for man's practical life, for the realization of values of life and their implicit biological purposes. But until now this result was seen only in light of the formal mechanical aspects of nature. On this basis, there remain for Scheler two questions to be resolved: (1) Does this productive knowledge occur merely accidentally in history, and (2) is it also accidental that knowledge of nature becomes purer the less it is relative to life, to biological purposes and to formal mechanics? In other words, are the ancient Greeks correct in holding that pure knowledge is always gained when the soul *turns away* from seeking power and control over nature and, accordingly, that one ought to direct oneself toward *love of the whole world?* Leibniz had the latter view in mind when he said, "*je ne méprise presque rien,*": "I despise almost nothing." This question of access to pure knowledge that pragmatism, on the one hand, and theoretical philosophy, on the other, necessarily bring with them can find a solution only if the *essence of reality* itself can be determined as resistance of internal and external states of affairs over against those human impulses of striving, drives and volitions.

If the essence of reality can be determined, then the essence is a pragmatically conditioned knowledge that controls nature and knowledge's relation to the primary experience of resistance. The essence of reality is not a relation of pure or theoretical knowledge to nature. If this were the case, it would also uncover a grave misconception in philosophy when idealism and realism are juxtaposed. Whereas idealism holds that the whatness itself of objects can in fact solely be given in the mind, it incorrectly infers that transcendent reality, too, must be in the mind. Idealism holds that there is no transcendent reality independent of the mind, as exemplified by Berkeley's equation *esse = percipi.* Whereas realism holds that the existence of objects is transcendent to the mind and, as such, is not given in it, it incorrectly infers that the whatness of objects is separate from mind and reflected in it only by way of symbols or images (VIII 287; IX 186).

If in light of Scheler's theory of reality *qua* resistance the tenets of idealism and realism are indeed misconceptions, then the techniques and methods that the mind uses in controlling and working with nature need to be examined. Husserl tried to do this in his "phenomenological reduction," but he failed completely because he conceived "something real" to be merely "having a place in time" (VIII 282).

On the basis of what he had established thus far in "Cognition and Work," Scheler informs us now with what the Husserlian reduction must be replaced: a technique for achieving levels of knowledge of essence. The technique will allow us (1) to set aside or *bracket the acts* in which resistance is given, and (2) the technique will allow us, conversely, *to infuse* the love of being and values that entities possess and in which they appear. A theory of reality is therefore the *foundation* for both pragmatic knowledge and pure, theoretical knowledge, in philosophy (VIII 282). It is for this reason that Scheler remained occupied with the theory of reality until the end of his life. The major treatment of it is contained in his 1926/27 five part treatise, "Idealismus—Realismus" (IX 183-340/PE 288-356).

What then does Scheler's theory of drive-conditioned perception look like? He frequently refers to it also as the theory of drive-motoric conditions of perception. He tells us that the theory is not his alone, but that traces of it can be found with Duns Scotus, Berkeley, Fichte, Dilthey, Reid, Jacobi, Bouterweck, Schopenhauer and Schelling (IX 209-210). In "Cognition and Work" he stresses again that Maine de Biran, Bergson and the psychologist Münsterberg are forerunners of it. Münsterberg was an early acquaintance of Scheler's who taught at Harvard. We mention especially these last three thinkers because Scheler considered them to be pragmatists on account of their involvement with the theory of reality *qua* resistance. This casts some light on the aforementioned observation that Scheler's very concept of pragmatism had not been sufficiently elaborated. But we now see that the theory of reality is perhaps part and parcel of Scheler's concept of pragmatism. If so, it goes beyond what he had learned from Peirce and James. In many respects this state of affairs will prove to be true.

Scheler makes a general statement when he begins to articulate his theory of perception that the functions of the senses of seeing, hearing, smelling, etc., and their respective organs are not to be regarded as "instruments" for gaining knowledge of nature. They are only the processes that regulate our actions toward nature and are thus not distinguished from other organic functions. All the senses function in the service of contributing to an optimal life of the whole of the organism.

Scheler distinguishes the *contents of perception* from sense functions. A content of perception is a *segment* that comprises a part of the content of the intuited whole of a thing's whatness. However, the perceived segment belongs only to things in the natural world-view or the human milieu. The segments of perceived contents are, therefore, vital-relative to both the organism and natural objects that have effects on the organism. Of central importance in Scheler's theory of perception is his well-founded contention that it presupposes at least a minimum of passive *attention* that is regulated by drives. Without drive-conditioned attention, without the concomitant "value-ception," and without an inception of a motoric (*motorische*) process there can be no perception. Scheler does not develop this line of thought in a systematic fashion. Accordingly, in our treatment we follow the order of foundation existing between the three components of general perception, namely, the phantasmic images of bodies, perception and sensation.

After having gone through an analysis of a number of false concepts of sensation that have prevailed in Western philosophy since Democritus, Scheler offers an explanation of the aforesaid phantasmic image and then makes distinctions in the concept of sensation. He does not go into the details of reality *qua* resistance as one would have expected at this point.

The phantasmic images of bodies (*Körperbilder*) must not be identified with the content of a perception. Phantasmic images are: (1) transcendent, in which case they stem from physical force centers, and (2) in given consciousness, but only inadequately. Their number seems to be as infinite as bodies themselves. Motion, space, time and extension are held to be phantasmic images. Scheler provides a definition of the image in his posthumous *Metaphysics*:

> I understand a phantasmic 'image' to be the quintessence of *all* possible visual, tactile, etc., segments of a thing but not in the division of their modality but in their concrete interwovenness. *This image we never have* but it is intended in every sensory intuition. It is the product of phantasy working in the impulsion from which it is continuously produced. It would continue to exist even if it were not perceived by humans (or animals).

> These images are 'ideal'—yet transcendent to consciousness, and objective—they are objective appearances, manifestations of the forces residual in impulsion which 'express' and 'represent' themselves in them. They can be understood (XI 132).

In *Formalism* an example for such an image is furnished, although Scheler in this first period of production rarely used the term "images" and "impulsion." He distinguishes the levels of perception of a cube (II 74-5/F 55). One "sees" a cube first as a "whole," that is not yet split into perspectival sides, inner material, etc. This whole also contains invisible aspects of the cube. That the cube is visually given pertains only to partially visual elements of the content of the perception of it. But the whole is not dependent on the senses in its initial presentation to us: it is the cube's phantasmic image. (This analysis is more or less comparable to a Husserlian *eidos* except that Husserl did not treat either the vital image's relativity to impulsion nor the absence of sensory data and the basis force centers have.) This initial phantasmic image does not give us any clue as to the cube's tangible materiality and its inside. In this whole image, the optical and physical aspects that are interwoven in the cube reveal its thingness only inasmuch as the cube is seen *as* this cube, *as* having colors and shadows on its surface. But *while* we are looking at it we are not aware of the act itself of seeing the cube. When we say that a thing is seen it always presupposes that the whole of the object is seen, no matter whether the whole is small, large, near or distant. Even in the field of sight, the differences of size and lengths and angles of perspectival sides are not measurable in the structure of the visual field itself. The differences are facets of the vital-relativity the cube has to a human lived body.

Scheler's argument that the phantasmic image of a body does not contain sense data depends, of course, on whether one sides with sensualism, which claims that sense data are indispensable for the cognition of objects. Scheler is certainly running counter with the general tendency of philosophy since Hume which either claims that sense data is indispensable to cognition or at least assigns sense data a cooperative function in the process of knowledge. Scheler would only agree with the latter point. He distinguishes the phantasmic image and a content of perception from "contents of sensation." Strictly speaking, sensations present themselves only when changes in the lived body occur. According to this model sounds and colors are not sensations, whereas hunger, thirst, pain, lust and fatigue are because they account for changes in parts of the lived body.

Sensations are actually "organic sensations" and cannot be precisely localized. For example, in the phenomenon known as referred pain, pain can be felt in places other than that where the pain originates. To enlarge the meaning of this, it can be said that sensations contain all those data of outer perception that can partake of changes of a given state of our lived body. Sensations are not objects or contents of intuition as are colors and sounds. In hearing a bell ring, the physical sound waves hitting the eardrum must be distinguished from the "sound." In the former level of stimuli there are no sounds; in the latter there are no waves. Yet, both do belong to the phantasmic image. Sensation is a "direction" of a change or variation of both exterior and interior (organic) appearances dependent on an individual's lived body. Therefore, a "pure" sensation, by and in itself, can *never be* given. It is only a "name" given for "variable relations" that obtain between a state of the lived body and appearances of our exterior and interior world (II 77/F 59; VIII, 316-327).

The elucidations of the phantasmic images of bodies presented in "Cognition and Work" converge in a general *gestalt*-philosophy within which Scheler explicates phantasmic images. Let a general remark be made concerning gestalt-philosophy. It is often hard to distinguish it from gestalt-psychology.

According to *gestalt*-philosophy, our natural view of the world consists of organized wholes that can be broken into various parts, down to the data of sensations. The organized wholes are not built up from data of sensations or discrete impressions. As a rule, reality in *gestalt*-philosophy is understood as that to which an organism can respond during perceptions and sensations. An example of a simple *gestalt* occurs when we drive toward blinking red railroad lights that warn of an oncoming train. In seeing the blinking lights they are perceived as *moving* right, left, right, left, etc., yet their mechanical functions are stationary. In seeing them in motion, however, their *gestalt*, is *more* than their stationary status.

The essential particulars of phantasmic images of bodies reveal the structure of what they convey. These particulars do not build a sum which would compose the image, nor are they the result of a sum of sensations—except in limited cases that depend upon the organization of a species. Perception does not bring images forth or create them: they are "trans-conscious." Ultimately, they are effects of physical force centers but decomposed as such in perception. For example, the image of an object of astronomy is an appearance of basic force centers in, say, the moon's physical and chemical makeup. As a whole, the scientific image is not the perception of the natural view of the world. But perceived according to the natural view of the world, the moon is a human "milieu-moon," sometimes full, crescent, white, reddish, romantic or an art-object. This image is not contained "in" the moon of astronomy. Our milieu-moon is relative to the life of our psycho-physical organization and our relative position to it. This allows in perception only a decomposed moon of the milieu-moon features.

But—and this is a challenging and arguable point throughout Scheler's philosophy—the image of our milieu-moon, that is vital-relative to the human organization, is *not* "immanent in consciousness," as Husserl maintained. Rather, the image of the milieu-moon is coupled with the astronomical satellite "moon" and its dynamic physical and chemical force centers. This point, one can argue, is justifiable only on the condition that one does not "bracket" the realty of the astronomical moon. If all reality is, in fact, resistance against the receiving capacity of individual and universal impulsion, it takes a technique, not a method, in order temporarily to suspend the moon's astronomical reality. But a temporary phenomenological suspension does not destroy the physical moon. In this way Scheler can still contend that phantasmic images *must* have "trans-conscious" existence no matter how hard this is to conceive, that lay, as it were, between force centers and decomposing perception.

For this reason, phantasmic images *"pre-exist"* perception, just as the image of the astronomical moon has pre-existed. Of course, the decomposed image of the moon as humanly perceived ceases to exist with the death of a human being or human race as a whole. This is because the natural world-view, on the one hand, and the morphological structure of the human organism, on the other hand, are reciprocally and mutually intercontained (*Einpassung*) and fit into each other (VIII 295). This intercontainment does not have any effect on the image of the moon that stems from its force centers. In this argumentation, there is no room for either an idealism based on an immanence of consciousness or for a sensualism found among some pragmatists which holds that sensations provide the ground for perceptions and images.

As concerns the specific structure of the whatness implicit in phantasmic images of bodies, Scheler mentions quite a few, but does not, except in one case, go into details. We just enumerate them briefly. He argues that their structures are composites of infinite spatial and temporal divisibility, of color and shades, of distance to other bodies, of position and place, all of them being part of the ontic essence of a body's image. These and the following structures provide the scope out of which possible perceptions take segments and make cuts. They are not to be taken as measurable structures in objective sequential time, but as residual in the whatness of phantasmic images themselves.

The structure *within* phantasmic images reveal an *order of foundation* joined to all fortuitously existing bodies. This order exists quite independently of the frequency of experience. The following aspects comprise the structural whole of phantasmic images of bodies: (1) All bodies have as their foundation "extension," understood as a state of being and as action of "spreading out." This extension is not yet homogenous because it varies from one whatness to another. (2) This extension is followed by irregular fluctuating variations or shimmering (*Wechsel*). This type of variation we discussed in our treatment of Scheler's phenomenology when we stated that (3) reversible fluctuating variation yields spatiality and irreversible fluctuating variation yields temporality. (4) Spatiality is the possibility of movement; temporality is the possibility of self-modification. Modification and movement are prior to spatially and temporally fixed points between which they occur. (6) Movement and self-modification are the foundation of objective space and objective time. (7) The pre-spatiotemporal expanse is the foundation for (8) the space-time-*gestalt*. (9) Spatial *gestalten* are the foundation of all qualities, such as color, sound, heat, taste, smell, etc. A spatial *gestalt* determines which sensations are possible, while the time-*gestalt*, or rhythm, is the foundation of all pure modification of qualities. (10) The primary quality of spatial and temporal gestalten are colorations in which (11) bright and dark are privileged. There are other aspects of phantasmic images but Scheler does not explore them in detail because their ontic status is revealed in the analysis of that structure which is most important in phantasmic images of bodies: the *gestalt*.

It is at this point that Scheler becomes more convincing in his assertion that the images pre-exist perception. First, he reminds us that any amount of elements of sensations that are felt cannot account for an image. The image "round," for example, cannot be produced by a continuous repetition of respective sensations. Black ink has the same number of optical elements of sensation as a pencil or a raven have. Their *gestalt* in perception simply does not admit of empirical reductions. This point is borrowed by Scheler from the *gestalt* psychologist Köhler. It also supports the fact that a *gestalt* "functionalizes" itself in subsequent *gestalten*, indicating that physical, physiological and psychological *gestalten* collectively possess common ontological features.

As we indicated earlier it is not humans alone that perceive *gestalten*. Among the species of the animal kingdom *gestalten* are perceived, but always relative to the type and pattern of their motion and the structure of their perceptual apparatus. The type of motion and perception *"correspond"* to each other in each species, including the human species. Each living being has *gestalten* that are relative to the structures of its organism and perception. All the spatial experiences that animals have are individually and *biologically* conditioned and vital-relative.

For example, a privileged human *gestalt* is, in contrast to many other animals, the shortest distance between two points: the straight line, or a circle gestalt; for a snake it is not. A circle-gestalt may appear in perception, for instance, when three points forming a triangle turn in accelerating rotation into a circle. They may not do so with a snake. Human geometry as based on Euclid's axioms pertains only to human milieu-space and the human natural world-view. This geometry is a geometry that is relative-to-human-life as constituted in the mutual intercontainment of an erect organism with its specific motility and the perceptual structure of three-dimensional space in the natural world-view. The long-assumed universal validity of Euclidean geometry had been superseded by Einstein (VIII 304). Nevertheless, the experience of standing between parallel railroad tracks that appear to meet at the horizon necessitates one to assume that there is still a trace of non-Euclidean geometry to perception. Scheler's description of impulsion states that it is non-Euclidian.

6) The Condition of Perception: Drives

Scheler summarizes the hinges of his theory of perception: the pre-existence of images prior to perception; the priority of perception with regard to functions of senses; the priority of sense functions with regard to sensations (VIII 331).

This order of foundation has to be kept in mind in order to understand the claim that perception is conditioned by drives. The role drives play in perception, their interconnection with feelings, affectations and attention, as well as their role in all perceptive life, including representations, recollections, phantasy, and thinking, has in the past been underestimated. The reason for this is to be seen in the fact that drives are indirectly given to us because they belong to a living being's "inwardness." Inwardness is a category of psychic life without regard to how different in kind it may be among various species. But inwardness itself has two sides: unmediated and non-perceivable inwardness.

Let us take an example to illustrate the point. When we are hungry we experience our inwardness directly in being hungry. The hunger is there: it is unmediated and no perception is necessary. Unmediated inwardness is, however, a *consequence* of an *un*perceivable inwardness of drives. The drives are pre-given to hunger. Although Scheler does not explicitly say so, unperceivable inwardness must encompass all other drives, such as those of propagation or power. This is to say that although we do notice wellings (*das Rühren*) in drives, we do not notice the wellings in their inceptions. We only notice drives working in us *after* their inception.

The distinction between unmediated inwardness and unperceived inwardness has another consequence, namely, physical movements. From this it follows that both unmediated inwardness and the accompanying physical movements are riveted in the *un*perceivable layers of inwardness, namely, the dynamic factors of impulses, drives, inclinations, needs and interests. They are all grounded in the vital energy of *spontaneous* self-motion of life or the unity of all drives: impulsion. Scheler claims that this point is tantamount to a new conception of life that is not the result of empirical inductions as found in pragmatism. Scheler, departing from pragmatism, claims that "life is *psycho-physically indifferent*" (VIII 335). At life's roots the empirical distinction between its psychic and physical side does not hold, even if these two sides of life are conceived—as Scheler does—as inseparably conjoined: one being figuratively speaking convex the other concave. But the essence of life is pre-empirical: it is pure "becoming-un-becoming" (*Werden und Entwerden*), a process in which its two empirical sides are not yet separated. It is easy to see that this concept of life necessitates the idea that all animal and human perception is conditioned by "motoric-dynamic" structures of drives.

The drive-conditioned theory of perception is also supported by the fact that the motility of an organism determines its sensory apparatus. A lizard, for example, remains undisturbed by a gun shot but runs away from the slightest noise in the grass. An organism has an alphabet of senses that can serve as signs of luring and noticing objects that are meaningful for its drive-motoric behavior.

The distinction made between unmediated and unperceivable inwardness is roughly analogous to phantasy, which Scheler always assigns to impulsion. There is a reproductive and an original phantasy. The former contains elements of perception and representation. For example, a "golden mountain" contains elements of the perception of gold and of a mountain. But original phantasy is not composed of such elements: it is a "surplus" coming from the depths of the vital soul. Even though Scheler does not explicitly do so, we may identify the vital soul with the vital principle of life in us. In its origins this vital soul does not contain any tendency toward usefulness in practical life. It is the surplus of the essence of the still undifferentiated life itself and it is the primordial form of all perceiving life. Taken in this sense, all forms of creative and productive imagination as they are addressed by Kant, Fichte and Schelling are without question justified speculative notions.

Phantasy is more active the younger a human being is. A child's world is replete with phantasy. Phantasy diminishes with growing age. Phantasy can also serve as a mental corrective. But in essence it remains the productive factor that spans the fortuitous world of entities and cognition of essences. It spans impulsion, drives, and mind and is for this reason indispensable in perception. As such, it is indifferent to all opposites inherent in cognition: to true-false, beautiful-ugly, evidence-deception. Phantasy is the highest form of representation that the vital soul possesses (XI 42).

Original phantasy is the main locus of all phantasmic images. Original phantasy is located in impulsion. Bearing this point in mind, the entire theory of phantasmic images and of perception reveals a uniform consistency. This consistency comes to the fore when Scheler's posthumous *Metaphysics* is taken into consideration. Here it is said that the origin of images in the phantasy of impulsion first carries forward into drives which themselves function as part of the original impulsion. Second, drive images carry forward into parts or segments of perception (XI 252, 260). The example of two parallel railroad tracks that appear to "meet" at the horizon shows that the axiom of parallels in Euclidian geometry does not hold in human perception. This *supports* Scheler's argument (1) that impulsion is itself four-dimensional, (2) that drive images are *gestalt*-like and not measurable by mechanical means, and (3) that drive images are *identical* with their partial projections in perception.

All phantasmic images, Scheler says, are made of the same fabric of which dreams are made. As was stated earlier, the images have no existence but only transcendent presence. Figuratively speaking, phantasmic images "exist" between reality and spiritual being. This is why they are difficult to describe. Repeatedly Scheler attempts to get at their ontological status but does not gain a description of them that could be supported by evidence. Perhaps this deficiency is rooted in the nature of phantasmic images themselves. After all, they are not innate ideas underlying perception and thinking.

Phantasy, rather, creates something that could satisfy us only if its images *were* real: they are not. Instead of innate ideas, phantasy has at its disposal any and all non-sensory *a priori* contents: those of intuition, love, preferring values, willing and acting and the logical forms and pure mathematics (VIII 354-355). Perhaps, Scheler could have cast some more light on phantasy had he not only referred to mathematics but to those manifestations of pure phantasy found in compositions in "absolute" music found in Bach's solo violin Chaconne, Beethoven's Fourth and Seventh symphonies, Schumann's Fourth Symphony or Chopin's Étude, opus 25, no.12, only to mention a few. It is in such manifestation of the human capacity to create "*ficta*" that one can catch a glimpse of the hidden workings of phantasy and the span between the still "mental-blind" phantasy in impulsion and the phantasy tethered to the mind's *logos*.

The maze of intersections between impulsion, drives, titillations, sensations, perception and cognition, through which Scheler ventures to walk his readers, leads, however, to yet more evaluations of pragmatism. Pragmatism is right, Scheler concludes, that all actions and deeds take their starting point in the practical relationship existing between man and world. It is this practical relationship that has the highest significance for perception and cognition. Man's initial attitude toward the world consists in "working on the world" (VIII 362). This defines the roots of science and technology. Hence, it is work, not contemplation, that characterizes these roots. But in this pragmatism underestimates the philosophical attitude of cognition that severs such roots and neutralizes practice by "peeking at" (*spähen*) the realm of essences and the stream of impulsions, drives and physical force centers that "manifest themselves" in their respective phantasmic images.

In summary, it is *not* work that can lead to philosophical cognition but the suspension of the impulsion, drives and drive-conditioned perception that can do so. Philosophical cognition has three starting points devoid of "working on the world": *"The whole spiritual person must love absolute value and being; the natural self and ego must be humbled; self-mastery must be achieved;* in this way it is possible to objectify the instinctual impulses of life, which are "given" and experienced as "of the flesh" and which must needs exert a constant influence on natural sensory perception." (V 89/E 95)

The overcoming of the tension between pragmatic and philosophical cognition initiated by these three basic attitudes of the mind is the place of the unity of person as the bearer of five value-ranks, ranging from those of divisibility to those of spirit, human or Divine.

CHAPTER IX

THE LAST VISION: THE BECOMING OF GOD, OF WORLD, AND THE COSMIC PLACE OF HUMAN EXISTENCE

Prefatory Remark

In the previous eight chapters, we have seen how Max Scheler cast light on various aspects and subject matters of philosophy such as ethics, love, intersubjectivity, religion, capitalism, phenomenology, sociology, and knowledge among others. We are now in the postion to see that there are two basic questions running through his thought which have been part and parcel of philosophy since ancient Greece: 1) What is the nature of the human being? and 2) What is the nature of the world in which we live? Or specifically, the question "What is Being?" Scheler shared with Kant the notion that all philosophy has laid too much emphasis on the question of Being at the expense of a clarification first of the nature of the human being.

In Chapter I, Scheler showed us how in his view the human being must be conceived primarily as a bearer of love. In Chapter II, we were shown how human beings are given to each other in certain kinds of intersubjective experiences. In Chapter III, the discussion continued by showing how humans live together in specific kinds of social forms said to be co-original in the constitution of the nature of the human. In chapter IV, we were told how human beings relate to a supreme, absolute and totally other existence, God. In Chapter V, a number of consequences were pointed out that result from the main tenet of the first chapter, namely, that human moral being rests on true or deceiving emotive experience which itself is primordial to will and reason. In Chapter VI, Scheler described the state of modern society as being largely determined by values of usefulness and pleasure values, which is part of the mind-set of "Capitalism." Chapter VII showed the basic tenets of Max Scheler's phenomenology on the basis of which he had gained the results accomplished during his first period of productivity.

Chapter VIII, however, pointed to the beginning of a fundamental change from what had thus far been discussed. Scheler began to search for general metaphysical foundations giving special attention to the human condition in the twentieth century. His struggle to this end is an unswerving and arduous attempt to get across for us the point that the human being, and being in general, must be comprehended as being anchored in two pairs of opposite principles: spirit (*Geist,*) and urge (*Drang*), or as we preferred to render the latter German term, "impulsion." As had been suggested in previous chapters, these principles manifest themselves in the human being first in terms of a very slowly growing interfusion of mind and life. This interfusion will have to be extended into their metaphysical dimension, without which their cannot be human beingness as such.

With this, Scheler divorced himself from Descartes and the beginnings of modern philosophy purporting that there is an unbridgeable gap between mind and body, a philosophy that held that there are two heterogeneous substances: *res cogitantes* and *res extensae*.

At this specific juncture, it must be our first task to explicate the very relationship between metaphysics and philosophical anthropology; Scheler was the first to establish the latter as a philosophical discipline. This procedure is called for because of two reasons: (1) philosophical anthropology was at the point of becoming a "fashion" during the twenties and later; (2) there have been many suggestions about what philosophical anthropology is supposed to be.

Paragraph 10 of Heidegger's *Being and Time* (1927)—the book that had one of the greatest impacts on twentieth century philosophy—speaks of contemporary tendencies toward philosophical anthropology. According to Heidegger, these tendencies are alleged to have two unfortunate presuppositions: the Aristotelian definition of the human being as a "rational being" and "Christian theology" that teaches that God created the human being in His own image. Concerning the latter's source, Heidegger specifically refers to Genesis I, 16. Having these two origins, philosophical anthropology, Heidegger asserts, cannot bring into view ontologically the very being of human existence.

It is obvious for us now that Heidegger's mistake lies in the fact that Scheler's philosophical anthropology can neither be based in Aristotle nor in Genesis I, 16. We already saw that both a Creator-God and the concept of an Aristotelian substance had been rejected by Scheler and, furthermore, that he was on the way of envisioning the becoming of God, and that earlier in his Ethics he had established the idea of a self-executing existence of the person bare of a substance. Heidegger may not have realized the negative impact he had made on understanding Scheler's intentions in the area of philosophical anthropology. Heidegger must, however, have been aware of his own mistaken position because he must have had some familiarity with Scheler's publications that were available at the time and

the growing publicity surrounding Scheler's philosophical anthropology and metaphysics projected in various lectures. Let me make
two points on the matter.

Heidegger told me an episode that he had personally witnessed.
There was a gathering among luminaries affiliated with phenomenological philosophy. Scheler was not present, but did arrive an hour or
so later. He did not offer the traditional European handshakes to all
present but remained standing in the door, proclaiming loudly, "God
is extended" ("*Gott ist ausgedehnt*"). He went on with a dramatic speech
that held all present spellbound, including Husserl who was standing in a corner of the room, one elbow resting on the other arm,
pensively holding his hand to his chin, according to Heidegger. The
very statement alone that "God is extended" could certainly not be
seen by any philosopher as coming from Aristotle or a traditional
Christian theology.

Another instance, too, would contradict Heidegger's false characterization of philosophical anthropology. On April 14 and April 30,
1927, there was a conference in Darmstadt under the title, "*Mensch
und Erde*" (Man and Earth) given by its sponsor Herr Graph von
Keyserling. Scheler was the keynote speaker and presented a paper
"*Die Sonderstellung des Menschen*" (Man's Special Place). The manuscript of the paper later served as the text of "*Die Stellung des Menschen
im Kosmos*" ("Man's Place in Nature"). The lecture-hall in Darmstadt
was packed and remained so until Scheler finished after over three
hours of lecturing on impulsion and spirit, the becoming Deity, and
the human being as "*weltoffen*." It is possible, of course, that the well
known "*Die Stellung des Menschen im Kosmos*" failed to get Heidegger's
attention. But this is unlikely because after Scheler's death in 1928,
Heidegger lead a group of scholars helping Scheler's widow to organize the posthumous materials in preparation for publications.

It is hard to imagine that *Die Stellung des Menschen im Kosmos* had
escaped Heidegger's attention. He never made the appropriate corrections in later editions of *Being and Time* concerning Scheler's philosophical anthropology. Heidegger also criticized Scheler's concept of
"resistance" in *Being and Time*. When Scheler read Heidegger's book,
he entered about two hundred marginal notes in his copy. Scheler's marginal pertaining to Heidegger's critique of resistance is crisp: "This does
not pertain to me." Heidegger appears to have remained unaware of
Scheler's concept of absolute time, which will be discussed below.

Throughout the investigation of Scheler's philosophy to this point
we have used the term "fragment" on various occasions implying
that his research in many areas remained unfinished. In particular,

both his projected major works, the *Philosophische Anthropologie* and *Metaphysik* indeed did remain fragments because he died while working on them. Since both remained fragments let us briefly look into the essence of a fragment. This will help us to grasp the unfinished character of these works.

It is the nature of a fragment that all the parts missing from it belong to a fragment itself. The reverse also holds: all the parts that are missing likewise belong to a fragment at hand. Concerning the philosophical fragments of Scheler's that we will discuss, this means that *whatever the missing parts do not tell us belong to what the given parts do tell.*

Fragments reach into a *whole* containing parts that no longer speak to us. This state of affairs pertains to all bits and pieces of fragments that once formed an indeterminate whole. Not only do broken up rocks and debris point to their wholes (for example, that of a temple); fragments of mind have the character of wholes that are concealed but to which the fragments once belonged. As an illustration we may say that whenever we ask a question like, "what do you mean?" we inquire into a whole of which the parts are not explicitly addressing us. Nevertheless, those parts do, in fact, address us somehow because otherwise we could not ask such a question as, "what do you mean." The concealed whole does address us through the very fragmentary bits and pieces that prompt the question.

In this sense, the whole of Max Scheler's later philosophy must be filled out with as many bits and pieces as possible: the pieces must be placed in the context of the whole that asks for its completion. In other words, the whole seeks to retrieve still missing parts from the fragments.

One must avoid, however, a preconception of a whole as given objectively, say, that of a picture-puzzle. Instead of filling an already given whole like a picture puzzle out with pieces belonging to it the whole we have in mind can only become translucent *in* the fragmented parts. Regarding the *Philosophische Anthroplogie* and *Metaphysik* the whole must in this sense itself come to the fore—no matter how vaguely—*through* its fragments. It is with this intention of making the whole translucent that we will concentrate on fragments in question, such as those on absolute time, the nature of an idea, evolution, the structure of spirit, meta-physics, meta-biology and impulsion, metaphysics, the ground of being, and death.

First, however, it is incumbent on us to clarify what Scheler's understanding of metaphysics and philosophical anthropology and on their interrelation.

1) Clarification of Terms:
Metaphysics, Philosophical Anthropology, Met-Anthropology.

In order to gain a suitable understanding of Scheler's last vision of the unity of man, world and the Deity we must first see what the disciplines of metaphysics, met-anthropology and philosophical anthropology themselves are.

Scheler entertains a rather traditional notion of metaphysics when it is seen in light of those thinkers who rejected metaphysics, such as Nietzsche and Heidegger, or by comparison with twentieth century analytic philosophy, existentialism and deconstruction.

Scheler draws a distinction between a metaphysics of first and one of second order. The metaphysics of the first order is based in Aristotle's "First Philosophy": it investigates the ontological structure of the world. For Scheler this is not yet metaphysics *per se*. According to him it only provides basic insights into "*Grenzprobleme*" (limit-problems) in that it confronts the question of the foundation of each particular discipline of knowledge. For example, such a question for biology is "what is life?"; for physics, "what is space?" or "what is matter?"; for mathematics, "what is a number?" or "what is infinity?" Such foundational questions cannot be answered in any particular discipline. In short, they cannot be answered in any discipline of knowledge outside metaphysics proper. What Scheler means by "*Grenzprobleme*" of the metaphysics of the first order pertains, therefore, to the limits of the foundation itself in each individual science or to the foundation of the objects of each discipline that are within its reach. Although the metaphysics of the first order is not metaphysics *per se*, it must of course have a link to the latter because the foundational questions can never be answered within their respective disciplines. For instance, the science of infinity, mathematics, need not raise nor claim to have an answer to the question of what infinity itself is. This question lies outside and beyond mathematical reaches of mathematical thinking. Therefore, the question of what infinity is one of "meta-mathematics." Metaphysics of the first order handles foundational questions as they are asked in meta-biology, meta-ethics, meta-history, meta-law or meta-physics. These meta-disciplines have the collective title of "meta-sciences," "*Metaszienzien*," as Scheler called them. He intended to investigate as many foundational question as possible, but left behind only fragments concerning meta-biology, meta-ethics and meta-physics. The linkage that metaphysics of the first order has to the metaphysics of the second order makes the former a "spring board" to the latter.

The diverse meta-disciplines demand a unity without which individual sciences would be hopelessly isolated. This unity makes possible such intersecting areas as chemical physics, physical biology, or in more recent times, bio-ethics, medical ethics and business ethics.

No matter how different the questions among the meta-disciplines, their unity is residual in *that* being in whom all foundational questions and quests intersect: the human being. The study of the place of this intersection is called "met-anthropology."

The human being is the bearer in whom all levels of being, namely, mind, soul, life and inanimate matter, meet. Scheler was relatively supportive of Aristotle's idea that man is quasi everything (XII 17). In addition to this, there is a partial correspondence between Being and the human being: Scheler did not elaborate this point. However, one can glean from his work a certain correspondence between Being and being human that holds for the successful application of scientific, logical and mathematical thinking relative to the universe. On the other hand, what does not correspond to Being are the exclusively human possessions or "monopolies" of freedom, language, domicile, building, conscience, duty, marriage, economics, law and clothing (XII 187-203). This brings us to the metaphysics of the second order.

What then is the function of met-anthropology? There are two functions. First, it is the "transition" leading from the unity that binds meta-disciplines and their various limit problems together to a metaphysics of the second order. Metaphysics of the second order is the metaphysics of the "absolute" or the metaphysics of an *ens a se*. Second, met-anthropology explicates the roots of and relations among, "*Letztsubjekte*" or "ultimate constituents." For example, how and in which order are the ultimate constituents of corporeal bodies, living beings, and persons, rooted in an *ens a se* ? Or how, for that matter, is the ultimate constituent of a physical field joined up with physical force centers and related to an *ens a se* or impulsion?

Surprisingly enough, Scheler does not question that there is an *ens a se*. He even tells us that the *ens a se* is the most evidential truth we have. This is because its existence follows from the evidentiality of the first metaphysical principle, namely, that there is something rather than nothing or "*nothing is not.*" The existence of all fortuitous entities in the world, that is, all relative beings, presupposes absolute Being. Despite the distinguished place this metaphysics of the second order has in philosophical thinking, it has nothing yet to do with the question of absolute Being itself: it elucidates only its attributes (XI 126).

We can now turn to the question: What is philosophical anthropology in Scheler's thought? Philosophical anthropology is intertwined with met-anthropology as the study of the intersections and the unity of all meta-disciplines. As such, philosophical anthropology is "between" the metaphysics of the first order and that of the second order. But in contrast to the many questions that are asked in them, philosophical anthropology asks only *one* question: it is *the* question of philosophy: "*Was ist der Mensch*," "What is the human being?" or "Who are we?" existing as we do on this tiny planet floating among billions of galaxies in an unimaginably vast universe.

This one question of who we human beings are suggests that it must not only be seen in light of pure philosophy but also within the context of the expansion of technology. We recall what we said earlier in this regard. We are familiar with pictures of our planet taken from outer space. Despite our planet's negligible size, it has the distinctive feature of shifting blue, white and sometimes reddish colors because of the life-giving layer of air. All scientific and literary visions, despite the human dreams of yore that there are other living beings somewhere else in the universe, we must face the possibility that Scheler faced, namely, that our planet alone possesses the subtle balance of life conditions.

If we are totally alone in the universe then philosophy would have to introduce a novel existential category of the human being: uncanny cosmic solitude. And if in a mental experiment, as we showed, we set aside for a moment the planet earth and all other celestial bodies and imagine human history floating alone through space and time, the question that immediately presents itself is why, in all the world, can humans be so destructive of their subtly balanced environment? Why do they hate and resent? Why are they so eager to make profit? Why can they be so selfish? The tranquillity of the skies and of celestial bodies visible from planet earth may be sublime, as Kant thought. Yet human history as seen floating through space and time is tragic. On the grounds of the tragedy of history is disorder of the heart that nevertheless points to something Divine that makes humans interiorly disquieted and prompts them to search for It.

Philosophical anthropology focuses on the essential nature of being human. In contrast to metaphysics and ontology, which pursue a path of thinking that is either directed toward Being or disclosed in or by Being, thinking in philosophical anthropology is a "reversed elongation" that extends from the constitution of the *human being* to absolute Being. In previous contexts, we have already become familiar with such principles and an implicit conceptualization of Being that these principles demand: the vital center of impulsion and the human spirit. It is these that Scheler seeks to "elongate" from the human being to an *ens a se.*

Scheler's philosophical anthropology accords with Kant's tenet that all philosophical questions meet in the question of who and what the human being is. Being itself and alone cannot provide a basis for an understanding of the "place" in the universe that human beings occupy. Hence, being must be seen from its very own base: the essential structure of the human being itself. The clarification of this structure is necessary because all previous attempts to determine both the essence and the origin of the human being have failed to lay it bare. Scheler writes that being human has become "problematical." We do not know who we are: yet we *know that* we do not know who we are (IX 120/P 65).

According to Scheler the question of "who we are" had been at the dawn of his thinking. Indeed, the question suffuses all his texts until his sudden demise (IX 9/M 3). This must be kept in mind in reading his posthumous philosophy. It must also be borne in mind that his last visions remained fragments, resembling scattered pieces of ruins whose original whole is given to us as a task.

In the texts of the philosophical anthropology, Scheler enumerates four areas that a determination of the essence of the human being has to cover:

(1) The relationship of the human being to inorganic nature, to plants and animals and to the "ground" of all things.
(2) The metaphysical origin of the human being and his physical, psychic and mental beginnings in the world.
(3) The clarification of the forces and powers that keep moving the human being, and the forces and powers that man himself moves.
(4) The possible and real basic directions of the human being's biological, psychic, mental, social and historic development, including the relation between body and soul (IX 120/P 64; XII 16-20).

A concerted effort in these areas will provide a firm foundation for all individual sciences that deal with the human being: the scientific sciences such as biology, the medical, pre-historical, ethnological, historical, social and psychological sciences and their subdivisions. All of these sciences converge in the nature of the human being which is to be clarified in a philosophical anthropology to be pursued without presuppositions.

Scheler's claim that a "reverse elongation" of the two principles of human existence, impulsion and spirit, implies that philosophical anthropology is a necessary foundation for both metaphysics and met-anthropology outlined above.

2) Philosophical Anthropology: General Discussion

There is a hidden order in the evolving complexity of Scheler's entire philosophy of the first and second period. This hidden order provides a footing for the unity of the life, mind and the spirituality of the human being. There is also another order that had already gradually emerged from the presentations thus far: an order in the unity of the becoming world and the becoming of God between which the human being is the dynamic transition (X 69/PE 5-6; X 236). Both orders consist in a *triad* of interrelated levels: (1) the level of what is relative to life or what is vital; (2) the mental level; and (3) a spiritual, divine level. These levels began to emerge in *Formalism* in terms of the stratification of vital, mental and spiritual values. This order of these levels reemerged in *Erkenntnis und Arbeit* as knowledge of control, knowledge of essences and knowledge of salvation. The triadic order is retained at the beginning of the posthumous manuscripts of both the *Philosophische Anthropologie* (XII 5-117), in *Die Stellung des Menschen im Kosmos* and in *Philosophische Weltanschauung* (*Philosophical Outlook*) (IX 7-71/M 3-95. IX 75-84/P 1-11).

Scheler also distinguished three types of humans. These types are primarily patterned after how humans have conceived, seen and understood themselves in the history of Western civilization. These three types of self-understanding are: (1) the idea that the human being has been created by God; 2) the idea that the human being is endowed with reason (*homo sapiens*); and (3) the idea that the human being is a tool-man (*homo faber*) as an end-product of evolution. These ideas largely determine a) the degrees of intensity and kind of faith in God, b) kinds of ethos, and c) social structures.

The triadic order pervades Scheler's works. Let us bring it into a relief.

Vital: acts - love - feelings - values - knowledge of control - tool man
Mental: acts - love - feelings - values - knowledge of essence - rational man
Spiritual: acts - love - feelings - values - knowledge of salvation - created man

This vital-mental-spiritual triad including the three forms of knowledge applies throughout the *Philosophische Anthropologie*. However, the main ideas that human beings have had of themselves, that is, human self-understanding in history, is not considered by Scheler to be the final word on the subject. The various historical aspects of self-understanding are too narrow. In light of his theory of the World-Era-of-Adjustment, all ideas of man will converge into one global human self-understanding that Scheler calls the "All-Man."

Scheler contends that the reason why the traditional ideas of man have been too narrow is that the human being must not be conceived exclusively philosophically, but also scientifically. Considerations should be given to aspects of evolution, biology, ethnology, psychology, the exact sciences, the medical science and sociology: they all belong to the unity of the human being and should not be omitted. One must, however, also face the fact that all the disciplines that deal with the human being reveal inconsistencies among one another. Therefore, one must avoid a fixed image of human existence suggested by these disciplines.

It can easily be seen that the philosophical ideas of human self-understanding are, like all scientific ideas, too narrow. The idea of the *homo faber*, for instance, fails inasmuch as it cannot account for the categories of good and evil. The same holds true for the idea of the *homo sapiens* which is too narrow in its explanation of the emotive character of moral existence. In particular, the idea of *homo sapiens* cannot account for the fact that the *ordo amoris* has "reasons of its own." While in *Erkenntnis und Arbeit* the idea that God created the human being had altogether been discarded, in the *Philosophical Anthropology* Scheler intensifies his own argument that God is in need of human existence in the first place to realize Himself historically.

Besides the ideas of human self-understanding, there had been many ideas that likewise proved to be insufficient. Some of them are La Mettrie's "*l'homme machine*," which is a self-understanding that appears in higher forms in the modern age of technology. Then there was Machiavelli's "power-man," Nietzsche's "over-man," Marx's "economic" man, Freud's "libido man" and Heidegger's "*homo curans*." All of these ideas designate particular aspects of what it means to be human. None of them is commensurate with the *flexibility* of human planetary existence. Scheler's main argument is that the nature of the human is not a "thing" that can be conceptualized. Human nature must be approached in the sense of a *direction* of cosmic becoming in which being human occupies a special, dynamic place. During a stay in Lausanne in September 1927, Scheler wrote the unfinished Part 5 of *Idealismus-Realismus*. He comes close to bringing into focus here the vision that the human being must be understood as a "direction" along with the becoming of world and the Deity:

Much as I assert that the being of 'world' is primarily history; much as I assert that access to all non historical forms of being can be gained from the nature of the world's essential historicity, and that historicity is rooted in both the constitution of the human being and that of the *ens a se* understood as the subject of the attributes of impulsion and spirit: I do assert that there is primordial time, and supremacy over history, in the being of the 'person' as a rational, spiritual individual. *A fortiori*, I assert also that this holds for the *ens a se*. Although the *ens a se* is in the state of becoming, it is not subject to time but becomes eternally by and for itself (IX 283).

The task of laying bare as many instances of human self-understanding as possible requires intense investigations into the various self-understandings we know, even when these appear to be far removed from philosophical thinking.

Scheler has sometimes been charged with going into elaborate scientific details instead of sticking to proper philosophical discourse. Heidegger charged him with biologism, while others regarded him primarily as a psychologist or sociologist. The fragment of his *Philosophische Anthropologie,* whose publication and scope has become known only in 1987 (XII, 5-382) gives textual underpinnings to a rethinking of Scheler's last vision and invalidate all premature criticism made of his last thoughts.

As to inconsistencies between philosophical anthropology and the natural sciences, we owe it to Scheler that they have at least been addressed. This, however, is one reason why Scheler had sometimes been charged with contradictions in his thought, in particular the idea of a dynamic human being advanced in *Philosophische Anthropologie*. On the one hand, we learn that the human cortex is the least developed phylogenetically in comparison to other organs. Vital functions have developed in unique ways. There are phylogenetic developments of parts of the brain that other animals do not show, as is the development of the forehead linked to human upright gait and the faculty of attention. The human brain uses tremendous amounts of heat energy which in turn channels energy away from other organs. The cortex itself is seen as the organ in which the development of life has come to a standstill. "Man is the slave of the cortex" and a "*dead end road*" of evolution (IX 94-6/P 23-25). In this most cerebral animal the longest of life-time of an individual is coupled with the shortest life-time of its species. The human species is an episode that did not exist long ago and which will soon cease to exist. Like any other species the human species, too, will fall victim to its natural "extinction" (*Artentod*) with the specification that the natural extinction of the human species will, by comparison to that of other species, occur at the fastest rate. The phylogenetic place of the human species reminds one of a caterpillar looking helplessly beyond the edge of a leaf near the top of a tree seeking rescue from a dreadful cosmic mechanism that surrounds it (V 105/E 109).

Yet, all such shortcomings are counterbalanced by traits that upon first sight look to be like contradictions to a human being as bearer of love and an *ordo amoris*, to the human being as invariably grounded in *both* spirit and impulsion, capable of knowledge of essence as well as being a bearer of the sphere of the Absolute.

Whereas the human being has the potential to bring under its control whatever is below its existence—energy, including the sun's, animals, plants and materials—it fails to bring under its control its very own existence. "For the first time, the human being feels *alone* in the universe" (V 105/E 109). This being also possesses, however, transcendence and the sphere of the Absolute. True, its existence as a whole is, phylogenetically, a *dead end road* but, ontologically, it is a "way out" (*Ausweg*) of it. Its "way out" is its "historicity." The human being does not only have a history but *is* historical. The historical aspect of the *Philosophische Anthropologie* describes the human's way out of its *dead end road*. Whereas the drive-life of the animal world is, as we saw, intercontained with the respective milieux in which animals live and which they can neither transcend nor change, the human being, can and does change adaptations to its milieu. *A fortiori*, the human being at every moment changes its historical world. Unlike any animal, the human being can emphatically hurl a "no" at its drives, its world and against God. The "*way out*" of the phylogenetic *dead end road* is the capacity of saying "*no.*" Therefore, as "*naysayer*" the human being is "world-open" (IX 32, 44/M 39, 52), that is, the opposite of the evolutionary *dead end road* of the cortex. Such are the incompatibilities that are inherent in human existence which Scheler, undaunted by their paradoxes, did not cease bravely to confront.

These antithetical traits in the nature of the human being are not contradictions. Scheler's view of the human being can account for these opposing traits in human nature and provide a glimpse of the breadth of his vision of man's dynamic place in nature.

3) Philosophical Anthropology: Specific Discussion
a) The Role of Human Self-Understanding in History

Because Scheler attaches so much significance to human self-understanding, which he argues lies beneath the various courses that history has taken and is taking, we must examine the reasons for this emphasis. There appear to be two reasons for stressing the argument of human self-understanding. (1) At no time in history has the determination of the essence and origin of the human race been more in question than it is today (IX 120/P 65). (2) In *Formalism* the pure exemplars of personhood were shown to be the quintessence of human history. They represent pure, personified outlines of the ranks of values. Through these outlines of exemplars humans also have a self-understanding in different ages and cultures (X 268/PV 140-141).

The first point provides a general and the second point the essential reason why the ideas of human self-understanding form the basis for the historical existence of the human race. At this point we can see that the triad of human self-understanding, namely, as being created, endowed with reason and the human being as a tool creature, must, because of the primacy of value-experience, be embedded in the three pure exemplars of person that are the personifications of a triad of the value-ranks of the sacred, the mental and of values relative to life: the saint, the genius, and the hero. The above diagram of the spiritual, mental and vital triadic structure of the human being can, therefore, be extended by the three exemplars of personhood.

One comment must be added with regard to the triadic order in Scheler's philosophy. We recall that Scheler did not list three but five personal exemplars that apparently correspond to the prism of the five ranks of values. He was not altogether clear in telling us whether the fourth and fifth "ideas" of human self-understanding given in his 1926 essay *Mensch und Geschichte* (Man and History) (IX 120-144/ P 65-93) correspond to the two lower ranks of utility and pleasure values. These two ideas are the human self-understanding as a disease of life's evolutionary direction and the human being as a godless entity responsible only to himself—the latter of which foreshadowed post World War II existentialism.

In any case these lower ranks are not treated in Scheler's list of "ideas" of self-understanding. He gave us only three at the beginning of the *Philosophische Anthropologie*. The imperfection in Scheler's texts as concerns the lower value-ranks and possibly as concerns the corresponding ideas of self-understanding is not, however, damning because these possible lower ideas of self-understanding are, like the third value rank, also relative to life. Nevertheless, the inconsistency deserves mention.

Our contention that the three ideas that humans can have of themselves presupposes the moral experience of the exemplars of the saint, the genius and the hero. This contention can be reinforced by the fact that the exemplars as "pure" are insufficient to nurture the mind and moral life. As "shadowy casts," Scheler said, they must drink the "blood" of historical experience. It is only then that they will become factual models in historical development (X, 268/PV 140-1). This, however, is only another way of saying that the exemplars must *functionalize* themselves with living individuals and their interpersonal experience.

The same point concerning this functionalization holds for the "ideas" that humans have of themselves. Strictly speaking, these ideas are *not* abstract and gained by abstraction from value ranks. They are given in a much "deeper" experience of how humans feel they are given to themselves without mediation and external influence (XII 16). This can be compared to the immediacy of the moral tenor of an individual or a group that sets the stage for the style, mores and trends of acts and actions. Because both the immediacy of ideas of self-understanding and the personal exemplars are inseparably linked to history and its epochs, (IX 123/P 68) there can be no substantial difference between human self-understanding and the prototypes of personal exemplars.

The immediacy of the givenness of self-understanding is not *a priori* in a traditional sense of the term. The immediacy is coupled to the triad of human drives. As we indicated in Chapter VIII, Scheler coupled the drive of procreation with mythology and origins of religion and their social form, the life-community. He coupled the power drive with society and the belief in rational powers and a human urge to dominate human beings and things. The nutritive drive he coupled with the rising age of economics and with unrestrained cravings for controlling nature and entities.

The result of the direction of the course of the alternating dominations of the three main drives is also reflected in yet another important factor. Even the idea of God is affected by the drive-mind link: the predominance of the drive of procreation is reflected in an idea of an "all loving" God that exists for the salvation of the people He created. The predominance of the power-drive effects the idea of God as the "all-mighty." The nutritive drive—itself gauged to the controlling things in nature—is reflected in the idea of an all-knowing or "omniscient" God. Our triad of the vital, mental and spiritual levels that are residual in the human being can, therefore, be even further extended by the three types of pure exemplars, the three aspects of the idea of God and the three main drives.

b) Absolute Time

Impressive as the hidden order of Scheler's philosophy may look at this point, the way that it has been described does not yet do justice to his actual intentions. This is because each of the elements of the order, described here as a footing to the *Philosophische Anthropologie*, is imbued with the intuition of the *becoming in absolute time*. In short, all terms in this order must be seen in light of Scheler's tenet that among all forms of being it is becoming that is *the* form of Being (XI 235-6). Scheler's philosophy is one of becoming, not of being.

This point calls for a brief comment on the ancient pre-Socratic issue of being and becoming, namely whether becoming presupposes, or is, being, or whether, conversely, being presupposes, or is, in its becoming. The issue first resurfaced in modern philosophy with Schleiermacher's compilation of pre-Socratic fragments of 1817. At issue is the argument between Parmenides's claim of the impossibility of becoming and Heraclitus's argument for the perpetual flux, and emergence or *physis*. Scheler is unmistakably clear on this matter: "...all 'being' is becoming in absolute time (Heraclitus was right in this)." (XI 250) All the same, we must bear in mind what had been said about absolute time thus far. "Becoming" can refer (1) to what will come to be in the future (*das Seinwerden*) and it can (2) refer to the inward self-becoming of a process (*das Werdesein*). The latter is the Schelerian meaning of "becoming" and absolute time. The conventional meaning of "what will be in the future" is associated only with measurable time as used in the sciences; it is simply clock-time. Throughout Scheler's philosophy, however, absolute time is the condition for the possibility of measurable or clock time.

Since absolute time began to play a central role in Scheler's metaphysics and philosophical anthropology, we must now expand on what had been said about it so far in Chapter VII, "Subliminal Phenomenology." In contrast to Husserl, time-consciousness for Scheler was seen as being founded on a *metaphysical* principle, namely, impulsion, which is itself characterized by absolute time. Absolute time, Scheler held, has three inherently interwoven aspects: 1) inseparable coincidence between meanings and their phases; 2) phases are simultaneously becoming and unbecoming; 3) the run-off of absolute time during transitions between an A and a B; for instance, during the transition between a phase A of potency to a phase B of the actualization of potency A.

Non-objectifiable absolute time as such looks like an undercurrent that suffuses all phases of growth and decline of both universal and individual life. It suffuses drive-life as well as the act-being of the person, historical development as much as the dynamic field forces of the atom, the becoming of the Deity as much as the becoming of consciousness (*Bewusstseinswerdung*) in any of its phases. It suffuses the becoming of the world and is also at the heart of evolution.

Let us focus on absolute time that runs off in the nutritional drive. The awareness of having to eat something comes at the end of a process that the nutritive drive had already been running off beneath our awareness of having to eat. After this run-off, the wellings in the drive have to rouse the lower thresholds of consciousness and solicit the intake of food that would accommodate the nutritional diet of humans. Whatever wells up in such a pre-conscious fashion has the character of absolute time. Each becoming phase simultaneously "unbecomes" in order to make room for new becoming and unbecoming phases. There is a difference between becoming hungry and feeling hungry. Becoming hungry is pure because the becoming temporalizes itself. Becoming hungry is sewn into an emerging, subliminal object in the drive. Its growth coincides with its phases of becoming and un-becoming. Such pre-temporal run-off of phases and their emerging contents holds for all vital motions: this is very different from motion that is measured in mechanics.

The vital motion that is manifest in the growth of a seed into a plant is perhaps the most apparent example of the becoming-unbecoming process of absolute time. Whereas the direction of a mechanical motion, for example that of a falling rock, is determined by the point of its impact on the ground which is its *terminus ad quem*, all vital motion is determined by its inception or its *terminus a quo*. The growth of a seed has no definite or calculable end point in contrast to the end point of a mechanical motion of the falling rock which is determined by gravity. The self-motion of living processes, however, allows only of "tendencies" that begin in the very *terminus a quo* of their motion. Branches can grow this way or that way, or might even not grow at all. Mechanical motion has no such relative freedom of motion.

All vital motion conquers, as it were, its own internal self-spatialization and self-temporalization. Mechanical motion of the falling rock falls "in" a measurable space and time. Space and time have the function here of boxes within which the rock is falling. Hence, mechanical motion and even inanimate bodies themselves are neither self-spatializing nor self-temporalizing. One would come close to a sufficient understanding of the simultaneous becoming and unbecoming of living processes only if one were able to place oneself into such growing process. This would make clear the immense difference between absolute time and objective time, a difference that is virtually ignored in our daily lives. We "observe" the objective growth of a seed from the outside; it begins to break through the surface of the ground in an experience of objective time. Saying that the seed has grown fourteen days in order to get out of the ground, however, presupposes all that was happening "in" the seed's own vital growth: the becoming and unbecoming phases beneath the visible growth.

Furthermore, "tendencies" in vital motion must be bound to a "void" into which the tendencies grow to fill it out, but only to be exposed to ever new voids "in," not in front of, them. This inward void of vital tendency is no spatial container like a box either. It is radically different from the usual empty space. Paradoxically, the seed is its own void, or the very space into which it grows.

The contention that absolute time runs through drives by way of self-activation of impulsion, through vital growth, through temporality of the consciousness and becoming in general is further supported by the argument that measurable, objective space and time have their foundation in the metaphysical principle of impulsion or "*Drang.*" Neither the absolute temporalization nor spatialization— nor the some twenty-four human drives in all Scheler assumed there to be—are separated from impulsion. Therefore, impulsion is maintained to be a four-dimensional manifold in which perceivable space and time are not yet separated but bringing their separation of an objective three-dimensional space and one-dimensional time about. This process of separation also has inherent vital powers that stem from impulsion: self-motion and self-modification.

Self-motion and self-modification are, as we saw, imbedded in the common principle of *Wechsel* which is a character of impulsion and was described in Chapter VII as "irregular fluctuating variation." Any *Wechsel* contains reversible movement that leads to *spatialization* and it has irreversible modification that leads to *temporalization*. In the human being, the first instance of the separation of spatialization and temporalization happens in drives. What makes a drive "in" the drive "urgent," say, a subliminal welling up (*Regungen*) for food in the nutritive drive, has priority over any other subliminal drive wellings. Subliminal wellings for the inner drive object "food" makes urgencies of other drives recede. Therefore a drive object that is welling up determines a subliminal "earlier" and a "later" of receding ones. In all this, drives temporalize themselves and pertain to both human beings and animals. But life also is manifest in plant-life that appears to be bare of animal drives. Scheler regarded plant-life to be a manifestation of life nearest to impulsion. It is in this regard that Scheler gives preference to the ontology of temporality of spatiality: Wherever there occurs "aging" and "death," even in the absence of drives, there is "absolute *earlier and later*" (XI 143). Drives do not only temporalize but also spatialize themselves. Like the "earlier" and "later" of their temporalization, the terms of their spatialization are "near" and "background," and occur along with the terms of temporalization. What is urgent is therefore both early and near, what is not is both later and in their background. All these terms are pre-perceptive, pre-conscious and self-constituting in the drives.

We mentioned above that tendencies of vital growth have a void "into" which tendencies go. The void is also "in" drives when they are dissatisfied and unfulfilled. For instance, the nutritive drive may be permeated with a "driving hunger" that is associated with a void toward which it is directed. Scheler makes the point but, as he frequently does, aggravates an already complex issue by linking it up with various other aspects of metaphysics and philosophical anthropology.

> We cannot represent to ourselves any sort of spatiality in which the peculiar phenomenon of the "void" does not appear, the phenomenon of that intuitive non-being [μὴ ὄν] or that "lack" which precedes from the factual datum itself. This phenomenon is, in any event, prelogical and certainly has nothing to do with the function of negative judgment. The phenomenon of the void is of the greatest interest. It arises, in the last analysis, from the experience that occurs when a driving hunger [*Triebhunger*] for spontaneous movement has not been satisfied or fulfilled. This hunger in the end conditions all perception [*Perzeptionen*] as well as representations and the spontaneous images of fantasy, which are independent of external perceptions. Thus, the phenomenon of the void, which is bound up with the power of self-movement (insofar as the latter is connected with this unsatisfied hunger) must be given as a stable background prior to all changing perceptions and even the material images of fantasy. The "emptiness" of the heart is, remarkably, the principle datum for all concepts of emptiness (empty time, empty space). The emptiness of the heart is, quite seriously, the source from which all emptiness springs. The empty path, the stationary empty path, so to speak, which our drives take as they reach out in every direction is constantly at hand. So, too, is the background of perceptions which is connected with this empty path. And it is only in man's urgent impulse to move, varying in force and direction, which reduces that rare marvel, the unheard-of fiction of man's natural world-view, that a particular kind of non-being [μὴ ὄν] seems to him to precede every positively determined being as its foundation: empty space (IX 219/PE 331).

The origins of temporality are analogous to that of space to which the above quote also referred:

> The central experience of temporality, like that of space, is originally given to us in a particular modality of our drive-based striving: in man's power, his experience of an ability as an animal to modify his qualitative conditions spontaneously, that is, "by himself." It is part of the primordial phenomenon of life that it exhibits not only self-movement but also self-modification [*Selbstveränderung*]. A creature that did not modify itself would have no access to time. Time, like space, is not originally given in intuition or perception but is a modification of our active and practical behavior. To have or to want to do "first" one thing, "then" another, to have barely enough time to do it, to have "already taken care of it," this dynamically experienced ordering of projects, not objects, is the basic experience of temporality (IX 227/PE 340).

Pre-temporal run-offs of absolute time also hold for ideas and insights of the mind *before* we are aware of them in their particularity and definability. All cognitions, for instance, those that are acquired during pragmatic experiences with things or those made during mathematical operations resulting in an insight that x=y, are in a "becoming" state. This amounts to saying that the pre-temporal emergence of an insight or of a failure was "not yet in sight," so to speak, while respective experiences were being made. In this particular regard, pragmatism is correct in holding that truth lies in the confirmation of states of affairs.

More directly, absolute time of the reader's mental processes had already been running off while reading these pages. Meanings, whether clear or obfuscated, were emerging in the reader's mind while at the same time they kept on fading away to make room for emerging ones. For this reason, Scheler's terminology concerning consciousness expresses it to be a continuous phenomenon of becoming and unbecoming (*Bewusst-werdung*) unlike Husserlian "consciousness" (*Bewusst-sein*), despite the predominant use of the latter term that was and still is *en vogue*. All consciousness is a continuous becoming and unbecoming. Its contents are simultaneously becoming and unbecoming: all mental insights, ideas, concepts, etc., are "becoming" and "unbecoming" in absolute time and therefore inseparably conjoined with their respective phases of running-off.

It is this important point, i.e., that the nature of the human mind and ideas are suffused with absolute time, that Scheler did not sufficiently develop in *Die Stellung des Menschen im Kosmos* (IX 9-71/M 3-95). Indeed, he intended to elaborate mostly on subhuman areas of anthropology, not specifically on the human mind and the meta-physical meaning of spirit. Moreover, the printed text does not re-flect the lecture that Scheler gave in Darmstadt upon which it is based. That Scheler did not address the emotive and subliminal dimensions of spirit, the religious dimensions of the person, and the nature of the human mind and ideas, is unfortunate. It affected negatively later appreciation of both the philosophical anthropology and metaphysics. Accordingly, the core of the *Philosophische Anthropologie* was eclipsed and confused by a large number of thinkers in the century. What follows is intended to rectify the state of affairs. We chose to bring into focus the very concept of an idea, its temporalization of and the nature of mind.

c) The Sketch: Emergence of Ideas

In one way or another, almost all philosophers have addressed the question of what precisely human ideas are: how they come about, whether they are pure or originate in perception or given by God or are simply interpretations of existence. The answer to the question of what ideas of the mind are is quintessential to understanding who or what we human beings are. Whichever theory is to be adopted must to some extent trace its roots to either Plato or Aristotle.

In order to become acquainted with Scheler's characterization of ideas,—unequalled in its peculiarity and challenge to philosophical theories of the past and present—let us first briefly recall Plato's and Aristotle's approach to the question.

If, according to Plato, we look at two equal things, say, two equal tents, the idea of "equality" must be in the mind prior to the perception of the two equal tents, because "equality" is not a tent. The idea of equality must be of another nature than perceivable things: it cannot originate in the tents. Hence, the idea of equality is inborn. It resides undisturbed by perceptions of equal things in the soul of the infant: the idea is inborn because ideas have not yet been spoiled by perception, say that of equal tents. For this reason, Plato refers to the infant as the greatest philosopher. During the lifetime of individuals, ideas in a mysterious way are recalled by the soul whenever perceivable things have the looks of a particular idea. All tents "look" like a tent although they are all different from each other. Heidegger point-edly showed that "idea" literally means the "look" of something that belongs to a class of particular things.

Plato's student, Aristotle, disagreed with his master, but not entirely. Aristotle's theory of what ideas are is often described in a pseudo-

Aristotelian way. He agrees with Plato on two essential points. (1) In Aristotle's distinction between a passive and active intellect he assigns to the latter the same attributes as Plato did to the soul: it is eternal and imperishable. (2) Aristotle attributes the same attributes to his "pure form" as Plato did to the Idea of the Good: it is eternal, non-moving, perfect and its purity is divorced from corporeity. The pseudo-Aristotelian theory—so named whenever the consensus between Plato and Aristotle is disregarded—always stresses that an idea like "equality" presupposes the perception of the aforementioned tents in that case. Without their perception they could not be known to be equal. In this sense, the equality of the tents is abstracted from sense data of the tents.

Scheler's contribution to the question of what an idea of the mind is can, at the outset of our explanations, be put in a nutshell: *an idea is a sketch*. Throughout the posthumous manuscripts, there are only two, albeit essential references made to this effect. They are contained in the *Zusätze aus den nachgelassenen Schriften* (*Appendices from Posthumous Manuscripts*) (IX 252) and in a manuscript entitled, *Entwurf und 'ideae ante res'* (*Rough Draft and 'ante res ideas'*) (XI 119-120).

Scheler's theory is very much at the core of his *Philosophische Anthropologie*, that is, of the question of the nature of human existence that is endowed with the ontological relation between knowledge and world. The theory remained undeveloped. It is for this reason that we want to interrupt the present discussion in order to find out first what exactly a sketch is. In doing so we take Scheler's brief remarks into account, but move beyond them by offering additional details so as to pinpoint its essence and, thereby, the nature of a human idea.

Both the Platonic and Aristotelian understanding of "ideas" presuppose that ideas are static, fixed and univocal. However, in a philosophy that shows that ideas occur only in the *functionalization* of them with things in practice and reality, there must be a departure from the Platonic and Aristotelian positions. For functionalization is, as we saw earlier, a *process* during which ideas are said to come about with things they are in tandem with, so to speak. If they fail to enter into practical functions with things and real factors to which they belong, ideas are lifeless, obsolete or defunct. All ideas that have not worked in this sense through history are in practice extinct.

There are three possible ways in which ideas occur. (1) The Platonic position claims that one already has ideas prior to perceived things or *ante res*. (2) The Aristotelian and empiricist position that claims ideas to be pursuant to the perception of things or *post res*. (3)

Scheler suggests a third possibility according to which ideas occur *during* their functionalization *with* things. They are real only *cum rebus*.

This last possibility is dynamic. Because functionalization is a process, ideas have to *emerge*. They "settle" with their proper states of affairs. Ideas emerge like sketches that are drawn out as rough designs. In this sense an idea is neither static nor an immutable essence. Indeed, we will see that there cannot be a so-called essence of an idea in the traditional sense of this term because ideas are never complete. This is due to their nature of a sketch. Let us now examine the nature of a sketch itself.

A first note on the variety of sketches is appropriate because sketches appear to be infinite in number. We are confronted with them consistently in our daily lives. Sketches can be rough outlines or plans of how we want to go about our activities of the day; they can pertain to outlines and programs intended to reduce unemployment. Art is replete with sketching, as is fashion design and architecture. Manufacturers, technologists, business leaders and managers, physicians, educators and politicians often refer to their sketches as "programs." Every program is, in essence, a sketch. We also sketch letters, speeches, wills, errands, discussions; we sketch our future, intentions, and our beliefs; sometimes we sketch even our afterlife. Sketches precede all scientific discoveries. Conceptualizations of the atom rest on sketches as do laws of physics that hold in outer space. The structure of sketches is also manifest in such things as agendas and medical diagnoses and research.

Do all sketches have something in common? Yes.

No matter how many types of sketches there are, all sketches have in common that they *beckon* or solicit their execution and completion. A sketch beckons to be filled out, most conspicuously so in drawings. How many times did Van Gogh resketch his famous "Shoes?" While sketches are being filled out and executed with details, their completion is relative to what is *possible* in individual cases. Sketches are "more" than any of their executions because they permit infinite variations of executions. The shortcomings of the execution of a sketch stem from various reasons: from materials used, such as paint; from the keys of melodies employed; from vocabulary or a style predominant in a certain period. How much different would Rubens have sketched "Shoes" at his own time? In short, the executions of a sketch depend on *real factors* with which a sketch is to be realized.

There are not only material sketches: sketches can be exclusively or almost exclusively in the mind of an individual, such as Beethoven's sketches of a tenth symphony. Sometimes both mental and material sketches are never executed. Others are executed by persons who live later than the original sketcher. A sketch is often later "filled out" by the students of an original artist.

We find numerous examples in literature where various executions of one and the same sketch is made by an author. H.G. Wells sketched *The Time Machine* (1895) over and over again, as did Dostoevski with his sketch "The Grand Inquisitor" in his *The Brothers Karamazov* (1879/80). Sophocles' *Antigone* was first presented in 441 B.C.; Jean Anouilh's was written in 1944. They are two executions of the same sketch of the tragic conflict.

At this point the following observation should be made: when we use the term "execution" of a sketch we refer to the process of execution itself, that is, *while* the sketch is drawn out. The execution of a sketch cannot actually be separated from the sketch. Once the pencil moves over paper to create a sketch the execution is already simultaneously underway. While we sketch and execute it, both the sketching and executing are tethered to the absolute time of the sketcher. It is only in the eye of the beholder that the executions become later subject to infinite "interpretations" made in discursive thinking and, therefore, measurable in clock-time.

What has been established up to this point makes it possible to formulate what I call the three laws inherent in sketches:

(1) The executions of a sketch are inexhaustible.

(2) Inherent in all sketching are two opposite extremes.

a) An execution can cover up a sketch. In this case the sketch remains opaque, unintelligible, such as the scribbles aimlessly drawn on a piece of paper during a lengthy telephone conversation, or the doodles drawn on paper while listening to a boring talk. A later examination of these scribbles does not by itself make such a sketch transparent, except perhaps for a psychiatrist who may find a clue in the scrawls for what has been going on in his patient's soul. Strokes of executions can be very bold and edgy, soft and round, depending on the patient's problems. In practice, however, all executions without an intelligible sketch remain cryptic.

b) The opposite of this is when a sketch shows little or nearly no execution at all. There appear just disconnected bits and pieces and segments of lines and curves. This, too, is unintelligible because there is a lack of execution. A painter who begins by drawing two or three thin lines only later gains an awareness of what he had initially been sketching. In this case, the sketch emerges from the early, rough and preliminary executions. Modern painting and drawing seems to be fond of these two extremes. A painter might just pour cans of multicolored paint on the canvas, that is, execute an act but without a sketch. Or he might paint a sketch so abstractly that its execution remains unfathomable and allows for infinite interpretations. A huge black canvas, for instance, that has an almost unnoticeable area of dark red at the lower right corner of the canvas makes it arguable as to whether the sketch or its executions can be fathomed. There appears to be an artistic shock value, or a deconstruction, occurring in this situation. The riddle implicit in the fusion of both sketch and execution provokes interest.

There is, then, either a maximum of executions covering up a sketch or a minimum of a sketch covering up executions. The essence of sketching, however, is situated between these extremes. There must be a *relative balance* of what the sketch is in its executions. If this does not occur, there cannot be a reasonable functionalization of a sketch with its appropriate real factors.

(3) A third law inherent in the nature of a sketch follows from the above: a sketch that has almost no executions is powerless to play a role in human realty. It does not realize itself in history because it remains an unsolvable puzzle. In *Formalism* Scheler refers to such cases as *unterhistorisch*, "sub-historical," meaning that ideas simply do not touch reality or get lost and remain ineffectual. He implies that most of human history remains sub-historical in this sense. By comparison, that portion of history that is knowable is only a small segment and resembles a narrow zone illuminated by a moving beam of a lighthouse that leaves a large part around it in darkness.

This leads to an essential interconnection between the dynamic nature of an idea as sketch and history. If ideas as sketches are never finished because they allow inexhaustible executions, then any historical fact or event, any moment in a life-time, too, must remain unfinished: events are open-ended (V 34/E 41; VIII 150/PR 151). Thus history itself is open-ended. This is the reason why the history of objective events cannot be measured in absolute time. The conception of history in light of absolute time is "historicity." It is constituted in humans and in their impulsion and spirit (IX 282).

Specifically, the dynamic theory of ideas must also pertain to the ideas that human beings have of themselves, or their self-understanding. The way humans understand themselves, their self-image, largely determines the character of an *ethos* and even of eras of human history. These ideas of a collective self-understanding are projections that humans develop of themselves, just as persons execute sketches of their individual self-understanding in terms of what they aim to be.

The argument can now be extended: if ideas have the nature of sketches, we must also attribute the factor of sketching to all subconscious *vital* development. The nature of ideas as sketches has to be ascribed to the *phantasy* in the principle of life, that is, impulsion. Impulsion infuses itself through drives and perception into the most abstract mental processes. The phantasy in impulsion must, however, have its own peculiar sketching process, namely, phantasmic sketching. Phantasmic sketching does not yet pertain to ideas on this subliminal level. Phantasmic sketching does not result in dynamic ideas either, but in phantasmic images (XI 130-2; 189) which, as we saw, are the base of drive-conditioned perception.

It is this line of thinking that must have prompted Scheler to conceive *all life* as having the structure of a sketch. During the process of evolution, the phantasy in impulsion sketches numerous forms of life, of which plants and animals are but a few. Plant and animal life are but a few examples of the execution of an immense but also largely futile phantasmic sketching that occurs in impulsion. The species known to us are only a part of the whole sketch of life that originates in impulsion. The portion of life known is like the remains of an ancient inscription, part of which has been lost over time (XI 196).

To borrow a Nietzschean expression, many executions of life's "Grand Design" are gone, some of which, perhaps, have been links between higher animals and the human species. However, the totality of all such missing executions that are generated in impulsion's phantasy are not buried under the surface of the earth waiting to be discovered by archeologist; rather, the executions of the universal phantasy of impulsion are inexhaustible because the nature of any sketch admits countless executions.

Our digression into the nature of a sketch has been necessary in order for us to gain an insight now into the whole of Scheler's philosophy as it emerged toward the end of his life. As stated, much of Scheler's philosophy remained fragmentary. The fragments of his later thought, however, point to an unarticulated whole.

The fragmentary character of Scheler's philosophy, however, reflects a similar fragmentation in life itself. Fragments, as we saw, always belong to a whole, as is seen not only in our personal lives but also in ancient architecture, literature, art, Holy Writings, etc. Thus, Scheler's theory of evolution, while admittedly fragmented, nevertheless admits of a hidden coherence.

d) Evolution: Vital Becoming

Scheler says that nineteenth century natural philosophy was guided by three presuppositions regarding evolution. Evolution was understood (1) as an empirical process having taken place in objective time, (2) as a process proceeding from the simple to the complicated, and (3) as a process proceeding from lower to higher life-forms. Charles Darwin's *On the Origin of the Species* (1859) and *The Descent of Man* (1871) bear out this myth (XII 83). Scheler does not accept these presuppositions. It could be argued that the reason he does not is because the three presuppositions are pre-conceived wholes. They are the result of a long tradition of two instances of man's self-understandings: (1) the belief of having been created by one source and (2) the idea of the *homo sapiens*, rational animal.

In light of the rise of science at his time, Scheler proposes an entirely new understanding of evolution, namely, that evolution does not take place in an objective, measurable cosmos: it is self-becoming process. Self-becoming is now understood as "historical" self-becoming (*geschichtliches Werdesein*) (XII 83) which is to be strictly distinguished from datable historical clock-time. Historical self-becoming does not only encompass life but inorganic nature as well (IX 236/PE 350). The world as a whole does not *have* history but *is* history, which includes life in general. Life in general must not be conceived as evolving amidst a huge inanimate and mechanical cosmos in objective time. Life is only part of the *all-becoming cosmos*. Becoming (*das Werdesein*) includes inorganic matter. Heraclitus's insight that everything is in flux and flows has been "victorious" everywhere, "*including inanimate being, ideas and gestalts*" (XII 83). Becoming thus pertains equally to ideas and laws of nature that science has told us rest on a quantum theory. The Quantum Theory allows only statistical laws and does not adopt a traditional concept of causality linked with objective time.

The unity of life must be seen in terms of absolute time. Life has no empirical unity: rather, the unity of life has at all times been a simultaneous plurality of species and life-forms. Scheler called this "polyphyletism." A polyphyletic concept of life tells us that the development of one living entity has *more* than one ancestral type. A group of animals can form a pluralist type. Rather than adhering to a genesis of life from one source, Scheler promotes such "polygenesis" of life (XII 83-116).

Some clarification in the usage of terms in Scheler is necessary. In his later texts, he often obscures the term "life-forms" by using it in conjunction with the term "species." For Scheler life-forms are plants, animals and humans. Species are subsets within such life-forms. For instance, races are said to be species of the human life-form (XIV 280).

Scheler replaces the concept of "origin" of species with the concept of "sustenance" that life-forms have maintained with one another throughout evolution. The evolutionary, interdependent sustenance is manifest, for example, in plants that sustain animals, insects that sustain birds, birds that sustain plants, etc.

The polyphyletic nature of life requires certain distributions of inorganic matter in order for life to exist. The distribution of inorganic matter cannot be explained by physical and chemical laws alone: it is guided by life itself. Scheler contends that the numbers of the forms of life and species does not diminish when one looks back into the remote past of the history of the earth. A monophyletic theory of evolution such as Darwin's suggests a decrease of life-forms the further back in life's history we look. Scheler argues that there has been an *unbroken balance* between those species that died out and those that came into existence. This suggests that there is not one but many origins of species.

From this it follows that two concepts of evolution must be discarded: the concept of an "origin" of the species and the concept of a "progress" of life toward ever higher forms. Scheler argues that origin should be replaced by two different concepts: (1) the "transformations of species" that takes place within the range of life's evolutionary direction going from plant and animal to human life. At the same time this evolutionary direction shows an increase toward gradual differences in gender. (2) A transformation of species takes place within the range of the forms of life, such as those of vertebrates and articulates. These transformations are said to occur from the death and the birth of a species. The birth of a species occurs by *mutations*, the beginnings of which are already laid out in a dying species.

What Scheler calls "directions of life" is also an incomplete chapter of his later theories. There is no biological organ responsible for the direction life takes toward its culmination in the human race. Each form of life has its own specific character or "direction." The specifically humanizing direction developed from primates to Neanderthal man and finally to the present human. Scheler conceives the essence of the human direction of life in terms of the immense amount of energy that is consumed by the human central nervous system in the supply it must give to organs. With all other animals this energy is used just for organic growth. It is therefore possible to think that the human being could at specific geological periods have resembled amphibious animals, reptiles, vertebrates, mammals or marsupials, Scheler held.

With these unelaborated notes Scheler began vehemently to refute any theory proposing or implying that the so-called origin of the species comes from nowhere or nothingness, from something that is not-yet or from a certain sub-species. It is not the case that the human is the highest biological being merely because it is the most recent animal that stems from primates. The human being is the highest biological being because it is a *microcosm*. The human being is a biological microcosm of all of life's stages of development. Scheler also considered the human to be the peak of life because it has similarity to all other animals: no other animal can be found to have such universal similarity.

One may argue for or against this view of evolution. What is peculiar about it, however, is the thread of thought running through it: on the basis of his polyphyletic theory all forms of life are *sketches* that life has tried out or made in its direction toward what was, at the polyphyletic and polygenetic outset, still rough and wanting of human completion. In evolutionary terms, the human being *itself* is a sketch of life that was likely drawn in the phantasy of impulsion once a human being made its first appearance on the planet. Nevertheless, the sketch of the human being that is still open to vital executions is a sketch distinct from all other life-forms and species: this sketch is a countenance (*Antlitz*) of a still unfinished God (XII 88, 92).

With regard to the idea of the essence of the human being as a microcosm and spiritual animal and with regard to the vital microcosm of human life, all empirical forms of the terrestrial human of the past, and possibly of other humanoid forms on other planets, are varying attempts that never succeeded during the process of the *becoming* of what the human is. This becoming possesses the direction of filling out the idea of the essence of being human (XII 93). The essence of the "idea" of being human pre-exists all vital evolution (XII 100), just as a sketch pre-exists the executions that realize it. Therefore, the human being did not pre-exist in a morphological, physiological, psychological, let alone in a Platonic sense of "pre-existence":

> How and when the earthly human came into existence was not determined by 'God as Spirit' but by life's impulsion even during its grappling with the inorganic level of impulsion and its images. In the formation of life-forms, there are numerous analogous forms and analogous rhythms suggesting that the human being is the richest conservation of the drafts and sketches of universal life which represent the idea of life and of which all life-forms are specifications. The existing human being represents the utilization of all the experiences life has made during its material and energetical manifestations. In certain stages of the ontogenesis, the human beingness wanted to turn into a "fish,"

but life "avoids errors" of the kind. Life is like an artist who draws countless sketches without prior conceptualizations of them. It is like an artist who, having arrived at the peak of his life-time sees at a propitious moment all his endeavors and sketches fall into their places; that is, they blend into something quite unexpected and new: containing the essence of all that had been going on. The human being, this "brief fest" grafted [*Aufgipfelung*] on top of organic nature, could not be without an earlier process of development. Nevertheless, the human being is not a summation of such development. He is "creative synthesis" of all of life's possibilities and tests to realize its possibilities (XII 100-101).

With Scheler's concept of evolution—no matter how fragmentary—the central notion in his metaphysics and philosophical anthropology, "becoming in absolute time," begins to return into view. Indeed, we can now say that absolute time spans his entire philosophy. It began from the moral and sympathetic dimensions of the human being as person. Just as the human person was not seen as a static substance but rather as the center of the self-realization of its existence, so also the human being is not a static substance in the evolutionary becoming of life. Not only as a personal center is the human being a *direction* of movement, but also in the becoming of life with its vital centers and force centers.

A theist "origin" of the human being cannot hold for this pattern of thought. Like any other species, the human being also arose from *mutation* (XII 112). The human mutation, which itself stems from a quantum leap, engendered a redirection of the general vital energy to the central nervous system. All the uniquely human advances that people enjoy over animals (such as language, clothing, etc.) are rooted in this redirection of energy to the brain. The old theory of evolution that is still oriented by causal chains that are supposed to further the development of life is thus overcome. It is replaced by mutational transitions of one species to another new species.

Mutational transition reminds us in particular of one of the three aspects of absolute time: the aspect of transition in which time is running between two terms. As such it is like its other two aspects: absolute time can neither be measured nor objectified.

Nevertheless, Scheler also holds that the general direction of life is not absolutely continuous but breaks off when the direction becomes mutational transition toward the human being. Life now takes a turn to "world-openness" and ideas and a turn toward "spirit." This turn that life takes toward world-openness is a turn beyond life. This beyond life status is compensated in life by surrogates such as intuition, concepts, signs, tools and culture. Life's developmental peak necessitates something that is "more than life," that is, spirit. Life had to negate itself at this peak in order to affirm the supra-vital (XII, 113). The ultimate turn of the general direction of life that goes beyond itself defies causal explanation because of the nature of a quantum leap in mutational transition.

Spirit occurred as soon as life reached its highest form in human beingness. This form was generated in the depths of life's own "suffering" of itself. According to this discussion of spirit, there is no room for a religious illumination as it is taught by churches. Human reason itself, as occurring in the form of the person, has become the locus of self-illumination and revelation of an attribute in the world-ground: the spiritual principle. Precisely at that point the human became open to a formal idea of God and of infinity. Precisely at this point of self-illumination and revelation the world-ground itself began to see one of its two attributes, spirit. Just as the human became aware of the Godhead, so also the Godhead become aware of Itself in the human being. Scheler describes this as "*one* act, *one* process of "mutual finding" of both God and man:

> Eternally impulsion struggles toward ideas. Eternally, the Deity—idea of ideas—awaits pulsations of the impulsion in order to gain distinctness of its idea and to realize itself through impulsion. The two eternal principles [of spirit and impulsion] must appear antagonistic to each other only for someone who is either an excessively sublimated ascetic or to someone who has excessive desires and a guilty conscience (XII 133).

The truth of the matter is that both the only seemingly antagonistic principles—life as form of impulsion and person as the form of spirit—are interdependent. It is in the embodied person that they have found each other in unison for the first time. Scheler's claim of this interdependence between spirit and life, between individual mind and individual body, abrogates all Cartesian dualism. The abrogation is not achieved by a preference of mind over body that so characterizes idealism and rationalism; nor is it achieved by a preference of the body over the mind as found in the philosophies of Nietzsche, Th. Lessing, Klages, and in varied forms in Spengler. The preference of body over mind continued to prevail among various twentieth century thinkers who, like Merleau-Ponty, stressed bodily existence over personal existence. The stress on bodily existence is quite obvious throughout modern society. But this stress on bodily experience reduces the body-mind relationship in the same manner as did

Descartes' insistence that the mind is mysteriously connected to the body.

Scheler abrogates the body-mind dualism by instituting the concept of *functionalization* between them: whereas impulsion and life are "blind" for spirit, so too spiritual values like good and evil, true and false, beautiful and ugly, sacred and profane are powerless without impulsion. The intersection of body and mind is reached when life in its development reaches beyond itself in the embodied person (XII 114). The human being has been a most unlikely result of the direction of vital evolution. There is no primate, Scheler says, from which one could have predicted the birth of a Goethe. Even God would not have been able to predict such a man from the existence of a primate (XII 110).

In his 1926 lecture *Leib und Seele* (*Lived Body and Soul*) Scheler presented an analogy that he said would best summarize the interrelation existing between spirit, person and impulsion, on the one hand, and the process of realization of an idea, on the other hand. The analogy may not only be the best clarification that Scheler presented to us on the matter, but it also connects the 1924 *Soziologie des Wissens* and the 1926 *Erkenntnis und Arbeit*, covered in Chapter VIII. Both works were sociological and metaphysical investigations into the processes of the realization of *ideal factors* by *real factors* and the role that human drives play in this process. Scheler's analogy as rendered below connects well also with his explanation of the realization of *values* that comes about only with things and with states of affairs.

Just as in Chapter I we learned that for Scheler values taken by themselves do not exist we now see that he has been telling us that ideas and the mind as such do not exist either. Ideas and mind by themselves, however, are said to be in a state that Scheler describes with a German verb that is not common in everyday German parlance which, however, many German philosophers, especially Heidegger, use. This verb is *wesen*. Ideas and mind are said only to "*wesen*": that is, they "are" even if only in potency. As such, ideas are formless and without any specification. When Scheler refers to "*in potentia*," however, he is not referring to Aristotle, for whom potential being is necessary for actualization. Rather, he appears to use the state of "*wesen*" in terms of potential existence here in the sense of what he called "relative nothingness." He distinguished three kinds of nothingness. (1) Absolute nothingness is the sense of there being nothing at all. Parmenides thought it unthinkable because thinking of absolute nothingness makes it already something in thought. On various occasions, Scheler held that absolute nothingness can, however, in contrast to Parmenides, indeed be thought, but he did not expand the point.

Scheler also speaks of (2) logical negation and (3) relative nothingness as the other two kinds of nothingness. Relative nothingness suffuses our whole existence. For example, when we say that there is "nothing" on the table or that there is "nothing" about a person. Nothing in such cases is relative to what could, potentially, be on the table or potentially be with a person, but is not the case.

Let us add that historically Scheler's position of the non-existence of mind and ideas as taken by themselves reminds one of a similar position taken by William James. In his essays "Does Consciousness Exist?" and "The Notion of Consciousness" (1904/05), James maintained the "non-existence" of consciousness but described it as showing through, as being translucent or "diaphanous." He also came close to Scheler's functionalism when he explained the relation between subject and object. There appears to be no indication that Scheler was familiar with these Jamesian essays.

e) The "Isomorphic Analogy" of the Structure of Spirit

The question to be answered then is how the existence of mind must, on the above premises, be explained and understood. Scheler proceeds by way of an analogy that will serve to summarize his philosophy of mind and the person that was proposed in his 1926 lecture on *Lived Body and Soul* (XII 148). He calls the analogy "isomorphic." This means that the analogy itself and that to which the analogy refers has the same forms of appearance, or that they have a one-to-one relation with each other. The analogy with the mind consists in the performance of a Beethoven symphony, although Scheler does not specify which symphony. Let us select Beethoven's Fourth Symphony for the sake of illustration.

The analogy between the ideas of the mind and the performance of this symphony has five distinct steps.

(1) The claim that mind by itself is powerless and historically ineffective is analogous to the Fourth Symphony that existed solely in the mind of its composer. As such, it remains unperformed: it is not real. The Fourth Symphony must be conducted and performed; it has no power strictly of itself to realize itself. This state of affairs also holds for innumerable moments in our life when we have ideas in mind that are not be realized in practice. These ideas are cloaked in darkness and will for the most part be forgotten. Some that may be remembered also remain unrealized.

(2) The realization of the Fourth Symphony is dependent on three factors: conductor, orchestra and performance. Without them there is no symphony. In this second step of the analogy Scheler lets the conductor stand for the principle that is the opposite of the mind: impulsion. It is through impulsion that mind and ideas can be realized. It is with impulsion as analogous to the conductor that Beethoven's symphonic ideas can enter into realizing function. Impulsion realizes Beethoven's ideas at each and every moment during the performance: the performance of the symphony realizes Beethoven's ideas by way of the functionalization they have with impulsion. In this step one can see that impulsion as analogous to the conductor is not a chaotic principle of life. Impulsion, Scheler says, possesses "eros." Eros is the central tendency of impulsion toward its spiritualization (XII 234-38).

(3) The reality of the symphony lies in the functionalization of ideas and impulsion. Beethoven composed the symphony during 1805/6 while at the same time composing the more famous Fifth Symphony. What made the Fourth audible and real for the first time was its first performance in March of 1807. Before that there was no reality to this symphony. Once the reality was established by functionalization, the symphony also became historical. Conversely, one can make the point that was argued in the *Sociology of Knowledge*, namely that whenever ideas cannot enter into functions with life they bite on "granite," remaining unhistorical (VIII 22/PR 38).

In this regard we can extend the analogy at this point by making use of the symbolism of light. Mind, reason and spirit have for ages been associated with symbols of illumination, as the light of reason, enlightenment, etc. However, light rays that do not strike a surface do not illumine anything: they remain dark. In order to realize their dormant possibility to illuminate there must be something else: a realizing principle, in this case a surface that is opposite the light source.

(4) The orchestra, like the conductor, is equally necessary for the performance. The players in the orchestra in Scheler's analogy stand for the various drive functions and unconscious factors. Without the conductor (impulsion) of the first performance the players would fail to be in rhythm with one another and the symphony would be hopelessly jumbled. Whereas the players are in need of a conductor for the unity of the performance, they make the conductor equally be dependent on them for the realization of the symphony.

(5) All the instruments in the orchestra are equally necessary for the performance. In the analogy, they stand for physical, mechanical

and chemical factors, especially for sound waves and the air that transmit them. In other words, there will not be a Fourth Symphony unless there are the scientific, physical fields and waves in the material of which the instruments are made. We again see that impulsion, even as the principle of life, must *also* contain inanimate elements that Scheler referred to as *Drangatome*, or atoms of impulsion (XI 157, 184).

This leads us to a metaphysical consideration of impulsion that is based in the metanthropology and science of physics itself.

f) Meta-Physics, Meta-Biology and the Inanimate Level of Impulsion

Up to this point the principle of impulsion has been described as the principle of life and as opposed to spirit or mind. Indeed, Scheler at times refers to impulsion as "All-Life," suggesting its universal nature. Despite this meta-biological aspect of impulsion, one cannot claim that Scheler represented a biological philosophy of life.

Throughout the history of philosophy, the concept of life itself has changed; one must be aware of its history in order to assess what Scheler has been saying. In Pre-Socratic thinking, life (*zoae*) meant being. From Aristotle on, however, life lost this meaning. With Aristotle life became actual only on the basis of potential being. Aristotle referred to this process as "entelechy," meaning to be actual or finished at and by its end or purpose. During the Middle Ages "life" was seen as a transient, earthly form having the purpose of preparation for "eternal" life. The concept life significantly narrowed in the modern period, especially at the hands of Descartes who understood it in terms of complex, mechanical extension. In the nineteenth century and after thinkers such as Bergson, Driesch, Nietzsche, Scheler and others tried to rescue the concept of life from Cartesian prejudices; yet the narrow understanding Descartes had of life persists to this day. Contemporary medical science depends on such an approach for its mechanical therapies and diagnostic methods.

There is another dimension to life. Human perception covers only a very small segment of the spectrum. Within this segment, the distinction usually made between organic and inorganic matter appears to be as evident as the distinction between space and time. But do these distinctions in human perception represent reality? This does not appear to be the case. Einstein showed that the unification of space and time, "space-time," is more commensurate with the reality of the four-dimensional structure of the universe. As we saw, Scheler also found it necessary to speak in a similar way of a pre-spatio-temporal expanse of impulsion in which space and time are not separated.

However, can a separation of organic and inorganic, of live and inanimate being also be analogously replaced by a unification of them? If so, would it lead one to accept concepts like "inanimate-organism," or "organic-mechanism"? Virology, for example, has shown that both animate and inanimate characteristics can be found in viruses.

Scheler thought that a fusion of the inorganic and organic has at least a "metaphysical probability," notwithstanding the fact that the realm of inanimate matter appears to be infinitely larger in the universe than the small span of life that exists on a single small planet that floats within a huge galaxy, but one of billions of galaxies.

There is, however, something that speaks against the huge imbalance of inanimate matter in the universe over against life and mind on the planet earth. This has been articulated by the pristine view of Pascal who, in his *Pensée* No. 348, says, "By space the universe encompasses and swallows me up like an atom, by thought I comprehend the world." The human being seen just as a "reed" by him is so feeble that the universe could crush it without effort at any time; but as a "thinking" reed the human being is more "noble," Pascal says, than the entire universe. The inanimate universe knows nothing of an all encompassing mind. Only the "thinking reed" does.

These arguments refer to the general problem of the distribution of matter, life and mind in the universe. Each of these terms may have considerable significance. The magnitude that Nietzsche, for instance, bestowed on the "Will to Power" of life lets the intellect dwindle into an insignificant X that makes nothing but errors and creates untruths.

The question now presents itself: how does Scheler's philosophy relate to the problem of the distribution of inanimate matter, life and spirit? The answer to the question has already been implied on several occasions: the metaphysical principles of spirit and impulsion exist in mutual interpenetration and functionalization that must keep them in a balance, including impulsion on the level of inanimate life. With this in mind, we can now address the role of the inanimate level in impulsion.

Scientific research has suggested that the relationship between physical energy and vital forces has to be rethought. Such rethinking has resulted, for example, in the claim also Scheler held, namely that mutations are the result of the aforementioned "quantum leaps." A quantum leap occurs when an atom's energy suddenly changes into a state of lesser energy or when an electron suddenly falls to an orbit of

lower energy. The energy lost is then transferred to an emitting pho-
ton. On a macro scale this quantum leap results in a sudden transfer
of one state of life to another. Already in Scheler's time and for Scheler
in particular, it was strongly suggested that the inorganic objects of
physics and organic objects of biology were in fact not as far apart as
had been thought.

As early as 1926, Scheler foresaw this rapprochement of physics
and biology, which was to become an area of research by the 1969
Nobel prize winner in physiology and medicine Max Delbrück in
California. According to Delbrück, the distinction between physical
and psychic nature is not a radical one and the distinction of external
and internal reality appears to be an illusion. He emphasized that
there is only one reality which cannot be split in two, as had been
done for centuries. In his 1989 book *Mind from Matter* Delbrück
argued that life cannot have come from outer space and ended up on
earth because exposure to cosmic rays would have destroyed life immediately. What did come from outer space, Delbrück argues, was
the "soup" from which organic molecules like those of H_2O, NH_3,
CH_2O, etc. are readily formed.

What Delbrück called "soup" has a likeness to Scheler's universal,
bio-energetic impulsion that underlies both organic and inorganic
material. According to Delbruck, organic molecules have an apparent similarity to atoms. Micro-organisms behave in patterns of "stop-
go" and "random-walk" as the result of rotational diffusions and ad-
aptation mechanisms. Delbruck even assigned the beginnings of perception to the micro-organic world. Again, to a certain degree this
appears to be a scientific point similar to Scheler's position that perception is conditioned by lower levels of life, that is, by the drives.

How can one clarify the similarities between non-organic atoms
and micro-organisms? In Delbruck's theory, we find that a *transition*
took place from non-life to life on earth. He considered explorations
into how this happened to be perhaps *the* question of the science of
biology.

Scheler had seen the importance of transition in life a few decades
earlier. Scheler saw that, first of all, the transition from non-life to
life must have taken place in absolute time. The nonliving micro-
material on which the existence of micro-organic matter rests functions as a base for life to grow. The micro-organic material of life,
Scheler says, is "engaged with" (*greift an*) this base. It does not engage
the phantasmic images of impulsion but engages *directly* with
impulsion's "atoms." The atoms of impulsion are not further explained, but they appear to be elements in impulsion on which ordi-

nary physical atoms rest. What is inanimate and what is alive are two directions of one and the same impulsion (XI 157, 181). In this engagement the atomic inorganic materials are extended centers of *field forces* that are generated from impulsion; all micro-organic materials are temporalizing *vital force centers.*

From this, Scheler draws the following conclusions. (1) In the shared engagement of extended field forces and temporalizing vital centers, the very *organ*-ization of extended field forces by the vital forces of impulsion must be both becoming and un-becoming because of the nature of self-temporalization itself. (2) Extended field forces result in "materialization" (*Materierung*); vital field forces result in "temporalization." This is not a successive process of one following upon the other but a simultaneous process of two aspects of impulsion *per se.* As we saw earlier, impulsion as such does not yet possess the separation between spatialization and temporalization. It is because of its pristine state of fluctuating variation (as discussed in Chapter VII) that such separation can follow from it.

Both force centers and vital centers obey only statistical laws. Let it be added that Scheler conceived the world as having actually three "centers": the field forces of physics, the vital forces of biology and the person-centers of philosophy. The former two centers must, however, presuppose the meta-physical and meta-biological force that generates both of them: cosmic impulsion. In a manner of speaking, impulsion is a principle that is convex on one side and necessarily concave on the other. Like the convex and concave inseparable counterparts of this principle, both sides of the principle of impulsion, namely the animate and the inanimate, are inseparable. Each is the necessary condition of the existence of the other.

g) Metaphysics and Science

Let us now address the place of the Relativity Theory and Quantum theory in Scheler's philosophy.

Scheler's dynamic metaphysics of inorganic nature received its orientation largely from the dynamic theory of matter proposed by the physicist Hermann Weyl (1885-1955). This orientation makes Scheler's metaphysics of impulsion more or less compatible with both the Theory of Relativity and Quantum Theory. In this regard, Scheler frequently acknowledged the pioneering work of Weyl as contained in Weyl's 1918 book *Raum, Zeit, und Materie* (Space, Time, Matter) and in the 1924 essays "*Was ist Materie? Zwei Aufsätze zur Naturphilosophie*" (What is Matter? Two Essays on the Philosophy of Nature).

Although Scheler died before providing a more detailed elaboration on the compatibility of his metaphysics with science, there are two elements that appear to support it. (1) His theory of resistance states that impulsion is the primordial capacity to resist and, therefore, impulsion in individual life alone has the capacity to posit reality. (2) Scheler argues that space must be reduced to motion, motion to variations of states of matter and both to forces.

In addition, the compatibility between Scheler's metaphysics and science is also supported by theoretical physics itself. Physics showed that the unity of electromagnetic field forces represents an ultimate logical subject of statements that are made in science. In 1900 classical mechanics came to be replaced by Max Planck's Quantum Theory and in 1905 by Einstein's Special Theory of Relativity. Planck's theory said that the emissions of luminous energy by an atom of matter can occur only in *discrete*, discontinuous packages or "quanta" that are the smallest possible units of energy. A quantum cannot be subdivided and remains a constant in the energy of the universe. Five years later, Einstein put forward the special theory of relativity. He showed that mass and energy must be equivalent and discovered the particles of light, called photons.

For our purposes, let us take a model that should show how these complicated scientific theories from early this century revolutionized our understanding of the macro- and microcosmic universe.

When one looks at a neo-impressionist painting that shows one area of a continuous green color, this green area will turn into discrete dots of blue and yellow when seen from a close distance. Neo-impressionists criticized the impressionists for their use of impure mixtures of colors that failed to do justice to true light and true brightness. Georges Seurat (1859-1891) and Paul Signac (1863-1935) accordingly suggested that only small, unmixed discrete points and dots of pure colors should be used to produce true light. In this art-form known as pointillism the human sense of sight remains at leisure either to blend the points by keeping a certain distance from the painting or to separate the points by looking at the painting up close.

By analogy energy which in classical mechanics was conceived as a continuous, not a discrete, phenomenon turned out to be discrete, however, in modern physics. Yet, it can still be shown also to have a continuous wave character. In our model this would compare to the points which when seen up close would again appear contiguous with each another. According to this model it is the distance of the onlooker of the painting and, analogously, the relative location of the observer and the type of the arrangement of a physical experiment that determine whether there are dots of atoms, if you will, or waves, respectively. In atomic physics "particles" can be turned into "waves," and vice versa. Thus, the ancient impasse of whether "there is no smallest" and that all is contiguous (Anaxagoras) or whether there are only disconnected atoms and material islands that float in the universe (Democritus) is still alive. However, the most recent discovery of a sixth quark leads one to be convinced today that Democritus was ultimately right.

Material particles seem conditionally to have both wave and particle properties. One sometimes speaks of "matter waves," which implies a welding of the concepts of particle and wave theory, or one speaks of Niels Bohr's "principle of complimentarily," that holds that the two phenomena are complementary to each other. Furthermore, one can speak of Erwin Schrödinger's tenet that reality is what you make it to be or subscribe to Werner Heisenberg's well known "uncertainty principle" that claims that at subatomic levels the very act of observation already affects what is being observed. Indeed, he argued that the closer an observation on this level, the less accurate the observation becomes: there is either the position of an observable particle *or* its momentum, but never both at the same time. The outcome of his discussion was that only statistical laws govern the micro-universe, thereby making the causal predictability of classical mechanics obsolete.

On the level of the macro-universe one also needs to take into account other novel concepts, namely, space and time, which were regarded by Newton and Kant as discrete. Now space and time blend into a four-dimensional "space-time continuum." Fields, space, time and forces come to be regarded as inseparably bound together according to Maxwell's equations. The Maxwell equations, Scheler held, are the final word on a "mathematical physics of images" and "principles" that validate all scientific observation.

For us it is important to note that the ultimate subject that is responsible for discrete quantum effects in nature are neither in objective space nor in objective time. That is, all variations of effects occur in what Scheler calls the "expanse" (*das Auseinander*) of a four-dimensional continuum. However,—and this is where Scheler draws a line between the science of physics and philosophy—this four-dimensional space-time expanse is *not* the ultimate subject for a dynamic metaphysics. The expanse is nothing but a "first manifestation" of field forces (XI, 129, 134). Hence, Scheler understands the ultimate force that underlies physical field forces not to be an object of physics: it is an object of a dynamic metaphysics only.

From the perspective of this ultimate force as an object of meta-physics, theoretical physics deals with secondary effects and their measurable properties only. But the *unity* of all physical field forces in the four-dimensional continuum do "point" to one and the same force without which the reality of field forces in their four-dimensional expanse would not be thinkable (XI, 129). This ultimate force is impulsion. All pulsations of this ultimate force form a four-dimensional fluctuating variation, the *Wechsel*. Already in his *Sociology of Knowledge* Scheler wrote:

> The philosophical theory whereby reality is nothing but resistance against acts of vital movement and given *prior to* all other qualities of "corporeal" things (duration, gestalt, color, etc.), coincides very closely with the results of *theoretical physics* concerning the ultimate subjects of physical statements (VIII 147/PR 148).

Scheler's later ideas on this subject remained even more fragmentary (XI 125-156), most likely because he suffered from increasing premonitions of his death, which his widow related to me more than once. Scheler's message, however, is clear: there cannot be any area of investigation in theoretical physics or, for that matter, in any other natural science, that does not presuppose a *ground* for the realities shown and verified in scientific experimentations. Indeed, Einstein himself believed in a God like Spinoza's who would reveal Himself in the harmony of the universe. It is well known, although never confirmed by Einstein himself, that he told Ben-Gurion that there has to be something behind all physical energy. Einstein's God appears to be the physical world itself in almost the same sense that the sum of a triangle's 360 degrees follows from Spinoza's God *qua* Nature. Both Einstein's and Spinoza's God, no matter how faintly, fall intuitably under the concept of a cosmic religion. For Scheler, the ground behind all energy is impulsion as one of the two attributes of the Deity, because impulsion is the primordial capacity of resistance, which posits and gives rise to reality as a whole.

Scheler also wanted to incorporate into his dynamic metaphysics the role of the phantasy in impulsion with its primal "objective appearances" or "phantasmic images" that occur in both animate and inanimate nature. We saw that phantasmic images do not reach only human drives but also the mind's highest forms of abstractions as found in pure mathematics. Phantasmic images, therefore, point to a basic tendency of impulsion itself: the tendency toward its own spiritualization. Scheler refers to this tendency, as we noted, as *eros* in distinction from *agape*, which, he thought, is spirit's tendency toward realization with impulsion. These overlapping tendencies both have the form of self-becoming in absolute time.

As we saw earlier, metaphysics must recognize that effects, waves and corpuscles have their own phantasmic images that exist separately from human consciousness because they originate in the principle of impulsion. The physical forces that underlie all inanimate nature are centers that determine physical fields. Physical fields determine a four-dimensional space-time-gestalt. Every such *gestalt* is of a purely statistical nature. The intensity of the pulsations in impulsion determine both magnitude and quality of any real body (XI 136). Subjective qualities are only a portion of the objective qualities, as had been discussed earlier with regard to the relationship between perception and phantasmic images.

According to what has been gleaned from respective fragments, a dynamic metaphysics recognizes the significance of theoretical physics and its dynamic theory of matter in which matter and energy are exchangeable. There is nothing like the traditional material substance, nor is there an objective space separate from an objective time. The traditional concepts of matter, empty space and time are "the greatest fictions," says Scheler, to which the human mind has ever given birth (IX 224, 230-231/PE 336, 344; XI 133, 137, 148).

In similar fashion, the traditional distinction between forces that either result or do not result in matter neglects the structure of impulsion. Impulsion does not allow such a distinction. Impulsion possesses its own teleology: it aims at *both* the inorganic and organic. Again, the inorganic and the organic are rooted in one and the same: impulsion. Hence, the difference between them is only phenomenally, not metaphysically valid.

h) Metaphysics and the Ground of Being

What, then, is supposed to be metaphysically valid? Metaphysics is made possible by two modes of participation that enable human existence to move toward the ground of being: (1) the partial identity that the human spirit shares with Divine spirit, and (2) the partial identity that human drives share with impulsion.

As the first attribute of the ground of being, referred to also as *ens a se*, spirit comes to know itself in the human spirit. Without the human being, or before the human spirit evolved in nature, spirit had no knowledge of itself. Impulsion, too, begins to sense itself (*empfindet sich*) on the animal level. Before there was any animality on earth, impulsion was nothing but *Gefühlstrieb*, a "feeling-drive" manifest first only in plants. But impulsion was already a force in inanimate nature. It was during the evolution of the human that both spirit and impulsion came to converge on each other by their interpenetration in an embodied spirit: the person (XI 90).

Scheler's manuscripts on metaphysics cover the period between 1923 and 1927. This time span coincides roughly with those of the treatises of *Probleme einer Soziologie des Wissens* and of *Erkenntnis und Arbeit* which Scheler referred to as "introductions" to his Metaphysics and philosophical anthropology underway. Metaphysics and philosophical anthropology are not separate disciplines. Both touch upon the ground of being as well as the essence of human existence. When Scheler writes that metaphysics is tantamount to "placing oneself" in both the continuous eternal production of nature in order for one to recreate to a certain extent all that had already developed, he implies that the common ground of metaphysics and of philosophical anthropology is the human being. Therefore the two cannot be separated from one another.

Scheler believed it possible to a certain extent to recreate the ground of being. This, however, also implies speculation. He does not shrink from admitting speculation to philosophy. He does not, however, use the term "speculation," without defining it. Speculation is described in two ways. (1) It is "immersion" of the human spirit into the emergence of ideas in absolute time, and (2) it is the "dionysian" phenomenological reduction that leads to a nullification of the inner vital capacity of resistance *qua* reality, that is, impulsion.

On this basis, metaphysics can recreate and reproduce a Divine ground of the world. The term "Divine" is still used loosely up to this point because Divine spirit is just a "potency" for the generation of ideas for a human spirit that is said to partake in that generation. Being only potential, Divine spirit cannot have the theistic character of being all-knowing or omniscient. Divine spirit does not exist "prior" to the world either: it did not create a world at a random moment in calendar-time. The concept of a Divine existence prior to creation had long been abandoned by Scheler because spirit, including Divine spirit, realizes itself only "with" a world in each phase of its absolute time of becoming. Hence, spirit like ideas, too, is becoming. Divine spirit and world—the latter sometimes referred to as God's lived body—are in a continuous state of a becoming functionalized with each other.

The last manuscripts of Scheler's metaphysics and philosophical anthropology, which had been made accessible only in recent times in the *Gesammelte Werke*, sometimes show a baffling use of terms.

One such use is that of All-Life that is said to be identical with impulsion (XI 181; XII 220), yet in other places it does not appear to have this identity (XI 221). Indeed, one can ask why this term is introduced in the first place when the meaning of impulsion had already been clarified. In addition, concepts of traditional philosophy are used with novel connotations, for example, when the term *ens a se* was suddenly introduced as the ground of being that has the two attributes of spirit and impulsion. All this makes Scheler's final texts difficult reading. Accordingly, some guidelines must be sought to assist general understanding of notions connected with such terms. The guidelines submitted here follow from practical examples found in the texts themselves.

Scheler preferred, for instance, "continuous creation," the *creatio continua*, to the theistic notion of creation. However, continuous creation is not understood in the meaning given by St. Augustine. Its meaning is now the continuous interpenetration of spirit and impulsion and their realizing themselves in this interpenetration. The interpenetration takes place in absolute time as Scheler understood it. Just as the human spirit can only realizes itself as an embodied spirit, that is, in the embodied person, so also Divine spirit requires a lived body for its realization. This lived body is understood also as "world" as we just mentioned, or as the "organism" of the cosmos said to be trans-individual (*überindividuell*) "All-Life."

All-Life, in turn, is seen in light of the Scholastic meaning of "*natura naturans*" (XI 199). In Scholasticism, *natura naturans* designated God. Literally, it meant "nature naturing" or "maturing nature." The naturing of nature is a process of the begetting of "*natura naturata*" or the "nature natured," or nature begotten from *natura naturans*. In using the medieval term "*natura naturans*," however, Scheler's use of it is close to Spinoza's. For Spinoza, all of God's attributes are infinite when seen in light of *natura naturans*, but finite when seen in light of *natura naturata*. Only two attributes of *natura naturata* are accessible: spirit and extension. Like Spinoza, Scheler also assumed there to be an infinite number of attributes in God, not only the two of spirit and impulsion.

Matters become even more blurred when Scheler uses the concept of substance, so much rejected in *Formalism*, in connection with the term "*ens a se*." Substance and *ens a se* are the point of coincidence of infinitely different attributes, whereas the universal substance itself is simple and without inherent differences. Indeed, this substance is also said to be Plotinus's "One" (XI 215) coming full circle to what

Scheler had stated on Plotinus with regard to his phenomenology of religious experience in 1915/16 (X 251).

It should also be mentioned that while Scheler's use of "spirit" becomes so prominent that he does not often speak about its form, the person. This is because Scheler looks predominantly at spirit from a metaphysical viewpoint. While he never abandoned the idea of the "person" as the form of spirit in which spirit realizes itself, he does tell us that ontologically spirit, as an attribute of the *ens a se*, precedes and concentrates in the center of the person (XII 181). He also stresses that both impulsion and spirit are unfinished and, therefore, continue growing through their real manifestations. The becoming Deity itself is a process of growth in its own works.

Despite the divergent use of these historical terms, impulsion is not a transcendent metaphysical principle independent of reality. It is one of the two knowable attributes *in* Divine becoming with which human becoming is also happening and in which impulsion is the necessary condition for the realization of God's and humanity's spirit in the history of humans and in the historicity of the world.

Given this state of affairs, one must ask whether Scheler's later thinking allowed for a moral attribute of the becoming Deity. Is this Deity, for example, a highest good? Scheler addressed this question very briefly: he answered no. Therefore, the theistic notion of a highest and perfect being is impossible. In a manner of speaking, he simply decrees that God's spirit cannot be made responsible for the existence of the world. It is equally incorrect to make God responsible for the existence of the world as it is to deny God's existence. It is not God but "All-Life" in God that in the sense of impulsion gives birth to the world. Impulsion as a vital force cannot be made "responsible" for anything, including the world's existence. The existence of the world cannot, therefore, be interpreted on moral grounds (XI 199).

This argumentation seems, however, to be flawed because moral existence is nowhere explained. One can find some justification with his argument, however, if the argument is examined more closely than Scheler himself did. One expects that a becoming Deity is a Deity that struggles with Itself, which Scheler quite forcefully held at the time (XIII 89). In this sense the Deity must be considered the primordial bearer of moral qualities and dimensions because its own struggle of becoming and its own impulsion exposes the potential for moral imperfection in the Deity. The best argument for moral existence with its dimensions of good and evil that Scheler presents is contained in his 1913 essay *Über Scham und Schamgefühl*. Here the human being is seen as a "bridge" between Satan and God. Scheler argued that neither God nor the devil can be both good and evil, but that man must because his ontological place is between God and Satan. Scheler now insists, however, that a moral status can be found in neither *natura naturans* nor in impulsion: neither possesses guilt or merit. He points out that all great minds of the century—he mentions among others William James, Tolstoi and M. Weber—pointed to this line of thinking by denying God's omnipotence (XI 199).

Having considered Scheler's rethinking of certain traditional notions, particularly the clarification of the meaning of speculation and of the explanation made earlier of pure phenomenological intuition, Scheler's late thinking nevertheless appears to have followed a clear path. The interpenetration of spirit and impulsion in God, in the human being, and the world as a whole, is intuited as a process of becoming and transition. This process happens in absolute time; its phases and historical meanings coincide *originaliter*. Their coincidence is "historicity" in which not only recordable history but the world itself is embedded.

We saw that Scheler's unremitting endeavor to gain insight into the nature of absolute time becomes more and more significant in his philosophy. This is partly because of the publication of Heidegger's *Being and Time*. After he read it, Scheler embarked on the third part of his essay *Idealismus-Realismus* in which he presented crucial visions of space and time. Clearly, Heidegger had no influence on Scheler's views in this regard. Scheler remained steadfast: there is no time without life, no matter how time can be thematized ontologically. Nevertheless, as the first person to whom Heidegger sent a copy of *Being and Time*, Scheler thought it to be of import. Indeed, he resolved to write a Part 5 of *Idealismus-Realismus* that would be designed exclusively as a critical debate with Heidegger's work (IX 235/ PE 349). When he was working on the project, Scheler died. Part 5 remained a fragment (IX 254-294).

Upon close scrutiny, one can again see traces of Scheler's thinking of absolute time. Of what significance, after all, is absolute time? Does it have the same degree of significance as temporality has for Heidegger, or time-consciousness has for Husserl? It does, but the significance is on another scale.

To begin, the significance of absolute time is seen in its various manifestations. First, absolute time occurs in living individuals of all organic forms. Second, absolute time in the character of transition was said to occur in mutations. Third, it occurs as social-historical time among coexisting humans, that is, as "We-Time." Forth, absolute time must be differentiated from measurable time. Absolute time that manifests itself in the above respects (as well as its occurring in historicity, the becoming of the Divine and of the world) has, therefore, *manifold* manifestations. These manifestations led Scheler to ask the question with regard to the temporality of Heidegger's *Dasein*,

> Is there also one, unique absolute time, a time in which the dimensions of past, present and future are preserved but are no longer relative to a particular living creature? Is there a unique time in which nature (*Sosein*) and temporal position are so linked to one another that a unique, absolutely irreversible process runs through its course in it and "the same" being and happening consequently could never recur? (IX 235/PE 349) (Tr. slightly changed)

It is not human *Dasein* or consciousness alone that is ontologically completely irreversible: it is life *itself* that is a "*temporal run-off*" (*selbst etwas zeithaft Ablaufendes*) (XII 215). Time as the empty time of classical mechanics or as a container *à la* Newton is rational fiction (XI 133). In the inorganic world of atomic micro-objects, Scheler agrees with the physicist Boltzmann that reversibility is at best thinkable. It is also to be noted that for Scheler, as it was for Heidegger and Husserl, time possesses a higher dignity than space. For Kant space and time had still an equal role to play in the forms of intuition as a result of the sway that science had upon him.

And yet, life as the condition for the possibility of both time and space makes time and space relative *to* life. How can this be? Through its ongoing becoming and unbecoming, its ever birth-giving and dying process, life "*posits its own flux*" (XII 215). Paradoxically, however, absolute time is still relative to life. How can something called "absolute" be at the same time "relative?"

It is not only the phenomenological technique of bracketing an individual's center of resistance, namely impulsion, that opens up the structure and essence of "world." In this, absolute time is still relative to an X that *can* inhibit its life-center in such a fashion that this X "overlooks" this center. This X—human spirit—for this reason cannot itself be wholly part of absolute time, let alone can it be forever incarcerated in the Kantian *Anschauungsformen* of space and time. Rather, spirit is able to place itself into the very center of the ceaselessly self-creating ground of all, the "divine substance" from which entities, the world and its phantasmic images emerge (XII 215).

Since the human spirit can truly tower above "continuous creation" and its absolute time process, it must also be able to account for the opposite of life's self-creating activity manifest in procreation: life's unbecoming or the phenomenon of death.

i) Death

As a subject of investigation, the problem of death can be traced in Scheler's work to 1911/12 (X 510). He presented a lecture on the subject in Göttingen in 1914 and published a lengthy essay entitled "*Tod und Fortleben*" ("Death and Afterlife") that is the only extant work of his dealing with a phenomenology of death (X 11-63). In it Scheler gave an outline of the tendency of the direction of the shifting experience of present, past and future in one's life time. We recall Scheler telling us in Chapter VII that the shifting tendency of the three horizons of temporal experience shows: that the past unremittingly "eats away" all of the life that has been lived; that the horizon of the future is getting ever smaller and squeezing the horizon of the present to extinction between the growing of the past and the diminishing horizon of the future. But what about death itself? It extinguishes the present, past and future horizons in both consciousness and vital experience. Scheler claimed in this essay that all that can be safely established phenomenologically are three points: (1) dying itself is an act *within* the process of life; (2) death is an intuitive certainty during everyone's life time; and (3) just as consciousness in its form of the person can "swing beyond" the lived body experiences during one's life time, so also the person can swing beyond the body's remains (*Leichnam*) during the act of dying and after death. Proving and disproving a continuation of the swinging-beyond-existence of the person after death are not appropriate methods for establishing the truth of this matter. A supra-temporality of a person's "swinging beyond" life's death is all one can establish phenomenologically.

While Scheler also confronted the problem of death in this essay from psychological and cultural viewpoints, he likewise addressed the phenomenon of angst of death, which he sees as a result of the modern calculating mind-set of the West.

After having delivered a lecture on "*Das Wesen des Todes*" (The Nature of Death) at the University of Cologne in 1923/24, Scheler's notes on metaphysical, scientific and medical theories on death show an increased occupation with the subject (XII 253-341). Notwithstanding his mastery of the literature on death at the time, especially that of medical literature, there appear conceptualizations of the nature of death central to the posthumous publications: namely that death is "harvest" (*die Ernte*). As seen from All-Life, death is a feast of accumulation and the giving away of what individual life had gained. Death is the complete victor over All-Life; death is eternal salvage of what All-Life has accumulated from the struggles of individual life.

Death is reversion to All-Life into itself. This is what, in a world of woman-rule (*die gynokratische Welt*), was expressed as a highest worship possible of All-Life: death is increase of power of the deceased souls; procreation is only the event designed toward this increase (XII 339). Womanhood is replete with the drive of death and the drive of procreation. For this reason, woman is born to serve, to suffer, to sacrifice, to be patient. But: "It is you—not us men—who have in possession the passkey to life" (XII 239). Woman represents impulsion; man represents spirit. Both demand one another. Scheler goes on to say that in their mutual love rises the disposition for the unification of Godhead with impulsion in the human being. Without women, man would fly into the skies of ideas. Without men, woman is bound to the earth like worms and remain blind; just as men remain paralysed without woman.

Despite the increasing range of the stream and the "waves" of All-life with its female and male sides, and despite the end of individual life with its disintegration of organs—because organs deteriorate in late age—*nothing gets lost*. All-life continuously enriches itself with the new functions that each vital individual, beginning with lowest one-cell organisms, had gained during an individual's natural span of life. Hence, we find expressions such as death being an "innovator" or a "revolutionary power" that prevents life from petrifying. Death in this sense is a sacrifice for the new life to come, just as history must have great revolutions for the same purpose. No matter what anybody's political orientations, we all have to admit that without the death of individuals and generations, without war and all destructive events in history, there is no chance for fresh and innovative happenings to surface, no chance for further development of humanity. In his early work *The Genius of War*, Scheler had likened destruction and war to a "moral thunderstorm" which is followed by an atmosphere of refreshment. Likewise, the meaning of death is to return a maximum of life (XII 337).

Because life is rooted in God's second attribute, impulsion, the becoming Godhead, too, dies and unbecomes with each individual's death but rises again in new life. Thus, the Godhead is present in the dying flesh and in the flesh reborn. In the waves of All-Life, death is like the receding of the water that makes way for new and higher waves. This symbolism of Scheler's follows from a slowly emerging majestic picture of a philosophy that encompasses the becoming of man, world and God sketching itself in this self-becoming process of absolute time. It is a process in which each of its phases contains the phenomenon of unbecoming or the death of individual life and of the death of species. But death is one side of a vital process whose other side is procreation (XII 91).

Since Scheler conceived dying one's death and death in general *within* the process of All-Life—that is, not as an end-point precipitating into nothingness—death cannot be equated with "absolute" nothingness. Death must be seen as "nothingness relative to something," that is, to life. It must be sharply distinguished absolute nothingness. Absolute nothingness would amount to complete absence of all: of man, the macro- and micro-universe and of God. While absolute nothingness is thus thinkable, it nevertheless defies the first principle of metaphysics according to which there is something rather than nothing, or that "nothing is not."

A 1927 note entitled *Zum Schluss der Anthropologie* (For the Conclusion of the Anthropology) Max Scheler gives us a hint of how much he was wrestling with the exposition of his final thoughts. He noted:

There is no human being bound by any culture, bound by any race, by any climate or by any countryside, tradition or myth. The human being is free—free to will what he wants, free to contemplate and to think whatever he wants to. Knowing that he is rooted in eternal substance—and that he has both drive-life and spirit that permeate all his bodily and psychic stirrings—being *open* to all nature, *open* to all cultures and *open* to his very own nature: the human being can rise above all nature and history. He is even free to accept, and can even truly will, his own death—knowing also that in such things he is a sacrifice for the becoming of the Godhead, and that his death amounts to the Godhead's own harvest and convalescence. He who loves, dies comfortably. He who took into himself enough of the life-giving nectar of the world, and who was both responsible and coresponsible for his fellow human beings: he, too, will die comfortably. And he who had been sensitive to the essential powers of ego-alien nature during his life time; and who felt borne by its *colossal wave* that he could control to a small extent, he, too, will succumb peacefully to all tides of nature.

Modern angst of death originates in the mistaken belief that "life" is a private property of one's organism like commodities and possessions are. Modern angst does not allow humans to see that life is flowing through us and that it gives itself as something that we must carry forward. Angst of death is also the mistaken belief that the soul is by itself an "isolated substance" to be saved and to be made appealing to a Divine judge. This very angst of death is, however, only the symptom

that ensues from bourgeois *loneliness* (society, bourgeois egoism). At
the same time, the angst inflates transient values of useful goods. Modern angst is a token of an *impoverished life.*

Death of the individual—what are you? "Dawn's resplendence; ascent;
harvest and onset in life's own endless revitalization through which it
grows and grows.

The cosmic-theogonic-solidary order of the becoming of world and
Deity will crush all angst of death. It will provide redemption from an
objectified ego. It will make us feel that we continue to live—in every
flower, insect, in all winds and clouds. This order will make us feel also
that our thinking, too, goes on in every other later mnd that links up
its ongoing thoughts with our's. (XII 340)

Originally, man lives in teh truth. (XV 155)

Soon after, during the night of May 12 to May 13, 1928, Scheler
suffered a heart attack. He was hospitalized. According to his widow,
he did not want to continue to live in such condition. He had longed
to have more children ever since his marriage to Maerit Furtwängler.
On May 17, 1928, his third wife Maria told him she was pregnant.
On May 19, Scheler suddenly became thirsty. He asked for a glass of
beer. The nurse hastened to get it for him. When she returned, death
had taken him away.

BIBLIOGRAPHIES

Collected Works (*Gesammelte Werke*) of Max Scheler

The Collected Works appeared in Bern: Francke Verlag, 1954-1985. Since 1986 it has been published in Bonn: Bouvier Verlag.

Vol. I   *Frühe Schriften.* Ed. Maria Scheler and Manfred S. Frings. Bern: Francke Verlag 1971.

Vol. II   *Der Formalismus in der Ethik und die matierale Wertethik. Neuer Versuch der Grundlegung eines ethischen Personalismus.* Ed. Maria Scheler, 1st to 5th Edition. Ed. Manfred S. Frings, 6th Edition. Bern: Francke Verlag, 1980.

Vol. III   *Vom Umsturz der Werte.* Ed. Maria Scheler, 5th Edition. Bern, Francke Verlag, 1972.

Vol. IV   *Politisch Pädagogische Schriften.* Ed. Manfred S. Frings. Bern: Francke Verlag, 1982.

Vol. V   *Vom Ewigen im Menschen.* Ed. Maria Scheler. Bern: Francke Verlag, 1954.

Vol. VI   *Schriften zur Soziologie und Weltanschauungslehre.* Ed. Maria Scheler. Bern: Francke Verlag, 1963.

Vol. VII   *Wesen und Formen der Sympathie.* Ed. Manfred S. Frings. Bern: Francke Verlag, 1973.

Vol. VIII   *Die Wissensformen und die Gesellschaft.* Ed. Maria Scheler, 1st and 2nd Edition. Ed. Manfred s. Frings, 3rd Edition. Bern: Francke Verlag, 1980.

Vol. IX   *Späte Schriften.* Ed. Manfred S. Frings. Bern: Francke Verlag, 1976.

Vol. X   *Schriften aus dem Nachlass, I. Zur Ethik und Erkenntnislehre.* Ed. Maria Scheler. Bern: Francke Verlag, 1957.

Vol. XI   *Schriften aus dem Nachlass, II. Erkenntnislehre und Metaphysik.* Ed. Manfred S. Frings. Bern: Francke Verlag, 1979.

Vol. XII   *Schriften aus dem Nachlass, III. Philosophische Anthropologie.* Ed. Manfred S. Frings. Bonn: Bouvier Verlag, 1987.

Vol. XIII   *Schriften aus dem Nachlass, IV. Philosophie und Geschichte.* Ed. Manfred S. Frings. Bonn: Bouvier Verlag, 1990.

Vol. XIV   *Schriften aus dem Nachlass, V. Varia I.* Ed. Manfred S. Frings. Bonn: Bouvier Verlag, 1993.

Vol. XV   *Schriften aus dem Nachlass, VI, Varia II.* Ed. Manfred S. Frings. Bonn: Bouvier Verlag, 1997.

Current English Translations
Books and Collections of Essays

Abbreviation   Work

E   *On the Eternal in Man.* Tr. Bernard Noble. London: SCM Press, 1960.

F   *Formalism in Ethics and Non-Formal Ethics of Values.* Tr. Manfred S. Frings and Roger L. Funk. Evanston, IL: Northwestern University Press, 1973.

M   *Man's Place in Nature.* Tr., Intro. Hans Meyerhoff. NY: Noonday, 1961.

N   *The Nature of Sympathy.* Tr. Peter Heath. Intr. Werner Stark. London: Routledge & Kegan Paul, 1954. Reprinted Hamden, CN: Archon Books, 1970.

P   *Philosophical Perspectives.* Tr. Oscar Haac. Boston: Beacon Press, 1958.

PE   *Selected Philosophical Essays.* Tr., intro. David Lachterman. Evanston, IL: Northwestern University Press, 1973.

PR   *Problems of a Sociology of Knowledge.* Tr. Manfred S. Frings. Ed., intro. Kenneth W. Stikkers. London: Routledge & Kegan Paul, 1980.

PV   *Person and Self-Value. Three Essays.* Ed., intro., partially translated Manfred Frings. Dordrecht, Netherlands: Martinus Nijhoff, 1987.

R   *Ressentiment.* Tr. William W. Holdheim. Intro. Manfred S. Frings. Milwaukee, WI: Marquette University Press, 1994.

Essays

A   "An a priori Hierarchy of Value-Modalities." Tr. Daniel O'Connor. In *Readings in Existential Phenomenology.* Ed. Nathaniel Lawrence and Daniel O'Connor. Englewood Cliffs, N.J: [Pub], 1967.

CM   "Concerning the Meaning of the Feminist Movement." Tr. Manfred S. Frings. *Philosophical Forum*, Fall 1978.

FU   "Future of Man." Tr. Howard Becker. *Monthly Criterion* 7, Feb. 1928.

HU   "Humility." Tr. Barbara Fiand. *Aletheia* II, 1981.

ID   "The Idea of Peace and Pacifism." Tr. Manfred S. Frings. *Journal of the British Society for Phenomenology* 8, October 1976, continued January 1977.

IM "The Idea of Man." Tr. Clyde Nabe. *Journal of the British Society for Phenomenology* 9, October 1978.

L "Love and Knowledge." Tr. Harold J.Bershady with Peter Haley. In *Max Scheler. On Feeling, Knowing, and Valuing. Selected Writings.* Ed., intro. Harold J. Bershady. Chicago: The University of Chicago Press, 1992.

MA "Metaphysics and Art." Tr. Manfred S. Frings. In *Max Scheler (1874-1928) Centennial Essays.* Ed. Manfred S. Frings. The Hague: [Pub] 1974.

MS "The Meaning of Suffering." Tr. Harold J.Bershady. In *Max Scheler. On Feeling, Knowing, and Valuing. Selected Writings.* Ed., intro. Harold J.Bershady. Chicago: The University of Chicago Press, 1992.

PC "The Psychology of So-Called Compensation Hysteria and the Real Battle against Illness." Tr. Edward Vacek, S.J. *Journal of Phenomenological Psychology,* 15, 2, Fall 1984.

PO "On the Positivistic Philosophy of the History of Knowledge and Its Laws of Three Stages." Tr. Rainer Koehne. In *The Sociology of Knowl-edge: A Reader.* Ed. James E.Curtis, John W. Petras. New York: [Pub], 1970.

RR "Reality and Resistance: On Being and Time, Section 43." Tr. Thomas Sheehan. *Listening* 12, 3, Fall 1977.

SC "The Thomist Ethic and the Spirit of Capitalsm." Tr. Gertrude Neuwith. *Sociological Analysis,* 25 1964.

ST "Toward a Stratification of the Emotional Life." Tr. Daniel O'Connor. In *Readings in Existential Phenomenology.* Ed. Nathaniel Lawrence, Daniel O'Connor. Englwood Cliffs, NJ: [Pub], 1967.

SW "Sociology and the Study and Formulation of Weltanschauung." Tr. R.C. Speirs. In Max Weber's *Science as a Vocation.* Ed. Peter Lassman, Irving Velody with Herminio Martins. London: [Pub], 1989.

T "On the Tragic." Tr. Bernard Stambler. *Cross Currents* 4, 1954. Reprinted in *Tragedy: Vision and Form.* Ed. R.W.Corrigan. San Francisco, [Pub], n.d.

W "Max Weber's Exclusion of Philosophy (on the Psychology and Sociology of Nominalist Thought." Tr. R.C.Speirs. In Max Weber's "Science as a Vocation." Ed. Peter Lassman, Irving Velody with Herminio Martins. London: [Pub], 1989.

SELECTED SECONDARY LITERATURE (1955 to Present)

(In a number of the book listings below, additional bibliographical data can be found. Listings below have been selected with regard to their direct or indirect relevance to the present book.)

Alphéus, Karl. *Kant und Scheler.* 2nd. ed. Ed. Barbara Wolandt. Bonn: Bouvier Verlag, 1981.

Avé-Lallemant, E. "Die phänomenologische Reduktion in der Philosophie Max Schelers." In *Max Scheler im Gegenwartsgeschehen der Philosophie.* Ed. Paul Good. Bern und München: Francke Verlag, 1975.

———. *Die Nachlässe der Münchener Phänomenologen in der Bayerischen Staatsbibliothek* Wiesbaden: Otto Harrassowitz, 1975.

———. "Bibliographisches Verzeichniss." *Max Scheler. Schriften aus dem Nachlass,* III. Ed. Manfred S. Frings. Bonn: Bouvier Verlag, 1978.

———. "Schelers Phänomenbegriff und die Idee der phänomenologischen Erfahrung." *Phänomenologische Forschungen,* IX. Freiburg-München, 1980.

———. "Religion und Metaphysik im Weltalter des Ausgleichs." *Tijdschrift voor Filosofie,* XLII, 2, 1980.

———. "Die Stellung des Menschen im Kosmos," "Vom Ewigen im Menschen," "Die Wissensformen und die Gesellschaft." In *Lexikon der philosophischen Werke.* Ed. T.Volpi, J. Nida-Rümelin. Stuttgart: Alfred Kröner Verlag, 1988.

———. "Die Aktualität von Schelers Politischer Philosophie." In *Phänomenologische Forschungen,* Bd. 28/29, 1994.

———. "Die Lebenswerte in der Rangordnung der Werte." In *Vom Umsturz der Werte in der modernen Gesellschaft.* Ed. Gerhard Pfafferott. Bonn: Bouvier Verlag, 1997.

Barber, M.D. *Guardian of Dialogue. Max Scheler's Phenomenology, Sociology, and Philosophy of Love.* Lewisburg, PA: Bucknell University Press, 1993.

Bershshady, H.J. *Max Scheler. On Feeling, Knowing, and Valuing. Selected Writings.* Chicago: The University of Chicago Press, 1992.

Bianco, F. "Die Gegebenheit der Werte. Max Schelers Stellung in der Werturteilsdiskussion der Gegenwart." In *Vom Umsturz der Werte in der mdernen Gesellschaft.* Ed. Gerhard Pfafferott. Bonn: Bouvier Verlag, 1997.

Blosser, Ph.E. "Kant and Phenomenology." *Philosophy Today,* 30, No. 2, 1986.

———. "Moral and Nonmoral Values: A Problem in Scheler's Ethics." *Philosophy and Phenomenological Research,* 48, No.1, 1987.

———. "Is Scheler's Ethic an Ethic of Virtues?" In: P.E.Blosser et al. (eds) *Japanese and Western Phenomenology.* The Hague: Kluwer Academic Publishers, 1993.

———, *Scheler's Critique of Kant's Ethics.* Athens, Ohio: Ohio University Press, 1995.

Bosio, F. "Eternità e storia nel pensiero di Max Scheler." *Il Pensiero*, No. 1, 1973.

——. *L'idea dell'uomo e la filsofia nel pensiero di Max Scheler*. Rome: Abete, 1976.

——. "Il significato della cultura e il fine della filosofia nel pensiero di Max Scheler." *Studie Ricerche*, 1977.

——. "Il fondamento metafisico dell'antropologia scheleriana." L'anima. Napoli: 1979.

——. "L'idea del fondamento filosofico della scienza e della tecnica in Husserl, Scheler, Heidegger." *Il Contributo*, 4, 1979.

——. *Borghesia, socialismo e intuitione del mondo*. Tr. ital. di tre saggi di Max Scheler, con introd. e note. Brescia: La Scuola Editrice, 1982.

——. "L'uomo e l'assoluto nel pensiero di Max Scheler." *Verifiche*, No.2, 1982.

——. "Max Scheler: il senso della storia." *Criterio, No.3*, 1987.

——. "Scheler interprete di Nietzsche." *Criterio 3*, 1987.

——. "Storia, valori e persona nel pensiero di Max Scheler." *Storia e valori*. *Il progresso del mezzogiorno*, Napoli, 1991.

——. "Religione e filosofia in Max Scheler." *Azione e contemplazione*. Milano, 1992.

——. "Il significato dell'antropologia filosofica nel pensiero di Max Scheler." *Fenomenologia e Società*, 2, 1992. (Introduzione a *Pagine scelte dalle opere di Max Scheler*, Roma, 1986).

——. *Invito al pensiero di Max Scheler*. Milano: Mursia, 1995.

——. *Max Scheler: Idealismo-Realismo*. Tr. ital. con introd. e note. Napoli: Il Tripode, 1995.

——. "Das Motiv des Umsturzes der Werte in der Erkenntnis der Welt und des Menschen in der Philosophie von Max Scheler." In *Vom Umsturz der Werte in der modernen Gesellschaft*. Ed. Gerhard Pfafferott. Bonn: Bouvier Verlag, 1997.

Brenk, B. *Metaphysik des einen und absoluten Seins. Mitdenkende Darstellung der metaphysichen Gottesidee des späten Max Scheler*. Meisenheim am Glan: Verlag Anton Hain, 1975.

——. "Ausgleich als solidarisches Werdeschicksal von Weltgrund, Welt- und Menschheitsprozess." *Siegener Studien*, 33, 1982/83.

Caronello, G. "Dallo spiritualismo al personalismo. Ipotesi sulla genesi del 'formalismo' di Max Scheler." (Introduction to italian tr. of *Der Formalismus in der Ethik und die matiarale Wertethik*.)

Catesson, J. "La valeur <materiale> et ses conséquences." *Critique*, 13. 1957.

Chang, M. "Valeur, personne et amour chez Max Scheler." *Revue philosophique de Louvain*, 69, 1971.

Cho Jeong-Ok. *Liebe bei Max Scheler unter besonderer Berücksichtigung des Begriffs "Eros." Eine kritische Interpretation insbesondere an Hand seines Werkes Wesen und Formen der Sympathie*. (Diss.) München, 1990.

Cusinato, G. "Intuizione e percezione: Bergon nella prospettiva di Scheler." *Annali*, 1986/87.

——. "La tesi dell'Ohnmacht del Geist e il problema del dualismo nell'ultimo Scheler." *Verifiche* 1995.

——. "'Ausgleich,' funzionalizzazione e critica all'illuminismo. La prospettiva di una filosofia 'inter-culturale in Max Scheler." In: Atti del convegno: *L'oggetto della storia della filosofia. Fisciano,* maggio, 1996.

——. "Die Historisierung des Apriori und der Funktionalisierungsbegriff im Denken Max Schelers." In *Cognitio humana. Dynamik des Wissens und der Werte* (Deutscher Kongress für Philosophie), Leibzig, September 1996.

——. *"Il superamento dell'egoismo e i gradi dell aperttura all'Assoluto. Sulle tracce di Max Scheler"* (in preparation).

——. "Absolute Rangordnung und Relativität der Werte im Denken Max Schelers. In *Vom Umsturz der Werte in der modernen Gesellschaft.* Ed. Gerhard Pfafferott. Bonn: Bouvier Verlag, 1997.

Da Re, A. "Die Tyrannei der Werte. Carl Schmitt und die phänomenologische Ethik. In *Vom Umsturz der Werte in der modernen Gesellschaft.* Ed. Gerhard Pfafferott. Bonn: Bouvier Verlag, 1997.

Deeken, A. *Process and Permanence in Ethics: Max Scheler's Moral Philosoophy.* New York: Paulist Press, 1974.

Dunlop, F. "Scheler's Theory of Punishment." *JBSP: Journal of the British Society for Phenomenology,* Vol 9, No.3, 1978.

——. "Scheler's Idea of Man: Phenomenology versus Metaphysics in the Late Works." *Aletheia,* 2, 1981.

Du Plessis, S.I.M. "Max Scheler's Concern with the Highest Perfection." In *Truth and Reality: Philosophical Perspectives on Reality.* Festschrift for Professor H.G. Stoker. Braamfontein, South Africa: De Jong's, 1971.

Dupuy, Maurice. *La philosophie de Max Scheler, son évolution et son unité.* 2 vols. Paris: Presses universitaires, 1959.

Escher Di Stephano, A. *Ill coraggio della verità. Max Scheler e la riflessione sull'uomo.* Napoli, 1991.

Ferretti, G. "Fenomenologia e teoria della conoscenza in Max Scheler." *Rivista di Filosofia Neo-Scolastica,* 1965.

——. "Rassegna di studi scheleriani in lingua tedesca." *Rivista di Filosofia Neo-Scolastica,* 1965.

——. *Filosofia della religione.* Milano, 1972.

——. *Max Scheler. Fenomenologia e antropologia personalistica.* Milano, 1972.

Filippone, V., *Società e cultura nel pensiero di Max Scheler., 2 vol.,* Milano, 1964-1969.

Findley, J.N. *Axiological Ethics.* London: Macmillan, 1970.

Frings, M.S. *Max Scheler. A Concise Introduction into the World of a Great Thinker.* Pittburgh: Duquesne University Press, 1965. 2nd. ed. Milwaukee: Marquette University Press, 1996.

——. "Der Ordo Amoris bei Max Scheler. Seine Beziehungen zur materialen Wertethik und zum Ressentimentbegriff." *Zeitschrift für Philosophische Forschung,* XX, 1, 1966, 57-76. (Transl. as "The Ordo Amoris in Max

Scheler." In *Facets of Eros*. Ed. F.J.Smith, E. Eng. The Hague: Martinus Nijhoff, 1973, 40-60).

——. "Max Scheler: On the Ground of Christian Thought." *Franciscan Studies,* Vol.27, Annual V, 1967.

——. *Person und Dasein. Zur Frage der Ontologie des Wertseins.* The Hague: Martinus Nijhoff. Phaenomenologica, Vol. 32, 1969.

——. "Max Scheler. Rarely Seen Complexities of Phenomenology." In: *Phenomenology in Perspective.* Ed. F.J. Smith. The Hague: Martinus Nijhoff, 1970.

——. *Zur Phänomenologie der Lebensgemeinschaft. Ein Versuch mit Max Scheler.* Meisenheim: Verlag Anton Hain, 1971.

——. "Toward the Constitution of the Unity of the Person." In *Linguistic Analysis and Phenomenology.* Eds. W.Mays, S.C.Brown. London: Macmillan, 1972.

——. *"Drang und Geist."* In: *Grundprobleme der grossen Philosophen. Philosophie der Gegenwart II.* Ed. J. Speck. Göttingen: Vandenhoeck & Ruprecht, 1973. 3rd Edition 1991.

——. "Humility and Existence." *Delta Epsilon Sigma BULLETIN,* Vol. XIX, 4, 1974, (German tr. as "Demut und Existenz." In *Die Wertkrise des Menschen. Philosophische Ethik in der heutigen Welt. Festschrift für Hans Reiner.* Ed. N. Huppertz. Meisenheim: Verlag Anton Hain, 1979).

——. "Max Scheler. Zur hundertsten Wiederkehr seines Geburtstags im August d.J." *Zeitschrift für philosophische Forschung,* 28, 2, 1974.

——. "Zur Idee des Friedens bei Kant und Max Scheler." *Kant-Studien,* 66, 1, 1975.

——. "Max Scheler. Vom Wesen des Dinges in wissenssoziologischer Sicht." *Proceedings of the XV World Congress of PHilosphy,* Vol 5, Sofia, Bulgaria, 1975.

——. "Nothingness and Being." A Schelerian Comment on Heidegger. In: *Radical Phenomenology: Essays in Honor of Martin Heidegger.* Ed. J. Sallis. *Humanities Press,* Atlantic Highlands, NJ, 1977.

——. "Gott und das Nichts. Zum Gedenken des 50. Todestags Max Schelers." *Phänomenologische Forschungen,* 6/7, 1979.

——. "Max Scheler. A Descriptive Analysis of the Concept of Ultimate Reality." *Ultimate Reality and Meaning.* Vol. 3, No. 2, 1980.

——. "Zum Problem des Ursprungs der Technik bei Max Scheler." *Phänomenologische Forschungen,* Vol. 15, 1983.

——. "Is Resentment the Venom of Society? An Example of Value Theory." In: *Essays in Memory of Aron Gurwitsch.* Ed. L.Embree. Washington: *The Center for Advanced Research in Phenomenology & University Press of America,* 1984.

——. "Time Structure in Social Communality." In: *Phenomenology and Science in Phenomenological Experience.* Ed.: Kah Kyung Cho. The Hague: Martinus Nijhoff, 1984.

——. "Max Scheler: The Human Person as Temporality." *Philosophy & Theology.* Marquette University Quarterly, Vol.1, No.1, Fall 1986.

——. "Max Scheler and Kant. Two Paths toward the Same: The Moral Good." In *Kant and Phenomenology*. Ed. J.Kockelmans, Thomas Seebohm. Washington D.C.: The Center for Advanced Phenomenology and University Press of America, 1984.

——. "Zur Soziologie der Zeiterfahrung bei Max Scheler. Mit einem Rückblick auf Heraklit. *Philosophisches Jahrbuch der Görres-Gesellschaft*, 1984.

——. *Philosophy of Prediction and Capitalism*. Dordrecht-Boston-Lancaster: Martinus Nijhoff Publishers, 1987.

——. "La fondation historico-philosophique du capitalism chez Max Scheler." *Cahier Internationaux de Sociologie*, Vol. LXXXV, 1988.

——. "Scheler, Max." *Encyclopédie Philosophique Universelle, III, Les Ouevres Philosophiques*. Paris: Presses Universitaires de France, Tome 2, 1992.

——. "The Background of Max Scheler's Reading of *Being and Time*. A Critique of a Critique Through Ethics." *Philosophy Today*, May, 1992, 99-113.

——. "Capitalism and Ethics. The World Era of Adjustment and the Call of the Hour." Studien zur Philosophie von Max Scheler. Ed. E.W. Orth, G. Pfafferot. *Phänomenologische Forschungen*, Vol. 28/29, 1994.

——. "Max Scheler." *Encyclopedia Americana*. Danbury, CT. Grolier, 1994.

——. "Max Scheler." *Encyclopaedia Brittanica*, 15th Edition, 1994.

——. "Max Scheler." *Dictionaire d'éthique et de philosophie morale*. Paris: Press Universitaire de France, 1996.

Gabel, M. *Intentionalität des Geistes. Der phänomenologische Denkansatz bei Max Scheler.* Erfurth: Benno Verlag, 1991.

——. "Ausgleich und Verzicht. Schelers 'später' Gedanke des Ausgleichs im Licht seines Phänomenologischen Ansatzes." *Phänomenologische Forschungen*, 28/29, 1994.

——. "Das Heilige in Schelers Systematik der Wertrangordnung." In *Vom Umsturz der Werte in der modernen Gesellschaft*. Ed. Gerhard Pfafferott. Bonn: Bouvier Verlag, 1997.

Good, P. Ed.: *Max Scheler im Gegenwartsgeschehen der Philosophie*. Bern: Francke Verlag, 1975.

Hammer, F. *Theonome Anthropologie? Max Schelers Menschenbild und seine Grenzen*. Den Haag: Martinus Nijhoff (Phaenomenologica 45), 1972.

——. "Glauben an den Menschen. Helmuth Plessners Religionskritik im Verlgeich mit Max Schelers Religionsphilosophie." *Dilthey-Jahrbuch, 7*, 1990/91.

Hartmann, W. *Max Scheler Bibliographie*. Stuttgart: Frommann, 1963.

——. "Max Scheler and the English Speaking World." *Philosophy Today*, Vol.12, 1968.

——. "Das Wesen der Person. Substanzialitat-Aktualitat zur Personlehre Max Schelers." *Salzburger Jahrbuch für Philosophie*. 1966-67.

Haskamp, R. *Spekulativer und phänomenologischer Personalismus. Einflüsse J.G.Fichtes und R. Eukens auf Max Schelers Philosophie der Person*. Freiburg, 1966.

Heidegger, Martin. "Max Scheler zum Gedächtnis." Tr. by Thomas Sheehan as "In Memory of Max Scheler." In *Heidegger: The Man and the Thinker.* Ed. Thomas Sheehan. Chicago: Precedent, 1981.

Henckmann, W. "Die Begründung der Wissenssoziologie bei Max Scheler." *Philosophisches Jahrbuch,* 85, 1978.

———. "Gesammelte Werke, Band 4." (Review) *Philosophisches Jahrbuch,* 91, 1984.

———. "Die Gesammelten Werke Max Schelers. Mit einer Nachlese unbekannter Buchbesprechungen." *Zeitschrift für philosophische Forschung,* 39, 1985.

———. "Schelers Lehre vom Apriori." In *Gewissheit und Gewissen.* Ed. W. Baumgartner. Festschrift fur F.Wiedmann. Würzburg, 1987.

———. "Max Scheler." In *Staatslexikon,* Band IV, 1988.

———. "Max Scheler." In *Metzler Philosophen Lexikon.* Ed. B.Lutz. Stuttgart, 1989.

———. "Max Scheler. Phänomenologie der Werte." *Philosophen des 20. Jahrhunderts.* Ed. M.Fleischer. Darmstadt, 1990.

———. "Das Intentionalitätsproblem bei Scheler." *Brentano-Studien* 3, 1990/1.

———. "Max Scheler." In *Literaturlexikon. Autoren und Werke deutscher Sprache.* Band 10, Ed. W. Killi. Gütersloh/München, 1991.

———. "Materiale Wertethik." In *Geschichte der neueren Ethik,* Band II. Ed. A. Pieper. Tübingen, 1992.

———. "Der Systemanspruch von Schelers Philosophie." In *Phänomenologische Forschungen,* 28/29, 1994.

———. "Schelers Begriff der Philosophie in der Zeit des 'Umsturzes der Werte.'"

In *Vom Umsturz der Werte in der modernen Gesellschaft.* Ed. Gerhard Pfafferott. Bonn: Bouvier Verlag, 1997.

Héring, Jean. "De Max Scheler a Hans Reiner: Remarques sur la theorie des valeurs Morales dans le Mouvement Phénoménologique." *Revue d'Histoire des Sciences et de leurs Application,* 40, 1960

Hufnagel, E. *Zum Problem des Wollens in Kant und Scheler.* Bonn, 1972.

———. "Aspekte der Schelerschen Personlehre." *Kant-Studien,* 65, 1974.

Ibana, Rainier. "The Essential Elements for the Possibility and Necessity of the Principle of Solidarity according to Max Scheler," *Philosophy Today,* 33, No.1/4, 1989.

———. The Principle of Solidarity in Max Scheler's Philosophy of Social Analysis. (Diss.) Fordham University, 1989.

Janssen, P. "Scheler's Wesens- und Wertphilosophie. In: *Phänomenologische Philosophie.* Ed: Ströker und P.Janssen. Freiburg/München: Albers, 1889.

———. "Die Verwandlung der phänomenologischen Reduktion im Werke Max Schelers und das Realitätsproblem." *Phänomenologische Forschungen,* Bd. 28/29, 1994.

——. "Ueber einige Schwierigkeiten einer zeitgemässen philosophischen Anthropologie – am Beispiel Schelers." *Jahrbücher der Staatlichen Universität Wolograd.* Moscow, 1995.

——. "Fühlen/Erkennen - Werte/Sein. Von verschiedenen Möglichkeiten, die Eigenart von Wissen zu bestimen." In *Vom Umsturz der Werte in der modernen Gesellschaft.* Ed. Gerhard Pfafferott. Bonn: Bouvier Verlag, 1997.

Kaehler K.E. "Selbsterkenntnis, Selbsttäuschung und das Subjektive der Werte." In *Vom Umsturz der Werte in der modernen Gesellschaft.* Ed. Gerhard Pfafferott. Bonn: Bouvier Verlag, 1996.

Kelly, E. "Ordo Amoris. The Moral Vision of Max Scheler." *Listening* XXI, 1986.

——. *Max Scheler.* Boston: Twayne Publishers, 1977.

——. *The Phenomenological Philosophy of Max Scheler.* Dordrecht: Kluwer, 1997.

——. "Virtue-Based Ethics and Moral Rules in the Non-Formal Ethics of Value." *Journal of Value Inquiry,* 1997.

——. "Education and Culture in Max Scheler." *Aitia,* Spring 1994.

——. "Sociology and Social Criticism in Max Scheler." *Journal of Social Philosophy,* 14 (4), Wnter 1983-84.

——. "Max Scheler." In *Ethics and the Search for Values.* Eds. L.E.Navia and E.Kelly. Buffalo: Prometheus Books, 1980.

Kiss, E. "Die Auseinandersetzung mit Max Scheler." *Hermann Broch. Das theoretische Werk.* Frankfurt/Main, 1988.

——, "Schelers 'Umsturz' als Interpretation der europaischen Moderne." In *Vom Umsturz der Werte in der modernen Gesellscahft.* Ed. Gerhard Pfafferott. Bonn: Bouvier Verlag, 1997.

Lambertino, A. *Max Scheler. Fondazione fenomenologica dell'etica dei valori.* Firenze, 1977. 2nd.ed. Bonn: Bouvier Verlag, 1996.

——. "Scheler und die psychoanalytische Freudsche Theorie." In *Vom Umsturz der Werte in der modernen Gesellschaft.* Ed. Gerhard Pfafferott. Bonn: Bouvier Verlag, 1996.

Lauer, Q. "The Phenomenological Ethics of Max Scheler." *International Philosophical Quarterly* 1, 1961.

Leonardy, H. *Liebe und Person: Max Scheler's Versuch eines "phänomeno-logischen" Personalismus.* The Hague: Martinus Nijhoff, 1976.

——. "Es ist schwer ein Mensch zu sein." Zur Anthropologie des späten Scheler." *Phänomenoloigsche Forschungen,* Bd. 28/29, 1994.

——. "Edition et traduction des 'Annotations dans le *Formalisme* de Max Scheler' d'Edmund Husserl." In *Edmund Husserl. Etudes Phénomeno-logiques,* 13/14, Louvain-la Neuve, 1991.

——. "La Philosophie de Max Scheler. Un essai de presentification." *Etudes d'Anthropologie,* 2, Bibliothèque philosophique de Louvain 30, Louvain-la-Neuve, Editions de l'I.S.P., 1984.

——. "La dernière philosophie de Max Scheler." *Revue philosophique de Louvain,* tome 79, 1981.

Lembeck, K.H. "Deutscher Weltberuf"? Natorps und Schelers Kriegsphilosophie." In *Vom Umsturz der Werte in der modernen Gesellschaft.* Ed. Gerhard Pfafferott. Bonn: Bouvier Verlag, 1997.

Leroux, H. "Sur quelques aspectes de la reception de Max Scheler en France." *Phänomenologische Forschungen* Bd.2 8/29, 1994.

———. Fonction herméneutique de la notion d'*Umsturz der Werte* en sociologie et en anthropologie." In *Vom Umsturz der Werte in der modernen Gesellschaft.* Ed. Gerhard Pfafferott. Bonn: Bouvier Verlag, 1997.

Lichtigfeld, A. "A Scheler-Renaissance." *Tijdschrift voor Filosofie,* 37, No 4, 1975.

Liu Xiaofeng. "Scheler's Christian Thought and the Phenomenology of Values." In *Christian Thought in the 20th Century.* Ed. Liu Xiaofeng. Hong Kong/Shanghai: *Joint Publishing House,* 1990. 3rd ed. 1993.

———. "Scheler's Sociology of Resentment and Modernity." *Hong Kong Journal of Social Sciences* 4, 1994.

———. "Scheler and Modernity." [Introduction to the Chinese translation of "*Die Zukunft des Kapitalismus*" (The Future of Capitalism). Tr.Lo Dilou.] In *Die Zukunft des Kapitalismus.* Liu Xiaofeng, ed. Oxford University Press (China) 1995.

———. "Scheler's and Heidegger's Debate on Ontik." *Chinese Review of Phenomenology and Philosophy,* Shanghai, 1995.

———. *Personwerdung: eine theologische Untersuchung zu Max Schelers Phänomenologie der "Person-Gefühle" mit besonderer Berücksichtigung seiner Kritik an der Moderne.* (Diss.:Basel). Bern: Peter Lang, 1996.

Llambias De Azevedo, J. *Exposicion sistematica y evolutiva de su filosofia, con algunas criticas y .* Buenos Aires, 1966.

Lützeler, H. *Persönlichkeiten. Konrad Adenauer, Paul Clemen, Kardinal Frings, Johannes XXIII, Erich Rothacker, Max Scheler.* Freiburg i.B.: Herder, 1978.

Luther, A.R. "Scheler's Interpretation of Being and Loving." *Philosophy Today.* 14, 1970.

———.*Persons in Love: A Study of Max Scheler's Wesen und Formen der Sympathie.* The Hague: Martinus Nijhoff, 1972.

———. "Scheler's Person and Nishida's Active Self as Centers of Creativity." *Philosophy Today* 21, 1977.

Macann, Ch.E. "Zu einer genetischen Ethik: Eine interpretative Transformation von Schelers Wertethik." In *Vom Umsturz der Werte in der modernen Gesellschaft.* Ed. Gerhard Pfafferott. Bonn: Bouvier Verlag, 1997.

Mader, W. *Die Geisteshaltung einer Philosophie und eines Philosophen.* (Diss.). Innsbruck: 1968.

———. *Max Scheler in Selbstzeugnissesn und Bilddokumenten.* Reinbeck bei Hamburg: Rowohlt, 1980. 2nd.ed. 1995.

———. *Die Leiden des Lebens und die Leidenschaft des Denkens bei Max Scheler.* (unpublished manuscript).

Mall, R.A. Schelers Konzept der kosmopolitischen Philosophie. *Trierer Beiträge,* 11, 1982.

——. "Schelers Idee einer werdenden Anthropologie und Geschichtsteleologie." *Phänomenologische Forschungen* Bd. 28/29, 1994.

Melle, U. "Schelers Motive in Husserls Freiburger Ethik." In *Vom Umsturz der Werte in der modernen Gesellschaft*. Ed. Gerhard Pfafferott. Bonn: Bouvier Verlag, 1997.

Métreau, A. *Introduction à Max Scheler ou la phénoménologie des valeurs (chois des textes)*, Paris, 1973.

Miller, G.D. "Ordo Amoris. The Heart of Scheler's Ethics." *Listening* Vol. 21, No.3, 1986.

Mikoshiba, Y. "Ueber den Begriff der Weltoffentheit bei Max Scheler." (Jap.). *Shisosi-wo-yomu*. Ed. Mineshima, Hideo. Tokyo: Hokujushuppan, 1995.

Morra, G. "Il primo Scheler. La nascita di uno moralisto." *Ethica*, XII, 1973.

——.*Max Scheler. Una introduzione*. Roma, 1987.

Nusser, K.H. "Wissenschaft, Weltanschauung und Charisma bei Max Scheler und Max Weber." In *Vom Umsturz der Werte in der modernen Gesellschaft*. Ed. Gerhard Pfafferott. Bonn: Bouvier Verlag, 1997.

Oh, Chang-Sun. *Sein und Herz – Die Personlehre Max Schelers in der metaphysisch-ontologischen Erhellung*. (Diss.:) München, 1986.

Ortega y Gasset. "Max Scheler. un ubriaco di essenze." *Ethica* 7, 1968.

Orth, E.W. "Husserl, Scheler, Heidegger. Eine Einführung in das Problem der philosophischen Komparatistik." In *Husserl, Scheler, Heidegger in der Sicht neuer Quellen*. Ed. E.W. Orth. *Phänomenologische Forschungen*, 6/7: Freiburg im Breisgau und München: Verlag Karl Alber, 1978.

——. Co-editor. "Studien zur Philosophie von Max Scheler. Internationales Max-Scheler-Colloquium "Der Mensch im Weltalter des Ausgleichs." *Phänomenoloigsche Forschungen*, 28/29, 1994. '

——. "Lebensformen und Werte." In *Vom Umsturz der Werte in der modernen Gesellschaft*. Ed. Gerhard Pfafferott. Bonn: Bouvier Verlag, 1997.

Perrin, R. *Max Scheler's Concept of the Person. An Ethics of Humanism*. New York: St. Martin's Press, 1991.

——. "A Commentary on Max Scheler's Critique of the Kantian Ethic." *Journal of the History of Philosophy* 12, 1974.

Pigalev, A. "Wertewandel, Phänomenologie der Liebe und die Frage nach dem fremden Ich im Denken Max Schelers." In *Vom Umsturz der Werte in der modernen Gesellschaft*. Ed. Gerhard Pfafferott. Bonn: Bouvier Verlag, 1997.

Pintor Ramos, A. "El risentiemento: Nietzsche y Scheler. *La Ciudad de Dios*, 183, 1970.

——.*El humanismo de Max Scheler*, Madrid, 1978.

Pfafferott, G. *Ethik und Hermeneutik. Mensch und Moral im Gefüge der Lebensform*. (Forum Academicum. Monographien zur philosophischen Forschung, Bd.208) Königstein/Ts., 1981.

——. Co-editor. Vorwort in: Studien zur Philosophie von Max Scheler. Internationales Max-Scheler-Colloquium "Der Mensch im Weltater des Ausgleichs." *Phänomenologische Forschungen*, 28-29, 1994.

——. "Präferenzwandel und sittliche Wertordnung." In *Vom Umsturz der Werte in der modernen Gesellschaft*. Ed. Gerhard Pfafferott. Bonn: Bouvier Verlag, 1997.

Platter, G. "Max Schelers Lehre von Politik und Moral." *Forum der Forschung*, No.1, 1995.

Pöggeler, O. "Scheler und die heutigen anthropologischen Ansätze zur Metaphysik." *Heidelberger Jahrbücher* XXXIII, 1989.

——. "Ausgleich und anderer Anfang. Scheler und Heidegger." *Phänomenologische Forschungen* Bd. 28/29. 1994. 166-203.

——. "Max Schelers Die Stellung des Menschen im Kosmos." *Interpretationen*, 1992.

——. "Ressentiment und Tugend bei Max Scheler." In *Vom Umsturz der Werte in der modernen Gesellschaft*. Ed. Gerhard Pfafferott. Bonn: Bouvier Verlag, 1997.

Pupi, A. "L'uomo <<resisto>> secondo l'analisi di Max Scheler." *Rivista Filosofia Neoscholastica*, 63, 1971.

Racinaro, R. *Il futuro della memoria*. Napoli: Guida editori, 1985. (Two chapters on Scheler: "Uno strano realismo: corpo, persona e intersoggettiva in Max Scheler;" and "Quotidianita e filosofia della domenica. Aporie tra il primo e il secondo Scheler.")

Ramos, A.P. "Schelers Einfluss auf das Denken der spanischsprachigen Welt." *Phänomenologische Forschungen* Bd. 28/29, 1994. 314-331.

Raensch-Tull, B. "Der Mensch als ens amans." *Philosophisches Jahrbuch*, 1995.

Ranly, E.W. *Scheler's Phenomenology of Community*. The Hague: Martinus Nijhoff, 1966.

Rutishauser, Bruno. *Max Schelers Phänomenologie des Fühlens*. Bern, München: Francke Verlag, 1969.

Sander, A. "Die Dezentrierung des Subjekts in der Philosophie Max Schelers." (Diss.) Hamburg, 1994.

——. "Askese und Weltbejahung. Zum Problem des Dualismus in der Anthropologie und Metaphysik Max Schelers." In *Vom Umsturz der Werte in der modernen Gesellschaft*. Ed. Gerhard Pfafferott. Bonn: Bouvier Verlag, 1997.

Schalow, F. "Religious Transcendence: Scheler's Forgotten Quest." *Philosophy and Theology*, Vol. 5 No. 2, May 1990.

——. "A Pre-Theological Phenomenology: Heidegger and Scheler." *International Philosophical Quarterly*, Vol. 28 No. 4, Dec. 1988.

——. "The Anomaly of World: From Scheler to Heidegger." *Man and World* 24, 1991.

Schneider, G. " 'Vorbilder' in Max Schelers wertfundiertem Elitekonzept." In *Vom Umsturz der Werte in der modernen Gesellschaft*. Ed. Gerhard Pfafferott. Bonn: Bouvier Verlag, 1997.

Schütz, A. "Max Scheler's Epistemology and Ethics." *Review of Metaphysics* 11, (1957-58). 304-314; 486-501.

——. "Scheler's Theory of Intersubjectivity and the General Thesis of the Alter-Ego." In *The Problem of Social Reality.* Vol. 1 of *Collected Papers.* Ed. Maurice Natanson. The Hague: Martinus Nijhoff, 1962.

——. "Max Scheler's Philosophy." In *Studies in Phenomenological Philosophy* Vol. 3 of *Collected Papers.* Ed. Ilse Schutz. The Hague: Martinus Nijhoff, 1975.

Schmuck, J. *Homo religiosus. Die religiöse Frage in der Wissenssoziologie Max Schelers.* München, 1983.

Schneck, St. F. *Person and Polis.* Albany: State University of New Press, 1987.

Schoenborn, A.v. "Max Scheler on Philosophy and Religion." *International Philosophical Quarterly* Vol XIV No.3, 1974.

Shimonisse, E., *Die Phänomenologie und das Problem der Grundlegung der Ethik: An Hand des Versuches von Max Scheler.* The Hague: Martinus Nijhoff, 1971.

——. "Welches ist primär, 'sittlich gut handeln' oder 'sittlich gut sein'? (mit besonderer Rücksicht auf Max Schelers Versuch der Grundlegung der Ethik)." In *Akten des XIV Internationalen Kongresses fur Philosophie*, Wien: Herder. 2-9 Sept. 1968. VI.

Smith, Q. "Max Scheler and the Classification of Feelings." *Journal of Phenomenological Psychology* 9, Nos 1-2, (1978), 114-138.

——. "Scheler's Critique of Husserl's Theory of the World of the Natural Standpoint." *Modern Schoolman* 55, No.4, 1977-1978.

——. "Scheler's Stratification of Emotional Life and Strawson's *Person.*" *Philosophical Studies* 25 (1977), 103-127.

Spader, P.H. "The Non-Formal Ethics of Max Scheler and the Shift in his Thought," *Philosophy Today*, Vol.18, No.3/4, 1974.

——. "A New Look at Scheler's Third Period," *The Modern Schoolman*, Vol. LI, No.2, 1974.

——. "Max Scheler, Phenomenology and Metaphysics," *The Philosophical Forum*, Vol.6, 1974-75.

——. "Aesthetics, Morals and Max Scheler's Non-formal Values," *The British Journal of Aesthetics.* Vol. 16, No.3, 1976.

——. "The Possibility of an Apriori in Non-Formal Ethics: Max Scheler's Task." *Man and World*, Vol.9, No.2, 1976.

——. "Scheler's Phenomenological Given," *JBSP: Journal of the British Society for Phenomenology*, Vol.9, No.3, 1978.

——. "The Facts of Max Scheler," *Philosophy Today*, Vol.23, No.3/4, 1979.

——. "Language and the Phenomenologically Given." *Philosophy Today*, 26, (Fall, 1982).

——. "The Primacy of the Heart: Scheler's Challenge to Phenomenology," *Philosophy Today*, XXIII, 1983.

——. "Scheler, Schutz, and Intersubjectivity, in *Reflections: Essays in Phenomenology* (Canada), Vol.4, 1983

——. "Person, Acts, and Meaning: Max Scheler's Insight," *The New Scholasticism*, Vol. LIX, No.2, 1985.

——. "A Change of Heart: Scheler's Ordo Amoris, Repentance and Rebirth," in *Listening*, XXI, 1986.

——, "Max Scheler;s Practical Ethics and the Model Person," *American Catholic Philosophical Quarterly*, Vol. LXIX, No 1, 1995.

Staude, St. *Max Scheler, 1874-1928: An Intellectual Portrait.* London: Collier-Macmillan, 1967.

Stein, E., *Aus dem Leben einer jüdischen Familie.* Freiburg i.Br., 1965.

Stickers, K. "Max Scheler. Toward a Sociology of Space." *JBSP: Journal of the British Society for Phenomenology* 9, 1978.

——, Introduction and ed. *Max Scheler. Problems of a Sociology of Knowledge.* Manfred S. Frings, Tr. London: Routledge and Kegan Paul, 1980.

——. "Phenomenology as Psychic Technique of Non-Resistance." In *Phenomenology in Practice and Theory: Essays for Herbert Spiegelberg.* Ed. W.S. Hemrick. Phaenomenologica 92. The Hague: Martinus Nijhoff, 1985.

——. "Ethos. Its Relationship to Real and Ideal Sociological Factors in Max Scheler's Sociology of Culture." *Listening* Vol. 21 No .3, 1986.

——. "Max Scheler's Contributions to Social Economics." *Review of Social Economy* 45, 1987.

——. "Goals, Values, and Community in the Social Economy: Some Implications from the Social Theories of Aristotle, Tönnies, and Scheler." *Forum for Social Economics*, 1988.

Strasser, St. "Phenomenological Trends in European Psychology (Husserl, Scheler, Pfänder, and others)." *Philosophy and Phenomenological Research* 9 (1957/1958), 18-34.

Suances Marcos, A.M. "Los valores y su jerarquia en la filosofia de Max Scheler." *Estudios Filosoficos,* 24, 1975.

Sweeney, R. "The Affective Apriori." In *Analecta Husserliana* III. Ed. A.-T. Tymnieiecka. The Hague: Rediel, 1974.

——. "Axiology in Scheler and Ingarden and the Question of Dialectics." *Dialectics and Humanism* 3, 1975.

——. "Affectivity and Life-World." In *Analecta Husserliana* V. Ed. A.-T. Tymieniecka. Dordrecht: Reidel, 1976.

——. "The 'Great Chain of Being' in Scheler's Philosoophy." In *Analecta Husserliana* XI Ed. A.S.Bello. Boston: Reidel, 1981.

——. "Cognition and Work." In *Analecta Husserliana* XIV. Ed. A.-T. Tymieniecha. Boston: Reidel, 1983.

——. "Value and Ideology." In *Analecta Husserliana* XV. Ed. A.-T Tymieniecka. Boston: Reidel, 1983.

——. "Scheler, Max 1874-1928." *Dictionaire des Philosophes*, K-Z. Paris: Press Universitaires de France, 1984.

Theisen, Marion. *Max Schelers Metapsychologie als Grundlage für einen integrativen anthropologischen Ansatz.* Frankfurt/Main: Peter Lang. Europäischer Verlag der Wissenschaften, 1994.

Trebicki, J. "Die Kant-Rezeption in der Axiologie Max Schelers." In *Wissenschaftliche Zeitschrift der Humboldt-Universität zu Berlin. Gesellschafts- und Sprachwissenschaftliche Reihe* 24, No.2 (1975).

Uchiyama, M. *Das Wertwidrige in der Ethik Max Schelers.* Mainzer Philosophische Forschungen, 4. Ed. Gerhard Funke. Bonn: H. Bouvier Verlag, 1966.

Vacek, Edward, S.J. "Anthropological Foundations of Scheler's Ethics of Love." Ann Arbor:, MI: University Microfilms, 1978.

———. "Max Scheler's Anthropology." *Philosophy Today* Vol. 23, No .3, Fall 1979.

———. "Scheler's Philosphy of Love." *The Journal of Religion* Vol. 62 No. 2, April 1982.

———. "A Schelerian Critique of 'The Moral Sense.'" *Phenomenology Information Bulletin* Vol. 8, October 1984.

———. "The Functions of Norms in Social Existence." *The Moral Sense in the Communal Significance of Life.* Ed. Anna-Teresa Tymieniecka. *Analecta Husserliana XX,* 1986.

———. "Personal Growth and the Ordo Amoris." *Listening* Vol. 21 No.3, 1986.

———. "Scheler's Evolving Methodologies." *Analecta Husserliana.* Vol. 22. *Morality within the Life- and Social World.* Ed. Anna-Teresa Tymieniecka. Boston: Reidel, 1987.

Waldenfels, B. "Wertqualitäten oder Erfahrungsansprüche?" In *Vom Umsturz der Werte in der modernen Gesellschaft.* Ed. Gerhard Pfafferott. Bonn: Bouvier Verlag, 1997.

Willer, J. "Der Bezug auf Husserl im Frühwerk Schelers." *Kant-Studien,* 72, 1981.

———. "Schröder–Husserl–Scheler. Zur formalen Logik." *Zeitschrift für philosophische Forschung,* Vol. 35, 1985.

Wojtyla, K. (Pope John Paul II) "The Problem of the Separation between Experience and Act in light of the Ideas of Kant and Max Scheler." *Roczniki Filozoficze,* 1955-1957.

———. "The Principle of Imitation, following the Sources of Revelation and the philosophical System of Max Scheler." *Ateneum Kaplanskie,* 1975.

———. "Concerning the metaphysical and phenomenological Foundation of the Moral Norm in the Conceptions of St. Thomas Aquinas and Max Scheler." *Roczniki teologiczno-kanonicze,* 1959.

———. *The Acting Person.* Analecta Husserliana X. Dordrecht, Boston, London: 1979.

———. *Primat des Geistes. Philosophische Schriften.* Einleitung (Introduction): Manfred S. Frings. Ed. Juliusz Stroynowski. Stuttgart: Seewald Verlag, 1980.

Wolff, Kurt. "Gedanken zu Schelers 'Erkenntnis und Arbeit.'" In *Wissenssoziologie. Sonderheft der Kölner Zeitschrift fur Soziologie und Sozialpsychologie* V. 22, 1980. Ed. N. Stehr, V. Meja.

———. "Scheler's Shadow on Us." *Analecta Husserliana* 14, 1983.

Index of Proper Names

Adler, 80
Aesop, 147
Anaxagoras, 287
Anouilh, 271
Aristotle, 19-20, 49, 60-61, 71, 79, 95, 116, 127, 149, 204, 250-51, 253-54, 268-69, 279, 282, 313

Bach, 78, 246
Bacon, 215
Bain, 152
Becker, 15, 17, 300
Beethoven, 78, 246, 270, 280-81
Bentham, 19, 71
Berdyaev, 16, 42
Bergson, 80, 222, 238, 282
Berkeley, 237-238
Biran, 238
Bismarck, 75
Boltzmann, 230-32, 294
Boole, 224
Bouterweck, 238
Brandt, 19
Brentano, 19
Buber, 99
Buddha, 78, 102, 128

Cairns, 181
Chopin, 246
Christ, 79, 92, 95, 102, 116, 153, 163, 174
Churchill, 169
Conrad, 10
Conrad-Martius, 10
Curtius, 13, 73

Dahlke, 17
Darwin, 274-75
Daubert, 182
Delbrück, 284
Democritus, 127, 239, 287

Derrida, 99
Descartes, 6, 25, 39, 86, 127, 156-57, 167, 189, 210, 228, 250, 279, 282
Dewey, 195
Dewitz-Krebs, 9
Dilthey, 222, 238
Dostoevski, 271
Dunker, 17
Duns Scotus, 238

Einstein, 228, 230, 233, 244, 282, 286, 288
Eucken, 9, 14, 186
Euclid, 61, 243

Farber, 17
Fichte, 78, 91, 222, 238, 245
Frankena, 19
Freud, 80, 258

Gadamer, 73, 181
Gauss, 215
Geiger, 182
Gelb, 225-226
Goethe, 279
Goldstein, 14, 225-226

Hafkesbrink, 17
Hartmann, 19, 306
Heidegger, 5, 11, 16, 20, 22, 25, 28-29, 36, 49, 60-61, 73, 83-84, 99, 106-07, 116, 129, 133, 145, 162, 176, 181, 217, 219, 221, 226-27, 250-51, 253, 258-59, 268, 279, 293-94, 303, 305, 307, 309-11
Heisenberg, 125, 287
Hepburn, 161
Herbart, 228
Héring, 10, 30
Hildebrand, 10, 182

Hitler, 11-12, 111, 144
Hobbes, 228
Homer, 28
House, 14, 169, 309
Hume, 152, 240
Husserl, 5, 9-10, 17, 20-22, 25, 36, 43, 49, 60, 78, 82, 84, 86, 91, 94, 99, 106-07, 121-22, 124, 129-31, 181-82, 184, 186, 188-92, 194, 203, 221-22, 237, 239, 241, 251, 263, 293-94, 303, 308, 310, 312-14
Hutchinson, 152

Ingarden, 10, 313

Jacobi, 238
James, 13-14, 19, 59, 214, 221-222, 236, 238, 280, 293, 301
Jeanne d'Arc, 28
Jerusalem, 14

Kant, 13, 19-21, 25, 42, 44-46, 49, 52, 59, 71, 146, 187, 200, 206, 210, 224, 228-30, 232, 245, 249, 255-56, 287, 294, 302, 305-07, 314
Kelvin, 230
Kerschensteiner, 195
Klages, 278
Koffka, 82
Köhler, 243
Koyré, 10

La Mettrie, 28, 258
Landgrebe, 181
Leibniz, 206, 237
Lessing, 278
Levinas, 5, 82, 99
Liebig, 215
Lipps, 10, 99, 182
Luther, 196, 309
Mach, 229-30
Maeder, 80
Marcel, 99
Marx, 75, 258

Maxwell, 230-31, 287
McGill, 17
Meinong, 19
Michelangelo, 78
Mill, 19
Mohammed, 78, 102
Moore, 19
Münsterberg, 14, 238

Newton, 232, 287, 294
Nietzsche, 5, 27-28, 32, 42, 49, 79, 88, 132-34, 142, 145, 151, 166, 222, 253, 258, 278, 282-83, 303, 310

Ortega y Gasset, 11, 59, 310
Otto, 131, 302

Parmenides, 128, 263, 279-80
Pascal, 6, 53, 59, 116, 140, 154, 167, 283
Peirce, 13, 221-24, 236, 238
Pfänder, 182, 313
Pfeiffer, 82
Planck, 229, 233, 286
Plato, 46, 61, 86, 95, 133, 149, 156, 163, 268-69
Plotinus, 291-92
Poe, 10-11, 148
Pope John Paul II, 29, 314
Protagoras, 152

Raphael, 78, 196
Rashdall, 19
Rathenau, 209
Reid, 238
Reinach, 10, 182
Reiner, 19, 89, 305, 307
Ricoeur, 19
Rodin, 78
Rubens, 78, 270

Sartre, 5, 20, 42, 49, 60, 99, 145, 181

Scheler, Maria, 11, 17, 73, 299

Schelling, 42, 78, 238, 245
Schilpp, 13
Schlick, 228
Schrödinger, 127, 287
Schumann, 246
Shuster, 17
Schütz, 17, 311
Seurat, 286
Shinn, 82
Signac, 286
Sigwart, 222
Sinclair, 209
Small, 14, 51, 95, 132-133, 170,
    189, 214, 240, 272, 282-83, 286,
    297
Smith, 152, 178, 207, 305, 312
Socrates, 19, 64
Sophocles, 271
Spengler, 28, 278
Spiegelberg, 17, 121, 181, 313
Spinoza, 19, 37, 228, 288, 291
St. Augustine, 49, 291
St. Francis, 50, 95, 174
St. Thomas, 116, 314
Stein, 10, 73, 182, 313
Stern, 82
Strauss, 181

Tolstoi, 293
Tönnies, 100, 313
Trotzki, 15
Tschitscherin, 15

Vaihinger, 222
Van Gogh, 270
Van Breda, 181

Weber, 142, 293, 301, 310
Wells, 54, 62, 76, 146, 264, 271
Williams, 17
Wodehouse, 12
Wojtyla, 29, 314

Wundt, 122-123, 228

Xenocrates, 20

Index of Subject Matter

a priori, 1, 31, 35-39, 59, 64, 70, 72, 74, 82-84, 126-27, 134, 138, 166, 183, 221, 223-24, 231, 246, 262, 300

abortion, 6, 20, 48-49, 144, 173

act, 2, 26, 37-38, 40, 42-45, 47, 54-56, 62, 66-67, 75-76, 81, 87, 96, 105, 110-111, 125, 129-32, 134, 136-39, 154, 161-163, 174, 189-90, 240, 271, 278, 287, 295, 314

agriculture, 159, 175

aliveness, 36-38, 125-27, 183-85, 225

at-handedness, 176, 227

atom, 127, 207, 232, 264, 270, 283, 286

becoming,
  absolute time, 263, 264, 296
  Deity, 292
  direction, 258
  ens a se, 259
  evolution, 274
  field, vital forces, 285
  human being, 276
  ideas, 61, 62
  impulsion, 187, 188
  inorganic matter, 274
  interdependence, 293
  life, 141, 245
  knowledge, 220
  man, world, God, 195, 198, 250, 257, 296, 298

buddhism, 115, 152, 186

child, 16, 45-46, 48, 57, 67, 79-80, 82, 85, 91-94, 96-97, 101, 106, 124, 126-27, 141, 158, 161, 204, 213, 245

christianity, 95, 115-16, 152, 163, 214

cognition, 3, 13-14, 26, 71-72, 116, 183-84, 190, 193-95, 208, 212-225, 230, 234-38, 240-41, 245-47, 313

collective personality, 109, 115, 118, 205

conscience,
  absolute, 70
  acts, 220
  call of, 52, 53;
  freedom, 50, 51, 54, 56, 67
  functionalization, 62, 63
  injustice, 27
  impulsion, spirit, 278
  mass, 100
  moral tenor, good, evil, 41, 42
  ordo amoris, 70, 132, 146, 151, 155, 167
  pre-logical, 59, 60
  repentance, 54, 56
  social, 154, 168

consciousness,
  absolute time, 188, 189, 264
  absence, 205
  acts, classes 43, 81
  a priori, 183
  attitude, 169, 170
  becoming, 267
  cognition, 218
  dream, 90
  identification, 94
  impotent, 192
  impulsion, 188, 263
  intuition, 185
  ontological rel., 217
  person, 22, 182, 189, 190
  phantasmic image, 239
  phenomenology, 35, 36, 122-124
    regions, 70, 125-127, 130, 137, 134, 139, 140, 182, 183
    pure, 78

religious act, exp., 121, 122 128-32; 134, 136-38
  self as object, 88
  social forms, 106, 117
  transcendence, 87
psychic contagion, 92-94, 97, 100-01, 103, 152
creatio continua, 291

dasein, 22, 25, 28-29, 68, 83-84, 129, 217, 294, 305
death, 4, 10-11, 13, 15, 17, 27, 57, 65, 67-68, 82, 86, 92, 103, 133-34, 139-41, 148, 159, 161, 174, 189, 242, 251-52, 266, 275, 288, 294-98
drives, 4, 80, 93, 176, 179-80, 188, 195-201, 206, 216, 223, 229-31, 235, 237-38, 244-47, 260, 262, 265-66, 273, 279, 284, 288-89

encompassing person, 2, 100, 108, 114-19
ens amans, 68-69, 192, 214, 311
entertainment, 21, 31, 33, 69, 75, 104, 159, 161-62
environment, 15, 27, 47, 65, 70, 85, 159, 176, 186, 214, 226, 235, 255
ethics, 1, 3, 6, 10-11, 19-24, 35, 39-40, 42, 45, 48-49, 51-52, 58-60, 62-64, 66-67, 71-72, 76, 80-81, 99, 149, 151, 156, 163, 167-168, 175, 177, 201, 222, 249-250, 254, 300, 302, 304, 306, 308, 310-314
ethos, 2, 37-38, 50-51, 94-95, 140, 151, 157, 160, 165, 174-75, 177, 195, 206-07, 215, 257, 272, 313
euthanasia, 20, 48
evolution, 4, 68, 200, 252, 257-59, 264, 273-77, 279, 290
exemplars of person, 1, 71, 73, 76-78, 203, 261
expanse, 86, 191, 243, 283, 287-88

fascism, 11, 16, 144
fate, 1, 63-65, 67, 69, 80, 85
feelings, 2, 10, 12, 21-22, 25-33, 39, 41-42, 51-56, 62, 68, 71, 76, 81, 84-85, 87, 91-93, 95-97, 100-101, 103, 107, 109, 114, 124, 144-49, 151-52, 155, 164, 166, 176, 189-90, 204, 219, 244, 257, 312
field forces, 264, 285-88
fluctuating variation, 186-88, 242, 265, 285, 288
functionalization,
  artist, geometry, reality, 61
  body, mind, 279
  childhood, 65
  divine spirit, 290
  exemplar, 77-79, 262
  ideas, impulsion, 269, 270, 281
  knowledge, 203, 224
  moral experience, 60
  real, ideal factors, 201
  sketch, 272
  values, 62

gestalt, 228, 233, 241, 243, 288-89
guilt, 11, 53, 55-57, 160-63, 293

hate, 68, 79, 81, 143, 145-47, 149, 154, 255
heart, 11, 15, 39, 45, 51, 56, 58-59, 63, 65, 67, 69, 74, 95, 138, 146, 148, 151, 157, 166-67, 174, 182, 190, 211, 224, 255, 264, 266, 298, 310, 312-13
holiness, 26, 28, 32, 40, 47, 69-71, 79, 118, 128, 131-32, 135, 138, 141, 153

ideal factors, 195-96, 201, 206-08, 210, 279
idealism, 13, 25, 50, 61, 78, 117, 237, 242, 278
impulsion,
  atoms, 282, 284-87, 294
  cosmic, 285

Deity, 278, 289
drives, 188, 245, 265
ergs, 281, 289;
ens a se, 291
forces, 234, 289
historicity, 272
inanimate,anmiate, 284, 285, 289
life, 235, 278
phantasmic image, 235, 239, 240, 276
phantasy, 245, 273, 276, 288
plants, 266, 290
reduction, 192
resistance, 286, 288
sketch, 276
space, time, 188, 234, 283
spirit, 195, 196, 200, 251, 252, 256, 272, 283, 289
    dormant spirit 281
    functionalization, 60
spirit and reality 217
    ontological rel. 216
    spirit grows 224
time 291, 293
steering, 202
suspension, 247
variation, 186, 187, 265
vital energy, 231
woman, 292
injustice, 6, 26-27, 32, 34
intuition, 67, 73-74, 121, 123-25, 156, 169, 181-86, 190-92, 195, 215, 218-19, 222, 225, 228-30, 232, 234-35, 239-40, 246, 263, 267, 277, 293-94
irreversible modification, 187-88, 265

kairos, 1, 20, 58, 67-68, 70
knowledge, 3, 10, 13-17, 30, 32, 48, 53, 83-84, 87, 90, 93, 99, 102, 106, 109, 116, 123, 126-27, 135, 138-39, 156, 175, 183, 185-86, 193-96, 202-07, 209-13, 216-17, 220-24, 231, 235-38, 240, 249, 253, 257, 260, 269, 281, 288-89, 300-01, 313

leaders, 73, 77, 79, 100, 203, 210-11, 270
life, 6, 9, 11-12, 16-17, 21, 26-28, 30-33, 38, 41-42, 49, 57, 61-63, 65, 67, 69-70, 73-75, 78-80, 84-85, 88-89, 92, 102-03, 112, 114, 118, 133-34, 139-41, 144, 150, 153, 155-59, 161-62, 167, 172-73, 178, 180, 182, 185-86, 188-90, 192, 194-96, 198-201, 206-07, 217, 219-22, 224-25, 227-30, 234-38, 241, 244-45, 247, 250, 253-55, 257, 259, 261-62, 264-67, 273-84, 286, 293-98, 301, 312, 314
life-community, 2, 85, 100-06, 108-15, 118, 160-63, 175, 198, 203, 205, 210, 227, 262
lived body, 2, 26, 30, 46-47, 83, 86-88, 95, 138-39, 186, 191, 208, 240, 279-80, 290-91, 295
logic, 20, 22, 25, 95, 137, 167, 190, 210, 222, 224, 227-28, 231-32, 235
love,
    at first sight, 38, 65
    capitalism, 173
    Christianity, 115, 116
    discloses, 69
    ens amens, 68
    foundation of preferring, 38
    of nature, 210
    ontology, 217
    person, 45
    see preferring
    quantity, 160
    solidarity, 161, 162
    unrequited, 66, 86, 162
    of world, 39

matter, 6, 21-22, 25-26, 39, 42, 46-47, 49, 58, 62, 64, 68, 81-82, 88,

93, 95-97, 106, 112, 116, 119, 122, 125, 127, 129, 134-35, 142, 155, 159, 165, 169, 171, 184-85, 191-93, 201, 220, 226, 229-31, 234, 240, 242, 251-54, 263, 270, 274-75, 277-79, 282-89, 293, 295-96

metaphysics, 4, 6, 11, 13, 15, 89, 125, 128-29, 175, 186, 188, 194-95, 202-03, 210-12, 214, 216-17, 220, 223-25, 229, 231-34, 236, 239, 246, 250-255, 257, 263, 266, 268, 277, 285-290, 297, 301, 304, 311-312

milieu, 64-66, 69, 87, 169, 176, 179, 186, 226, 235, 238, 260

mind-set, 14, 105, 114, 145, 152, 158, 163, 168-76, 179, 207, 214-15, 249, 295

murder, 48, 93

mutation, 277

narcotics, 33

national socialism, 11, 145

ontological relation, 213, 216-17, 220, 222, 269

ordo amoris, 1, 55, 58-60, 63-67, 69-70, 73-74, 132, 138, 145-46, 151, 155, 166-67, 190, 258, 260, 304, 308, 310, 313-14

ought, 19, 22, 33-34, 48, 50-56, 59, 62-63, 66-68, 71, 74, 76, 80-81, 160, 168, 170, 237

oughtness, 20, 22, 33-34, 52, 59, 66, 71, 74

perception, 4, 21, 24, 31, 37, 86-87, 89-90, 125, 167, 176-81, 183, 187-91, 194, 200, 208, 211, 216, 218-19, 223, 225-26, 228, 231-32, 234-36, 238-47, 266-69, 273, 282, 284, 289

person,
    act execution, 43, 44, 66, 87, 137, 138, 163, 189, 250

bearer of values, 21, 23, 42, 48, 66, 247

becoming, 220

being of person, 42, 43, 54, 189

coresponsibility, 160-62

deception, 40

form of consciousness, spirit, 22, 276, 292

kairos, 67, 68, 70, 88

moral tenor, will, 45-47, 50- 52
    its change, 58; 68, 74, 139, 140, 142, 151, 161, 168, (Francis) 174, 222; 262

origin, 85

qualitative direction, temporality, 47, 53, 54, 65-67, 117, 164, 167, 190

self-illumination, 278

self-disclosure, 138

social forms, 100, 103, 110-13, 115, 117

uniform sense, 65-68

phantasy, 239, 244-46, 273, 276, 288

phantasmic image, 239-240

phenomenology, 2-3, 9-12, 17, 25, 35-36, 76, 81, 107, 121-25, 129-30, 181-86, 189-92, 221, 225, 242, 249, 263, 292, 295, 300-02, 304-06, 309, 311-14

physics, 20, 125, 225, 227, 229-34, 253-54, 270, 282, 284-89

pragmatism, 3-4, 13-14, 60, 165, 176, 194, 212-14, 216, 221-227, 35-238, 245, 247, 267

preferring, 27, 30-31, 33, 37-41, 43-45, 64, 190, 223, 246

quantum theory, 229, 233, 274, 285-86

quantum leap, 277-278, 283-284

real factors, 195-202, 207, 269-270, 272, 279

region, 2, 60, 125-31, 133-34, 136-40, 204-05, 220

relativity theory, 285
religion, 6, 10-11, 26-27, 51-52, 63, 78, 115-18, 121-22, 128-29, 135, 139, 142, 160, 164, 185, 194-96, 202-03, 209, 211, 217, 220, 225, 249, 262, 288, 302, 312, 314
resistance, 86, 183, 185, 189, 217, 233, 237-39, 241, 251, 286, 288, 290, 294, 301
reversible movement, 187-88, 265
role model, 74, 160, 201

salvation, 118, 142, 155, 194, 220, 223, 257, 262
self, 2, 35, 81-91, 94, 96, 101, 110, 114, 126, 136, 150, 154, 229, 247, 309
self-givenness, 37, 122-24, 218-19
self-understanding, 4, 28, 211, 257-62, 272
sensation, 4, 30, 123, 229-30, 236, 239-40, 243
shame, 42-43, 56, 86, 95, 124, 185
sketch, 4, 47, 62, 268-73, 276
socialism, 11, 145, 168-69, 172-75, 211
society, 2-3, 9, 19, 21, 27-29, 32-33, 40, 42, 48, 51-52, 56-58, 63, 75, 79, 90, 93, 96, 100-15, 118, 139, 145, 148-51, 154-58, 160-163, 165, 167-68, 172-73, 175, 177, 179, 193-95, 198, 202-12, 214, 217, 249, 262, 278, 298, 300-01, 304-05, 312-13
sociology of knowledge, 3, 13-15, 17, 32, 48, 84, 106, 109, 126, 156, 175, 193-96, 202, 204-07, 281, 288, 300, 313
solidarity, 3, 58, 101-05, 109-11, 114, 118-19, 159-63, 174, 198, 205, 307
space,
    bracketing, 185
    impulsion, 186
    lived body, 86, 88
    motion, 232, 233, 236

objective, see time
ontological rel. 216
ordo amoris, 64
phantasmic images, 239, 242
science, 125
society, 113
space-time, 125, 282, 287
spatialization, 188, 264-66, 285
sphere, 21, 43, 47, 70, 83, 86-88, 91, 103, 125, 128-29, 132-34, 153, 160-61, 183, 189, 192, 204-05, 260
spirit, 4, 12, 42, 50-51, 60, 78, 95, 128, 141-42, 174, 193, 195-97, 200-02, 212, 216-17, 224, 227, 247, 250-52, 256, 259-260, 268, 272, 276-83, 289-94, 296-97, 301
steering, 202

technology, 3, 6, 19-20, 27, 31, 108, 143, 145, 154, 156-57, 159, 169, 173, 175, 195, 207, 210-11, 214-215, 247, 255, 258
tenor, basic moral, 1, 41, 45-46, 50
theory of knowledge, 10, 16, 186, 193, 212
Thou, 34, 82-84, 87-88, 99, 126-127, 162, 179, 204-205
time,
    absolute, temporalization, 188, 251, 264-68, 285
    becoming, growth, 263-65
    bracketing, 185
    clock, empty, objective time and space, 47, 184, 191, 221, 235, 243, 263, 265, 266, 271, 274, 282, 289, 290
    fate, 63-65, 67, 69
    history, 272, 274
    horizons, 189, 295
    ideas, 267
    intersubjective, 84, 88
    life, 274, 284
    manifestations, 293
    materialism, 228

motion, 232, 233, 236
mutation, 277
ontological rel., 216
phantasmic images, 239, 242
sketch 271
vital ref., 229
tradition, 42, 54, 84, 103-105, 274,
   297

value,
   a priori, 31; (transverse) 37-41, 74,
      166
   communality, 83, 84, 143, 147,
      151, 154, 155, 159, 162
   colors, things, 23, 24
   criteria, 31-33, 178
   deception, 36, 38, 68, 70, 72, 74,
      146
   essence, 31
   foundation of ethics, 22
   functionalization, 62
   ideas, 258
   good,evil, 30, 39-41
   life-values, 27, 28, 31, 32
   inversion, 139, 154 156, 157, 159,
      172, 224
   non-existence, 22-26
   non-logical, 59, 70, 166, 175
   order, disorder, 24, 25, 27, 31, 33,
      39, 40, 44, 49, 54, 64, 66, 67, 69,
      70, 74, 108 148, 151, 165-68
   ought, 22, 34, 52, 71, 74
   ranks, 26-28, 38, 49, 77, 79, 91,
      190, 247
   riding on back, 44-46
   temporality, 44, 64
   tradition, 105
   transfinite numbers, 98
   see preferring
   social forms, 99
   ref. act, 132
   vital center, 223, 256

willing, 25, 37, 42-44, 46, 50, 53,
   63, 69, 74, 103, 111, 154, 164,
189, 246
will, 9-10, 13, 15, 21-25, 28, 32, 35,
   38, 40, 42-49, 55-56, 58-62, 64-
   65, 67-68, 71-72, 74, 77-81, 85,
   88-89, 94, 97, 99-104, 107-11,
   113, 116-17, 124-27, 129-30,
   132-33, 143, 145, 149-50, 156,
   158-59, 165-67, 175-78, 180,
   182, 185, 187, 193, 195-99, 201,
   203-04, 207, 209-10, 212, 215-
   16, 222-23, 227-28, 233-34, 236-
   238, 249-52, 256, 258-60, 262-
   63, 270, 280, 282-83, 286-87,
   297-98
work, 3, 5, 10-15, 17, 20, 22, 30,
   32, 35, 52-54, 59-61, 72-73, 76,
   80, 82, 90-91, 108, 121, 140-42,
   150, 154, 156-57, 160, 164, 168,
   170, 178, 181, 189-90, 192-95,
   198, 200, 204, 206-08, 210-16,
   230, 234, 236-38, 241, 247, 254,
   285, 293, 295-96, 300, 313